NARRATING UTOPIA

Liverpool Science Fiction Texts and Studies
General Editor DAVID SEED

Series Advisers I.F. Clarke, Edward James, Patrick Parrinder
and Brian Stableford

Chris Ferns

NARRATING UTOPIA

Ideology, Gender, Form in Utopian Literature

LIVERPOOL UNIVERSITY PRESS

First published 1999 by
LIVERPOOL UNIVERSITY PRESS
Liverpool L69 3BX

British Library Cataloguing-in-Publication Data
A British Library CIP record is available

ISBN 0-85323-594-5 (hardback)
ISBN 0-85323-604-6 (paperback)

Typeset in 10/12.5pt Meridien by
XL Publishing Services, Lurley, Tiverton
Printed by Bell & Bain, Glasgow

FOR
JEANNETTE

Contents

Acknowledgments

During the apparently endless process of writing and rewriting this book I was assisted by advice, comments, and criticism from numerous friends and colleagues. For especially helpful commentary on earlier drafts of the manuscript I would like to thank Steven Bruhm, Ruth Levitas, Maureen McNeil, Peter Schwenger, Anna Smol, and (last but certainly not least) Rhoda Zuk. Maurice Michaud's computer skills were of invaluable assistance, and I am also grateful to the students in my courses on utopian literature at Brock University and Mount Saint Vincent University, whose questions, ideas, and sometimes violent arguments forced me to clarify my own thinking.

Parts of Chapters 1 and 7 originally appeared in *English Studies in Canada* 14.4, an earlier version of part of Chapter 4 in *Dalhousie Review* 69.3, and part of Chapter 6 in *A Very Different Story: Studies on the Fiction of Charlotte Perkins Gilman*, ed. Val Gough and Jill Rudd (Liverpool, 1998).

This book is dedicated to the memory of Jeannette Mitchell, to whose ideas, and whose living, I owe more than I can say.

Preface

This is a book not so much about utopia, as about the stories people tell about utopia. It does not set out to provide a survey of utopian thought (of which there are already a number of excellent studies), nor indeed an exhaustive history of utopian literature. Rather, its preoccupation is with the nature of utopian narrative—with that curious hybrid of the traveller's tale and the classical dialogue which emerges in the Renaissance, and whose outlines remain clearly apparent even in some of the most recent utopian writing.

Utopia itself, unsurprisingly, exhibits an enormous range of configurations. Embodying as it does social and political alternatives to the society of the writer's own time, its nature is obviously affected by numerous variables: the historical circumstances prevailing at the time and place of composition; the writer's gender and class background; psychological factors—variables which in turn give rise to a bewildering assortment of imagined social structures. Utopian society may be centralized and regimented, or anarchic and diverse; it may be religious, or secular; there may be free love, or rigid control of sexuality; the family may be central to its operation, or abolished altogether. Some utopias have detailed provisions for the division and distribution of wealth and possessions, while in others money and private property have been done away with. In terms of its extent, utopia may be confined to a remote island, or embrace the entire globe. Yet for all this diversity, one thing that exhibits far less variation—at least so far as literary utopias are concerned—is the story, the framing narrative which accounts for how the narrator or central character reaches the more perfect society and obtains the opportunity to witness its distinctive excellences. This study sets out to examine the nature of that story, and its relation to the social structures that utopia depicts.

Given that a central premise of utopian fiction is that the world could be changed for the better—that it might be possible to create a society preferable to that which exists—it is understandable that the first concern of many readers is with the nature of that society. How does it work? *Would* it work? If it worked, would it be desirable—and if so, for whom? Beyond that, however, arises the further question of the purpose served by the representation of such a society. What function does the imagining of utopian alternatives serve? What is the effect on the reader? Is the purpose of utopian fiction narrowly didactic, aimed at securing the reader's assent to a particular sociopolitical vision? Or is it more broadly concerned, as Ernst Bloch suggests, with the education of hope, the stimulation in the reader of the desire for and belief in new possibilities? Does the imagining of utopian alternatives provide the impetus to work for radical social change, or merely serve as a safety valve, reinforcing the status quo by diverting attention from practical possibilities for change in the here and now?[1] Yet while these are perhaps the most immediate questions that utopia poses, in recent years increasing attention has been given not simply to the nature of the alternatives utopia presents, but to the *ways* in which they are presented. Critics such as Darko Suvin and Gary Saul Morson have pointed out the pitfalls that await the reader who sees utopian fiction as merely the uncomplicated expression of the writer's political ideals, indistinguishable in effect from any other kind of political platform; while Suvin, Morson, and more recently, Tom Moylan have examined the ways in which it is possible for utopian fiction to fulfil more than a purely didactic function, where narrative serves mainly as a kind of sugar coating designed to ease the swallowing of an otherwise indigestible bolus of political theory. In their discussions of what Morson terms 'meta-utopia' and Moylan 'critical utopia', they investigate the ways in which the narrative devices of utopian fiction—or at least more recent utopian fiction—involve the reader in a complex dialogue, rather than merely aiming to secure his or her unquestioning assent to the writer's sociopolitical agenda.[2]

What emerges from these, as well as a number of other recent studies, is a growing consensus that, while utopian fiction has its inherent problems, these are capable of being resolved, provided one first abandons the old notion of utopia as a static ideal. Rather than a monolithic ideal, whose unquestionable superiority to existing society is taken for granted, utopia becomes more a matter of exploring possibilities, indicating new directions, offering glimpses—or what Angelika Bammer calls 'partial visions'—of how things might be otherwise. This in its turn, it has been suggested, also involves modification, or even abandonment of the traditional accompanying narrative paradigm, in which a visitor to utopia is provided with a guided tour of the more perfect society. Where such a narrative presents a largely static picture—a series of tableaux, in effect—the critical or meta-utopia restores a sense of process, and by doing so seeks to involve the reader in a critical consideration of the utopian enterprise, rather than simply aiming to secure his or her passive assent.

Yet while there is much to be said for this view, it remains problematic in certain respects. In the first place, it may be argued that while the critical or meta-utopia avoids many of the pitfalls of traditional utopian narrative, it risks doing so at the cost of sacrificing something valuable, namely, the notion of a functioning utopian society as a practical possibility, rather than merely a locus of desire.[3] In addition, while it is true that a number of writers have set out to represent utopia as other than a prescriptive and authoritarian ideal, the influence of the traditional utopian narrative paradigm has proved more difficult to escape. It is the nature of that influence, the reasons for its persistence, and its effect on the sociopolitical character of the imagined utopia, that constitute the main focus of this study.

What this study seeks to show is, first, that specific narratives have their own ideological implications and, second, that in the case of utopian narrative, these are by no means entirely congruent with those of the utopian society described. As Pierre Macherey suggests, while narrative forms may change in response to the ideas they embody, they are also capable of resisting or transforming some of the implications of those ideas. What is proposed here is that the traditional utopian narrative possesses ideological implications of its own, which continue to influence the character of utopian fiction until well into the modern era.

To explore what these are, and how they interact with a range of widely differing utopian ideals, this study begins with a discussion of some of the generally acknowledged problems and contradictions inherent in utopian narrative—problems which have led some commentators to conclude that utopia has reached a dead end, and others to dismiss it as, for example, 'a relatively minor genre never quite detached from political theory' (Frye, 'Varieties' p.40). This is followed by an examination of the ways in which more recent studies of utopia have sought to broaden the scope of utopian inquiry, to clarify its terms of reference, and to explore new ways of articulating utopian desire. It is within this context that the study introduces its consideration of the ideological implications of narrative, and of utopian narrative in particular.

Following this introductory chapter, the main body of the discussion falls into two sections, roughly chronological in sequence, which are structured primarily in terms of the content of the utopias under discussion. The first, under the heading 'Dreams of Order', comprises three chapters all dealing with utopias whose character is centralized and regimented. Chapter Two examines the origins of the traditional narrative paradigm in the Renaissance, when theories as to how a more perfect society might be organized (which date back to before the time of Plato) first find fictional representation. It begins, naturally enough, with a study of More's *Utopia*, and then moves on to a discussion of two of the most influential utopias of the later Renaissance: Campanella's *The City of the Sun* and Bacon's *New Atlantis*. Taken together, these works reveal a number of common narrative features which may be seen as distinctive of the genre. Yet while it is scarcely surprising that the resultant narrative paradigm should clearly reflect the ideological climate of the period in which it emerges, what is harder to account for is its stubborn persistence in the very different historical context of the modern era—particularly given the range of alternative narrative models available—and it is the reasons for, and implications of its persistence in a modern context that the remainder of this study sets out to explore. Chapter Three moves forward to examine a number of utopias of the late nineteenth and early twentieth century in which the traditional paradigm is still clearly evident, and considers some of the consequences of its interaction with the very different social and political ideals embodied in the utopian societies depicted. Chapter Four concludes the section with an examination of the dystopian reaction to the centralized utopias of writers such as Bellamy and Wells. As a parodic counter-genre, dystopia is characterized by a very different narrative dynamic than its utopian counterpart; yet for all that, it will argued, is often unable to avoid reinscribing many of the very values implicit in the object of its parody.

Section Two, under the heading 'Dreams of Freedom', looks at a range of attempts to imagine a utopia based on libertarian, rather than authoritarian premises, and examines the extent to which these too remain constrained by the limitations of the traditional narrative paradigm. Chapter Five deals with William Morris's attempt to imagine a utopia as far as possible removed from the regimented vision of Edward Bellamy, with Alexander Bogdanov's *Red Star*, written to keep alive the vision of revolutionary possibility in the aftermath of the failure of the Russian Revolution of 1905, and with the much later attempt of Aldous Huxley to imagine a utopian alternative to the centralized nightmare depicted in *Brave New World*—all attempts, it will be argued, that are undermined by the narrative model they continue to deploy. In the final two chapters the gendered character of that model will be explored, along with the ways in which a number of women authors seek to transcend the limitations of a genre hitherto overwhelmingly dominated by men. Chapter Six examines the separatist visions of Charlotte Perkins Gilman and Sally Miller Gearhart, while Chapter Seven moves into the territory of the 'critical utopia', with a discussion of the utopian fiction of Marge Piercy and Ursula Le Guin, and includes a further reflection on the contemporary trends in both utopian fiction and utopian studies addressed in the Introduction. Like utopian fiction, the criticism of utopian literature also involves a narrative— whether of the death of utopia or of its salvation—and the study concludes with a consideration of the implications of such critical narratives.

1. Introduction

When future intellectual historians come to examine the second half of the twentieth century, they may well be struck by what might seem a widespread penchant for premature obituaries. During this period there have been announced not only the Death of the Novel, and of the Author, but also the End of Ideology, and even—in the aftermath of the collapse of the Soviet bloc—the End of History. Yet while all the above appear to be carrying on their way unperturbed by announcements of their demise, the status of another alleged casualty—utopia—is more questionable. It is significant, for example, that two of the most important surveys of utopian writing in recent years, the Manuels' *Utopian Thought in the Western World* (1979), and Krishan Kumar's *Utopia and Anti-Utopia in Modern Times* (1987), while reflecting widely differing ideological stances, should both reach pessimistic conclusions as to the future of utopia. Against this, of course, one might cite such phenomena as the new wave of feminist utopian writing during the 1970s, the re-evaluation of utopianism by Marxist theorists such as Ernst Bloch, or the significant expansion of the field of utopian studies over the past twenty years. Yet while this has led some commentators to conclude, more optimistically, that new approaches to utopia have opened up a promising new field of oppositional struggle on the cultural front, a more cynical assessment of such renewed critical interest in utopian studies might be that the academy is where ideas end up when they have nowhere else to go.

Contradictory viewpoints, however, are scarcely new in the field of utopian studies: indeed, it has become something of a commonplace that the very concept of utopia itself is one fraught with contradictions and ambiguity. Whether such contradictions and ambiguity are disabling, or enabling, however, is another matter. Whether utopia's inherent contradictions inevitably undermine the social alternatives portrayed, leading to an equally inevitable reinscription of most of the inequities it seeks to resolve, or whether by contrast such contradictions open the way to the fruitful exploration of diverse possibilities remains open to debate— although in recent discussions of utopia an increasingly common critical narrative appears to be that, while the former used to be the case, new ways of both writing and reading utopias are now making the latter increasingly possible. Before exploring the ways in which this bears on a study of utopian narrative as such, however, it might be helpful to first examine the nature of the impasse from which escape is seen as necessary.

The Death of Utopia?

The term 'utopia', of course, notoriously embodies a pun; Sir Thomas More's coinage is deliberately ambiguous in its derivation. Its root may be taken as either *ou-topos*—'no place', or *eu-topos*—'good place'. Utopia then, may be defined as both a good place, an ideal (or at any rate, more perfect) society, yet at the same time one that does not exist—desirable, perhaps, but at the same time unattainable. In utopian fictions this is reflected in the society's location, almost invariably remote or well insulated from the actual world to which it proposes an alternative: More and Francis Bacon are only two of the many writers who place their utopias on islands; Tomasso Campanella's City of the Sun is rendered impregnable by its sevenfold walls; while more recent writers have set their fictions in the future, on other planets, or both. What does tend to change with the passage of time, however, is the scope of utopia: where earlier utopias were conceived of as isolated bastions of sanity in the midst of a world of chaos and unreason, their more recent counterparts have tended to become more all-embracing—the Wellsian world state being a case in point. While there are exceptions to this rule (such as Charlotte Perkins Gilman's *Herland*, Aldous Huxley's *Island*, or Ernest Callenbach's *Ecotopia*), the overall trend has been toward utopian fictions where the more perfect society, rather than cutting itself off from the real world, seeks instead to replace it. In Marge Piercy's feminist utopia, *Woman on the Edge of Time*, the forces of sexism and technocracy have been marginalized to the arctic regions and outer space; while in *Always Coming Home*, Ursula Le Guin's anarchist vision of freely interacting communities is set so far in the future that our own society is barely even a memory.

Yet this separation of utopia from the all-too-imperfect real world can never wholly obscure the links between the two. In theorizing a more perfect world, the writer remains governed by the realities of his or her own society, extrapolating from its more positive aspects, reacting against its more negative ones, recasting it in the light of social and political theories generated by the imperfect reality from which utopia separates itself. Equally, in narrative terms, there has to be some link, some fictional mechanism to render plausible the transmission of information regarding utopia to the non-utopian reader (to whom utopian fiction is, after all, addressed). Thus, no matter how inaccessible utopia might be, it always finds room for at least one visitor, a traveller, whether in time or space, who can observe and later testify to the wonders of the more perfect society. Although utopia's isolation is clearly designed to protect it from contamination by the squalor and disorder of the real world, it can never be *so* isolated as to be inaccessible to the privileged individual who will eventually return to bear witness to the superiority of the utopian way. However exclusive the writer's concentration on the distinctive excellences of utopia, however contemptuous he or she (more often he) may be of the defects of contemporary society, the fact of the connection remains: no matter how deeply buried in the text, the *relation* between utopia and reality is always a crucial aspect of utopian fiction.

More perfect than the real world, yet nonexistent; separate, yet connected: the more closely one examines utopian fiction, the more its ambiguities become apparent. Not the least of these is what might best be described as an ambiguity of *intention*: often it seems that the writers themselves are not entirely sure what effect they are aiming at. (Indeed, when one considers the range of critical responses to utopian fiction, it becomes clear that this uncertainty is also shared by the audience.) More's *Utopia*, for instance, contains what are surely deeply serious considerations of both the nature of good government and the role of the philosopher in society—yet it also contains elements suggesting that the whole work is little more than an elaborate scholarly joke (an impression which More's subsequent correspondence reinforces).[1] In later utopian fictions, serious, even mundane descriptions of political reforms and their consequences coexist with narrative devices whose fantastic nature works to heighten the reader's sense of the *fictional* character of what is described. The incredible (the century-long trance of the narrator in Edward Bellamy's *Looking Backward*, the gas which transforms human nature in H.G. Wells's *In the Days of the Comet*) go hand-in-hand with practical proposals for social and political reform. While commentators such as Darko Suvin and Gary Saul Morson rightly warn against the dangers of confusing utopian fiction with mere blueprints for social change[2], it is only fair to say that the confusion is one that writers of utopian fiction often do little to discourage. Campanella, writing in his Italian prison, clearly saw *The City of the Sun* as embodying a practical basis for the establishment of an ideal society, while contemporary responses to Bellamy's *Looking Backward*, ranging from William Morris's vehement denunciation to the enthusiastic reactions of those thousands of people who formed Bellamy societies, indicate that, for all its fantastic elements, it was seen as far more than merely wishful speculation. Both its threat and its promise lay in the fact that a substantial part of Bellamy's utopian vision was seen as at least potentially realizable. Still more recently, B.F. Skinner's *Walden Two* (1948), while vilified by a large number of critics, nevertheless prompted the foundation of several actual communities based on its principles.

Yet even where the element of practical social and political programme is less obtrusive, some degree of persuasive intent remains a fundamental characteristic of utopian fiction. Although, as we shall see, a good deal of recent criticism has tended to focus on the ways in which utopian fiction may be seen as a kind of 'thought experiment', presenting alternative forms of social organization to the reader in order to establish a creative dialogue in which the reader questions both his/her own assumptions and those of the author[3]—even here problems remain. While there *are* works of utopian fiction—mainly recent ones—which seek to create an open-ended format conducive to such continuing dialogue, there is also a powerful tendency, in many cases, for utopian fiction to resort to narrative strategies whose effect is to foreclose such dialogue, rather than stimulate it. Utopian fiction is often characterized by a certain *prescriptive* quality, suggesting, not simply that things might be otherwise, but that they *ought* to conform to a specific vision. While utopian fiction may have the potential to open up wider horizons, to suggest the sheer extent of the possible, its *effect* is often impoverishing rather than enriching: instead of opening up space for the imagination, the utopian vision merely fills it with a construct, to use Ernst Bloch's phrase, 'made banal by the fulfilment' (*Utopian Function* , p.2).

This is not to say, of course, that writers of utopian fiction are not aware of the problems inherent in the genre. As Wells suggests, in *A Modern Utopia:*

> There must always be a certain effect of hardness and thinness about Utopian speculations. Their common fault is to be comprehensively jejune. That which is the blood and warmth and reality of life is largely absent; there are no individualities, but only generalized people ... Too often the prospect resembles the key to one of those large pictures of coronations, royal weddings, parliaments, conferences and gatherings so popular in Victorian times, in which, instead of a face, each figure bears a neat oval with its index number legibly inscribed. [pp.9–10]

On the other hand, to recognize a problem is not necessarily to resolve it: the inhabitants of Wells's own utopias are for the most part as bloodless and one-dimensional as the denizens of Bacon's Bensalem or Campanella's City of the Sun. As in any fiction, utopian or otherwise, there are inherent problems in presenting characters who are merely ideals. Too often the reader's experience of utopian fiction is akin to that of reading a novel whose entire cast is composed of Dickensian heroines.

Psychologically speaking, it has been suggested that at least some of these deficiencies are rooted in what may be seen as the essentially regressive character of the fantasy underlying even those utopian visions which purport to describe societies of the future. In the Manuels' monumental survey of utopian thought, for example, it is suggested that for all its apparently rational character, utopia embodies the longstanding human dream of a return to paradise—a paradise which is in its turn a metaphor for the prenatal security of the womb. Other critics have pointed to the infantile dependency to which the citizens of many utopias of the authoritarian variety are reduced—a dependency ruthlessly satirized by Huxley in his dystopian *Brave New World*—while David Bleich argues that utopia is informed by a desire for immediate gratification that is typical of adolescence, not to mention being 'peculiarly masculine' (p.3) in character. The failure of utopian fiction to provide what Wells describes as 'the blood and warmth and reality of life', then, might be seen to reflect a desire to turn away from, or inability to deal with the complexities of adult experience.

The validity of such interpretations is a question to which we shall return; on the purely formal level, however, perhaps the basic problem lies in the hybrid character of utopian fiction. Whatever the psychological motivations involved, its aspirations are both political (to convince the reader of the desirability of its particular social vision) and aesthetic (to do so in an artistically convincing manner[4]). And in trying to do two things at once, it often succeeds in doing neither: the utopian vision is dismissed by political theorists as naïvely impractical, and by the literary critics as bad art. From a Marxist perspective, for instance, the main weakness of utopian theories is their tendency to make their goal the imposition of a static and often subjective ideal on society, disregarding the fact that historical development is a process involving the conflict and interaction of economic, social, and political forces. Progress is a *process*, not a finite goal to be attained once and for all—and while the utopian vision may well offer a valid critique of society as it exists at a specific time, its static character inevitably dooms it to obsolescence. However radical its initial impulse, the utopian dream is continually outstripped by the course of history. As Engels suggests, the writer or theorist who pursues utopian solutions in a modern context is rather like:

> ... someone who, after the discovery and establishment of the laws of modern chemistry, reestablished the old alchemy, and who seeks to utilize the atomic weights, the molecular formulae, the quantivalence of atoms, crystallography and spectral analysis, solely for the discovery—of the philosopher's stone. [p.276]

Or as Marx puts it, rather more bluntly: 'the man who draws up a programme for the future is a reactionary.'[5]

Of course, it is not only Marxists who are critical of utopian speculation: in much contemporary political discourse the term 'utopian' is a pejorative one—to label a scheme 'utopian' is often little more than a rhetorical device to rule it unworthy of serious consideration. Yet while the strictures cited above are addressed to utopian theorizing in general, rather than utopian fiction in particular, their application to the latter is hard to refute. Even so comparatively recent a utopia as Huxley's *Island* (1962), whose blend of pacifism, eastern mysticism, free love, and the sacramental use of psychedelic drugs seemed briefly prescient in the later 1960s, now appears increasingly quaint—a period piece—while earlier fictions, such as those of Bellamy and Wells, at least insofar as they embody what were once seen as practical programmes of social engineering, now seem not so much desirable ideals, as recipes for disaster. Such relevance as they continue to possess for a modern audience lies in what they reveal about the ideology of their specific historical period, and in such aesthetic merit as they may or may not exhibit.

In this last regard, however, utopian fiction is often seen as just as deficient as it is when considered in the light of practical politics. Bernard Bergonzi's lament that Wells should have deserted the realms of imaginative scientific fantasies such as *The Time Machine* or *The War of the Worlds* in favour of arid utopian speculation (p.165), or Frank Kermode's assessment of *Island* as 'one of the worst novels ever written' (p.472) are scarcely atypical pronouncements. For Northrop Frye, utopian literature remains 'a relatively minor genre never quite detached from political theory' ('Varieties', p.40), while Krishan Kumar suggests that 'few utopias stand out as great works of literature ... and in many cases utopian authors are perfunctory in the extreme in their selection and use of the form. The didactic purpose overwhelms any literary aspiration' (*Utopia*, p.25). And, once again, such criticisms are hard to refute. Considered in purely aesthetic terms, Wells's utopian fictions do represent, one must admit, a falling-off from his earlier science fiction, Huxley's last utopian vision a decline from the vigour of some of his earlier satire[6]—while Bellamy frankly admitted that in *Looking Backward* 'barely enough story was left to decently drape the skeleton of the argument and not enough, I fear, in spots, for even that purpose' (quoted in Kumar, p.151). And yet—the question remains whether or not this standpoint is really the most helpful one from which to examine utopian fiction. As with the political criticism that utopian speculation ignores the realities of the historical process, or the psychological reduction of utopia to a regressive fantasy, there remains the nagging suspicion that such readings—rather like that of the clergyman who, on reading *Gulliver's Travels*, allegedly declared that for his part he didn't believe a word of it—may be missing the point.

The Survival of Utopia

While the problems and contradictions which bedevil utopian literature are real enough, the discussion so far leaves a number of questions unanswered. Why, given the extent of the problems involved, do writers go on writing utopias? Why, given the often unsatisfactory character of the end product, do readers go on reading them? And what is it that motivates both writers and readers alike to seek ways out of this (at least apparent) impasse? Certainly, presented in the terms above, the problems inherent in utopian narrative may well appear insoluble. Nevertheless, more recent discussions of utopian fiction have gone some way towards either addressing the problems involved, or else finding ways of looking beyond them.

To begin with, it is clear that within a political context, while 'utopian' remains a pejorative term, at least within the discourse of those with an interest in the preservation of the status quo, the radical potential of utopianism is considerably greater than might appear from the Marxist strictures cited above. While, as we have seen, both Marx and Engels were critical of utopianism, there has been a growing awareness that this criticism needs to be located in the context of contemporary debates within socialism; and that it by no means rules out a sympathetic consideration of utopia as an enabling vision, rather than a static ideal. Far from dismissing utopianism *tout court*, in fact, both Marx and Engels were sympathetic to it in many of its aspects, and its compatibility with Marxist thinking is evident in the recuperation of utopianism within a Marxist tradition by writers such as Ernst Bloch[7] (although it should be said that Bloch himself remained critical of much utopian literature: witness his scathing dismissal of Wells's *Men Like Gods* as reducing utopia to 'a frolicking life like that of naked piano-teachers in Arcadia' (*Principle of Hope*, p.617).) As Ruth Levitas suggests:

> The roots of Marxist objections to utopia can be found in the writings of Marx and Engels; however, their criticisms of utopian socialism have been used illegitimately as a justification of a general rejection of descriptions of the future socialist society. The concept of utopia deployed in this rejection ... confounds two issues: speculation about the future, and the possibility and means of transition to socialism. The real dispute between Marx and Engels and the utopian socialists is not about the merit of goals or of images of the future but about the process of transformation, and particularly about the belief that propaganda alone would result in the realisation of socialism.'
> [*Concept of Utopia*, p.35]

Or, as Vincent Geoghegan argues, 'what is under attack ... is not anticipation as such, but rather the failure to root this anticipation in a theoretical framework cognizant of the essential dynamics of capitalism' (p.27).[8]

The recovery of a sense that utopia continues to possess at least radical *potential* has led in its turn to an exploration of ways in which utopian writing might escape the limitations evident in the examples of the past. In critical terms, perhaps the most radical strategy takes the form of what is in itself the highly utopian gesture of drawing a line between past and present, and starting again—acknowledging the failure of utopia as traditionally conceived, and charting a new path altogether. Angelika Bammer, for example, argues that:

> Those who declared that utopia was dead were, of course, in a structural sense, right. In that sense, utopia had always been dead. Rather than describe a vital impulse toward change, utopia as it has traditionally been defined represents a static and, in the most literal sense, reactionary stance: a place which, being 'perfect', does not need to—and will not—change. Conventional utopias thus embody an inherent contradiction. In their vision of a state in which change seems neither desirable nor possible, and even more significantly in their reconstruction of precisely the kind of dichotomous categories (notably the distinction between the 'actual real' and the 'impossible ideal') that they claim to refute, they tend to reinforce established ways of thinking even as they set out to challenge them. [p.2]

Against this, she suggests a range of possible revitalizing approaches, whose common feature is a moving away from the conception of utopia as total system. In place of the traditional utopia's detailed description of the workings of an entire alternative sociopolitical structure, she sees more recent utopian writing as offering glimpses, 'partial visions' of utopian possibility—a utopianism 'experimental rather than prescriptive, speculative rather than predictive ... propos[ing] a politics of change cast in the subjunctive instead of the imperative mode' (p.51). Tom Moylan, while similarly critical of the traditional utopia's 'narrative reduction of the multiple levels of utopian desire to the single, relatively abstract, field of social planning' (*Demand the Impossible*, p.24), also exemplifies the growing tendency to examine utopian fiction in the context of the generic norms of fantasy and science fiction, rather than those of representational realism. Taking a number of examples of recent utopian science fiction, he argues that such writing 'breaks with the limits of the traditional genre and becomes a self-critical and disturbingly open form that articulates the deep tensions within the political unconscious at the present moment' (p.210). The result is what he sees as an entirely new category—the 'critical utopia'— in which 'the imposed totality of the single utopian text gives way to the contradictory and diverse multiplicity of a broad utopian dialogue' (p.210). Yet if both Bammer and Moylan argue not only the possibility but the necessity of a radical break with the past, others have suggested that at least some earlier utopias encourage precisely the 'broad utopian dialogue' which Moylan identifies as distinctively new. Morson, for example, while acknowledging that a large number of traditional utopias are essentially monologic in character, attempting to establish the absolute authority of a particular viewpoint, points to both More's *Utopia* and Wells's *A Modern Utopia* as examples of what he terms 'meta-utopias'—works which, notwithstanding the authoritarian character of their imaginary sociopolitical structures, are designedly open to multiple and contradictory readings. Even if the utopian societies described may seem to embody a static ideal, rather than an active principle, they are nevertheless situated in a narrative context that holds that ideal up to critical inspection as one of a range of utopian possibilities. Peter Ruppert, examining the utopian tradition in the light of reader-response theory, goes still further, suggesting that this kind of reading can—even ought—to be the basis of reading *all* literary utopias. Where Bammer sees the traditional utopia's insistence on closure, both in narrative terms and in terms of the total system it describes, as undermining its 'transformative potential' (p.18), Ruppert argues that 'even though literary utopias are constructed like closed texts that try to elicit a precise response, they also force us to assume a more critical and detached position toward all social propositions, including the ones they offer' (p.62). Seen in this light, it might be argued that all utopias are in a sense 'critical utopias'—although pursuing this argument leads to a markedly ahistorical disregard for the fact that (for example) the huge success of works such as *Looking Backward* with contemporary audiences was based on reader responses radically unlike those which Ruppert proposes as normative.

Nevertheless, *how* one reads utopian literature does seem to be at the root of at least some of the problems inherent in utopian narrative—and what is also clear, more broadly, is the extent to which some of these problems derive from definition. When Kermode criticizes *Island* as 'one of the worst novels ever written', he is obviously electing to read it in a particular *kind* of way, within the interpretive conventions of representational realism—a decision not without its own ideological implications, and one which, as Wayne Booth points out, does not necessarily provide the most helpful context within which to read utopian fiction (p.631). Conversely, as Morson argues, disregarding the fictional aspect of utopian literature, and regarding it as merely the 'literary mould' into which utopian political theory is poured, leads to equally skewed critical judgements:[9] clearly, to read More's *Utopia* as though there were no real generic distinction between it and, say, Gerrard Winstanley's *The Law of Freedom in a Platform* is to ignore a crucial dimension of the work as a whole.

Prior to the act of reading, then, it would seem that some kind of informed generic definition is necessary—yet here, once again, problems arise.

That utopian fiction, pervaded as it is by ambiguity and contradiction, should present problems of definition is scarcely surprising. The very concept of utopia itself is an oddly slippery one, not only embracing a vast range of possible alternatives to existing society, but also often shading into kindred conceptions of a better world—the earthly paradise, the Arcadian idyll, the millennium[10]—and utopian fiction has likewise proved resistant to generic classification. It has variously been categorized as a kind of novel (however unsatisfactory), a type of romance, or, more recently, as a sub-genre of science fiction.[11] Yet, as Suvin has shown, even some of the most apparently commonsensical definitions prove, on closer examination, to be fraught with contradictions and unanalysed assumptions (*Metamorphoses*, pp.37–62).[12] Indeed, as Levitas argues, not only is there no real consensus regarding the definition of utopia, there is not even any general agreement as to the basis on which definition might be made: some commentators see utopia as primarily a formal category; others are more concerned with its content—the nature of the society imagined; while others still focus on the function which utopian imagining is designed to fulfill. Thus, while in practice

> … most commentators limit what they consider to be properly utopia … without agreement as to what the proper limits, if any, are, there is a danger of researchers in the area making arbitrary and subjective selections of material; or, even if they are clear and methodical in their own use of the term, using it in an idiosyncratic way and talking past each other; or, indeed, wasting too much time arguing over what is or is not utopian. [*Concept of Utopia*, p.4]

Unsurprisingly, therefore, even when the field is narrowed down to literary utopias alone, some of the most carefully crafted definitions continue to present difficulties. Morson, for example, while acutely aware of the problems involved, avoids the vagueness of some of the other commentators he discusses only at the cost of narrowing his generic definition to the point where it excludes a range of works that most would agree are clearly utopian:

> A work is a literary utopia if and only if it satisfies each of the following criteria: (1) it was written (or presumed to have been written) in the tradition of previous utopian literary works; (2) it depicts (or is taken to depict) an ideal society; and (3) regarded as a whole, it advocates (or is taken to advocate) the realization of that society. [p.72]

The difficulty with this is that, while it works well enough with most works written up until the early twentieth century, it excludes a whole range of more recent examples: those that consciously challenge the tradition of previous utopian works, like Samuel R. Delany's *Triton*; those that represent societies that, while utopian, are clearly far from ideal, like Le Guin's *The Dispossessed*; or those which, while presenting visions that are clearly utopian, can hardly be taken as advocating their realization, such as Gilman's *Herland*, or Sally Miller Gearhart's *The Wanderground*.

Suvin, by contrast, offers what would appear to be a more inclusive formula:

> Utopia is the verbal construction of a particular quasi-human community where sociopolitical institutions, norms, and individual relationships are organized according to a more perfect principle than in the author's community, this construction being based on estrangement arising out of an alternative historical hypothesis. [*Metamorphoses*, p.49]

Yet while the 'more perfect' formulation has the virtue of greater comprehensiveness, its effect is at the same time to downplay that prescriptive quality noted earlier—the tendency of many utopian fictions to present their visions not just as better alternatives, but as ideal solutions. Equally, one may question the utility, if not the logic, of a definition which results in the making of generic distinctions between works as closely related as *Looking Backward* and *News from Nowhere*—denying the latter the status of a utopia (p.182), while according it to the former.[13] Which brings us back to the formal problem alluded to earlier: the fact that utopian fiction is an inherently hybrid genre, incorporating so many features of contiguous modes that definition inevitably becomes problematic. Although distinct from the 'blueprint', or utopian treatise, utopian fiction nevertheless often contains many of its elements; likewise, while distinct from the novel, it often verges on the novelistic. Indeed, one of the recurrent problems in utopian fictions—its often awkward blend of the fantastic with the stolidly mimetic—may be seen as rooted in writers' own uneasy consciousness of the novel as a desirable model to emulate. Wells, Huxley, and Le Guin have all suggested that utopian fiction would benefit from being *more* novelistic, each attempting (albeit with varying success) to work in that direction.[14]

Whether this is the *best* way of resolving the problems inherent in the composition of utopian fiction is a different matter; nevertheless, for the purposes of definition, it is as well to bear in mind that the boundaries between utopian fiction and other genres would appear to be more than usually permeable. Indeed, it might be argued that it is only by crossing these boundaries that the problems inherent in utopian narrative can be resolved. Two of Moylan's main examples of the 'critical utopia', for instance, Delany's *Triton* and Joanna Russ's *The Female Man*, both move away from the straightforward delineation of the more perfect society to an exploration of varying social alternatives, both desirable and undesirable, an exploration more characteristic of the broader genre of science fiction. Delany, indeed (adopting Foucault's terminology), dubs his fiction a 'heterotopia', rather than a utopia—prompting the question whether it is in fact possible to resolve the problems inherent in the utopian genre without at the same time abandoning most of those elements that render it utopian.[15]

Yet while approaches such as these do much to recover the possibilities inherent in the category of utopia, and to resolve some of the problems attendant on utopian narrative, it is important to bear in mind that they themselves are *also* narratives—and, moreover, ones which rehearse a number of typically utopian narrative strategies. In contrast to the critical narrative of the death of utopia, the story they tell is effectively one of its salvation. In one account, utopia does indeed die, but only to be reborn under the new category of the utopia*n*, or the 'critical utopia'—a fresh start which draws a line between utopia and its past history in a manner very much characteristic of traditional utopian narrative. Ruppert uses reader-response theory to tell a somewhat different story, one in which the contradictions and loose ends of utopian narrative find resolution and completion in a dialectical relationship with the reader,[16] yet here again it is possible to detect the old utopian desire for wholeness, for a coherent total system. Even such moves as broadening the scope of utopian inquiry to encompass a whole range of utopian possibilities that go beyond the traditional 'ideal commonwealth' conceived in isolation exhibit what Suvin refers to as 'a somewhat overweening imperialism' (*Metamorphoses*, p.61) which might be read as parallel to the colonizing impulse of much utopian narrative, in which the problems inherent in the establishment of utopia in isolation are resolved by expanding it to embrace the wider territory of the world itself.

While sharing some of the same assumptions, this study seeks to offer not so much a counter, as a counterpoint to the narratives above. Where they are concerned with ways forward, with ways of escaping the pitfalls of the traditional utopia, this study is more concerned with the connectedness of new utopian directions with what went before—and in particular with the obstinate persistence of some of the characteristic patterns of traditional utopian narrative even into the radically different historical context of the present day. As the study of utopian literature has repeatedly shown, even those utopias which seek to break most radically with the norms of existing society often end up reinscribing many of the values they purport to oppose, and one question that clearly arises is whether the new approaches to both the study and writing of utopias are any more successful in transcending the limitations of the traditional model. Before that can be addressed, however, it is necessary to examine in more detail the nature of utopian narrative as such.

The Nature of Utopian Narrative

Unusually, given the diversity of opinion to which the discussion of utopia itself normally gives rise, there would appear to be something approaching consensus as to the nature of the traditional utopian narrative.[17] What Angelika Bammer describes as the 'rudimentary plot' (p.17) takes the form of a narrative which 'begins as the narrator/protagonist leaves his world to visit utopia and ... ends when he leaves utopia to return home' (p.17)— the choice of pronouns, incidentally, reflecting the fact that the protagonist in such narratives is nearly always male. Barbara Goodwin suggests that 'the traditional utopian form' is that of 'a voyage to a lost island or into the future' (p.15), in which the visitor is introduced to 'a perfect society which is viewed as an integrated totality' (p.16); while Frye offers a slightly more elaborate account:

> In utopian stories a frequent device is for someone, generally a first-person narrator, to enter the utopia and be shown around it by a sort of Intourist guide. The story is made up largely of a Socratic dialogue between guide and narrator, in which the narrator asks questions or thinks up objections and the guide answers them ... As a rule the guide is completely identified with his society and seldom admits to any discrepancy between the reality and the appearance of what he is describing. ['Varieties', p.26]

Originating in the Renaissance, it was a narrative model which at first proved serviceable enough; with the passage of time, however, its weaknesses begin to become more apparent. Comments on the shortcomings, literary or otherwise, of utopian narrative are, as we have seen, a recurrent phenomenon, and Frye is hardly alone in complaining that '[o]ne gets a little weary, in reading a series of such stories, of what seems a pervading smugness of tone' (p.26). Nevertheless, notwithstanding such criticisms, and despite radical changes over time in both the ideological character of the utopian societies imagined, and the range of alternative narrative models available, this curious hybrid of classical dialogue and traveller's tale has proved remarkably resilient. Full-blown examples, such as Huxley's *Island* or Callenbach's *Ecotopia*, can be found as late as the second half of the twentieth century; substantial elements of the form are present in a 'critical utopia' such as Piercy's *Woman on the Edge of Time*; while even dystopias such as Huxley's *Brave New World* and Orwell's *Nineteen Eighty-Four* are by no means free of its influence. A narrative model, in other words, that evolved to articulate a particular sociopolitical vision in a specific historical context, continues to be deployed in very different historical circumstances, and in the service of a vision whose ideological implications are in many cases virtually antithetical.

In order to account for this, a helpful starting point might be to examine the relation between narrative form and utopian content in more detail. In terms of content, for example, it is possible to distinguish, within the broader category of utopian fiction, between three main types—each characterized by its own distinctive ideological orientation. The first, with roots which go back to Plato and beyond, may be identified as primarily centralist and authoritarian in orientation—a dream of order conceived of in a world of disorder. The vast majority of utopias written prior to the twentieth century (*News from Nowhere* being a notable exception) conform to this pattern, portraying utopian society as something to be imposed on humanity in its own best interests. To modern eyes, of course, this traditional utopia seems regimented, lacking in freedom—yet it clearly possessed a considerable appeal in the historical context surrounding its emergence. To a contemporary of More or Campanella, their more perfect societies offered in fact a great deal of freedom—albeit mainly a freedom *from* a range of existing constraints, rather than 'individual freedom' as it is currently conceived of in western society. What such utopias offered was stability, security, freedom from hunger, from endless toil, from war. More, in the early 1500s, posited a society sufficiently rationally organized as to allow for a six-hour working day; Campanella, writing a century later, reduced it to four hours[18]—and it requires little exercise of the historical imagination to envisage the degree of liberation which this would have offered to members of nearly all levels of society. Moreover, many of the earlier utopias emerged from historical contexts in which the promise of civil order must have seemed especially appealing. For Plato, writing against the background of constant bickering and warfare between rival city states, for More, with the memory of the Wars of the Roses still relatively fresh, for Campanella, living in an Italy torn apart by civil strife and foreign invasion, the notion of a sane, orderly, rational, and above all peaceful society must clearly have exerted an almost irresistible appeal.

Ironically, the decline in the appeal of this type of utopia coincides with the development of many of the means—political, economic, technological—which might make such a social ideal a practical possibility. The utopian model of social control is, of course, predicated on the notion that such control would be used wisely, in the best interests of the citizen—

whereas modern experience of strong central authority has tended almost invariably to contradict this. While writers such as Bellamy and Wells carry the old, centralist, authoritarian tradition into the late nineteenth and early twentieth century, since then much of the gloss has vanished from the old utopian dream. The realities of modern dictatorship have made enthusiasm for the traditional model hard to sustain—and this has in turn given rise to both reactions against, and rethinking of the premises of the traditional utopia.

Reactions against the traditional utopian ideal take a variety of forms, the most significant being the dystopia—or anti-utopia—which both parodies and subverts the traditional utopian model as a means of satirizing and warning against some of the more alarming trends in contemporary society. Yevgeny Zamyatin's We and Huxley's Brave New World push the premises of the centralist utopia to the point where dream is transformed into nightmare—a nightmare in which technological progress, hitherto glorified by writers from Bacon to Wells as central to the realization of the utopian vision, becomes the means to a totalitarian end. Rather than liberating humanity from the constraints imposed by nature, technology becomes the instrument for the imposition of a far more rigorous tyranny— a tyranny of purely human agency. Citing Berdiaeff in the epigraph to Brave New World, Huxley implies that it is the growing practicability of utopia that renders it so threatening: from being an impossible ideal of perfection, it has been transformed (not least by technological progress) into a possible future—but one to be avoided at all costs.[19] What makes utopia a nightmare, in effect, is the fact that it is no longer merely a dream. With the proliferation of increasingly effective mechanisms for social control, in fact, dystopian fantasy has become in the modern era almost a myth in its own right—as expressive of the deep-seated dreams and anticipations of modern society as was utopia in the Renaissance—and as such it continues to flourish.[20] George Orwell's Nineteen Eighty-Four and, still more recently, Margaret Atwood's The Handmaid's Tale continue this tradition, extrapolating from such apparently disparate starting points as State Socialism and fundamentalist Christianity, yet arriving at visions of a future society which bear a marked family resemblance—much as do the more perfect societies presented in earlier utopian fiction.

Yet reaction against the utopian ideal is not the only direction writers have explored. Another alternative which has been pursued is the possibility of a utopia which is no longer predicated on order. Writing from a range of libertarian perspectives, writers from Morris to Le Guin and Piercy have created utopian visions which are not so much dreams of order in a world of disorder as dreams of freedom in a world of oppression. Individual freedom and self-fulfilment become the main goals of the more perfect society, rather than the imposition of a static, centralized order, however perfect in theory.

Which brings us to the question of the *relation* between narrative structures and ideology, and the extent to which radically different ideological assumptions are accompanied by the evolution of radically different narrative strategies. Obviously, there *are* differences in narrative approach: to begin with, in both dystopian fiction and the science-fictional devices of the 'critical utopia' one may see reflected the changing character of the literary models available at the time of writing—a transformation which in its turn reflects the changing character of the social formations which produce them. Nevertheless, this fails to account for why certain narrative patterns seem stubbornly to persist even when the literary model from which they derive has become outmoded. In the case of utopian narrative, for example, there is a clear correlation between its character and that of other narrative models prevalent at the time of its emergence— and the prevalence of those models is in turn a reflection of the surrounding historical context. Thus the traveller's tale format of so many Renaissance utopias (the 'sailor's yarn', as Bloch terms it) clearly reflects the popularity of this form during the age of exploration which constitutes part of the historical context in which they were produced. Equally, the massive resurgence of interest in Greek learning which characterized the Renaissance may be seen as reflected in the influence of the classical dialogue on the narrative practice of writers such as More and Campanella. Likewise, it is evident that the growing influence of the novel with the passage of time determines many of the modifications (greater emphasis on characterization, plot, and dramatic interaction) which utopian fiction comes to exhibit—although it is at the same time worth noting that, until the early twentieth century, these remain for the most part *only* modifications, rather than transformations of the original pattern. Dystopian fiction, however, originating at a time when the novel constitutes the dominant narrative model, moves much further in this direction, its typical theme of the struggle of the individual against an oppressive society lending itself readily to a more novelistic treatment. And while some of the earlier efforts at writing utopian fiction from a libertarian perspective (*News from Nowhere, Island*) may struggle to find an appropriate form, later works have clearly benefited from the example of modernist and postmodernist narrative experiment, as well as from the broader revaluation of fantasy and speculative fiction in recent years.

Yet it is not simply a question of writers making use of whatever narrative conventions happen to be current at the time. To begin with, it would seem that, as a genre, utopian fiction is particularly strongly influenced by a sense of its own specific tradition—by the writer's consciousness of what has gone before. However much it may be the product of its own time, utopian fiction is also, as Gary Saul Morson puts it, 'designed to be interpreted in the tradition of previous utopian works' (p.74). Not only do writers of utopian fiction engage in an ongoing debate with the ideas of earlier writers, they are often clearly very much aware of the *narrative* example of their predecessors. (*The Handmaid's Tale* is a striking instance of a work which makes self-conscious use of specific episodes in earlier fictions—rewriting, and ultimately subverting them.)

This becomes especially significant when one considers the fact that narrative forms themselves possess their own ideological implications—implications which in the case of utopian narrative are not always consistent with the ideological message inherent in the nature of the utopian society which that narrative depicts. Now clearly, every narrative has *some* ideological implications, however deeply buried: the decision to tell one story rather than another, to present a story in one way rather than another, is always to some extent—however indirectly—conditioned by ideological assumptions. The traditional folktale, with its recurrent message of the possibility of individual self-fulfilment within a rigidly hierarchical social structure, or the Victorian novel which examines the phenomenon of social unrest within the reconciling framework of a bourgeois love story are both cases in point. What utopian fiction does is reveal still more nakedly the nature of the relationship between ideology and narrative strategy—not least because of the gaps and contradictions which emerge when the two are considered together.

In discussing this relationship, however, it is important to guard against making too simplistic an equation between form and ideological content: to avoid, for instance, a crudely mechanical cause-and-effect model, where ideological base manifests itself in narrative superstructure; or, conversely, the assumption that specific forms *necessarily* possess corresponding ideological implications—that fragmentary and open-ended narratives are *ipso facto* subversive, for instance, or that narratives characterized by formal coherence and narrative closure are inevitably conventional. (Such assumptions would seem to inform the almost ritual lambasting of Le Guin in which a number of recent studies have engaged.)[21] A more sophisticated model of the relationship between ideology and narrative form is proposed by Pierre Macherey, who suggests that, while 'the history of forms ... corresponds to the history of ideological themes' (p.91), their interaction is in fact a complex one:

> The form takes shape or changes in response to new imperatives of the idea: but it is also capable of independent transformations, or of an inertia, which bends the path of ideological history. [p.91]

While the implications of a specific narrative form may be closely congruent with the ideology prevailing at the time of its inception, the relationship between them often changes with the passage of time: their development does not necessarily proceed in harmonious parallel. To take the example of the detective tale: in the hands of Edgar Allan Poe it is initially expressive of a prevailing ideological ambivalence—of anxiety regarding the dark forces unleashed by the loosening of traditional social constraints under the impact of capitalism, yet at the same time of a countervailing faith in the capacity of unaided human reason to deal with them. In its subsequent manifestations, however, there can be little doubt that the form most often lends itself to the expression of a more conservative ideology. In the tales of Sir Arthur Conan Doyle, the role of the detective as defender of society is emphasized to a greater extent, as is the sense of the social order as a good to be defended; while the detective himself may be a maverick, the end result of his efforts is the affirmation of the existing order. Even the relative ineptness of the police serves only to reinforce faith in the ability of their social superiors: the ruling class can always produce a Holmes—whose brilliance also communicates the comforting message that significant *individual* action is still possible, notwithstanding the complexities of mass society. In tales where the detective is himself a policeman, the reinforcement of confidence in authority is stronger still. This is not to say, however, that the form itself is *inevitably* conservative in its implications: while it certainly lends itself more easily to the expression of an essentially conservative ideology, it can also be used for rather different ends. In works such as Jorge Luis Borges' 'Death and the Compass', or Stanislaw Lem's *The Chain of Chance*, the form acquires a renewed ambivalence, communicating a sense of the limitations of human reason in the face of the infinite complexity of reality, rather than a complacent confidence in the resilience of the existing order. The form, in effect, contains its own matrix of sedimented ideological implications,[22] some (though not necessarily all) of which can be potentiated even where they run counter to prevailing ideological trends. Yet at the same time, the form is not *wholly* malleable: it can still undermine or deform the writer's intentions, as in the case of designedly 'progressive' detective fictions, where the villain is a policeman, or a corrupt politician, but where the threat they pose is nevertheless susceptible to a comforting resolution, in which their excision from the order of which they constitute part is enough to preserve its structure intact. What in effect becomes apparent, as Fredric Jameson argues, is the extent to which 'an already constituted "narrative paradigm" emits an ideological message in its own right' (*Political Unconscious*, p.88).

In the case of utopian fiction, a similar pattern is evident. Originally cast in the form of the traveller's tale, the utopian narrative has continued over the years to manifest many of the form's characteristic features—radical changes in the surrounding ideological context notwithstanding. The original appeal of this particular narrative model, as we have seen, is not hard to understand. As Frank and Fritzie Manuel observe:

> As strange lands were penetrated, the windows of credibility were opened wide. Authentic narratives about new nations and kingdoms with hitherto unheard-of customs were in themselves so marvellous that they lent verisimilitude to the imaginary utopia, however wild it might be. The boundary line between the real and unreal, possible and impossible, faded. [p.82]

In an age of exploration, such narratives had a particular immediacy. Indeed, for More and his circle, one senses that this was not simply part of the appeal, but also part of the joke: it was actually *possible* that someone might take it seriously, as a factual account. More's Raphael Hythloday, in the account he gives of his travels, is hardly less credible than many other visitors to exotic parts who returned home to tell the world of the wonders they had witnessed.

So long as exploration persists—so long as the traveller may, potentially, have something new to say—so too does the appeal of the traveller's tale, the 'sailor's yarn', as a narrative model. The utopian tale, be its narrator More's Hythloday or Campanella's Genoese mariner, has both exoticism and plausibility to commend it: it is incredible, certainly, but hardly more so than a variety of competing narratives which purport to be authentic. In effect, it is a narrative format almost equally suited to the representation of fact or fantasy, inasmuch as both are capable of embodying the radically new—and a mode which proceeds by sequentially unveiling the unknown is as apt for articulating the utopian dream, as for relating the wonders of new discovery.

Nevertheless, as the age of exploration draws to a close, the fictionality of utopian narrative becomes increasingly transparent. Colonized by the old, known world, the infinite possibilities of the new become closed and finite. Gradually, the traveller gives way to the rather less glamorous figure of the tourist: a cataloguer, not of the new and unknown, but of the meaninglessly exotic; returning home not with news from nowhere, but with holiday snaps—souvenirs of an experience of little relevance, or even interest to the reluctant viewer. This transition, in its turn, finds an almost comical reflection in utopian narrative, where, while the *form* of the traveller's tale is preserved well into the twentieth century, the intrepid explorer of the Renaissance utopia is replaced by the more prosaic figure of the holiday-maker. It is no coincidence, for example, that two of Wells's utopian fictions begin with the central character going on vacation—while in Huxley's *Island*, Will Farnaby reaches the mysterious utopian island of Pala, not in the course of a voyage of discovery, but when a recreational boating trip goes disastrously awry. At the same time, the emergence of the novel as the dominant form of fictional discourse, and the changing expectations on the part of the reader to which this gives rise, serve to render the limitations of the traditional format more apparent: compared to the novel, the traveller's tale appears linear, episodic, lacking in dramatic interaction—deficiencies which only become more obvious when, as is often the case in more recent utopian fiction, the writer introduces novelistic elements (attempts at individual characterization, a love interest, and so forth) in an effort to remedy the problem.

The continued survival of this narrative pattern, then, even in a world where the traveller's tale seems more suggestive of the guided tour or the advertising brochure than of the exploration of new worlds, might well seem puzzling. Given its persistence even in some of the most recent utopian narratives, however, a consideration of the form's ideological implications may prove helpful. To begin with, it is clear that one essential feature of the traveller's tale is that it is already *finished*: the experience it relates has to be completed before it can be narrated. The very presence of the traveller before his audience indicates his separation from the experience he is about to relate. For him (as has been observed, the traveller in such narratives is almost invariably male), the experience of utopia lies in the past, elsewhere in time, as well as in space. And because that experience has been completed, it can be presented as a whole, a static entirety. In a Renaissance context, where the notion of a static society seemed neither implausible nor undesirable, this presents few problems: while with hindsight we may see the process of historical change leading to the emergence of the modern world as well under way, neither process nor change would have seemed inherent features of society to the writers or readers of the period. While the Renaissance imagination was quite capable of conceiving of alternative, indeed better forms of society, there was less concern with the process of how they might come into being. Indeed, it is significant that a good deal of radical political dissent at the time was informed by millennialist fantasies, not simply of the transformation of society, but of its immediate, and above all, *final* transformation—after which further change would be unnecessary. It is only with the passage of time, once again, that problems arise: when writers such as Bellamy or Wells, writing in the context of a *perceptibly* changing world, continue to conceive of utopia in basically static terms.

What is it, then, about a static social vision that should prove so problematic in terms of fictional representation? It has, to begin with, radical implications with regard to the depiction of time: if the utopian society is static, immune to change, or at least sufficiently perfect that only minor tinkering is needed to sustain it, then time is deprived of much of its meaning, since nothing that happens in time has any real effect. Mikhail Bakhtin's concept of chronotope is helpful in this context: given the mutual interdependence of time and space which this posits, it is clear that the virtual elimination of time as a significant factor will have profound implications for the writer's depiction of space. Which is precisely what we find: in the traditional utopian narrative, the absence of any real sense of time can only be compensated for by a corresponding extension in space. All the traveller can really do is *visit*, moving from place to place in a random and arbitrary order so as to witness the various excellences of utopian society. Since in such a society nothing of significance ever happens (everything of significance has *already* happened), it is of little consequence whether the visitor learns first about education and health care, and then about domestic arrangements, or *vice versa*. In addition, the fact that time in any meaningful sense has come to a stop often lends to the traditional utopian narrative a millenarian character which makes still more marked its separation from the reality to which it proposes an alternative. The virtual abolition of time leads to a corresponding lack of interest in *process*: as Bakhtin puts it, such fiction '... always sees the segment of a future separating the present from the end as lacking value; this separating segment of time loses its significance and interest, it is merely an unnecessary continuation of an indefinitely prolonged present ' (*Dialogic Imagination*, p.148). Which again has obvious narrative repercussions: in a context where time and historical causation have lost all meaning, the concept of individual character likewise becomes meaningless. Where the birth, life, death of the individual make no difference, individual distinguishing characteristics become insignificant; in narrative terms, this tends to result in the replacement of the individual character by that more durable construct, the typical citizen. As Frye remarks, in most cases 'the utopia-writer is concerned only with the typical actions which are significant of those social elements he is stressing' ('Varieties', p.26). In *Looking Backward*, for instance, Edith Leete is characterized (if that is the right word) as 'an indefatigable shopper' (p.52), and it often seems as though her function as love interest is secondary to her utility as a narrative mechanism for taking the narrator shopping, thus opening his eyes to the wonders of utopian commerce. (Although the prevalence in North America of bumper stickers reading 'Born to Shop' might be seen as indicating that such complete lack of character is not unique to utopia.) Interaction between such ciphers inevitably becomes equally meaningless, while that other dramatic staple of the novel, the conflict between individual and society, is likewise precluded—for who would wish to oppose the utopian order?[23] (Interestingly enough, however, many utopias provide for just such an eventuality, the penalties for dissidence ranging from exile or slavery to treatment in a mental institution—not to mention Bellamy's enlightened solution of solitary confinement on a diet of bread and water.)

Dystopian fiction, by contrast, would seem to suffer from fewer limitations. Although it too posits the *existence* of a static social order, its parodic elements serve to imply an alternative value system in the light of which utopian society is judged and found wanting. There is an implicit dialectic between the imaginary and the actual which enlivens and gives depth even to so close a parody as Huxley's *Brave New World* constitutes of the Wellsian world state. In addition, the abandonment of the notion that utopia is desirable make possible that very element of dramatic interaction which the traditional utopian narrative so signally lacks. Since the utopian ideal is no longer seen as positive, the concept of opposition to it is no longer unthinkable. And in resisting the authoritarian aspirations of the State, dystopian dissidents may be seen as offering, at a narrative level, an embodiment of the reader's own resistance to the closure and over-determination which so often characterizes the traditional utopia. Even where the dissident elements are defeated (as they almost invariably are), there remains a degree of conflict, of dramatic process, which gives rise to a very different narrative pattern. Instead of the traveller's bland report on the wonders of utopian society, we are given the portrayal of individuals in conflict with society—a theme so often central to the novel. Where the static society is presented from a critical perspective, its existence is no longer inimical to successful narrative experiment. And, as a number of commentators have argued, where the concept of utopian stasis is also abandoned, as is the case in much recent utopian fiction, the range of possible narrative experiment is still further extended.

All of which might seem to suggest that, in the case of the traditional utopian narrative, the problem is largely one of ideology—that the static character of such utopian visions is not so much a function of the narrative vehicle, but rather inherent in the writer's own ideological assumptions. While Wells, for example, whose assertion that utopia should be 'not static but kinetic' (*A Modern Utopia*, p.5) suggests a keen awareness of the problem, tries to address the issue primarily by means of narrative experiment, the effect of the static social vision he presents serves to neutralize those narrative elements which are freighted with different chronotopic and dramatic implications. His attempts to combine a portrait of utopian society with novelistic elements in *In the Days of the Comet*, or with social satire in *Men Like Gods* result in rather awkward hybrid narratives, whose non-utopian elements seem designed more to mask the limitations of utopian narrative than to resolve them. Even *A Modern Utopia*, which several critics have seen as a more successful attempt to create an open-ended and non-prescriptive utopian vision,[24] never entirely succeeds in avoiding the pitfalls of the traditional utopia. For all its elaborate narrative framework and self-consciously speculative tone, the actual portrait of utopian *society* that emerges remains static, rather than kinetic; as in *Men Like Gods* and *In the Days of the Comet*, the impact of the narrative innovations is neutralized by the authoritarian implications of the utopian vision which they accompany.

Yet consideration of another aspect of the traditional utopian narrative suggests that its limitations are by no means an *automatic* reflection of the writer's ideological assumptions—that the actual narrative itself possesses characteristics which may either reinforce or run counter to the writer's ideological intent. For example, the earliest utopian narratives are not only modelled on the traveller's tale, they are also, as Ruppert observes, 'structured and organized as dialogues' (p.xi). Campanella's *The City of the Sun*, for instance, is laid out as a formal dialogue—and even where this is not the case, it is clear that the dialogue is a fundamental feature of utopian narrative, whether the interlocutors are More and Hythloday, Julian West and Dr Leete, or Morris's William Guest and Old Hammond. Such dialogue, of course, may be seen as serving a purely functional purpose. Just as the traveller's tale is a convenient narrative vehicle, in that it accounts for the process of witnessing utopia and returning to describe it, so the dialogue allows for the efficient transmission of the mass of factual detail required to flesh out the outlines of the more perfect society. Nevertheless, a number of critics (Ruppert included) have adduced from this a broader principle: that utopian narrative, by virtue of its origins, is *inherently* dialogic, even dialectical, inviting readers into active participation in the text, rather than relegating them to the status of passive observers. Yet while it is certainly true that a number of *recent* utopian fictions invite such interaction, a consideration of the conventions of the Renaissance dialogue, in which the traditional utopian narrative is rooted, might suggest that it is more often designed to have precisely the opposite effect—to produce the illusion, rather than the reality of dialogue. Functioning primarily as a rhetorical device, it serves rather to reinforce the authority of a single viewpoint than to reflect a genuine process of debate. More's *Utopia* is in fact most unusual in the degree of tension that exists between the conflicting points of view espoused by the narrator and Hythloday; more generally, the Renaissance dialogue (to a far greater extent than the Socratic model from which it derives) uses the appearance of debate or discussion as a rhetorical tool. One speaker either asks questions designed purely to set up the authoritative statements of the other (as is glaringly the case in *The City of the Sun*), or else voices reservations or opposing arguments whose rebuttal only strengthens the case of the speaker who represents the author's own point of view. As Bakhtin observes: 'when the genre of the Socratic dialogue entered the service of ... established, dogmatic worldviews ... [it] was transformed into a simple form for expounding already found, ready-made irrefutable truth; ultimately, it degenerated completely into a question and answer form for training neophytes' (*Problems*, p.110). Looking at some of the examples referred to above, it would appear that much of the discussion in *Looking Backward* or *News from Nowhere* bears this out. Serving a mainly didactic intent, its effect is to foreclose dialogue, rather than encourage it; confronted by such devices, the reader is likelier to feel that the debate has been rigged than that his or her active participation is invited. Rooted in such conventions, utopian narrative is often in fact anti-dialogic, rather than dialectical, enacting the suppression and marginalization of other voices, rather than allowing them free and creative interaction. Utopian narratives may seek to challenge 'established worldviews', but the alternatives they propose are often presented in a manner hardly less dogmatic.

To this extent, then, the traditional utopian narrative may be seen to bear out Jameson's contention that 'in its generic form, a specific narrative paradigm continues to emit its ideological signals long after its original content has become historically obsolete' (*Political Unconscious*, p.186)—in this case serving to reinforce the writer's own ideological assumptions, where these are authoritarian in essence, yet also to undercut those of a more libertarian cast. If Wells's attempts to resolve the narrative problems of utopian fiction are thwarted by the ideological limitations of his essentially static conception of utopian society, it might equally be said that the libertarian visions of Morris, and later Huxley, are undermined by the authoritarian implications inherent in their narrative format.

A tension between ideology and narrative form, then, is often manifest in utopian fiction, with the one frequently at odds with the other. Utopian narratives, as Bammer argues, are 'texts in which an oppositional impulse is embedded in an essentially conservative form', and as a result 'are *generically* ambiguous' (p.45). Yet this tension is reflected not just at the level of structure, but also in matters of detail. Detail, in fact, is a recurrent preoccupation of utopian fiction. Not only are the broad outlines of the utopian social system provided, but also all manner of minutiae whose relevance is not always readily apparent. While More's explicit account of the seating plan for utopian mealtimes can be seen to have at least *some* function in the wider scheme of his description of utopian education, it is harder to see the justification for Bacon's obsession with the smallest details of utopian clothing and personal jewellery—still less the insistence, in

James Harrington's *Oceana*, on specifying the precise heights of the various ballot boxes! Writers of utopias often seem reluctant to leave anything to chance, and their resultant propensity to systematize even the most trivial aspects of social organization can, as Roland Barthes argues, end up undermining itself—if it is only pursued *far enough*. In his discussion of the French utopian theorist, Charles Fourier, Barthes suggests that Fourier's mania for classifying everything from social institutions to sexual proclivities (Fourier calculates, for example, that 'at the rate of 33 per million' there are roughly 26,400 males in the world who—like him—are predominantly attracted to lesbians) is carried to such extremes that it ultimately subverts the utopian impulse toward rational order (Barthes, p.93). So all-embracing is Fourier's system of classification that, rather than separating and distinguishing categories, it paradoxically suggests potential connections between even the most disparate objects. What, for example, do horses, cats, and fertilizer have in common? Each functions to consume the global surplus of watermelons produced by the utopian state: an infinite system of classification ultimately establishes an infinite series of connections, thereby undermining the whole purpose which classification is designed to serve.

Of course, few writers go to such extremes as Fourier—whose theories, incredible though it may seem, were intended, not as fictions, but as the basis for a practical programme of action. It may be that he felt the writing of fiction to be superfluous, given the blossoming of art he envisaged as following inevitably on the realization of his utopian vision:

> When the globe shall have been organized and brought to a total of three billion inhabitants, there will normally be on earth thirty-seven million poets the equal of Homer, thirty-seven million mathematicians the equal of Newton, thirty-seven million authors of comedies the equal of Molière, and the same number in all other conceivable talents (these are estimates) ... [Quoted in Manuel and Manuel, p.667]

Yet this kind of excess,[25] the capacity to imagine possibilities extending so far beyond the actual, is in fact relatively uncommon in utopian fiction, which, at least until relatively recently has tended to limit itself to horizons dictated by what might *rationally* be anticipated. As opposed to the inventions of Fourier, which in Barthes' view 'address[es] the absolutely new, that about which nothing has yet been said' and which 'preach[es] only what Opinion holds to be *impossible*' (p.88), utopian fiction for the most part remains constrained by a concern for what is at least plausible—displaying in the process a caution that Bloch sees as typical of the bourgeois imagination.[26] The impulse toward systematization remains, however, as does the obsession with specifying the smallest details of utopian social organization. Underlying much utopian fiction is the implicit assumption that if only everything can be determined, every contingency anticipated, every space within the boundaries of utopia filled, then the disorder and consequent imperfection of reality can somehow be avoided. Yet the completeness to which such fiction aspires invariably proves an unattainable goal. No matter how clear its presentation, how comprehensive its scope, how coherent its organization, there are always contradictions, places where, as we shall see, utopia frays at the edges, revealing conflicting assumptions, incompatible agendas.

Given this aspiration to completeness, to say everything, Macherey's suggestion, that 'what is important in the work is what it does not say' (p.87), is particularly apt. Underlying any fictional text are the shadows of what might have been said, even perhaps of what was intended or hoped to have been said, and an examination of the nature of the gap that exists between the text and its shadow, the word and the often more suggestive silence that surrounds it is often fruitful. But it is particularly so in the case of utopian fiction: committed as it is to a coherence and order more perfect than that which actually exists, its incoherences and inconsistencies are especially instructive. What *does* utopian fiction not say? With its stress on the difference, the superiority of its alternative society, it often glosses over the extent to which it continues to resemble the world to which it is designed to be superior. Hence, one question to be asked is—what aspects of the writer's own world does s/he choose *not* to address, *not* to reform? As well as examining what is different in utopia, we must also ask what remains the same. For even where it is most coherent, consistent, complete, utopia can never wholly cut itself off from the world of the writer who creates it, or of the reader to whom it is addressed. Equally, on the formal level, it is necessary to examine whether attempts to break away from the traditional narrative pattern are wholly successful, or whether in some of the apparently gratuitous details of the text its shadow remains apparent.

When it comes to examining what is *not* said, however, it is striking that for all the wealth of detail that utopian fiction customarily provides, one area where such detail is conspicuously lacking is that surrounding the question of how the utopian society originated—a question which is generally given only the most perfunctory treatment, or even avoided altogether. There are exceptions, of course: in *News from Nowhere* in particular, and to a lesser extent in *Island*, there is some attempt to account for the process whereby the more perfect society came into being. But in most cases utopia is achieved by *fiat*—created once and for all, whole and perfect, by some King Utopus or Solamona; or else simply emerging from circumstances which are never made clear. In *Looking Backward*, for example, utopia just *happens*, inevitably, we are told, while the narrator is conveniently asleep; while Wells resorts to a whole battery of narrative devices—redemptive gases, parallel universes, a twin earth with an alternative history—to avoid altogether the practical issue of *how* a better society might be created.

Such evasion is in itself revealing, suggestive of a reluctance to confront the nature of the relation between the real world and the utopian dream. Indeed, we are often given more detail about the barriers and boundaries that *separate* utopia from the real world—the vast earthmoving project with which King Utopus severs Utopia from the mainland, or the sevenfold walls which enclose the City of the Sun—than is provided concerning the origins of the more perfect society. But it is not just the fact of the evasion which is significant: equally revealing is the compensatory elaboration of what might be termed the *metaphors of transition* which utopian fiction contains. While the question of how utopia came about is often evaded, there is no lack of detailed (and often extremely bizarre) explanations of its *narrative* link to the real world: although the reader may be starved of details concerning utopia's creation, there is frequently a compensatory mass of detail concerning how the visitor to utopia got there. Once again, a characteristic chronotope is evident—one in which the spatial displaces the temporal: descriptions of utopian history may be perfunctory or nonexistent, but utopian *geography*, and the problems this poses for the traveller, are given extensive treatment. And when these metaphors of transition are examined, they often exhibit a striking family resemblance, suggestive not simply of ideological, but also psychological parallels. What is not said, and still more, what is said *instead* of what is not said, prove highly revealing of some of the most deep-seated impulses underlying utopian projections. Which in its turn, as this study will seek to demonstrate, points to the need to add one further term to the matrix of historical context, ideological orientation, and narrative structure which has so far been examined: the question of gender. For if the overwhelming majority of utopian dreams of order have been written by men, it is equally the case that the recent resurgence in utopian dreams of freedom has been predominantly the work of women. In the more detailed textual analysis that follows, it will be argued that this is no accident.

DREAMS OF ORDER

2. The Utopian Dream of Order: More and his Successors

Reference has already been made to the emergence of a distinctive pattern of utopian narrative during the Renaissance, and to its relation to some of the other available narrative models of the period. Before exploring its later transformations, however, it would be helpful to examine its distinguishing features in more detail. As has already been argued, utopian fiction reflects not just the ideological climate of its day, not just the influence of available literary models, but also the writer's own awareness of and response to a specifically utopian literary tradition. This being so, an examination of the earliest exemplars of this tradition, of the works which in so many ways set the agenda for subsequent utopian fiction, may be seen as an essential prerequisite for an understanding of the radical changes in both ideology and narrative structure which such fiction has undergone in the past hundred years.

The obvious starting point for such an examination, of course, is More's *Utopia*: the work from which the genre itself takes its name. Yet to examine it in isolation presents some equally obvious problems. While, as Morson observes, the whole notion of genre presupposes shared assumptions on the part of both author and reader as to its nature and ruling conventions, it follows that:

> ... the exemplars of a genre occupy a unique status. For a genre's first works cannot have been designed to be read in the tradition of previous works, nor can they have been designed to be interpreted according to the conventions of a generic tradition that began only with them ... works become exemplars only through the unforeseen creation of later works and the unanticipated emergence of a common hermeneutic approach to the entire class. History makes the exemplar; and tradition, insofar as it directs readers to take the exemplar *as a member of the genre* that it fathers, changes its semiotic nature: the original text is, in effect, re-created by its own progeny. [pp.74–5]

Subsequent utopian fictions, in other words, by their common pursuit of some, but not all of the possibilities adumbrated by More, have served to establish a generic model with which the exemplar—*Utopia*—is only partially congruent. *Utopia*, in short, unlike its successors, is by no means *only* a work of utopian fiction—witness the volume and diversity of critical commentary to which it has given rise, much of it devoted to the question of just what *kind* of work it is. It is only when examined in the context of subsequent works—of its utopian 'progeny'—that its distinctive generic characteristics become clear. By way of establishing those aspects of More's fiction that are specific to the traditional utopian narrative model, rather than peculiar to *Utopia* alone, the present discussion will therefore also focus on two of the most influential utopias of the later Renaissance: Campanella's *The City of the Sun* (1623), and Bacon's *The New Atlantis* (1627).

The Historical Context of *Utopia*

Utopia itself was first published in 1516, but it is clear that what one might term the utopian impulse—the urge to dream or speculate about a more perfect social order—was hardly something new. Theories as to the nature of an ideal state go back to the time of Plato and beyond, while the basic human yearning for a better world, whether expressed in nostalgia for a lost Eden or vanished Golden Age, or in dreams of a heavenly afterlife, seems practically coterminous with civilization itself. Nevertheless, there can be little doubt that in More's hands the *expression* of this impulse takes on a new and distinctive form. *Utopia* is neither a manifestation of nostalgia for the past nor a millennial dream. It is not an abstract, theoretical discussion of the mechanisms of an ideal state, after the fashion of Plato's *Republic*, and still less is it a pastoral fantasy, whether of the temperate bliss of Arcadia, or the riotous overindulgence of the land of Cockaigne. What More offers is not a blueprint, but the portrait of a more perfect society in operation, and one which has been created by the unaided use of human reason. And it is this last which is perhaps the main source of *Utopia's* lasting appeal, the reason why 'utopia' has passed into the language as word signifying a fundamental cultural concept—the fact that More's fiction depicts the real possibility of humanity taking control of its own destiny and, in doing so, creating a world that—above all—*makes sense*.

This is not to say that in Utopia's more perfect society individual human beings have become wholly rational: it is accepted that irrational and instinctual impulses will persist; however, such impulses are channelled and controlled by a social order that is, at all levels, rationally explicable. (Even its rituals and customs are, as Frye observes, susceptible to rational explanation.)[1] *Utopia* portrays a society that is *fundamentally* orderly, part of its appeal lying in the fact that there is an explanation for everything. Unlike More's own world, with its frequent lapses into chaos and anarchy which could only be made sense of by recourse to such essentially irrational concepts as the inscrutable workings of Divine Providence, Utopia could be explained (and justified) in terms of reason alone. As a social construct, Utopia was simpler, more orderly, more elegant, and perhaps for that very reason more aesthetically appealing than any existing social system—in much the same way that the Copernican model of the universe was more appealing, in its orderly simplicity, than the old Ptolemaic version, with its untidy jumble of planetary epicycles. Nor was the appeal of that simplicity lessened by More's shrewd decision to preface his purportedly eyewitness' description of utopian society by a vivid portrait of some of the real-life alternatives to the rule of reason: the first book of *Utopia* depicts a world full of ignorant lawyers, foolish priests, grasping landowners, and power-mad monarchs—a satiric *tour de force* which inevitably prompts, on the reader's part, a sympathetic predisposition toward the discourse that follows.

A number of questions remain, however: what, for instance, prompts the emergence of this vision of human and social possibilities at this *particular* moment in time? And, having emerged, why should it then be so eagerly seized upon as a model for so many reworkings of the theme (many of which would doubtless have horrified the author of the original version)? Clearly, no discussion of the nature and appeal of *Utopia* can be divorced from a consideration of the historical and intellectual context within which it was composed—and while one can scarcely hope, given the present study's terms of reference, to do anything like justice to the appalling complexity of the conflicting beliefs and ideologies underlying Renaissance thought, it might be helpful to point to some of the more significant connections between *Utopia* and the social and intellectual milieu within which More was writing.

Considering when it was written, one of *Utopia's* most striking features is—at least at first sight—the unusual degree of what might be termed cultural relativism it displays. In More's fiction, the society of his own day is judged and found wanting, not in the light of absolute and divinely ordained moral standards, but rather in comparison to specific (if hypothetical) instances of other human societies doing things differently—and *better*. Far from exhibiting a xenophobic preference for the English (or even European) way of doing things, More appears to look to his imaginary foreign societies (Achorians, Macarians, Utopians) for examples from which his own society might profitably learn. And this apparent willingness to judge society by alternative *human* standards may be seen as, at least in part, the product of a quite literal widening of horizons—both geographical and intellectual. In intellectual terms, More was both beneficiary and proponent of the resurgence of interest in classical Greek learning—a phenomenon which, while prompted by renewed access to the wisdom of the past, rapidly came to offer a challenge to many of the received intellectual assumptions of the present. The influence of Plato, in particular, proved a powerful stimulus to new ways of looking at the world, reinforcing as it did the sense that contemporary society had much to learn from the example of a past civilization whose intellectual accomplishments and modes of political organization were at least as sophisticated as those sixteenth century Europe. The revival of interest in Greek learning, in other words, inspired More with the sense of there being alternative models of social organization which, even if impractical in terms of the political realities of his own day, certainly bore thinking about.

The expansion of intellectual horizons, however, might equally be seen as representing a shift in society's temporal perspectives: the opening of a new window on the past, together with the accompanying sense of another time as not only different, but also having value, opens the way to an awareness that the present is by no means immutable, that change inspired by the example of past human achievement is not only possible, but even desirable. And this potential challenge to human acceptance of the world's existing order is of course reinforced by the simultaneous expansion of geographical horizons—to which More was equally responsive. Writing in the immediate aftermath of the discovery of the New World, and in the dawn of a new era of exploration, More could not help but respond imaginatively to the fact that different forms of social organization were not merely a feature of the past, but actually existed in the world of his own day. Admittedly, the information available concerning the actual *nature* of such different societies was scanty at best at the time he was writing, but this scarcely mattered: what was important was not so much the details, as the *possibility*—as may be seen from the way in which More seizes on a throwaway remark in one of Amerigo Vespucci's letters regarding the indigenous South Americans' contempt for riches, and extrapolates from this an entire society based on the absence of private property. The expansion of geographical horizons provided a physical space into which the more perfect society could be projected, not merely as an abstract formulation, but as a concrete fictional portrayal, presented in the words of someone who claimed actually to have been there, and seen it with his own eyes.

All of which suggests—and rightly so—that More was someone who responded eagerly to new thinking, to new ideas and possibilities: in both its vigorous attack on the shortcomings of the existing order, and its lively exploration of radical alternatives, *Utopia* is a work clearly reflective of the age of transition in which it was written. Yet it would be wrong to see More, as some critics have done, as therefore progressive. While he was very much a man of his time, that time was characterized by an extraordinary ferment of ideas, quite as many of which were backward-looking as progressive. Indeed, even some of the most apparently radical ideas and attitudes prove, on closer inspection, to possess startlingly retrogressive implications. Thus, for example, while More's was a period when Western society was on the threshold of an era of far-reaching religious reform (a process in which More himself was shortly to become embroiled, and not on the 'progressive' side), an examination of the writings of the would-be reformers themselves suggests that it is doubtful whether their intention was to take religion in a new direction. Rather, it would seem that what is now termed the Reformation was initially conceived of in terms of the recovery of lost purity, of a return to principles and values which had been obscured by latter-day corruption—as a restoration, rather than a revolution.

The revival of interest in Greek learning, likewise, was seen in More's time in a somewhat different light. Where, to the modern eye, its most important aspect might seem to be the stimulus which it gave to new discovery, or the challenge which Platonic philosophy represented to the longstanding primacy of Aristotelianism, at the time the emphasis was rather different. When, for instance, in the early 1460s, Cosimo de' Medici ordered Marcilio Ficino to begin translating the Greek manuscripts which his agents had been busy collecting following the fall of Byzantium, he instructed him to begin, not with the works of Plato (manuscripts of which he possessed), but with the *Corpus Hermeticum*, a collection of mystical and magical writings dating from between AD 100 and 300, but thought at the time to be the work of Hermes Trismegistus, a sage supposed to have been a near contemporary of Moses.[2] And while hermetic philosophy, to the modern eye, might appear to be largely mumbo-jumbo, based on a catastrophic misdating (which caused passing references to Christianity to be interpreted as evidence of astonishing prophetic wisdom), it proved at the time to be enormously influential—as influential in its way as the work of Plato. When Copernicus produced his revolutionary heliocentric hypothesis, he appealed to the authority of Trismegistus for support; and when Giordano Bruno defended the Copernican hypothesis at the University of Oxford, he did so primarily because he saw heliocentricity as consistent with and supportive of the greater truths of hermetic philosophy.[3] While there is little evidence that More had much sympathy for hermetic thought, he was none the less a great admirer of Pico della Mirandola, whose biography he had earlier translated into English. It was doubtless Pico's exemplary piety and immense learning that chiefly commended him to More, but at the same time he can hardly have been unaware that Pico was also a magician, steeped in hermetic and Cabalist lore. Paradoxically, therefore, some of the most apparently progressive ideas of the Renaissance had their roots in dreams of a magical transformation of the world—dreams which had as their goal, not progress, but the restoration of an order, a harmony, an innocence that had once existed, but had long since been lost.

Even the scientific and geographical discoveries of the period were by no means immune to interpretations which saw them less as signs of progress than as fulfilments of biblical prophecy, indicative of the imminence of the second coming. Charles Webster's study of science in Puritan England, *The Great Instauration*, reveals that much of the scientific investigation during the first part of the seventeenth century was prompted by the belief that it formed part of the essential preparation for the recovery of wisdom which would accompany the millennium (as prophesied in Daniel 12, 4).[4] Even Bacon, so often hailed as one of the most important pioneers of 'modern' science, appears to have believed that scientific discovery could help repair the damage done by the Fall of Adam:

> For man by the fall fell at the same time from his state of innocency and dominion over creation. Both of these losses however can even in this life be in some part repaired; the former by religion and faith, the latter by arts and sciences. [p.387]

Columbus, likewise, while his search for a new trade route to Asia was clearly motivated in part by pragmatic commercial considerations, claimed that the real purpose of the enterprise was to raise funds for the liberation of Jerusalem,[5] and even appears to have seriously believed he had discovered the location of the earthly paradise in the course of his voyages.[6]

Viewed in the light of such grandiose visions of humanity bringing—or restoring—harmony to the world through its own efforts, More's *Utopia* might be seen, in fact, as characterized by a certain modesty, inasmuch as it proposes a harmony which is primarily merely *social* in character. Later writers, however, such as Campanella and Bacon, clearly had more ambitious designs in mind: designs in which social harmony would be integrated into a larger cosmic pattern—yet even then, a pattern which human enterprise might well be able to influence.

Against such a background, the ambiguity which has been pointed to as a central characteristic of utopian fiction seems less surprising. Emerging from a context where the possibility of religious, scientific, and social transformation seemed increasingly real, but where the direction it might take was less than clear, any attempt to envisage a complete alternative society could scarcely avoid some degree of ambiguity. In the case of *Utopia*, however, the ambivalence is compounded by the complex and sometimes contradictory character of the author himself—which is also reflected in both the nature, and the presentation of the alternative society he proposes. As might be expected of a writer who has been both canonized by the

Roman Catholic church and hailed by Nikita Khruschev as an honoured precursor of Soviet Communism (Gilison, p.24), his vision of an ideal commonwealth is one which, even by utopian standards, is particularly ambiguous in its implications

The element of paradox in *Utopia* has, of course, frequently been commented on. It is the work of a devout Christian, yet one which portrays a non-Christian society as being in most respects far superior to those of Christian Europe. It proposes as desirable a degree of religious toleration unusual for its time, yet comes from the pen of a man who, in his public capacity, soon proved a fierce and intolerant persecutor of heretics. In the first book, there is a debate concerning the utility of the wise man involving himself in government, in which Hythloday argues forcibly that it is impossible to do so without sacrificing one's principles; yet while, in the book, Hythloday gets much the better of the argument, More himself went on to enter the public service—and later to die over his refusal to compromise over a question of principle. Nor do the paradoxes end there, for while the issues the work raises could scarcely be more serious (in the last instance, quite literally involving matters of life and death), *Utopia* is at the same time disconcertingly full of elements—puns, wordplay, ironies—suggestive of an intent which is anything *but* serious. More's often ludicrous choice of names for people and places, together with some of his comments, both in the work itself, and in subsequent correspondence, seem explicitly designed to undercut the impact of the radical ideas it contains—as, for example, when Hythloday's lengthy description of Utopian society is immediately followed by the narrator's *caveat*:

> ... it seemed to me that not a few of the customs and laws he had described as existing among the Utopians were quite absurd. Their methods of waging war, their religious ceremonies, and their social customs were some of these, but my chief objection was to the basis of their whole system, that is, their communal living and their moneyless economy. [p.91]

What is 'quite absurd', in other words, is the entire society!

Not all of More's readers, of course, can be said to have got the joke—least of all, perhaps, the modern critic who seriously argued that *Utopia* was in fact an actual description of the society of the Incas.[7] But such spectacular misinterpretations only serve to underline the extent to which the boundaries between fiction and nonfiction become blurred in utopian narrative. While More was clearly concerned to *avoid* such misunderstandings, deliberately writing in Latin for a select group of friends and acquaintances, all of whom could confidently be expected to recognize the scholarly humour, and enjoy the speculative freedom of its often radical suggestions without mistaking them for a practical programme of action, perhaps the greatest paradox of all is that such a work, although designed for a limited audience, should have gone on to achieve a degree of recognition and influence far beyond anything its author could have intended—or indeed, desired.

The Narrative of *Utopia*

Written at the dawn of an age of exploration, *Utopia* takes as its starting point the *Voyages* of Amerigo Vespucci: purportedly factual accounts (although ones, interestingly enough, whose authenticity has often been disputed).[8] Raphael Hythloday, the visitor to Utopia, is supposed to have accompanied Vespucci on his alleged fourth voyage, and to have been one of those left behind in a fort on the coast of Brazil—from which he then set out to engage in further exploration. Hythloday's account of his travels is presented, in effect, as an extension of what More believed to have been a real voyage of discovery, its form modelled on that of travel narratives which lay claim to some degree of plausibility and authenticity.

In form, then, *Utopia* takes as its model a narrative of travel and discovery—it is a fiction which begins by describing an actual voyage, and goes on to imagine a further one. Nevertheless, the details provided concerning the latter are curiously sparse. From their starting point on the coast of Brazil, we are told, Hythloday and five companions 'travelled through many countries ... At last, by strange good fortune, he got, via Ceylon, to Calcutta, where by good luck he found some Portuguese ships; and so, beyond anyone's expectation, he returned to his own country' (p.7). Where the regular travel narrative (and Vespucci's is no exception) is customarily full of concrete details concerning distances travelled, and the time taken to cover them, *Utopia* is conspicuously vague in its treatment of both time and space. As Robert Adams remarks, in a footnote to the passage cited above: 'More covers in a prepositional phrase the distance from Eastern Brazil to Ceylon, a distance of about fifteen thousand miles. Somewhere in there is Utopia' (p.7 n.).[9] Yet while this is tantalizingly imprecise, the text does provide us elsewhere with some oddly suggestive details.

Utopia is located, as are the ideal commonwealths of Campanella and Bacon, in the southern hemisphere, to speak in literal geographical terms— but also in the 'south land', that quasi-mythical locale which was the half serious goal even of real-life explorers of the New World: both Columbus, as we have seen, and later Ponce de Leon had dreams of locating, not just the Indies, but the Earthly Paradise itself.[10] Remote from, and also (as it would be visually represented) *below* the known world, Utopia is only reached after an arduous journey through an equatorial region described as 'desolate and squalid, grim and uncultivated, inhabited by wild beasts, serpents, and also by men no less wild and dangerous than the beasts themselves' (*Utopia*, p.8). Beyond this region, however, the conditions grow milder: 'The heat was less fierce, the earth greener, men and even beasts less savage' (p.8). There are increasing signs of civilization: ships, primitive at first, but later just as sophisticated as those of Europe. Hythloday and his companions encounter 'towns and cities ... commonwealths that were both populous and not badly governed' (p.7). Nearer still to Utopia are nations—the Achorians and Macarians—whose societies, while not perfect, are both cited as examples from which European civilization might well profit. Finally, there is Utopia itself: remote from the known world, separated by an almost impassable barrier, yet at the same time able to diffuse its influence over a wide area. The closer the approach to the ideal, the more its influence (in the best Platonic tradition) becomes apparent, affecting not only humanity, but even nature—even the beasts grow tamer.

The *precise* location of Utopia, however, is never revealed. As its name suggests, it is both (enticingly) the good place and (infuriatingly) no place: desirable, yet unattainable. Its location is the one piece of information conspicuously absent from an account which Hythloday's listeners beg him to make as thorough and exhaustive as possible:

> 'Do not try to be brief, but explain in order everything relating to their land, their rivers, towns, people, manors, institutions, laws— everything, in short, that you think we would like to know. And you can take it for granted that we want to know everything that we don't know yet.' [p.33]

Yet while Hythloday does respond, in Book Two, with a comprehensive account of utopian society, this very comprehensiveness serves, paradoxically, to highlight the narrative's omissions—to draw attention, as Macherey puts it, to 'what [the work] does not say' (p.87). Given his audience's expressed desire to know 'everything' (a desire, moreover, which Hythloday agrees to satisfy), the omission of the elementary fact of Utopia's whereabouts seems all the more glaring. Indeed, in a subsequent letter to Peter Giles, More even makes joking reference to this:

> ... it didn't occur to us to ask, nor to him to say, in what area of the New World Utopia is to be found. I wouldn't have missed hearing about this for a sizable sum of money, for I'm quite ashamed not to know even the name of the ocean where this island lies about which I've written so much. [p.111][11]

Giles, in his turn, takes up the running joke in a subsequent letter to Jerome
Busleyden:

> Raphael did not try in any way to suppress that information, but he
> mentioned it only briefly and in passing, as if saving it for another
> occasion. And then an unlucky accident caused both of us to miss
> what he said. For while Raphael was speaking of it, one of More's
> servants came in to whisper something in his ear; and though I was
> listening, for that very reason, more intently than ever, one of the
> company, who I suppose had caught cold on shipboard, coughed so
> loudly that some of Raphael's words escaped me. [p.114]

Humour, obviously, can have a wide range of functions—but there is
surely something suggestive about this *kind* of humour, which depends for
its effect on a tantalizing refusal to reveal information, both drawing
attention to, yet refusing to disclose a secret. The commonest use of such
humour, of course, is in the service of sexual innuendo, where a pose of
innocence is combined with the implication of knowingness to create a
complicity between speaker and audience: at the literal level, the statement
can be taken at its (innocent) face value, yet both speaker and audience
understand its true significance—to which, however, neither can allude
overtly without the risk of disturbing the delicate balance on which the
humour of dealing with the taboo depends. This is not to say, of course,
that the humour which More and his circle deploy is *identical* in character:
Utopia is scarcely a work of sexual innuendo; nevertheless, there would
seem to be at least some element of the taboo involved in its humour.
Utopia can be thought about, but is physically unattainable; the pretence
of its existence is sustained by a knowing complicity between author and
audience; and the secrecy surrounding it is maintained by barrier of an
essentially *defensive* humour—the kind designed to forestall awkward
questions.

What, then, is there about Utopia that might involve an element of the
taboo, representing unconscious or unavowable desires? Eric Rabkin
suggests that part of the appeal of utopian fiction lies in its indulgence of
'our atavistic desire for a special kind of orderliness, the simple, calm
orderliness found in childhood, a bliss ignorant of sex and ignorant of the
full knowledge of personal autonomy' (Rabkin, 1983, p.10). Yet while this
gives some sense of the regressive element inherent in much utopian
fantasy, a mere yearning for the simplicity of childhood is hardly sufficient
to account for the degree of evasiveness encountered here. More to the
point, surely, is the frequently drawn parallel between the actual
geography of Utopia and the womb. Formerly a peninsula, we are told,
Utopia was transformed into an island at the behest of King Utopus, whose

first act on coming to power was to sever the link with the mainland by decreeing the excavation of a fifteen-mile-wide channel. By doing so, in Angelika Bammer's view, 'King Utopus symbolically births his own utopia by cutting off the umbilical cord that had joined it to the mainland' (p.14). Yet this is surely to miss the point, since what is suggested by the geographical details that More *does* supply is not so much the birth process, as a *return* to the womb. What King Utopus's prodigious feat of engineering in fact accomplishes is the creation of an island shaped like a crescent whose horns nearly meet, enclosing a large, placid bay, which can only be entered (and even then with difficulty) by way of a narrow channel:

> What with shallows on one side, and rocks on the other, the entrance into the bay is very dangerous. Near the middle of the channel, there is one rock that rises above the water, and so presents no dangers in itself; on top of it a tower has been built, and there a garrison is kept. Since the other rocks lie under water, they are very dangerous to navigation. The channels are known only to the Utopians, so hardly any strangers enter the bay without one of their pilots ... [p.34]

If More's evasiveness concerning Utopia's actual location may be seen as suggestive, then the compensatory wealth of physical detail provided in the description of its appearance is still more so—particularly when taken in conjunction with his account of the nature of Utopian society.

The analogy between human visions of an ideal world and the mother's womb is by no means a new one: long before Freud—indeed, as early as the first century AD—the Gnostic heretic, Simon Magus, proposed that the Garden of Eden had no literal, physical existence, but was merely an allegory of the womb, where the individual was innocent, happy, idle, and plentifully supplied with food.[12] And this same ideal persists through any number of fantasized paradises, from Eden, the land of Cockaigne (where geese fly ready-roasted through the air, crying 'Geese, al hot, al hot!), down to contemporary television advertisements for Caribbean holidays. As Frank and Fritzie Manuel suggest:

> The human fetus is an island, and in their island utopias men have often expressed a longing for the protective fluid that once surrounded them. The maternal symbols of most Elysian, golden-age, and paradisaical utopias are compelling and need not be laboured. The enclosed gardens, islands, valleys have reappeared with constancy through the ages. There is free feeding, security, peace, plenitude, and no rivalry. [p.76]

While it may fairly be objected that the ideal commonwealth depicted in *Utopia* is neither Elysian, paradisaical, nor golden-age, it nevertheless shares many of their distinctive features. Where *Utopia* differs is not so much in the *character* of the dream it represents, as in the fact that it seeks to put that dream on a more rational, plausible footing. If food is not free, there is at any rate a sufficiency: 'their working hours are ample to provide not only enough but more than enough of the necessities and even the conveniences of life' (p.42). And while work is still necessary, to the average Tudor artisan or agricultural labourer, the Utopian six-hour day would surely have seemed, if not paradisaical, then the next best thing to it. There is peace, maintained by the ruthless efficiency with which the otherwise pacific Utopians wage war on aggressors. And there is security, provided by an ordered social hierarchy, clearly defined laws and customs, and the strict routine that governs day-to-day living. It is, as has often been remarked, a highly institutionalized society, and one strongly influenced by the ideals of monasticism—yet it also goes a long way toward providing, albeit in a more temperate fashion, many of the essential features of the fantasized paradise.

Paradise, however, like the womb, offers something more: a freedom from guilt, the promise—or is it the memory?—of an innocence lost by the Fall. And here, at least at first sight, Utopia might seem to diverge from the pattern of the paradisaical fantasy. For there *is* evil in Utopia: its citizens have to be controlled—educated to do right, restrained from doing wrong. The effects of Original Sin are only mitigated, not abolished by its institutions, and while the legal system seems in most respects milder and more civilized than that of Tudor England, some of its provisions are, to say the least, Draconian—witness the Utopian penalty of death for a second conviction of adultery. Yet even here there is evidence that Utopia represents a rationalized version of the underlying Edenic dream. While guilt cannot be eradicated altogether—any more than can hunger, the need to work, or the possibility of war—it can, like them, be minimized. Utopian religion, unlike Christianity, lays little stress on humanity's fallen nature; the legal system places, at least by the standards of the time, less emphasis on punishment, more on rehabilitation; and there are, quite simply, far fewer opportunities to do anything one might feel guilty *about*. The absence of money and private property frees the Utopians from greed and covetousness, and there are few chances of indulging in any of the usual social vices:

> ... there is no chance to loaf or kill time, nor pretext for evading work; no taverns, or alehouses, or brothels; no chances for corruption; no hiding places; no spots for secret meetings. But because they live in the full view of all, they are bound to be either

working at their usual trades, or enjoying their leisure in a respectable way. [p.49]

As Utopia's provisions concerning adultery would seem to indicate, human sexual instincts remain a problem—yet even here every attempt is made to strip sexuality of its mystery and aura of forbidden delight. The notorious provision of opportunities for potential marital partners to view one another naked before finalizing their vows may be seen as a step (however naïve) in this direction. But the Utopian obsession with living life entirely in the open clearly has another function: in a world where everything is known, the causes of fear and anxiety are minimized. Indeed, while *Utopia* depicts a world radically different from that of its author, one of its most striking aspects is the extent to which the element of novelty is downplayed. Not only are there few opportunities to do anything wrong, there are scarcely any opportunities to do anything *new*. While travel is permitted within Utopia (although only with an official license: the penalty for unlicenced travel is enslavement for a second offence!), there seems little point in it, given that all their cities are 'exactly alike' (p.36). In Hythloday's words, they are 'identical in language, customs, institutions, and laws. So far as the location permits, all of them are built on the same plan, and have the same appearance' (p.35). Everything in Utopia is familiar; everything in Utopia makes sense: there are no surprises. While there are elements of the carnivalesque inversion of customary values which Bakhtin sees as a central element in the Renaissance utopia[13] (the use of gold for chamberpots and convicts' chains; the mockery of the Anemolian ambassadors, while their servants are treated with respect), these remain subordinate, in More's scheme of things, to the emphasis on official hierarchical order. What Utopia offers its citizens, above all, is security. Albeit in a rational form, it might be argued, Utopian society offers many of the same attractions as does the fantasized paradise: so far as is humanly possible, the Utopians attempt to rectify the negative consequences of birth, of belonging to a human society, rather than dwelling in the Garden of Eden.

The risk of such an interpretation, of course, as with all attempts to psychologize desires for, or attempts to imagine social reform, is that of reductionism: the desire for the radically new is all too readily decoded as mere nostalgia. Nevertheless, to argue that there are powerful, and in many respects regressive unconscious drives underlying the utopian vision is not necessarily to reduce it to a compensatory fantasy of returning to the past, in the face of one's inability to deal with the present. As Bloch suggests, an acceptance of the *existence* of such drives does not imply automatic acceptance of the Freudian goal of securing the individual's adjustment to the norms of society (which are themselves historically contingent)—still less commit one to a Jungian pursuit of primeval archetypes. To suggest that humans are profoundly influenced at an unconscious level by the experience of prenatal security, or by the trauma of birth is not necessarily to argue that such experience is not subsequently socially mediated.[14] In addition, even granted that utopian visions have at their roots a regressive fantasy, this does not necessarily render them reactionary *per se*. Whatever the roots of the desire for a better world, the real issue is the use made of that desire. Indeed, history is full of examples of the past, however fantasized or mythical, being used to legitimate radical political action in the present: witness, for example, Gerrard Winstanley's utopian appeal to the historically quite unfounded, but nevertheless enabling vision of a formerly egalitarian English society that had fallen from grace as the result of the imposition of the 'Norman Yoke'. As Miguel de Unamuno argues: '[e]veryone who fights for any ideal whatever, although his ideal may seem to lie in the past, is driving the world on to the future' (p.321). Utopian fantasy *to the extent that* it is merely compensatory, may be reactionary in tendency; to the extent that it uses the gap between the joys of even a mythologised past and the inadequacies of the present as a starting point for the imagining of new alternatives, it contains radical potential.

However, this is not to say that the underlying presence of such regressive elements is entirely unproblematic, either—as becomes apparent when one examines some of the parallels with the discovery narratives on which *Utopia* is partly modelled. As numerous commentators have pointed out, a striking feature of such narratives is the consistency with which the territory of desire is also conceived of as female.[15] For Columbus, as we have seen, the enterprise of discovery was inextricably bound up with fantasies of regaining the paradise of which utopia offers a rationalized version. In his account of his third voyage, indeed, he advanced the singular theory that the earth, far from being spherical, was in fact pear-shaped, or else like a round ball on which there was a protuberance resembling a woman's nipple (Jane, Vol. 2, pp.30–1). This theory, in addition to accounting for apparent anomalies in his observations of the pole star, which he regarded as proof that he was sailing uphill (pp.30–1), led him to believe that he had actually located the earthly paradise—situated on top of the nipple-like summit of the world, somewhere upriver from the mouth of the Orinoco (which he took to be one of the life-giving streams issuing from paradise itself). Paradoxically, however, it was this dream, along with the no less regressive fantasy of recapturing Jerusalem—formerly held to be the geographical centre of the world—that informed Columbus's discovery of an altogether new world. Nevertheless, as Annette

Kolodny points out, the recurrent gendering of the land as female in narratives of discovery has a range of implications:

> Implicit in the metaphor of the land-as-woman was both the regressive pull of maternal containment *and* the seductive invitation to sexual assertion: if the Mother demands passivity, and threatens regression, the Virgin apparently invites sexual assertion and awaits impregnation. [p.67]

While Columbus sees the newly discovered territories as the site of a paradise conceived of in maternal terms, a very different relationship with the land is implied by Sir Walter Ralegh's celebrated claim that 'Guiana is a countrey that hath yet her maydenhead' (p.347)—not to mention the contention of his lieutenant, Laurence Keymis, that 'whole shires of fruitfull grounds, lying now waste for want of people, do prostitute themselves unto us, like a faire and beautifull woman, in the pride and floure of desired yeeres' (p.391).[16] Along with what Marcuse describes as the fantasy of 'the land as woman, the total female principle of gratification—enclosing the individual in an environment of receptivity, repose, and painless and integral satisfaction' *(Eros and Civilization,* pp.246–7)[17] often goes the desire to assert masculine dominance over that domain. While the project of exploration, although informed in part by regressive fantasies, makes possible the discovery of the genuinely new, it also opens the way for the exercise of traditional modes of domination.

Seen in this light, the parallels between *Utopia* and the discovery narratives to which it owes part of its inspiration become more, rather than less troubling. For while the underlying symbolism of Utopia—its shape and location, its peace, fertility, and security—may well be maternal in character, indicative of deep-seated and barely acknowledged subconscious yearnings, it is, as Bammer points out, 'not a world in which women are empowered. On the contrary, male hegemony is reinscribed as normative' (p.14). For all the maternal attributes of the underlying utopian dream, the social superstructure erected on these foundations is, by contrast, distinctively patriarchal.

This, of course, it might be argued, is hardly surprising: Tudor society, after, was likewise highly patriarchal—and to this extent More might be seen as simply reflecting the social realities of his own era. Yet while this is certainly true, it leaves a number of questions unanswered. If More's own society was patriarchal, it was also a society in which a money economy, the institution of private property, and Christian belief were equally fundamental. Given the extremely radical social transformation which *Utopia* proposes, it is surely not without significance that there are aspects of the author's own society which he chooses to leave unchanged.

Indeed, it might be argued that More (and he is not alone in this: the same might be said of Campanella and Bacon) does not *simply* reflect the realities of his own world when he envisages utopian society as patriarchal; rather, this is an element which he chooses to reinforce. Utopia is a society in which patriarchy is, one might say, raised to a higher power.[18]

In discussions of Utopian society, much attention has been given to the political organization of its upper echelons—its hierarchy of syphogrants, tranibors, and so forth. Yet this often serves to obscure (as do the frequent references to the influence on More of mediaeval monasticism) the fact that, as J.H. Hexter observes, the fundamental organizational unit of Utopian society is the patriarchal family (pp.40–5). The family provides the basic unit of agricultural production; it is the family heads who elect the syphogrants who constitute the lowest tier of government; and it is the family which instils into Utopian citizens the habit of obedience to authority on which the stability of society as a whole depends. 'Husbands chastise their wives,' we are told, 'and parents their children, unless the offense is so serious that public punishment seems to be in the public interest' (p.67). In addition, we learn that:

> Each city ... consists of households, the households consisting generally of blood-relations. When the women grow up and are married, they move into their husbands' households. On the other hand, male children and after them grandchildren remain in the family, and are subject to the oldest parent, unless his [sic] mind has started to fail, in which case, the next oldest takes his place ... Wives are subject to their husbands, children to their parents, and generally the younger to the elders. [pp.44–5]

In themselves, such provisions are not far removed from the realities of family life in Tudor England—although the monthly ritual where 'wives kneel before their husbands ... to confess their various failures and negligences, and beg forgiveness for their offenses' (p.86) is surely less than typical. Nevertheless, there is a difference. What is striking is that *Utopia* makes explicit aspects of social organization that would more commonly be taken for granted: the patriarchal family, in other words, is represented as being *just as* fundamental to the workings of Utopian society as any of the sweeping changes that are evident; its maintenance is *as* crucial as the abolition of money and private property, or as the radically different laws, customs, and rituals which are described in such detail. In *Utopia*, as in any portrait of a more perfect society, it is not merely what changes that is important: equally significant is what remains the same. And it is here that we encounter one of the essential contradictions inherent in the traditional utopia: the fact that, although suffused by a yearning for the security of the maternal womb, it sets out to achieve that security by the imposition of a distinctively masculine order. This is manifested not only in the forms of social organization which utopian narrative depicts, but also at the deeper level of symbol: in the description of Utopia's geography already cited, for example, one may see the erasure of the feminine by the masculine enacted in such telling details as the superimposition of the potently phallic tower full of armed men upon the harmless clitoral rock which rises in the entrance to Utopia's womb-like bay. Equally, in the decisive act of authority with which the male King Utopus establishes Utopia, severing it from the mainland, one may see a further rewriting of the primal myth. While, as we have seen, some critics view this action as analogous to the severing of the umbilical cord, its implications are actually more ambiguous. Where the cord linking mother and child is severed *after* the birth process, here the analogous action is a *prelude* to the womb's creation: the direction of time, in effect, is reversed, as if the hidden intent of the utopian fantasy were to reach back beyond the birth process, beyond the fall into independent conscious life, and start over again—only with the male firmly in control. If the earthly paradise constitutes an allegory of the womb, the utopian dream—at least as first formulated—is rather one of recreating its security by distinctively male means.

The articulation of such a dream at this particular point in time, of course, can hardly be seen as purely coincidental. The ambiguity of direction evident in the utopian dream is scarcely an isolated phenomenon: even the process of discovery which revealed the existence of the New World was, as we have seen, similarly informed by dreams of the recovery of a lost paradise. And the utopian vision, which seeks to recover a lost harmony by the creation of a new order, may likewise be seen as looking both forward and backward at the same time. Yet the parallels do not end there. If, in geographical terms, the process of discovery (the disclosure of the new) was informed by a dream of recovery (the regaining of what had been lost), what followed was an entirely different project: that of *colonization*—the superimposition of the existing upon the new. As Christina Thürmer-Rohr points out, while Bloch sees Columbus as exemplifying utopian desire in his search for a lost paradise

> ... he does not mention that such a quest for paradise always initiated male campaigns of conquest and domination. The paradises of western men—and of their wives, mostly sent for later—are their colonies, large and small. Bloch describes them not as the sites of robbery, of oppression, of presumption, of rape and murder, but rather as 'geographic utopias', earthly paradises, since heavenly paradise had proved unattainable. [p.23]

Which in its turn poses the uncomfortable question as to how far one of the goals of the utopian dream is not also, in a sense, the colonization of *terra incognita*.

In the case of More's *Utopia*, of course, it might be argued that nothing could be further removed from the colonialist enterprise than his depiction of an indigenous (albeit hypothetical) New World civilization as in almost every respect superior to that of Europe. In representing such a society as a model, not merely of wisdom and good government, but of tolerance, even—or rather, especially—in matters of religion, More would appear to evince an outlook radically at odds with that informing the process of conquest and colonization with which discovery soon becomes inextricably linked, whereby the indigene is commonly demonized as prelude either to forcible conversion or extermination. As has already been suggested, such apparent openness to the example of other societies would seem to indicate a degree of cultural relativism unusual for the time. Nevertheless, as Stephen Greenblatt argues, such essentially *theoretical* tolerance is ultimately a meaningless abstraction:

> ... the customs of those at a vast distance in space or time or of imaginary beings may be admired or despised, but such responses are independent of tolerance. They are, in effect, the attitudinal equivalent of the act of categorizing: one may decide that other peoples scarcely merit the name of human beings or that they are models of virtue. In neither case do significant life choices, entailing political decisions with historical consequences, have to be made. A metaphoric embrace of the other is no doubt wonderful, but what is its exigency in the real world? What is to keep it from vanishing into thin air? [pp.45–6]

Indeed, the gap between the degree of religious toleration proposed in More's utopian vision and his own practice as a fierce and intolerant persecutor of heretics would seem to bear this out. Yet while the perceived contradiction between More's actions and the apparent implications of the text has attracted voluminous critical comment, of perhaps greater relevance to the present discussion is another, somewhat less obvious contradiction.

As has already been observed, *Utopia* (in common with the overwhelming majority of subsequent utopian narratives) provides an abundance of specific detail concerning the actual workings of a more perfect society, yet remains tantalizingly vague concerning the processes whereby it came into being. What we *are* offered, however, is in essence a fiction of conquest. Formerly a nation of 'rude and uncouth inhabitants' (p.35), the land of Abraxa is conquered by King Utopus, who, having subdued the indigenous population, promptly puts his subjects to work excavating a fifteen-mile-wide channel through the isthmus formerly linking them to the mainland. Having renamed the resultant island after himself, he then proceeds to raise his subjects 'to such a high level of culture and humanity that they now excel in that regard almost every other people' (p.35). Where King Utopus came from, however, and where he acquired his ideals of civic harmony are left as obscure as the actual geographic location of Utopia. In any event, what follows the establishment of the utopian state is a process strikingly similar to that of colonization. While the Utopians, we are told, never fight except in self-defence, or to help 'various of their neighbours to throw off the yoke of tyranny' (p.69), one side-effect of their conspicuous virtue is that their neighbours have 'made a practice of asking for Utopians to rule over them' (p.69).[19] Utopian administrators are sent out, in consequence, to serve either one or five year terms, after which 'others are sent in their place' (p.69)—for all the world like colonial governors.

What emerges, in effect, is less an imaginative response to the example of the other, than to the possibilities inherent in the *space* opened up by the voyages of discovery—a space wherein the values of the Old World could be reconfigured. Where an indigenous population exists, its function is to be moulded in the image of a King Utopus; neighbouring races are portrayed either as enemies to be destroyed, or else as eager to be governed by the superior wisdom of the Utopians. Like the native Americans described by Peter Martyr as 'rased or vnpaynted tables …apte to receaue what formes soo euer are fyrst drawne theron by the hande of the paynter' (quoted in Greenblatt, p.95), the indigenous population serves effectively as *tabula rasa*—a blank page on which the patterns of what Michel de Certeau characterizes as 'Western desire' (p.xxv) can be inscribed. As coined by More, the term 'utopia' is, as we have seen, deliberately ambiguous: both *eu-topos*, the good place, and *ou-topos*, no place—an ideal impossible of attainment. Yet in the actual context of More's narrative, it becomes something rather different—the name imposed by a conquering king, remaking the world in his own image. The parallels with Columbus, renaming Guanahani 'San Salvador', or Ralegh, rechristening Wingandaco 'Virginia' at the behest of Queen Elizabeth,[20] are hard to escape.

Utopias of the Later Renaissance

That these are characteristics of utopian narrative in general, rather than merely features peculiar to More's *Utopia*, becomes apparent when one turns to the work of his successors. Published just over a century later, neither Campanella's *The City of the Sun* nor Bacon's *The New Atlantis* exhibit the narrative complexity or, indeed, possess the narrative fascination of their predecessor: Campanella's work, written in prison, shows signs of having been composed in haste, ending abruptly with its narrator breaking off his account as he rushes to catch his ship; while Bacon's is no more than a fragment,[21] which leaves many features of his utopian society unclear. Yet while the complex interaction between reality and imagined alternative which emerges from the juxtaposition of Hythloday's narration with the dialogue which prefaces it is lacking, both *The City of the Sun* and *The New Atlantis* share much of *Utopia*'s pervasive ambiguity. At the same time, however, perhaps by virtue of their greater narrative straightforwardness, they serve to give focus and emphasis to certain elements which the complex ironies of More's fiction tend to obscure.

Campanella, *The City of the Sun*

Campanella, especially, shares with More an ideological ambiguity which is likewise reflected in the conflicting responses of his readers. Although at times an advocate of papal supremacy, not only in religious, but also secular matters, Campanella has also been conscripted, along with More, into the Communist pantheon of honoured precursors of socialism[22]— and, as in More's case, there has been no lack of critics anxious to defend him from so terrible a slur. Bernardino Bonansea argues that, like More, Campanella was simply attempting to portray in his ideal society the virtue possible to natural man—to show the best that could be achieved by reason alone—which should in no way detract from his being seen as a good Catholic (p.265). Nevertheless, to present Campanella in this light is problematic, to say the least. Unlike More, who died a martyr for the Catholic faith, Campanella was very nearly martyred *by* the Catholic church, spending over thirty years in the prisons of the Inquisition, undergoing torture on several occasions, and only avoiding execution by feigning insanity. His thinking is described by D.P. Walker as 'drenched in hermetic ideas' (p.234), and while he did, in the later years of his life, find favour with the papacy, this in itself can scarcely be taken as evidence of Catholic orthodoxy, given that one of his chief services to the Holy See was to perform ceremonies of astral magic with Pope Urban VIII in order to protect him from the ill-effects of an eclipse.[23] Clearly Campanella presents almost as many problems to the Catholic apologist as he does to the socialist in search of forerunners of Marx.

One important respect in which Campanella does differ from More, however, is in his introduction of what is to become an increasingly central preoccupation in utopian fiction: scientific and technological discoveries become for the first time integral to the creation of a more perfect society.

Like the inhabitants of Bacon's Bensalem, Campanella's Solarians have made extraordinary advances in the fields of medicine and astronomy, and have even discovered the art of flying. Prescient though this may seem, however, the actual *role* of such discoveries is once again by no means unambiguously forward looking. The Solarians' expertise in astronomy, for example, is used primarily in the service of the practice of astrology, which in turn plays a large role both in Solarian medicine and—as will be seen—eugenics. While clearly important, science remains subordinate, in Campanella's scheme of things, to religion and astral magic. Thus the 'progressive' elements in *The City of the Sun* remain part of a larger order which is anything but modern. As with *Utopia*, the orientation of Campanella's ideal commonwealth remains ambiguous, seeming to look both forwards and backwards simultaneously.

No such ambiguity, however, surrounds the question of Campanella's intent. Whereas More seemed concerned to ensure that his often radical speculations were seen as just that—speculations, rather than proposals to be acted upon—in Campanella's case there can be little doubt that *The City of the Sun* expressed what he saw as an ideal toward which practical progress could be made. If More's vision of a better society may be compared to the contemporary theory of Copernicus, insofar as both remained at the relatively unalarming level of hypothesis, Campanella may be seen as comparable to his contemporary, Galileo, in his activation of the hypothesis' radical implications. Thus, while the composition of *Utopia* in Latin was designed to restrict it to an audience sufficiently educated (and ideologically reliable) to take its speculations in the sense they were meant (More was unwilling to have it translated into English), Campanella translated his work from the vernacular *into* Latin precisely because his admirers felt this would secure it a wider audience. While *The City of the Sun* depicts what may now seem an unrealizable ideal, it is one whose premises are wholly consistent with the political activism which got its author into trouble with the Inquisition in the first place. If there are doubts as to the *direction* in which Campanella wanted society to move, he clearly had no problems with the subversive implications of utopian speculation. As his actions testify, he was only too eager to offer a challenge to established authority.

Perhaps for this reason, we find none of the irony, the wordplay, the somewhat defensive humour with which More seeks to undercut the radical implications of his narrative. Nor, indeed, is there any of the rather coy mystification surrounding the location of the more perfect society—which is not to say, however, that Campanella is much more informative. In response to an initial question from a Knight Hospitaller, Campanella's Genoese mariner responds:

> I have already told you how I sailed around the world and came to
> Taprobana, where I was forced to put ashore, how I hid in a forest
> to escape the fury of the natives, and how I came out onto a great
> plain just below the equator. [p.27]

Which is all we learn about how utopia is reached: the narrator has already
gone into the details, and does not propose to discuss the matter further.
Within less than half a page, he is embarked instead on a detailed
description of the city itself. What Campanella provides, in other words,
is another *form* of evasion: while elsewhere the mariner is only too happy
to respond to the knight's eager inquiries ('Tell me more, I beg you, tell
me more' (p.29)) with detailed and explicit accounts of the most minute
aspects of Solarian life, his reticence here—his uncharacteristic brevity—
is all the more striking. Nor are we told much more concerning the origins
of Campanella's utopia: all we learn of its foundation is that its inhabitants
are 'a people from India, many of them being philosophers, who fled before
the depredations of the Tartars and other plunderers and tyrants, and they
resolved to live in a philosophic community' (pp.37–9). Yet, scanty though
these details are, one significant parallel between the process of *creating* a
utopian society and that of *reaching* it does emerge. Both processes take
place after exposure to the unbridled hostile impulses of man in his 'natural'
state: the Solarians flee from the savage Tartars and 'other plunderers',
while the mariner hides from the 'fury of the natives'. Both find refuge
within the circular walls of the City of the Sun: as is the case with *Utopia*,
one of its most essential features is the security it provides.

    What follows is the depiction of an order whose comprehensiveness
surpasses even that of More. Campanella himself was obsessed by order
and correspondence (he even believed that seven bumps on his head
corresponded to the seven planets), and this passion is reflected in almost
every aspect of his imagined society. The city, we learn, is built in a series
of concentric circles, seven in number, each named after one of the seven
planets, and each girdled by a formidable wall. Since it is built on a hill,
each circle is higher than the one which encloses it, and at the summit,
within the innermost circle, stands the vast temple of the Sun. This design
serves a number of purposes, the most obvious being that of defence:

> It is constructed in such a way that if the first circuit were taken by
> assault, more effort would be required to take the second, likewise
> again the third, and so forth, so that seven assaults would be need
> to conquer it all. But in my opinion not even the first assault would
> be successful, so thick is the wall … [pp.27–9]

Like Utopia, the City of the Sun is impregnable. Yet this is only one function
of its design: as well as protection, the walls also provide education—their

surfaces, apart from those of the outermost, are adorned with paintings illustrating every aspect of knowledge. The City, in fact, forms a kind of encyclopaedia: on the outer walls of the temple are depicted the stars in order; on the inner wall of the first circuit all the mathematical figures; and so outward to the exterior of the sixth circuit, on which appear pictures of great men—'founders of laws and of sciences and inventors of weapons' (p.37). Living in such an environment, Solarian children 'without effort, merely while playing ... come to know all the sciences pictorially before they [are] ten years old' (p.37).

Most important of all, however, the symmetry and harmony of the city's design is clearly intended to reflect the broader harmony of the universe. With its seven circuits, named after the planets, centred on the Temple of the Sun, the city itself constitutes a microcosm; while within the temple the process repeats itself on a smaller scale, with the stars depicted on the vault of its dome and seven lamps burning to represent the planets. The purpose of Solarian architecture, in other words, is not only defensive and educational, but also religious.

Given this preoccupation with celestial design, it comes as little surprise to discover that Solarian religion is inextricably bound up with astrology. Their Priest-Ruler, called interchangeably either Sun or Metaphysic, is invariably a man of great learning, and heads a body of priests who, when not engaged in affairs of state, divide their time between prayer and astrology:

> Twenty-four priests are stationed high in the temple to sing certain psalms in praise of God in the morning and evening, at midnight and noon. Their task is to gaze at the stars and, using astrolabes, note all their movements and the effects these produce. In this manner, they learn what changes have taken place or are likely to take place in every country. They establish the hour in which conception should take place, the day on which sowing and harvesting should be done, and in general, serve as mediators between God and man. [p.103]

Both prayer and astrology are presented as basically similar in purpose, merely constituting different aspects of the priestly task—which is to keep the human microcosm attuned to the harmonies of the universe. Even the city's political organization has a religious dimension: the chief officials, we learn, are all priests as well—and it is clear from their preoccupation with astrology that the task of securing social harmony is, once again, merely part of the larger enterprise of integrating the human with the celestial order. By the institution of an elaborate system of social control, the Solarians seek to re-establish an unalienated union between the individual and the natural world which may be seen as echoing the organic prenatal connection between mother and foetus, where the rhythms of the foetus are synchronous with those of its surrounding environment. It is an archetypal utopian dream.

Nevertheless, just as in More's *Utopia*, the emphasis of the social order which Campanella outlines remains resolutely masculine. This is to some extent prefigured in the city's actual design, its womb-like geography being overlaid by the exclusively male symbolism of the pictures that adorn the walls: in the outermost circle of illustrations, for example, the portraits of legislators, scientists, and inventors of weapons are supplemented by images of 'Moses, Osiris, Jupiter, Mercury, Muhammad ... Jesus Christ and the twelve Apostles ... Caesar, Alexander, Pyrrhus, and all the Romans' (p.37). Yet in marked contrast to More, for whom the fundamental instrument of patriarchal authority is the family, Campanella's social order is constructed on radically different principles. In the City of the Sun, the family is quite simply abolished—on the grounds that its existence is detrimental to the individual's commitment to the community:

> They claim that property comes into existence when men have separate homes with their children and wives. From this self-love is born; for in order to increase the wealth or dignity of his offspring or leave him heir to his goods, every man becomes publicly rapacious if he is strong and fearless, or avaricious, deceitful, and hypocritical if he is weak. When self-love is destroyed, only concern for the community remains. [p.39]

In this, Campanella is clearly influenced—and to a far greater extent than More—by the ideals of monasticism; yet at the same time he articulates, and in an extreme form, what is to become an increasingly prominent trend in utopian writing: the tendency to do away with all institutions that might mediate between the individual and the monolithic state. It is striking, in fact, how seldom utopias allow for the existence of intermediate groups or organizations—associations, unions, guilds, clubs, political parties—that have any degree of independence of the state. In abolishing the family as well, Campanella merely goes farther than most.

But if the family in More's *Utopia* is the chief mechanism for the maintenance of patriarchal authority, its absence in *The City of the Sun* by no means signifies that Campanella's emphasis is any less patriarchal. What does emerge, however, is a striking contradiction between the theory and practice of his utopian state. At first sight, it would appear that the quasi-monastic social organization of the Solarians serves significantly to diminish sexual inequality: 'both sexes are trained in all pursuits' (p.41), we are told—including warfare—while later it is explicitly stated that men and women do the same work, 'whether of a mental or mechanical nature' (p.49). Yet while, by seventeenth century standards, this would seem to represent a revolutionary extension of women's freedom, once Campanella goes into more detail some telling gaps between theory and practice become apparent: all the priests and officials are male, to begin with; while the contention that men and women do the same work is subsequently qualified to the point of outright contradiction. 'One distinction is observed' (p.49), we are told:

> ... that is that such tasks as involve hard work or a good deal of walking, like plowing, sowing, harvesting, sheep herding, are performed by the men. Threshing, grape gathering, cheese making, milking, tending to the kitchen gardens, and other light duties [*servizi facili*], on the other hand, are usually assigned to women. These include weaving, sewing, barbering, pharmacy, every kind of clothes making, but exclude the work of the blacksmith or the arms maker. If a woman has skill in painting she is not forbidden to pursue it. Music, except for the playing of trumpets and drums, is reserved to women and children, since they give the most pleasure by it. Women also prepare food and lay the tables ... [p.49]

Compared to the society of Campanella's day, this still offers *some* modest extension of women's sphere of activities, but the 'one distinction' referred to does rather more than simply modify the initial assertion. The radical promise of sexual equality proves to be merely an abstraction, translating in practical terms into what is tantamount to a reinscription of the existing order.

Nor do the notorious sexual provisions of Campanella's utopia offer women much by way of liberation. Solarian women may not be obliged to confess their failings to their husbands on bended knee, but they are no less subject to the will of the State, in the eyes of which they appear to be little more than a sexual resource, to be disposed of as its officials see fit:

> No female ever submits to a male until she is nineteen years of age, nor does any male seek to have children until he is twenty-one or, if he is pale and delicate, even older. Before that age some of them are permitted to have intercourse with barren or pregnant women so as to avoid illicit usages. [p.53]

Such women are provided by the 'matrons and seniors in charge of procreation', who first consult with a doctor as to the advisability of the proceeding. The provisions regarding procreational sex are even more specific:

> Since both males and females, in the manner of the ancient Greeks,

are completely naked when they engage in wrestling exercises, their teachers may readily distinguish those who are able to have intercourse from those who are not and can determine whose sexual organs may best be matched with whose. Consequently, every third night, after they have all bathed, the young people are paired off for intercourse. Tall handsome girls are not matched with any but tall, brave men, while fat girls are matched with thin men and thin girls with fat ones, so as to avoid extremes in their offspring. On the appointed evening, the boys and girls prepare their beds and go to bed where the matron and senior direct them. Nor may they have intercourse until they have completely digested their food and have said their prayers ... They sleep in neighbouring cells until they are to have intercourse. At the proper time, the matron goes around and opens the cell doors. The exact time when this must be done is determined by the Astrologer and the Physician ... [p.55]

It must be conceded that men do not appear to have much choice in the matter either, but elsewhere it becomes clear where the balance of power lies. While men are free to copulate with sterile or pregnant women (or ones of 'scant worth' (p.57)), sterile women are barred from a range of privileges, 'to discourage any woman from making herself sterile in order to become a wanton' (p.59). These customs Campanella refers to as 'community of women' (p.65); Solarians, we are told, 'share their women with respect to both obedience and the bed' (p.67). Women are just as subordinate to the male-dominated State in Campanella's utopia as they are to their husbands in More's; their theoretical equality is repeatedly undercut by details revealing that underlying assumptions as to their inferiority remain unchanged.

It may be tempting to write off the sexual provisions of *The City of the Sun* as merely the heated imaginings of a Dominican monk. Indeed, Thomas Halliday's frequently reprinted 1885 translation omits them altogether—an expurgation which one editor rather airily refers to as 'one or two omissions of detail which can well be spared.'[24] Nevertheless, they may be seen as representing yet another attempt to restore human innocence by freeing sexuality from guilt—in this case by employing astrological means to bring human instinctual drives into harmony with the divine order of the universe. At the same time, however, Campanella's emphasis on selective breeding as integral to the creation of a more perfect society introduces what is to become a recurrent theme in utopian fiction. In many later utopias, in particular those of Bellamy and Wells, the aim is to transform not merely the social institutions which govern humanity, but also the raw human material itself. If human unpredictability and imperfection prove an obstacle to the establishment of a rational, ordered ociety, then the answer is very simple: humans themselves must be altered, usually by means of some form of eugenic control. It is a view which, as we shall see, has alarming implications.

In the City of the Sun, however, the transformation of humanity is not yet complete; while Campanella is somewhat equivocal concerning the doctrine of the Fall, his Solarians are still sufficiently imperfect to need laws and legal penalties to deter them from wrongdoing. Like More's, Campanella's legal provisions are, by the standards of the time, relatively humane—yet there are also (again as in More's case) some odd exceptions. Indeed, in several places the account we are given of Solarian law is actually contradictory. Although we are told at first that 'theft, murder, rape, incest, adultery' are unknown among them (p.41), we later learn that homicide is punishable by death—as are offences involving 'injury to the freedom of the public, or to God, or to the highest officials' (p.99). We are, however, assured that 'only a person found guilty of one of these crimes is punished with death' (p.99). So far, so enlightened, it would seem—except that in the course of the discussion of sexuality two further capital offences emerge. Repeated sodomy, it appears, is also punishable by death, as is the wearing by women of cosmetics, high heels, or gowns that cover the heels!

Even by the standards of the sumptuary laws of the period, this last is quite extraordinarily Draconian—yet when the two offences are considered side by side, it becomes apparent that they do have something in common. Both might be seen as 'unnatural' insofar as they involve—at least to the innocent utopian eye—an element of deception. A recurrent feature in utopias is their emphasis, not simply on order, but on an order that is absolutely clear, wholly explicable. Confusion and uncertainty threaten the very foundations of utopian order: hence perhaps the insistence that everything should be open, easily knowable, not liable to errors of interpretation. As we have seen, there is in utopian narrative a tendency to try to determine *every* detail, an unwillingness to leave *anything* to chance. In such a context, a woman wearing make-up, disguising her 'real' appearance, or a sodomite, engaging in sexual conduct other than that conventionally expected of a 'real' man, both require an effort of interpretation not normally expected of the utopian citizen. In a society where everything is transparent, they represent enigmas which require deciphering. Yet even so, the extremity of the penalty, the disparity between offence and punishment, particularly in the context of a legal code otherwise lenient by the standards of the time, prompts further questions. Just who, or what is so threatened by sodomy, or by a woman's use of cosmetics? Whose interests are being safeguarded? The answer in both cases would seem to be—men. While in Campanella's day sodomy did not necessarily specifically imply homosexual conduct, the sodomite represented at least a potential threat to a stable male sexual identity, in that sodomy could transform the recipient into a passive sexual victim. Likewise, a woman's use of make-up, with its connotations of sexual display, could be seen as suggesting a degree of predatory sexual aggression again threatening to male sexual dominance. While 'normal' male sexual drives are catered to by the provision of women 'so as to avoid illicit usages' (p.53), conduct which threatens the norm is punishable by death. For all the radical character of Campanella's challenge to the sexual institutions of his day, the emphasis of his alternatives remains distinctively masculine.

Nor is this all: as in More's *Utopia*, the fantasy of masculine dominance extends beyond the boundaries of the utopian state itself. While, like More, Campanella is capable of imagining a more perfect society *located* somewhere other than in Europe, it is once again a social structure to be imposed on the indigenous inhabitants in their own interest. Indeed, it would appear from the Genoese mariner's account of his first encounter with the *natives* of the region (from whose 'fury' he has to flee), that Campanella's conception of the indigene owes much to the demonizing accounts of the inhabitants of the Americas found in so many discovery narratives—accounts, of course, which are then used to legitimate the process of colonization, conversion, or even extermination. In the case of Campanella's utopia, however, there seems to be an inherent contradiction between the representation of the local inhabitants as savages, and what we are subsequently told concerning the City of the Sun's relations with its neighbours. The Solarians, it turns out, are constantly at war (although once again, always in self-defence), and, due largely to their sophisticated military skills, invariably win. Conquered cities and their inhabitants, we are told

> ...immediately change over to the system of communal ownership of all goods. They receive Solarian officials and a garrison from the City of the Sun and proceed to model their institutions after those of that city, which is henceforth their guide. [p.77]

Given this pattern of constant warfare, uninterrupted military success, and the subsequent imposition of the utopian system on conquered territory, it becomes hard to understand how there can be any furious natives left to escape from.

One further contradiction remains to be explored. As has already been remarked, Campanella differs from More in his emphasis on the importance of scientific discovery as integral to the creation of a more perfect society. Besides discovering the art of flying, the Solarians have invented 'vessels that move without wind or oar' (p.87), a device which allows them to listen to the music of the spheres, and 'a secret, marvellous art by which they can renew their bodies painlessly every seven years' (p.93), which, along with their healthy diet and habits, has led to an average lifespan of roughly a hundred and seventy.[25] Marvellous as these may seem, however, it is clear that Campanella sees them as plausible possibilities, given the advances in knowledge the world of his own day had already seen. The Genoese mariner boasts that the previous hundred years 'has produced more history ... than the whole world did in the preceding four thousand' (p.121),[26] citing the invention of the compass, the printing press, and the arquebus. Yet such apparent enthusiasm for change and innovation is difficult to reconcile with the static ideal which the City of the Sun embodies. Indeed, it is hard to see *how* new knowledge and its implications can actually be incorporated into a structure already complete and perfect. While the startling inventions of the Solarians may be partly attributable to the excellence of their educational system— 'without effort, merely while playing, their children come to know all the sciences pictorially before they are ten years old' (p.37)—its central feature, the illustration of all human knowledge on the city walls, has problematic implications. As Judah Bierman points out, 'there is no place for exploring new knowledge; in effect, knowledge is fully known, codified and exhibited' ('Science and Society', p.495). The City of the Sun is not just the title of a book: it *is* a book, written on stone, rather than paper—and like a book's, its contents are finite, fixed and immutable. To extend the city to make space for the depiction of new knowledge would be to violate the archaic principles of harmony and correspondence which are fundamental to its very existence. While the Genoese mariner acknowledges the dynamic principle of new discovery, which has produced more history in a hundred years than did the previous four thousand, the City of the Sun is an embodiment of the end of history: already perfect, its order is immune to change. If there is a dynamic element, it consists rather in the Solarians' colonialist project of imposing that order on its neighbours.

Bacon, *The New Atlantis*

A similar tension is evident in Bacon's *The New Atlantis*, where the dynamic implications of scientific discovery are again hard to reconcile with the static character of a society portrayed as already perfected.[27] While the role of such discovery is still more important (the celebrated account of the wonders of Salomon's House comprises roughly one third of the text), a marked ambivalence with regard to its function and *direction* is likewise evident. Ambivalence, indeed, has been seen by several commentators as an essential aspect of Bacon's thinking. J.C. Davis, for example, describes him as:

[A] scientific modernist consigning all past philosophy to oblivion yet unable to shake off the mental habits of the scholastic, the jargon of the alchemist and magician; the analyst of the imperfections of the human mind, carefully planning the retrieval of its dominion over nature ... pessimistic and optimistic, conservative and radical, timid and bold ... [p.106]

While science and scientific research are clearly crucial to Bacon's vision of a utopian society, the traditional view of Bacon as perhaps the first truly 'modern' scientist is somewhat misleading, ignoring as it does the complexity and ambiguity of Bacon's thought. As Frances Yates observes:

Bacon's view of the future of science was not that of progress in a straight line. His 'great instauration' of science was directed towards a return to the state of Adam before the Fall, a state of pure and sinless contact with nature and knowledge of her powers. [Rosicrucian, p.119]

Thus, while The New Atlantis contains an extensive catalogue of scientific discoveries, they are presented in a context which is anything but suggestive of a modern scientific outlook. The scientists of the House of Salomon, like Campanella's Solarians, have developed the art of flying and the means of prolonging human life—as well as inventing the submarine, a form of perpetual motion machine, and what sounds like a kind of telephone, which 'convey[s] sounds in trunks and pipes, in strange lines and distances' (p.730). Yet, as in The City of the Sun, these startling innovations are hard to reconcile with some of the other details of the text. In describing the history of Bensalem, for instance, the governor of the Strangers' House where the narrator and his companions are lodged indicates that Bensalem has done little more than preserve a level of civilization that was formally global, rather than progressing beyond it. With reference to navigation, for example, he declares:

'You shall understand (that which perhaps you will scarce think credible) that about three thousand years ago, or somewhat more, the navigation of the world, (especially for remote voyages), was greater than at this day. Do not think with yourselves that I know not how much it is increased with you within these six-score years: I know it well: and yet I say greater then than now ...' [p.718]

Given such a starting point, however, it seems curious that so little appears to have changed since. As Davis remarks, it is remarkable that the nineteen hundred years of uninterrupted research following the foundation of Salomon's House should have produced so few technological innovations, or indeed so little social impact. Like the discoveries of the Solarians, the esearch of Bacon's scientists appears to have few practical applications; ather, the main goal of scientific research would seem to be the restoration f a harmonious union between humanity and nature, which will only be chieved when the latter is fully known.

To further complicate the issue, *The New Atlantis*, for all its emphasis on cience, is one of the few utopias in which the supernatural plays an ssential role. While astrology and astral magic are integral to the workings f Campanella's ideal society, it is clear that these are seen as having a ational basis; whereas in Bacon's case one of the fundamental haracteristics of his society—its Christianity—is portrayed as the product f a full-blown miracle. Given that neither the Catholic saint, More, nor he Dominican monk, Campanella, found it necessary to make Christianity he religion of their utopian societies, the fact that Bacon *did* is in itself not vithout interest[28]—but what is particularly interesting is the nature of the 1arrative mechanism which he devises to account for it. In sheerly 1arrative terms, it must be said that the miracle is considerably in excess f requirements: indeed, if mere plausibility were the only consideration and the desire for plausibility is surely at the root of the relentless specificity f details which characterizes so much utopian fiction, Bacon's included) hen the navigational prowess of the Bensalemites would surely have ufficed to account for their coming into contact with the revealed truths f the Christian religion. Bacon, however, resorts to a miracle—what Bloch erms 'the blasting apart of the accustomed status quo' (*Principle of Hope*, .1304)—and doing so he opens a space for a freer play of the imagination han the constraints of utopian fiction (which is designed to persuade its udience that a specific alternative is workable) normally afford. What he roceeds to imagine, given the limitless possibilities of the miraculous, is evealing.

The miracle, we are told, coincided with Christ's ascension—at which ime there appeared off the coast of Bensalem an enormous pillar of light, not sharp, but in the form of a column or cylinder, rising from the sea a reat way up towards heaven' (p.716), the whole surmounted by a cross ven 'brighter and more resplendent than the body of the pillar' (p.716). Vhat then follows is surely one of the oddest scenes in utopian literature. Jumerous concerned citizens put to sea to investigate the apparition, but ind themselves unable to get any closer than some sixty yards away. One oat, however, contains a scientist of the House of Salomon, who prostrates himself before the pillar, and then, raising himself to his knees, utters the ollowing prayer:

> 'Lord God of heaven and earth, thou hast vouchsafed of thy grace to those of our order, to know thy works of creation, and the secrets of

them; and to discern (as far as appertaineth to the generations of
men) between divine miracles, works of nature, works of art, and
impostures and illusions of all sorts. I do here acknowledge and testify
before this people, that the thing which we now see before our eyes
is thy Finger and a true miracle ...' [pp.716–17]

What is presented, in other words, is the spectacle of a trained scientist
solemnly affirming a miracle to be miraculous. Having thus acknowledged
the phallic pillar's divine origin, the scientist is allowed to proceed past the
invisible barrier, at which the pillar promptly explodes into "a firmament
of many stars' (p.717), which then vanish, leaving behind only a 'small ark
or chest of cedar', which opens to reveal what proves to be the seed of
Christianity: 'all the canonical books of the Old and New Testament' (p.717),
even including the ones that had not yet been written—which at the time
of the ascension must have been rather a lot. All of which goes to explain
why Bensalem, unlike Utopia or the City of the Sun, is a Christian
community; extending the analogy between utopia and the womb, Bacon's
account depicts a process of impregnation by the word of God as the result
of what reads remarkably like a symbolic representation of the male orgasm.

In most other respects, for all its fragmentary character, *The New Atlantis*
conforms to the pattern already evident in *Utopia* and *The City of the Sun*.
Bensalem is likewise remote, southerly in location, and unknown to the
rest of the world—an isolation decreed some nineteen hundred years
before by King Solamona, in the belief that contact with the outside world
could only harm a society that 'might be a thousand ways altered to the
worse, but scarce any one way to the better' (p.720). Lost, sick and starving,
the narrator and his companions reach the coast of Bensalem, there to find
many of the characteristic features of the womb-like paradisaical utopia.
Entering a safe harbour, their initial attempt at landing is repulsed by the
threatening presence of men waving batons, phallic symbols which, as in
Utopia, bar entry to the safe haven beyond. Once it emerges that they are
Christian, however, they are permitted to land, and are given food and
lodging, free of charge, in the Strangers' House. A period of quarantine
then ensues, during which their sick (who constitute precisely one third
of the ship's company) are provided with appropriate diet and medicine,
and make so rapid a recovery that they 'thought themselves cast into some
divine pool of healing, they mended so kindly and so fast' (p.715).

Reduced to a state of total dependence, the travellers remain passive
and submissive throughout, appreciative of the 'gracious and parent-like
usage' (715) they receive, and often prostrating themselves at the feet and
kissing the robes of the various authority figures they encounter. When
they are finally sufficiently recovered to be allowed to explore their

surroundings—within the strict limits laid down by their hosts—they discover a world that is, once again, stable, prosperous, happy, and at peace. And while, compared to More and Campanella, Bacon provides relatively few details of the social organization of his ideal commonwealth, it is clearly characterized by, if possible, an even greater degree of purity and moral rectitude on the part of its inhabitants: 'there is not under the heavens so chaste a nation as this of Bensalem; nor so free from all pollution or foulness. It is the virgin of the world ...' (p.724). Despite a few passing indications that individual conduct may occasionally require correction, it would appear that Bacon's society is, again, one in which innocence has in large measure been recovered.

Yet it is also a society in which the maternal security it provides is the product of an order if possible still more exclusively male-dominated than those of Utopia or the City of the Sun. While the brevity of *The New Atlantis* precludes more than a brief glimpse of its workings, one feature that *is* described in what seems almost redundant detail is the so-called 'Feast of the Family', a ceremony held to honour 'any man that shall live to see thirty persons descended of his body alive together, and all above three years old' (p.722). This feast, which is paid for by the state, follows two days of consultations during which the father of the family (called the tirsan) settles any outstanding family disputes, and offers advice or assistance to such members of the family who seem in need of it. He then chooses one of his sons to live with him, who is thereafter called 'the Son of the Vine', and the feast ensues, after which prayers are offered to the patriarchs, Adam, Noah, and Abraham. The tirsan is served exclusively by his male children, while 'the women only stand about him, leaning against the wall' (p.723), and the ceremony concludes with the tirsan giving his blessing. There is, however, one notable absentee:

> ... if there be a mother, from whose body the whole lineage is descended, there is a travers placed in a loft above on the right hand of the chair, with a privy door, and a carved window of glass, leaded with gold and blue; where she sitteth, but is not seen. [p.723]

It would be hard to imagine a more explicit image of the displacement of the female by the male, with the mother reduced to peering down, unseen, as the power of the father is celebrated; yet it is an image very much in keeping with the emphasis of the work as a whole—elsewhere, although women presumably do exist, they remain invisible. In such a context, it is perhaps unsurprising that among the discoveries made by the scientists of the House of Salomon is a method of artificially creating life. Not only are women invisible in Bacon's utopia, the technology exists to render them superfluous.

The Utopian Narrative Paradigm

A range of features, then, begin to emerge as characteristic of the utopian narrative model. As has been seen, the ideological ferment of the Renaissance finds a reflection in a series of distinctive ambiguities. In all three of the works so far examined, the *direction* of the utopian impulse remains unclear: the question of whether utopia embodies the desire to create a genuinely new order, or to recover one that has been lost is in each case difficult to resolve. And while the utopian vision is of a society radically different from that of the writer, it nevertheless excludes any consideration of the process of *change*. Not only are the utopian societies of More, Campanella, and Bacon fundamentally static, leaving little or no room for alteration (unless for the worse), the process whereby they came into being is passed over or evaded. More's Utopia is simply decreed; Campanella's is apparently the fruit of a collective resolution; while Bacon's was apparently already in existence when King Solamona instituted a policy of isolation designed to preserve it in its perfection. The emphasis of the Renaissance utopian narrative is on stasis rather than process, security rather than change. And while the *nature* of that security may be seen as distinctively maternal, it is in each case sustained by the imposition of an explicitly patriarchal order. Although utopias may sweep away such fundamental existing institutions as private property, money, or the Christian religion, they rely as heavily on the maintenance of patriarchy for their distinctive character as on the abolition or transformation of other aspects of society. In this regard, there are also clear parallels with the contemporaneous discovery narratives, in whose language a similar fantasy of masculine dominance over territory gendered as female is likewise inscribed, and in which the opening up of the new is only the prelude to the superimposition of existing hierarchies and modes of domination. In both *Utopia* and *The City of the Sun* it is significant that, albeit with the best of apparent intentions, one of the major projects of the utopian state is the colonization of its neighbours.

Lastly, while utopia proposes an order which appears on the surface distinctively rational, although one which at the same time reproduces significant aspects of existing society, this apparent reasonableness should not be allowed to disguise its essentially fantastic character. As Bloch remarks, the apparent modesty of some aspects of the utopian dream conceals 'a basic utopia ... which is much too fantastic to manifest itself ... openly' (*Principle of Hope*, p.751). Underlying the concrete, even mundane detail of utopian systems for the production and distribution of food, underlying More's six hour and Campanella's four hour working day, is the old paradisaical dream of free feeding and idleness; while the common utopian preoccupation with hygiene, diet, and improved medical techniques conceals an aspiration still more grandiose. Beyond the Solarian life span of between one hundred and two hundred years lies the ultimate dream of eternal life.

In narrative terms, the tensions and contradictions inherent in the *content* of the utopian dream also manifest themselves at the formal level. As has been suggested, the peculiarly static character of the utopian vision gives rise to a distinctive chronotope, in which plenitude in space seems designed to compensate for the virtual erasure of time. While both More and Bacon indicate time-frames presumably intended to enhance the reader's sense of utopia's permanence (1760 years have elapsed since the foundation of Utopia, 1900 since the reign of Solamona), the fact that nothing of any significance appears to have happened *during* that time strips it of any real meaning. Time, no matter how extensive, is empty of content; whereas the *space* of utopia is full. Within the confines of the City of the Sun *all* human knowledge is encoded, while the House of Salomon has achieved a similar exhaustive mastery of the secrets of nature. The very architecture of utopia, whether More's or Campanella's, is designed to create an environment in which everything (and everyone) is *known*. Yet this fullness is lacking in any dynamic quality: it remains, as Wells puts it, static rather than kinetic. The description of utopian geography, while it possesses a concreteness that the account of utopian history so signally lacks, has the quality of a tableau—a space frozen in time. Utopian narrative consists primarily of a single process: that of unveiling the tableau to the non-utopian audience. And it is here that one may see the emerging utopian narrative model as in a sense more restrictive than its first exemplar. Where More does provide some sense of narrative *interaction* between utopia and his own world, both in the vigorous debate which occupies the first book, and in the complex dialectic between the actual account of utopia and the narrative which frames it, this element is far less evident in the work of his successors. In the fictions of Campanella and Bacon, the tension between Hythloday's unequivocal enthusiasm for Utopia and the scepticism of the narrator disappears. Campanella's Knight Hospitaller eagerly interrogates the Genoese mariner, but accepts all he is told with uncritical wonder; while the narrator of *The New Atlantis* provides a more passive, but equally sympathetic audience for the authoritative discourse of the utopians. While in More's case there *is* a sense of genuine dialogue, of an interaction between conflicting viewpoints, the work of his successors serves largely to foreclose such exchanges. The complicating irony of *Utopia* almost entirely disappears, giving way to a more straightforwardly didactic intent. Even where the form of the dialogue is preserved, albeit in vestigial form, it only serves to highlight the extent to which, as Bakhtin puts it, 'the content ...assume[s] a monologic character that contradict[s] the form shaping idea of the genre' (*Problems*, p.110). Dialogue becomes merely 'a simple means for expounding ready-made ideas' (p.110). With the passage of time, then, the purpose of utopian narrative become clearer: its function is primarily to persuade.

Such didactic intent is, of course, quite in keeping with the norms of Renaissance narrative practice; it is only later, with the rise of the novel, and the emergence of interpretative conventions rooted in the growing influence of representational realism, that finding a fictional vehicle for such overt didacticism becomes more problematic. Thus, while the most obvious challenge facing later writers of utopian fiction is that of conceiving more desirable sociopolitical alternatives in a context where innovation and growth, rather than stasis, have become evidently the norm, the problem of how such alternatives are to be represented becomes a more pressing one. Moving forward to the modern era, it becomes clear that, despite the ingenuity which writers such as Bellamy and Wells bring to bear on both the ideological and narrative problems involved in the production of literary utopias, the influence of the traditional, and essentially static utopian model is by no means easy to escape. In examining the very different narrative strategies which they adopt, it becomes necessary, once again, to ask not only what changes with the passage of time, but what remains the same.

3. Bellamy and Wells: The Dream of Order in the Modern World

If a certain degree of tension and ambiguity can be seen as inherent in the utopian model as such, it is also clear that much of the complex and contradictory character of the utopian fictions of the Renaissance is a direct reflection of the ideological ferment of the period in which they were written. Indeed, the intellectual exercise of projecting a more desirable alternative to the society of the day often has the effect of highlighting precisely those aspects of Renaissance thinking that are most ambivalent and fraught with contradiction. In an era where new and potentially revolutionary ideas co-exist with a powerful commitment to tradition, the utopian vision, offering the promise of stability while at the same time implying the desirability of change, almost inevitably exposes gaps and disjunctures—the points where conflicting impulses become impossible to reconcile.

That not only the utopian dream of order as such, but also the characteristic narrative paradigm associated with it should survive into the modern era raises a number of issues with regard to the relation between ideology and form. While the endurance of the utopian impulse itself requires little explanation—so long as society remains imperfect, more perfect alternatives will always have an appeal—the persistence of so many specific features of the Renaissance utopia, in terms both of content *and* form, is less easy to account for. Obviously, there is the question of direct influence to consider: in many cases later writers are clearly aware of, and respond to the example of their predecessors; nevertheless, as we shall see, that example is one which becomes increasingly problematic with the passage of time.

To begin with, it is clear that the writer of utopian fiction at the close of the nineteenth century (which sees the first major flowering of utopian fiction since the Renaissance) is faced with a radically different relationship between text and context. That dramatic changes in the nature of society are likely to dictate changes in the nature of the alternatives envisaged to it goes without saying: a utopia designed to resolve problems of scarcity in a pre-industrial economy will clearly differ radically from one which addresses issues arising from the contradictions of industrial capitalism and the organizational needs of a mass society. What also changes, however, is the nature of the *connection* between the writer's society and the utopian alternatives proposed. For example, when Campanella's Genoese mariner remarks that the past hundred years had seen more history than the preceding four thousand, the implications of his statement had not yet become fully apparent. While to a modern eye it might seem singularly prescient, indicative of an awareness that a process of far-reaching historical change had now begun, in a Renaissance context it might equally be taken as suggesting that history was now hastening to its end—towards a final state of millennial perfection, of which the City of the Sun is an emblem. By the close of the nineteenth century, however, the notion of progress—of history as a process of continuous advance, with change as the norm, rather than the exception—had become commonplace. Writing in 1890, Sidney Webb (whose thinking clearly influenced Wells, notwithstanding his subsequent break with the Fabians) declared:

> ... we can no longer think of the future society as an unchanging state. The social ideal from being statical has become dynamic. The necessity of constant growth and development of the social organism has become axiomatic. [p.5]

Given such assumptions, much that in a Renaissance context seemed relatively fixed (social institutions, the relation of human society to nature) now appears provisional, susceptible to modification by human agency. The largely speculative premise of the Renaissance utopia—that human beings, by the unaided use of their powers of reason, might create a more perfect society—begins to seem increasingly plausible. As the evidence mounts that changes once envisaged solely in a utopian context are capable of being embodied in reality, the assumption that social engineering is not only desirable, but practicable becomes more and more widely accepted. The manifest influence of utopian ideas during such historic conflicts as the English Civil War, the American War of Independence, or the French Revolution clearly demonstrates the practical impact of notions once seen as largely hypothetical. Change, in other words, is no longer a dream, but a real possibility, and the increasingly widespread belief in the feasibility of creating, if not an ideal, at any rate a better society obviously affects the ways in which utopian fiction is both imagined and read. If the establishment of a better society is seen as possible, even likely, then the concept of a still more perfect society becomes that much more plausible.

In addition, the plausibility of the *content* of utopian fiction is further enhanced by the fact that accompanying developments in science and technology give substance to another aspect of the utopian dream: that of humanity gaining control over nature. By 1888, when Bellamy's *Looking Backward* was first published, many of the wishful imaginings of Campanella and Bacon had already become realities, with dramatic advances in hygiene, medicine, long-range transport and communications, and even 'some degrees of flying in the air' (Bacon, p.731). Far from being confined to a research institute such as the House of Salomon, with only minimal effect on the surrounding society, invention becomes instrumental in the process of societal change, which in turn lends a very different resonance to its depiction in a utopian context. In portraying technology as central to the creation of their utopian societies, writers such as Bellamy and Wells are in essence only reflecting the realities of their own world. Not only technological advance, but its impact are depicted with a degree of concreteness wholly lacking in the utopias of Campanella and Bacon: in contrast to their rather abstract formulations, even the most futuristic aspects of Bellamy's and Wells's utopias (the underground network of pneumatic tubes in *Looking Backward*, the genetic engineering of *Men Like Gods*) are presented in detail, and as integral to the functioning of utopian society as a whole.

Yet while it might therefore seem reasonable to conclude that one effect of the passage of time is to render utopian fiction more plausible, in other respects the radically different historical circumstances render the writing of such fiction more, rather than less problematic. As Kumar suggests, where the Renaissance utopia embodied an essentially static ideal—a society where change was not merely unnecessary, but an actual threat—those of the modern era 'had perforce to be open-ended, to a degree never before attempted or thought necessary. They had to accommodate the requirement for ceaseless innovation and growth, individual and social' (*Utopia*, pp.47–8). This necessity, however, creates some undeniable formal problems. As Wells was among the first to acknowledge, in order to portray a society in which change is integral, rather than representing a threat of degeneration, it becomes necessary to incorporate a much greater element of process—to dramatize what *happens* in such a society, as opposed to merely describing its outlines. Such an essentially novelistic approach, utilizing the techniques of a genre evolved to represent precisely such a changing society, might seem the obvious solution, yet it is not without its own difficulties—for if the development of both new technologies and new forms of political organization serve to render the actual *content* of utopian literature more plausible, in other respects its fictionality becomes more transparent. With the end of the age of exploration, the space into which earlier writers were able to project their utopias disappears. The unknown becomes known; the possible is colonized by the actual: in the end, imperfect reality fills all the territory on the map where utopian perfection could once be imagined. Forced to look elsewhere for a locale, writers of utopias turn increasingly to the space provided by the extension of temporal, rather than geographical horizons. As the old, finite time-frame in which history was conceived of as a matter of a few thousand years, bounded by the creation at one end and the millennium at the other, gives way to the far vaster perspectives afforded by evolutionary theory, the future becomes a new *terra incognita* into which utopia can be projected.

This has certain attendant drawbacks, however: while the emergent genre of science fiction takes full advantage of the imaginative perspectives provided by this larger future, (not to mention the corresponding extension of spatial horizons to which speculation as to the feasibility of space travel gives rise), utopian fiction seems less successful at exploiting the creative possibilities that arise. The exuberance with which Wells uses the techniques of representational realism to lend a veneer of plausibility to such futuristic fantasies as *The Time Machine* and *The War of the Worlds* is notably lacking in both his own utopian fictions and those of most of his contemporaries. In part, this may be attributable to the constraints imposed by the more earnest, even didactic intent which utopian fiction evinces; yet this is not the only factor. What is also clear is the extent to which even the most radical fictional experiments (such as Wells's own *A Modern Utopia*) remain tied to the characteristic narrative paradigm of the Renaissance utopia—that of the traveller's tale, in which the visitor explores the more perfect society, and then reports back on the wonders he has seen. Indeed, while it has become something of a critical commonplace that temporal, rather than geographical displacement becomes the norm,[1] it is curious how many modern utopias, from Gilman's *Herland* to Huxley's *Island*, in fact retain the traditional premise of a utopian society isolated from, but contemporaneous with the writer's own: even Wells, a pioneer of futuristic fiction in works such as *The Time Machine* and *The War in the Air*, chooses for the most part to locate his utopias in worlds parallel to, rather than chronologically separated from his own.

None the less, what does emerge at this period is a recognizable variant of the old form—a narrative in which the traditional voyage to utopia is replaced by the process of going to sleep and reawakening in a utopian future. Used by both Bellamy and Morris in their utopias, not to mention Wells, in his far-from-utopian *When the Sleeper Wakes* (1899), what Peter Beilharz refers to as 'the Rip Van Winkle genre typically associated with the term [utopia]' (p.x)[2] soon becomes a narrative device sufficiently familiar as to become an object of parody—witness Stephen Leacock's *Afternoons in Utopia* (1932), which begins:

> ... let us reproduce the familiar scene of the long sleep and the arrival of the awakened sleeper in dear old Utopia. We will introduce, however, the slight, but novel, innovation of supposing that the

narrator in this case arrives with—and not, as usually depicted, without—his brains. [p.3]

In a modern context, however, the adequacy of this narrative paradigm, whether modified or not, seems open to doubt. At least part of the Renaissance utopia's narrative fascination, as we have seen, lay in its capacity to exploit the conventions of a narrative model that was factual and documentary in origin. At the same time that More, Campanella, and Bacon were writing, there were also *actual* travellers' accounts from the southern hemisphere, allowing the writer of utopias to play with the notion (as More does most teasingly) that the ideal society might actually exist. This is not to say that any but the most literal-minded reader believed it really *did* exist: the point is that the possibility remained intriguingly plausible. In the case of fictions set in the future, however, in a parallel universe (*Men Like Gods*), or 'out beyond Sirius' (*A Modern Utopia*, p.12), the fantasy is unequivocal, thereby bringing into play a rather different set of interpretive conventions. Whereas the actual utopian *societies* outlined may seem more plausible, more susceptible to practical realization, the narrative form in which they are represented becomes self-evidently fantastic. As a result, the fruitful ambiguity which pervades both the content and the form of the Renaissance utopia gives way, in a modern context, to a certain sense of generic discontinuity, rooted in what Morson describes as 'the double encoding of utopias as both fiction and non-fiction, literature and nonliterature' (p.93). Where More's manipulation of the conventions of a purportedly factual narrative mode is well suited to his apparent ambivalence of intent, the fantastic narrative mechanisms of the utopias of Bellamy and Wells seem rather less in keeping with the evident seriousness of their sociopolitical prescriptions. The result is often a certain confusion as to how such hybrid fictions are meant to be read. As Morson suggests, problems arise when

> the ... set of instructions, which characterizes the text as not a fiction or not 'just literature', is delayed and the reader consequently led astray. It is not surprising, then, that readers of utopias often feel exploited as well as perplexed. That feeling may be the result not so much of having been led to read a literary work that turned out to be bad as having been led to read one that turned out—or did it?— to be no literary work at all. Belatedly discovering that the literary and fictional contracts had hidden clauses, readers may feel themselves to be victims of literary fraud. [p.93]

Such problems, of course, stem in part from the changing nature of fiction's interpretive conventions. In an era when fiction is dominated by the norms of high realism and naturalism, by what Fredric Jameson describes as 'the threefold imperatives of authorial depersonalization, unity of point of view, and restriction to scenic representation' (*Political Unconscious*, p.104), the formal heterogeneity and tendentiousness of utopian fiction is always liable to appear anomalous. And while Jameson argues that the re-emergence of genres such as the utopian is symptomatic of a reaction against the stifling constraints imposed by such realism's celebration of the merely existing, it is nevertheless the case that writers of utopias seem uneasily aware of the extent to which their fictions fail to secure the consistent suspension of disbelief at which realist fiction aims. Both Bellamy and Wells, for example, while preserving the central features of the traditional narrative paradigm, seek to supplement its by now somewhat limited attractions by the incorporation of more 'novelistic' elements: individual characterization, for example, or plot features such as a love interest. Such window dressing, however, scarcely resolves the underlying narrative problem.

Not the least of the difficulties that arises from the use of novelistic elements is an essential incompatibility between utopian narrative and the conventions of a genre which had evolved primarily to register the complex texture of existing reality. As Morson argues:

> The interpretive conventions of utopias are radically different from those of novels—a difference which, as we shall see, reflects the two genres' antithetical philosophical assumptions. First, in the novel, unlike the utopia, the narrative is to be taken as representing a plausible sequence of events (i.e., as designed to be 'realistic'). Second, in a novel, the statements, actions, and beliefs of any principal character (or the narrator) are to be understood as a reflection of his or her personality, and of the biographical events and social milieu that have shaped it. An important corollary for our discussion of utopias follows from this second interpretive convention. The sort of unqualified, absolute truths about morality and society that constantly occur in utopias have no place in novels.
> [p.77]

While novels are by no means invariably free of didactic intent, that intent normally presupposes some common assumptions on the part of both writer and reader as to both the nature of reality and the validity of the value system informing it; where alternative assumptions have to be spelled out, as is the case in most traditional utopian narratives, an unavoidable tension arises between the utopian and novelistic elements in the text. Thus, while characters in a novel may *utter* 'unqualified, absolute truths about morality and society' they remain utterances made in a particular context. As Morson goes on to suggest:

In novels, but not in utopias, each truth is *someone*'s truth, qualified by what might be called an 'irony of origins'—that is, by our knowledge that it reflects a particular person's (or character's) experience and a given set of personal and contextual circumstances. They are consequently understood to be *partial*—that is, both limited and biased—even if we (or the author) are inclined to share that partiality. [p.77]

Yet it is precisely this awareness that the traditional utopian narrative seeks to discourage: whereas the partial, limited awareness of the inhabitants of *existing* society may be the target of utopian critique—as is the case in the utopias of both Bellamy and Wells—the underlying assumption is that in the more perfect society such limitations have largely vanished, enabling the utopians to see the truth as it is.

Given the difficulties associated with the reproduction in a modern context of the Renaissance utopia's narrative paradigm, its persistence raises a number of questions. To begin with, the survival of a generic structure rooted in very different historical circumstances should alert us to the possibility that, for all its shortcomings in a modern *narrative* context, it nevertheless continues to embody some ideological message of enduring relevance. Are there, in other words, any parallels between the differing historical situations which might encourage a *specific* narrative formulation of utopian alternatives? Equally, the continued evasion by writers such as Bellamy and Wells of the issue of utopia's origins (accompanied once again by an often extravagant compensatory elaboration of metaphors of transition), poses a further question: how far is the characteristic psychological pattern of the Renaissance utopia, in which a recurrent element is the reconstitution of the maternal security of the womb under a system of patriarchal control, *inherent* in the traditional paradigm? If, as we have seen, the very process of exploration and discovery is bound up with primal fantasies of the recovery of Eden, is the traveller's tale itself not likely to lend itself particularly easily to the embodiment of this dream? Finally, given the contradictions inherent in the content of Renaissance and modern utopia alike, it must be asked whether, paradoxically, the problematic aspect of its form, its inscription of conflicting impulses in an unresolved tension, is not also a source of its lasting appeal.

Yet if a detailed examination of more modern articulations of the utopian dream may help to account for the resilience of the traditional narrative format, it should likewise be borne in mind that the continuing use of a specific narrative form is liable to have ideological consequences in terms of content. As Macherey argues, the relationship between ideology and narrative is by no means a simple one of cause and effect: the form also has its effect on the narrative's ideological implications. How far a form originally used for the expression of the static, authoritarian vision of the Renaissance utopian writers affects the avowedly 'progressive' content of the works of Bellamy and Wells—or, as Jameson puts it, how far 'an already constituted narrative paradigm emits an ideological message in its own right' (*Political Unconscious*, p.88)—is a question which the following discussion will address.

Bellamy, *Looking Backward*

Bellamy's *Looking Backward*, as we shall see, adheres particularly closely to the traditional narrative paradigm. While the chosen locale for the ideal society is no longer an imaginary island or walled city, but the rather more prosaic setting of Boston, Massachusetts, it is none the less a Boston transfigured by its displacement more than a hundred years into the future—into the year 2000—by which time it has become literally unrecognizable.[3] Nevertheless, the fantastic nature of its narrative premise does not appear to have detracted from what was widely seen as the plausibility of its social prescriptions. Indeed, in its day, *Looking Backward* enjoyed a degree of influence and popularity which now seems barely credible, not only enjoying enormous sales, but inspiring the foundation of Bellamy societies as far afield as Holland, South Africa, Indonesia, and New Zealand. Even as late as the 1930s it was cited by both the philosopher John Dewey and the historian Charles Beard as being second in importance only to *Das Kapital* among books published in the preceding half-century.[4] And for all that *Looking Backward* now appears terribly dated in most respects, its appeal clearly has much in common with that exerted by the earlier utopias of More, Campanella, and Bacon. Like theirs, Bellamy's vision of an ordered society offers a telling, even seductive contrast to the chaos of the actual world to which it proposes an alternative. Endeavouring to account for the appeal of such utopias, Northrop Frye suggests that:

> ... the utopian form flourishes best when anarchy seems most a social threat. Since More, utopias have appeared regularly but sporadically in literature, with a great increase around the close of the nineteenth century. This later vogue clearly had much to do with the distrust and dismay aroused by extreme laissez-faire version of capitalism, which were thought of as manifestations of anarchy, ['Varieties', p.27]

In the case of *Looking Backward*, this would seem to be particularly true: indeed, some of the most powerful passages in the work occur in the introductory section where, like More before him, Bellamy offers a vivid depiction of the social evils of his day. It is here, in his portrayal of the period's recurrent financial crises, its often brutal conflicts between capital and labour, its glaring divisions between the conditions of rich and poor, that Bellamy is at his most bitterly satirical—most notably in the celebrated allegorical passage where society is depicted as a coach, drawn by the mass of humanity:

> The driver was hunger, and permitted no lagging, though the pace was necessarily very slow. Despite the difficulty of drawing the coach at all along so hard a road, the top was covered with passengers who never got down, even at the steepest ascents. These seats on top were very breezy and comfortable. Well up out of the dust, their occupants could enjoy the scenery at their leisure, or critically discuss the merits of the straining team ... It was naturally regarded as a terrible misfortune to lose one's seat, and the apprehension that this might happen to them or their friends was a constant cloud upon the happiness of those who rode ... When the vehicle came to a bad place in the road, as it was constantly doing, or to a particularly steep hill ... the desperate straining of the team, their agonizing leaping and plunging under the pitiless lash of hunger, the many who fainted at the rope and were trampled in the mire, made a very distressing spectacle, which often called forth highly creditable displays of feeling on the top of the coach ... It was agreed that it was a great pity that the coach should be so hard to pull, and there was a sense of general relief when the specially bad piece of road was gotten over. The relief was not, indeed, wholly on account of the team, for there was always some danger at these bad places of a general overturn in which all would lose their seats. [pp.10–11]

Yet while the forcefulness of Bellamy's satire on contemporary society recalls the spirit of the first book of More's *Utopia*, what follows is closer to the letter of the second.

The basic scenario is simple enough. The narrator, Julian West, is a young Bostonian who goes to sleep one May night in 1887, but (due to a somewhat bizarre combination of circumstances) fails to awake until September of the year 2000. While he finds himself still in Boston, the reality he confronts is otherwise wholly unfamiliar. Physically, there are no vestiges of the city of his own day, and it soon becomes clear that the squalor and industrial strife of the 1880s have given way to utopian co-operation. During his century-long slumber the laissez-faire capitalism of the late nineteenth-century has evolved—painlessly, it would appear—into a full-blown command economy: employers and trade unions alike have been superseded by the monopolistic state, and (most other nations having followed the lead of the United States) the world is as a result governed by reason and justice. As Julian West discovers, in a series of lengthy discussions with his utopian host, Dr Leete, there is universal peace, the spread of prosperity and enlightenment having rendered it unnecessary for nations to make war in order to divert attention from suffering and unrest at home, while the combination of centralized economic planning with the elimination of wasteful competition and needless duplication of services ensures a sufficiency of goods for all. Liberation from the demands of unceasing labour is also provided, although in this case by early retirement, rather than the reduction of hours: 'industrial service', as it is called, terminates at the age of forty-five. What is offered, in other words, is very much the same basic agenda as that of the Renaissance utopia: the technology of Bellamy's society is more advanced, the vocabulary he employs rather different, but the end product is remarkably similar.

Even where obvious differences occur, they often prove superficial. While peace, in the Renaissance utopia, is only secured by vigorous defensive precautions—witness the ruthlessness with which the otherwise pacific Utopians wage war, or the detailed account we are given of the Solarians' sophisticated military tactics—one might think the extension of utopian society worldwide would render such military preoccupations redundant. In *Looking Backward*, however, while warfare no longer takes place, the military impulse is simply displaced elsewhere: if international harmony has rendered external defence superfluous, the society's internal organization exhibits a strikingly militaristic character. Indeed, the entire system of industrial organization in the United States of the future is explicitly based on a military model: 'the principle of universal military service', we are told, has simply been applied to 'the labour question' (p.32).[5] Bellamy even goes so far as to state—approvingly—that the efficiency of the utopian workforce is comparable to that of 'the German army in the time of Von Moltke' (p.135)![6] Given that his latter-day Americans 'were already accustomed to the idea that the obligation of every citizen, not physically disabled, to contribute to the defence of the nation was equal and absolute' (p.32), it follows that it is 'equally the duty of every citizen to contribute his quota of industrial or intellectual services to the maintenance of the nation' (p.32). Hence the institution of what Bellamy refers to as 'the industrial army', whose discipline and efficiency are central to the harmony and prosperity of his utopian future. Even the contrasting chaos of late nineteenth-century society is represented in terms of the same all-pervasive military metaphor. As Dr Leete puts it:

> People would be prompt enough to ridicule an army in which there
> were neither companies, battalions, regiments, brigades, divisions,

or army corps—no unit of organization, in fact, larger than the corporal's squad, with no officer higher than a corporal, and all the corporals equal in authority. And yet just such an army were the manufacturing industries of nineteenth-century Boston, an army of four thousand independent squads led by four thousand independent corporals, each with a separate plan of campaign. [p.178]

No such independence, of course, is either possible or desired in the Boston of the year 2000: all citizens are subject to the central authority of the industrial army, into which recruits are inducted at the age of twenty-one on what is significantly called 'Muster Day'. Or rather, almost all: like its Renaissance predecessors, Bellamy's utopia has its élite, who form a separate caste.[7] 'The liberal professions', we learn, do not form part of the industrial army, and it is they alone—doctors, teachers, artists, men of letters—who, along with retired males over the age of forty-five, are eligible to vote. The industrial army itself is disenfranchised—as indeed are all women.

In the case of women, of course, it may fairly be objected that Bellamy is merely reflecting the political realities of his day: women in late nineteenth-century North America did not have the vote, either. Nevertheless, as has already become evident, the features of his own society which the utopian writer chooses to preserve are no less significant than those he transforms. As with the Renaissance utopia's maintenance of patriarchy, Bellamy's relatively traditional conception of the role of women needs to be set against the sweeping transformations of society proposed elsewhere. For while, like Campanella, Bellamy seems at first sight to be proposing a radical extension of women's existing rights and freedoms, on closer examination a similar ambiguity becomes apparent. As does Campanella, Bellamy offers a freedom which proves increasingly illusory, undermined and contradicted as it is by other evidence in the text. While some recent critics have praised Bellamy for his commitment to feminism,[8] his utopia is hardly less male-dominated than those of the Renaissance.

For example, while women work in Bellamy's Boston of the future, just as they do in the City of the Sun, the narrative's initial assertion of equality in principle ('women, as well as ... men, are members of the industrial army' (p.142)) is subject to a series of progressively more disabling qualifications, whose ultimate effect is to restore women to a subordinate role. Just as in Campanella's utopia, the actual range of jobs open to women is restricted, due to their being 'inferior in strength, and further disqualified industrially in special ways' (p.142):

Under no circumstances is a woman permitted to follow any employment not perfectly adapted, both as to kind and degree of labour, to her sex. Moreover, the hours of women's work are considerably shorter than those of men's, more frequent vacations are granted, and the most careful provision is made for rest when needed. The men of this day so well appreciate that they owe to the beauty and grace of women the chief zest of their lives and their main incentive to effort, that they permit them to work at all only because it is fully understood that a certain regular requirement of labour, of a sort adapted to their powers, is well for body and mind ... [pp.142–3]

What becomes clear, in effect, is that the power dynamic underlying Bellamy's system of utopian gender relations is not radically different from that obtaining in the society to which his utopia proposes an alternative. While there are some real improvements in the lot of women, not least their liberation from most domestic labour by the institution of public kitchens, laundries, and facilities for clothes repair, the basic social structure remains clearly patriarchal. As Bammer argues, one way in which utopias of the period sought to allay anxieties aroused by the sweeping changes they imagined in society's public institutions was by their insistence that the structures of private life would remain reassuringly unchanged—and that in particular 'gender would remain constant: a woman, no matter what else might change, would still remain "every inch a woman". And a man, by implication, a man' (p.30). Thus, in *Looking Backward*, while men 'permit' women to work, it is 'only' for health reasons: the principal value of their labour is that it renders them more desirable to the men. And the marginal status of women's labour is still further underscored when it transpires that women, notwithstanding Dr Leete's initial assertion, are not in fact part of the industrial army after all: they 'constitute rather an allied force than an integral part of the army of the men. They have a woman general-in-chief and are under exclusively feminine régime' (p.143).[9]

The motives for this segregation, however, are less puritanical than they might seem at first sight. Bellamy's main concern, it would appear, is for the preservation of industrial discipline. Outside the workplace, relations between the sexes are not merely permitted, but actively encouraged: love, it turns out, is regarded as essential to the welfare of the state. In the course of yet another lengthy conversation with Dr Leete, the narrator learns that 'the independence of women' has ensured that economic considerations no longer influence the woman's choice of marital partner, with the result that 'there are nothing but matches of pure love' (p.148). Yet while the narrator is appropriately impressed by this 'astonishing phenomenon', Dr Leete is more concerned to spell out its implications:

It means that for the first time in human history the principle of sexual selection, with its tendency to preserve and transmit the better types of the race, and let the inferior types drop out, has unhindered operation. The necessities of poverty, the need of having a home, no longer tempt women to accept as the fathers of their children men whom they neither can love nor respect. Wealth and rank no longer divert attention from personal qualities. Gold no longer 'gilds the straitened forehead of the fool.' The gifts of person, mind, and disposition; beauty, wit, eloquence, kindness, generosity, geniality, courage, are sure of transmission to posterity. Each generation is sifted through a little finer mesh than the last. [p.148]

It is the effect of such 'untrammelled sexual selection' as 'tending to race purification' (pp.148–9) that really matters. As in *The City of the Sun*, the sexual provisions of *Looking Backward* have selective breeding as their ultimate goal. Nevertheless, Bellamy's is a distinctively nineteenth-century reworking of a longstanding utopian preoccupation: an end which Campanella seeks to attain by the imposition of rigorous state control, with appropriate medical and astrological supervision, is here left to the unhindered operation of the forces of the sexual free market.

Yet purification of the race is not the only benefit, it turns out. In addition, Dr Leete reveals, the fact that merit alone inspires love also proves conducive to industrial efficiency, since the best (indeed virtually the only) way of demonstrating the desirable qualities Bellamy lists is by being a good worker:

...not all the encouragements and incentives of every sort which we have provided to develop industry, talent, genius, excellence of whatever kind, are comparable in their effect on our young men with the fact that our women sit aloft as judges of the race and reserve themselves to reward the winners. Of all the whips, and spurs, and baits, and prizes, there is none like the thought of the radiant faces which the laggards will find averted. [p.149]

In the name of a saner, more rational organization of society, woman is still more nakedly reduced to the status not merely of consumer (Dr Leete's daughter, it will be recalled, is characterized as 'an indefatigable shopper'), but of commodity—the prize awarded for success in the race of life. What Bellamy offers is not so much an alternative structure of gender relations, as an unmasking of the process whereby sexual gratification becomes a reward for economic success. Where the difference lies is that in his utopia there is no longer any mediation: the rewards for the productive capacity of the individual are now sexual *instead* of economic. While many of *Looking Backward*'s most traditionally utopian provisions—the abolition of money, state control of the means of production and distribution—might seem antithetical to the values of late nineteenth-century capitalism, what is enacted, in effect, is the compensatory displacement of the economic into the realm of the sexual.

In this instance, Bellamy's underlying assumptions become only too overt; yet what he *shows* is perhaps less interesting than what he seeks to conceal. As in the Renaissance utopias, a relentless specificity of detail regarding the workings of the more perfect society is accompanied by an equally telling lack of detail concerning the process whereby it came into being. As Jean Pfaelzer remarks, despite the wealth of detail which Bellamy provides in other areas, he remains 'vague and imprecise about the transition to utopia' ('Immanence', p.53). Although he portrays late nineteenth-century America as being on the brink of anarchy, for example, it is significant that the utopian command economy of the year 2000 appears to have been established without any form of struggle or conflict whatsoever. Despite the competitive greed of the business community, and labour unrest so acute that it causes some observers to 'predict an impending social cataclysm' (p.7), and to surmise that, having emerged from barbarism, the human race had 'attained the perihelion of civilization only to plunge downward once more to its nether goal in the regions of chaos' (p.7),[10] it transpires that the subsequent amalgamation of all businesses into a single nationwide corporation has been accomplished with none of the 'great bloodshed and terrible convulsions' (p.29) that might reasonably have been expected. Instead, as Dr Leete is at pains to assure the narrator:

> '... there was absolutely no violence. The change had been long foreseen. Public opinion had become fully ripe for it, and the whole mass of people was behind it. There was no more possibility of opposing it by force than by argument.' [p.29]

And that is all we learn concerning the transition to a utopian society: it just happened, apparently inevitably. Brief as this is, however, it serves to emphasize the extent to which security, above all, remains the fundamental object of Bellamy's utopian desire. The transition is not merely non-violent, but there is *absolutely no* violence (not a single landlord or capitalist forcibly resists dispossession, we must assume, nor does a single member of the proletariat resort to violence out of resentment or a desire for vengeance). Yet that is not all: not only is there no violence—there is not even any dialogue. Argument, like resistance, is futile in the face of the absolute, self-evident persuasive authority of the utopian ideal. Utopia is achieved, not by revolutionary struggle, but by consensus—by a painless, automatic process which, for a late nineteenth-century middle-class liberal such as Bellamy was doubtless a profoundly consoling fiction. While Bellamy was frequently accused of being a socialist, it should be noted that he himself vehemently rejected the label, declaring the very word 'socialist' to be

> a foreign word in itself, and equally foreign in all its suggestions. It smells to the average American of petroleum, suggests the red flag and all manner of sexual novelties, and an abusive tone about God and religion, which in this country we at least treat with decent respect. [Quoted in Bowman, p.31][11]

This reluctance to deal with the process whereby utopia comes into being, however, is symptomatic of a broader pattern of evasion. What Bellamy seems to dislike, in fact, is explicitness about process of *any* kind. For example, while the predictive element in utopian fiction is not in itself of any great interest (witness the tedious journalistic debates in 1984 over how far Orwell's fiction had 'come true'), there is nevertheless a certain significance in what the futuristic details which Bellamy *does* get right have in common. Like More, for instance, Bellamy banishes money from his utopia—but instead of making his gold into chamberpots, he replaces it by credit cards. Piped music is the norm, live concerts having been replaced by a sort of musical telephone, on which one calls up a 24 hour concert service—the narrator is woken one morning by a spirited reveille: 'the airs played during the waking hours of morning were always of the inspiring type' (p.76). (In fact, what Bellamy calls the 'telephone' more closely resembles the radio—although it might equally be seen as fulfilling the Baconian dream of conveying 'sounds in trunks and pipes, in strange lines and distances'.) Shops no longer exist, their place having been taken by central warehouses similar to the Argos or Consumers' Distributing networks, the one difference being that, instead of consumers collecting their purchases, they are despatched directly to the consumer's house via a subterranean system of pneumatic tubes!

What all these details have in common is that they serve to mask the actual process involved. Money, itself a mere signifier of value, is replaced by a token of itself, thereby obscuring the commercial transaction involved; the producers of music have been rendered invisible, leaving only the product itself—the actual music; while the pneumatic tube, for all its period charm, effectively serves the same purpose—one never actually sees or touches the goods one buys: they simply arrive, as if by magic, in the home. Moreover, for all the extended discussion of how industrial production is organized, there is never any depiction of work as such: the narrator visits only places of consumption, never of production.[12] Taking all this along with the fact that in the utopian household no-one cooks, meals being either provided in communal restaurants, or sent to the home, it begins to appear that for Bellamy the mechanisms of production are very much like those of reproduction—something to be kept decently veiled at all costs.

This distaste for too much reality is further reflected in the odd extravagance of some of Bellamy's language, and in particular in the often curious similes and analogies with which he seeks to emphasize the contrast between utopian perfection and the squalor of reality. For example, while Bellamy's insistence on the fundamental importance of universal culture and education to the establishment of utopian society is in itself unremarkable—indeed, very much in keeping with the norms of the Renaissance utopia—his justification for it is rather more idiosyncratic. As Dr Leete tells the narrator:

> '... we should not consider life worth living if we had to be surrounded by a population of ignorant, boorish, coarse, wholly uncultivated men and women, as was the plight of the few educated in your day. Is a man satisfied, merely because he is perfumed himself, to mingle with a malodorous crowd? Could he take more than a very limited satisfaction, even in a palatial apartment, if the windows on all four sides opened into stable yards? And yet just that was the situation of those considered most fortunate as to culture and refinement in your day. I know that the poor and ignorant envied the rich and cultured then; but to us the latter, living as they did, surrounded by squalor and brutishness, seem little better off than the former. The cultured man in your age was like one up to the neck in a nauseous bog solacing himself with a smelling bottle.' [p.122]

The principal benefit conferred by universal education and the availability of culture to all, in other words, is that it protects the cultivated from the unpleasant spectacle (not to mention smell) of ignorance. And, to judge by the terms in which the 'poor and ignorant' are described ('boorish', 'coarse', 'malodorous', etc.) , there can be little doubt that it is the plight of the 'rich and cultured' for which Dr Leete feels most sympathy.

Dr Leete and his family, in fact, provide an interesting perspective on the true nature of Bellamy's utopian ideal—a perspective which, in part, emerges from one of the features of *Looking Backward* that renders it distinct from its predecessors. Whereas the Renaissance utopia contents itself with simply *describing* the more perfect society (Bacon is the only author to portray individual utopians, and then only in the most cursory fashion), Bellamy sets out both to describe and dramatize his utopia, to tell a story which will show the utopian society in action. Yet it is precisely here that a new contradiction emerges, a contradiction revealed by the significant gap between what is described and what is dramatized. While the emphasis of Bellamy's description is heavily on *work*, on how it is organized, by whom it is performed, and so forth, his portrayal of how utopian life is *lived* shows only the utopians at leisure. As his sole representatives of utopian society, he chooses a retired couple and their daughter who, while she must surely be of working age (Dr Leete and his wife are both about sixty), never appears to work at all.[13] The resultant picture of utopian society in operation portrays a lifestyle virtually indistinguishable from that of the wealthy middle-class of Bellamy's own day. Dr Leete, with his wine and cigars, his novel-loving wife, and Edith, with her taste for classical music and fine muslin, would, one feels, be equally at home in the drawing-rooms of 1887. The main benefit which utopia has brought them is precisely that freedom from the spectacle of squalor, brutishness, and ignorance to which Dr Leete refers—a freedom which is, in essence, a freedom from guilt. In contrast to the acute discomfort which Julian West experiences when confronted by the disparity between his wealth and the poverty and suffering of the masses, the Leetes lead a placid existence, free from any such qualms. The elimination of poverty and injustice allows them to live the good life of the nineteenth-century bourgeoisie, only with a clear conscience. While Frye is no doubt correct in his assertion that utopias such as Bellamy's were prompted in part by 'the distrust and dismay aroused by extreme laissez-faire versions of capitalism' ('Varieties', p.27), Bellamy's utopian vision remains, in Kumar's words, 'irretrievably bourgeois', depicting a world where 'leisure (and consumption) are still seen in relation, and opposition, to work' (*Utopia*, p.163). What *Looking Backward* offers is in effect a middle-class fantasy of a classless society—one created not by the transformation of society as a whole, but rather through the elimination of the lower orders by their absorption *into* the middle-class, whose values become the values of utopia. In this context, it becomes less surprising that the process of production is nowhere shown; while it may be *described* at great length, what is dramatized is very much the stuff of the traditional utopia: a life of leisure, plenty, innocence, and security—a life in many respects more paradisaical than any encountered in the utopias of the Renaissance.

There remains the question of how the narrator gets to utopia. As we have seen, *Looking Backward* shares the reticence of the Renaissance utopia regarding the origins of utopian society; where it differs is in the nature of the compensatory elaboration which the text exhibits. Where the Renaissance utopia offers a wealth of often suggestive geographical detail in place of the historical specification which it evades, the basic narrative premise of *Looking Backward* renders this particular kind of displacement more difficult. Locating utopia elsewhere in time rather than in space clearly demands a little more by way of narrative explanation than is afforded by More's prepositional phrase or Campanella's few impatient lines. Nevertheless, the account which Bellamy provides goes *so* far beyond what might be seen as necessary to secure the reader's willing suspension of disbelief, particularly when its lavish detail is contrasted to the perfunctory treatment given to utopia's historical origins, that it is hard not to see it, again, as precisely a *metaphor* of transition—a narrative in which the psychological, rather than historical origins of utopia are encoded.

To reach utopia, as we have seen, the narrator falls asleep, awakening in the year 2000 after a slumber of one hundred and thirteen years—during which time the construction of utopia has conveniently been taken care of. Nevertheless, this still leaves the cause of this spectacular case of oversleeping to be accounted for. In his former, non-utopian existence, it transpires that the narrator suffered from insomnia, a problem he sought to palliate by a number of precautions whose abnormality is not entirely concealed by the matter-of-fact tone in which they are related. Unable to sleep in an upstairs room due to the noise of the city, he has a sleeping chamber specially constructed beneath the foundations of his house:

> ... to this subterranean room no murmur from the upper world ever penetrated. When I had entered it and closed the door I was surrounded by the silence of the tomb. In order to prevent the dampness of the subsoil from penetrating the chamber, the walls had been laid in hydraulic cement and were very thick, and the floor was likewise protected. In order that the room might serve also as a vault equally proof against violence and flames, for the storage of valuables, I had roofed it with stone slabs hermetically sealed, and the outer door was of iron with a thick coating of asbestos. A small pipe, communicating with a windmill on the top of the house, insured the renewal of air. [p.10]

Yet what is perhaps most striking about these quite obsessional provisions for a good night's sleep—so reasonable in their every detail, so utterly bizarre when taken as a whole—is that they *don't work*!

> It might seem that the tenant of such a chamber ought to be able to command slumber, but it was rare that I slept well, even there, two nights in succession. So accustomed was I to wakefulness that I minded little the loss of one night's rest. A second night, however, spent in my reading chair instead of my bed, tired me out, and I never allowed myself to go longer than that without slumber ... If after two sleepless nights I found myself on the approach of the third without sensations of drowsiness, I called in Dr. Pillsbury. [p.10]

Dr Pillsbury, it turns out, is a 'Professor of Animal Magnetism'—or in other words, a hypnotist.

To cut a long story short, the narrator goes to visit his fiancée, who, concerned at his having gone two nights without sleep, sends him home at nine o'clock sharp, 'with strict orders to go to bed at once' (p.9). Dr Pillsbury is summoned, and puts him into a hypnotic trance. During the night the house burns down (leaving, however, the cement-encased, hermetically sealed, asbestos-coated sleeping chamber unharmed), and the narrator remains entranced until the year 2000, when his subterranean refuge is finally excavated in preparation for the construction of, of all things, a laboratory.

Considered in its purely functional aspect, as a plot mechanism for the transference of the narrator to the utopian future, it is a scenario which goes so far beyond the minimum demands of narrative plausibility as to prompt a number of questions as to its deeper significance. What are the implications of the narrator's inability to sleep, for example? Or of the bizarre measures he takes to counter his insomnia? While Bellamy's chief concern in *Looking Backward* is surely the exposition of a rational alternative to existing society, it seems curious to find this surrounded by narrative trappings more reminiscent of the world of Edgar Allan Poe. Here, as in Poe, we encounter hermetically sealed subterranean chambers: Julian West's sleeping quarters seem like a lineal descendant of the copper-sheathed vault that lies far beneath the bedroom of the narrator in 'The Fall of the House of Usher'. There is the same fascination with hypnosis, with its capacity to render the individual passive, open to suggestion, deprived of agency. The distinction between dream and reality is deliberately blurred, as in so many of Poe's tales: the utopia to which the narrator awakens seems at first like a dream, but proves a reality; while in a subsequent nightmare he returns to his own past, only to find that its hallucinatory vividness is mercifully an illusion. And there is even the same confusion of the roles of lover and mother. The narrator's fiancée sends him to bed early, like a little boy (and to a bedroom which seems more like a tomb), and her maternal role is promptly taken over in utopia by her great-granddaughter, who turns out to be Edith Leete.

Nor is this the only feature of the narrator's previous existence to reproduce itself in utopia. The hypnotist of 1887, Dr Pillsbury, finds a utopian equivalent in Dr Leete, whose medical treatment of the bewildered narrator consists largely of giving him sleeping draughts, and whose discourse holds him virtually mesmerized for the remainder of the book. While utopia is only a dream in 1887, by the year 2000 it is the past, as we have seen, that is a figment of the imagination. Even the process of the narrator's emergence into utopia (as if the initial metaphor of transition were not enough) is re-enacted, not once, but *twice*. On the first occasion, Julian West, lonely and depressed despite all that utopia has to offer, returns to his subterranean chamber: '"This," I muttered to myself, "is the only home I have. Let me stay here, and not go forth any more"' (p.165). But he is rescued from this fit of self-pity by Edith, who appears at the door, having followed him there. He goes to meet her, and a short conversation discloses their mutual love. It turns out, in fact, that Edith had already known of the narrator, having read his love-letters to her great-grandmother, and become fascinated by him. Discovering his identity from a locket of her great-grandmother which he had worn on his breast during his long sleep, she already feels a maternal solicitude for him before he awakes—or is reborn—into utopia. Now, on his second emergence from the womb-like chamber, it is to find mother and lover innocently united into one, his for the asking. Amid all the rational features of Bellamy's utopia, its carefully thought-out legal, social, and economic provisions, there is the promise of guilt-free oedipal gratification.[14]

Yet even this is not the last occasion on which the transition to utopia is re-enacted. Shortly after, although enchanted by his new-found love, Julian West suffers a recurrence of his sleeping problems, and when he finally does fall asleep, it is only to suffer an extended nightmare of waking back in his old world. So vivid is the nightmare, in fact, that it is only with the utmost difficulty that he succeeds in arousing himself from it:

> Tears poured from my eyes. In my vehemence I became inarticulate. I panted, I sobbed, I groaned, and immediately afterward found myself sitting upright in my bed in my room in Dr. Leete's house, and the morning sun shining through the open window into my eyes. I was gasping. The tears were streaming down my face, and I quivered in every nerve. [p.185]

While Bellamy asserts that the emergence of his more perfect society was smooth, inevitable, untroubled by violence or even opposition, it is clear that the transition to utopia is by no means as free from trauma as he might wish it to appear. In the narrator's anguish and hysteria are surely signs that the birth pangs of the new society have been displaced and given a fictional embodiment elsewhere.

It would appear, then, that Bellamy's attempt to recast the traditional utopian paradigm in the light of more recent narrative practice causes at least as many problems as it resolves. In the gaps that emerge between the traditional *description* of the more perfect society and the more novelistic attempt to dramatize its workings, between what is told and what is shown, the familiar contradictions and disjunctures that characterize the Renaissance utopia become all the more apparent; while the narrative trappings that surround the outline of utopian society—the elements of futuristic fantasy, the gestures towards a fuller characterization of ndividuals—only serve to render more evident the psychological underpinnings of the utopian dream.[15] At the same time, many of the features most typical of the Renaissance utopia persist. The womb-like topography of *Utopia* is reproduced in Bellamy's description of the narrator's sleeping quarters; there is the familiar reluctance to deal with utopia's origins, or indeed with history in any form; and there is a similar rationalization of the essentially paradisaical dream of long life, leisure, freedom from guilt, and total security. Taking this along with the ambivalence of Bellamy's presentation of the role of women, whose ostensibly enhanced freedom seems scarcely compatible with their effective status as commodities in a society no less male-dominated than the author's own, and it begins to appear that the constraints of the traditional narrative paradigm are more difficult to escape than might be imagined. Andrew Delbanco describes *Looking Backward* as 'both progressive in its politics and conservative in its artistic strategy' (p.xi), yet not the least striking feature of Bellamy's utopia is the extent to which it reproduces not simply the narrative form, but much of the authoritarian character of its Renaissance predecessors. Less, rather than more democratic than the society to which it proposes an alternative, its militaristic social organization is accompanied by the traditional emphasis on universal surveillance to ensure that utopian ideals are adhered to: one of the ways in which industrial efficiency is maintained, for instance, is through a system of quality control so stringent that any flaw in a specific product can be traced back to the individual worker responsible for it. Which raises anew the issue of the extent to which a work's narrative form and ideological implications are in fact related. As we have seen, Bammer argues that 'as texts in which an oppositional impulse is embedded in an essentially conservative form, utopias are *generically* ambiguous' (p.45)— and in the case of *Looking Backward* that ambiguity prompts one to question whether 'progressive politics' are in fact reconcilable with a 'conservative artistic strategy', or whether the authoritarian tendency of the Renaissance utopia is not actually inherent in the narrative paradigm in which it is embodied.

Here the considerably more sophisticated narrative practice of H.G. Wells—to whom the 'progressive' label is also often applied—is instructive. Unlike Bellamy, whose other fictional efforts are now largely forgotten,[16] Wells reveals in his non-utopian fiction a mastery of a variety of narrative modes, ranging from realism, through social satire, to speculative fantasy. Well aware, as we have seen, of the problems which writing utopian fiction poses, his attempts to resolve them exhibit a correspondingly greater narrative resourcefulness. Thus, while the same basic narrative paradigm— journey, followed by a relation of the wonders of utopia—still lies at the heart of *A Modern Utopia* (1905), *In the Days of the Comet* (1906), and *Me* *Like Gods* (1923), each represents a different approach to the problem c creating a utopia that is 'not static but kinetic' (*A Modern Utopia*, p.5), an where 'the blood and warmth and reality of life' (p.9) are no longer absen

H.G. Wells and Utopian Narrative

Of the three examples under discussion, *A Modern Utopia* is the mos ambitious—both the most comprehensive in its outline of a more perfec society, and the most radical in its narrative experimentation. Rejectin both 'the form of the argumentative essay' (p.xxxi) and 'the vulgar appetit for stark stories' (p.xxxii), Wells creates instead a complex hybrid, in whic both a fictional narrative and essayistic speculation are contained withi multiple framing narratives in which, as in More's *Utopia*, the voices c author and narrator are carefully distinguished. In the fictional narrativ the narrator (along with his travelling companion, the rather patheti Botanist) is holidaying in the Swiss Alps, when the two are magicall translated to another world—which turns out to be the utopian mirro image of our own; there then follows the familiar guided tour of the mor perfect society. Yet while this, taken by itself, may seem little different fror the traditional paradigm, the fictional narrative is interspersed wit extended passages where the storyline is abandoned altogether in favou of something closer to a speculative treatise on the nature of utopia. Here acknowledging the difficulty of successfully imagining a social orde radically different from the one by which we have ourselves bee conditioned, Wells attempts to present, not the traditional account of a already established utopia, but rather a carefully phrased and rathe tentative exploration of the form it *might* take. Instead of the confiden present tense in which the Renaissance utopia is described, Wells resor to the uncertainties of the subjunctive mood or future tense. There i frequent recourse to formations such as 'Let us suppose', or 'In utopia w should ...', which further reinforce the work's speculative character; whil on occasions Wells deliberately employs frame-breaking devic apparently designed to undermine the fictional illusion altogether:

> The whole world will surely have a common language, that is quit elementarily Utopian, and since we are free of the trammels c convincing story-telling, we may suppose that language to b sufficiently our own to understand. [p.17]

In *Men Like Gods*, the traditional paradigm is more clearly evident, wit the central character, Mr Barnstaple, fulfilling the conventional role of th visitor to utopia. Driving off on his holidays, he is abruptly whisked into parallel, utopian universe—to whose wonders he is then introduced in the customary detail. Here Wells relies on a rather different kind of fictional sleight-of-hand, trusting to his skill as a satirist to distract attention from problems inherent in the depiction of a more perfect society. Mr Barnstaple's fate, it turns out, is shared by a group of other motorists, which includes, among others, recognizable caricatures of Arthur Balfour, Lord Beaverbrook, and Winston Churchill—and it is in contrast to their antics that the virtues of utopian society are allowed to appear. Given the way that the existing ruling class behave, Wells seems to be saying, is not even the almost inhuman calm of utopia preferable? *In the Days of the Comet* takes yet another tack, preparing the way for a relatively brief vision of utopia with a lengthy realistic account of the life of petty oppression and tormenting sexual jealousy experienced by the narrator prior to its advent (here occasioned by a passing comet, which releases a gas that transforms human nature).

Whether any of these solutions is entirely successful, however, remains debatable. *A Modern Utopia*, in particular, has been widely praised for its success in avoiding many of the pitfalls of the traditional utopia,[17] yet while Wells is clearly aware of the problematic character of utopian narrative, the paradigm embedded in each of the works under discussion is by no means the only traditional feature that is reproduced. Just as in *Looking Backward*, for example, the preoccupation with military attributes resurfaces even in a worldwide utopia without enemies. In *Men Like Gods*, such narrative suspense as exists resides in the armed conflict between the utopians and the party of the Churchillian Rupert Catskill, and Wells appears to derive considerable vicarious satisfaction from the spectacle of the latter's helplessness in the face of the utopians' vastly superior technological resources. *In the Days of the Comet*, while its final section sets out to depict the construction of the new utopian world-order, focuses as much on the 'vast exultant dust of house-breaking' (p.200) which accompanies the wholesale destruction of London, Philadelphia, Chicago, and even Edinburgh that precedes it—not to mention the 'Year of Tents', when humanity lives in a vast encampment while demolishing the cities of the past and building those of the future. Yet it is *A Modern Utopia*, for all its attempts to circumvent the prescriptive character of the conventional utopia, that is perhaps most interesting in this regard. While Wells elsewhere describes his utopian ideal as 'a scientifically organized classless society',[18] here there is envisaged a ruling élite called, tellingly, the *samurai*—a name whose warlike connotations seem strangely at odds with the otherwise pacific tenor of the utopian society described in the text. The *samurai* are explicitly compared to Plato's guardians, and are elsewhere referred to as 'a voluntary nobility' (p.259). Becoming a member of this élite involves passing a competitive examination, meditation, physical fitness, and a variety of rather oddly-assorted ascetic practices, which include bathing in cold water, and sleeping alone 'at least four nights in five' (p.297). In return, they receive a number of privileges, including the right to wear a distinctive uniform, sole access to the careers of lawyer, doctor, and public administrator, and the right to vote—a right denied the rest of the population. There are also certain restrictions: members of the *samurai* class may not act on stage, perform menial tasks such as waiting, barbering, and so forth, and are forbidden either to play or watch competitive sports—which Wells appears to regard as little more than ignoble spectacles for the degenerate masses.

The bias of Wells's vision, in other words, is very much akin to that of Bellamy's: once again, we find a utopian society substantially less democratic than that to which it offers an alternative, and (for all its talk of 'a voluntary nobility') representing an ideal that is fundamentally—as Wells himself admitted[19]—that of the educated middle class, albeit a middle class not averse to strong government and firm treatment of undesirables. If poverty and oppression are to be eliminated, it is once again primarily because of the offence they give to society's cultured upper echelons. Even in the extreme case of slavery, we are told that the 'true objection' is 'not that it is unjust to the inferior but that it corrupts the superior' (p.337)! If inequality in society is to be remedied, it will be through a levelling-up process, ultimately brought about not so much by political or economic reform as by selective breeding.

In *Men Like Gods*, as in *Looking Backward*, it would appear that the removal of barriers to the unhindered operation of love is sufficient to achieve the desired end. Socially undesirable qualities, such as indolence, are steadily being bred out of humanity, since their possessors will neither find lovers nor bear children, 'because no one in Utopia loves those who have neither energy nor distinction. There is much pride of the mate in Utopian love' (p.64). In *A Modern Utopia*, however, the mechanisms of selective breeding are far more explicitly set out: in its initial stages, we are told, utopian society will retain a class system—the difference being that it will be biologically based, rather than socially constructed.[20] This will consist of four classes, labelled (with Fourier-like arbitrariness) the poietic, the kinetic, the base, and the dull: a structure which Frye describes as 'like an uncharitable version of the four Indian castes' (1967, p.35).[21] What is clear, however, is that the long-term goal of utopian eugenics is to move towards a classless society by the elimination of the latter two—which will be achieved primarily by the provision that it will be necessary to reach certain pre-set earning levels in order to prove one's fitness to have children. Thus, while in the short term society will have to take into account the flaws and limitations of fallen humanity, in the long run the necessity for most laws, restrictions, and regulations will be eliminated by the evolution of a superior race—the 'cleaned and perfected humanity' of *Men Like Gods*—in comparison with whom even the best representatives of our world (Mr Barnstaple, for example, or the narrator of *A Modern Utopia*) will feel hopelessly inferior.

Where Wells differs from Bellamy, at least at first sight (and still more so from the utopian writers of the Renaissance), is in his representation of the role of women in utopian society. While Bellamy, in direct contradiction of what he asserts to be the norms of his future society, only actually portrays women in stereotypically passive roles, Wells does not hesitate to show women in a markedly non-traditional light. We see women in *A Modern Utopia* as leaders and administrators, as scientists and inventors in *Men Like Gods*; while in *In the Days of the Comet* (where much the most complex and interesting character, Nettie, is female) it is a woman who most clearly articulates the sexual politics of the new utopia. Yet once again, there are some striking contradictions: as in *Looking Backward*, there is a telling gap between what we are told and what we are shown—although in Wells's case it is the former that undermines the latter. In *A Modern Utopia*, for instance, the *effect* of Wells's attempt at a radical reassessment of society's sexual institutions is often to reinscribe, often more overtly, the assumptions that underlie them. As in his utopian revision of the class system, Wells's account of gender relations serves primarily to reinstate existing structures of domination by naturalizing them—giving them a biological, rather than socially constructed foundation. For example, in the context of what purports to be an argument in *favour* of liberating women from social discrimination, we are told that:

> It is a fact that almost every point in which a woman differs from a man is an economic disadvantage to her, her incapacity for great stresses of exertion, her frequent liability to slight illnesses, her weaker initiative, her inferior invention and resourcefulness, her relative incapacity for organization and combination, and the possibility of emotional complications whenever she is in economic dependence on men. [p.187]

Nor does Wells end there: women with children in the modern utopia would be forbidden to work 'unless they are in a position to employ qualified efficient substitutes to take care of their offspring' (p.188)—child care apparently being 'naturally' a woman's task—while as the producers of children, who constitute the future of the species, they are subject to more severe moral restraints. Given that only the fittest are allowed to breed, we are told, logic dictates that 'one unavoidable condition' of the utopian marriage contract 'will be the chastity of the wife' (p.194):

> Her infidelity being demonstrated, must at once terminate the marriage and release both her husband and the State from any liability for the support of her illegitimate offspring. That, at any rate, is beyond controversy ... It will be obvious that under Utopian conditions it is the State that will suffer injury by a wife's misconduct, and that a husband who condones anything of the sort will participate in her offence. A woman, therefore, who is divorced on this account will be divorced as a public offender, and not in the key of a personal quarrel; not as one who has inflicted a private and personal wrong. [p.194]

Even in the non-utopian world, it would be hard to imagine a more explicit statement of the sexual double standard—particularly given the subsequent declaration that 'a reciprocal restraint on the part of the husband is clearly of no importance whatever' (p.195). As in *The City of the Sun*, the project of total social transformation is undermined by a fundamental contradiction—the fact that it is an embodiment of specifically *male* desire. Wells's utopia not only frees men from sexual guilt regarding their own conduct: it also reassures them that women's sexual fidelity is an objective social requirement. Once again, the effect of utopian logic is to unmask the essential identity between its premises and those of the patriarchal order to which it proposes an ostensible alternative.

Such contradictions, like those evident in the utopias of Campanella and Bellamy, are perhaps unsurprising in view of the tension inevitably inherent in the traditional utopian project of recreating maternal security through the imposition of a masculine order. In Wells's case, however, they are symptomatic of a broader ambivalence—an ambivalence strongly reminiscent of that which Kolodny points to as characteristic of the discovery narrative. On the one hand, the utopian longing for maternal security is repeatedly reflected in passages which suggests a strong attraction to the idea of returning to a childlike passive dependence on the mother. In *In the Days of the Comet*, for example, the narrator, despairing over his loss of Nettie and the death of his mother, finds unexpected solace in the arms of Anna, who has nursed his mother through her final illness. 'A miserable attraction' (p.243) draws him back for a last look at his mother, and he finds Anna at the bedside:

> 'Willie,' she whispered, and eyes and body seemed incarnate pity.
> An unseen presence drew us together. My mother's face became resolute, commanding. I turned to Anna as a child may turn to its nurse. I put my hands on her strong shoulders, she folded me to her,

and my heart gave way. I buried my face in her breast and clung to her weakly, and burst into a passion of weeping ...

She held me with hungry arms. She whispered to me, 'There, there!' as one whispers comfort to a child ... [p.244]

As in *Looking Backward*, the line between mother and lover becomes blurred: they marry, and within a year she has borne him a son. Coming as it does in the midst of the turmoil of demolition and construction attending the birth of the new utopian order, the implications of the passage are hard to ignore. It is as though the birth pangs of the new society find a psychological equivalent in the narrator's temporary return to infantile dependency, swiftly followed by the reassertion of male authority: the motherly Anna is 'given [him] in marriage' (p.244) and bears him a son.

A similar instance of temporary regression occurs in *Men Like Gods*, when Mr Barnstaple escapes from the castle where he has been immured with the other Earthlings—effectively choosing utopia in preference to their efforts to assert the old order. At the very moment that he sees the castle blasted out of existence, he collapses unconscious, awakening to find himself back among the utopians:

Then people had stood about him and talked about him. He remembered their feet. He must have been lying on his face with his face very close to the ground. Then they had turned him over, and the light of the rising sun had been blinding in his eyes.

Two gentle goddesses had given him some restorative in a gorge at the foot of high cliffs. He had been carried in a woman's arms as a child is carried. [p.180]

Yet while such passages speak powerfully of a yearning to be restored to the lost mother, to experience a form of rebirth in the arms of a stronger and more capable woman, Wells elsewhere seems to react strongly against this impulse. Underlying the passion for order which characterizes all Wells's utopian writings there is often evident a distaste for weakness which goes so far as to include a suspicion of any form of emotion which might soften the 'hard, clean' lines of the utopian vision. In *Men Like Gods*, for instance, it is suggested that while the Utopians still experience love, it is no longer the same emotion as that experienced in our imperfect world:

And they loved no doubt—subtly and deliciously—but perhaps a little hardly. Perhaps in those distant plains there was not much pity nor tenderness. Bright and lovely beings they were—in no way pitiful. There would be no need for those qualities ... [p.127]

The stereotypically 'feminine' qualities of pity and tenderness are disavowed, and due to their absence the terrestrial visitor finds himself sadly neglected, since there is little about him to interest the superior beings who surround him. Yet when one Utopian, Lychnis, does take an interest in him after his spell of childlike dependence, Mr Barnstaple shies away from her sympathy. He begins to see her as 'a lingering romantic type', as 'one of Utopia's failures' (p.204), whose 'dark sacrificial disposition' is surely evidence of 'some underlying racial taint ... something that Utopia was still breeding out' (p.205). She represents the persistence of all that Utopia is seeking to outgrow: even after a short stay, Mr Barnstaple comes to the conclusion that 'he was a better Utopian than she was' (p.205). All that is most motherly about her now seems to him distasteful, and as if to underscore the threat she represents to his aspirations to grow into someone worthy of utopia, Wells even provides the quite gratuitous detail that she was responsible for the deaths of her own two sons:

> She had had two children whom she had loved passionately. They were adorably fearless, and out of foolish pride she had urged them to swim out to sea and they had been taken by a current and drowned. Their father had been drowned in attempting their rescue and Lychnis had very nearly shared their fate. [p.204]

The mother, whose allure is so powerfully portrayed elsewhere, is ultimately a danger to be resisted. In a particularly telling formulation, given the extent to which utopias may be seen as opening up space for the play of desire, she is described as filling 'more than her legitimate space in the Utopian spectacle. She lay across it like a shadow' (p.205).

In *In the Days of the Comet* the desire for the reassertion of male authority in the face of what is represented as female entrapment is still more apparent. Following the magical transformation of human nature by the vapours unleashed by a comet, the narrator's personal transition from the old, imperfect world into the new, utopian one is significantly accompanied by the symbolic displacement of Nettie, the female who embodies all the disorder in his life (and whose name, one feels, is hardly coincidental), by Melmount (Male-mount?), the male epitome of order and control. His last memory before the comet descends is of pursuing Nettie, revolver in hand, through the thickening mist; when he awakens from the sleep into which the entire world has been plunged, the symbolically phallic pistol discarded,[22] the first person he encounters is the famous politician—whose appearance, he declares, he will remember to his dying day:

> I believe, for instance, I could match the fur upon the collar of his great motoring coat now, could paint the dull red tinge of his big cheek with his fair eyelashes just catching the light and showing beyond. His hat was off, his dome-shaped head, with its smooth hair

between red and extreme fairness, was bent forward in scrutiny of his twisted foot. His back seemed enormous. And there was something about the mere massive sight of him that filled me with liking. [p.161]

Yet there is more involved than simple liking: indeed, one of the very first new, utopian perceptions of which the narrator becomes aware is the fact that:

> ... without servility or any insincerity whatever, as if it were a first fruit of the Change, I found myself in the presence of a human being towards whom I perceived myself inferior and subordinate, before whom I stood without servility or any insincerity whatever, in an attitude of respect and attention. [p.165]

While the longing for maternal security is always represented in an ambiguous light, as a desire to which surrender can never be more than temporary, no such reservations attend the acknowledgement of the authority of this archetypal father-figure—which is further emphasized by the quasi-biblical language in which it is articulated.[23]

In *A Modern Utopia*, leaving aside the peculiarities of the Utopian marriage contract, the reaction against the feminine manifests itself rather differently, in a broader distaste for sexuality in general. The appeal of the *samurai*'s sexual abstinence is emphasized by the description of the narrator's Utopian *alter ego*—the person he would have been in Utopia: a *samurai*, unsurprisingly, his self-discipline is reflected in his appearance—as taller, more youthful, 'sounder looking' (p.247). Of course, his physical and mental superiority are not merely the product of his spending four out of five nights sleeping alone, but one feels that this is not the least of the facets of his life which the narrator envies—especially given his earlier eulogy of the cleanliness of the Utopian bedroom, which contrasts starkly with 'the foetid disorder of many an earthly bedroom after a night's use' (p.105). Physical, or indeed emotional involvement, insofar as it is portrayed at all, is seen as messy, self-indulgent: the bright, clean, unsentimental love of *Men Like Gods* is clearly foreshadowed. Indeed, part of the appeal of Utopia for the narrator is that it will clearly have no place for people like his travelling-companion, the Botanist, for whose love-affair he shows undisguised contempt. So far as the Botanist serves a narrative purpose, it is largely to illustrate most of the flaws which a utopian society will eliminate—emotional indulgence clearly being one of them.

Yet it is not merely the inadequacies of the Botanist's love life that are significant: why, one wonders, of all possible professions, does Wells make the narrator's travelling companion a botanist? A botanist is, in effect, a classifier of nature—and as such represents the virtual antithesis of the

Wellsian attitude towards it, which involves not so much accepting and describing nature as it exists, but rather taking control of and transforming it. And it is this aggressive imposition of order on the natural world that is one of the most distinctive features of Wells's utopian vision. Where the Renaissance utopias describe societies sufficiently rationally organized as to offer their citizens a large measure of protection from natural disasters such as famine and disease, Wells proposes a far more radical policy of intervention.[24] In part, of course, this is simply a reflection of the very different historical context in which he was writing—of the fact that his was a world where the transformation of the natural environment by human technology was now an established fact. Nevertheless, it may be argued that, even by early twentieth century standards, Wells's vision of just how far human dominion over nature might be carried is an extravagant one.[25]

In *Men Like Gods*, for example—the most extreme of Wells's utopian projections—it appears that nature has been almost wholly domesticated. Human health and hygiene have been improved by the elimination of virtually all disease-carrying insects, all rats and mice, and even 'the untidier sorts of small bird' (p.122). To be fair, most of the human pollution of the environment has been eliminated as well (a process vividly described in *In the Days of the Comet*), but this appears to be more a matter of human convenience than of environmental concern. In essence, Wells's utopian vision is of a natural environment entirely controlled by and at the service of humanity. Insects are largely eliminated, as are such 'big annoyances' (p.73) as the wolf and hyena. Trees and plants have been hybridized: 'trained and bred to make new and unprecedented secretions, waxes, gums, essential oils and the like, of the most desirable quality' (p.73). Indeed, one of the first and most striking indications of the extent to which the utopian society depicted in *Men Like Gods* differs is the appearance of a tame leopard (which subsequently dies of an infection it catches from Wells's fictional portrait of Winston Churchill), and it later becomes clear that this is merely one product of a much larger-scale 'befriending and taming of big animals' (p.73):

> ... the larger carnivora, combed and cleaned, reduced to a milk dietary, emasculated in spirit and altogether becatted, were pets and ornaments in Utopia. The almost extinct elephant had increased again and Utopia had saved her giraffes. The brown bear had always been disposed to sweets and vegetarianism and had greatly improved in intelligence. The dog had given up barking and was comparatively rare. [pp.73–4]

With its beautifully manicured landscapes, in which human and beast peacefully co-exist, the utopia described in *Men Like Gods* possesses a decidedly Edenic character. Yet it is, once again, very much an Eden recreated on rational principles, with man firmly in control, manipulating nature to suit his own convenience. And while Mr Barnstaple consciously alludes to that first garden, remarking that 'it was a good invention to say that man was created a gardener' (p.74), he also describes the utopian reduction of wild animals to the status of harmless pets as a process of 'revision and editing' (p.74)—an intriguing metaphor, with its implicit comparison of nature to a provisional and still fluid draft which only utopia can transform into the static finality of the completed text. Nature, whose power over humanity the Renaissance utopia sought primarily to mitigate, is here transformed into the ultimate colony, entirely subject to human command.

The desire to impose order on nature, however, constitutes only one aspect of a larger dream of order: Wells's utopias, like their predecessors, are in essence patterns for *human* existence—for the best, but also the most efficient mechanisms of social control. And in this respect, Wells's utopias are if possible still more regimented than Bellamy's future Boston. While the measures outlined in *Looking Backward* to ensure individual adherence to the utopian ideal are far-reaching enough, Wells goes still further. Even in *Men Like Gods*, where formal government as such scarcely seems to exist, there is 'complete knowledge of the whereabouts of every soul upon the planet' (p.193): everyone, we are told (in another literary metaphor) is 'indexed and noted' (p.193). In *A Modern Utopia* the efficient functioning of utopian society relies heavily on the central card index which records the identity and whereabouts of every citizen of the world state—rather as if its members were so many books in an enormous library. In this index are recorded the name, location, and thumbprint of each individual, while, in tribute to the distinctive qualities of the French intellect, the privilege of housing it is given to Paris. Yet while this may seem a bureaucratic nightmare—the kind of thing routinely parodied in any number of dystopian fictions, from Zamyatin's *We* on—the detail of the thumbprint is revealing, given its implications concerning Wells's conception, not just of utopia, but of human nature.

Utopia, for Wells, embodies an ideal, rational order—planned, centralized, and secure from disruptive forces—and to maintain it, his utopian state seeks to control its citizens by the very fact of their individuality, the distinguishing characteristics that separate them from the rest of their fellows. To an even greater extent than in Bellamy's utopia, there is a notable absence of structures which might mediate between the individual and the monolithic State: no unions or corporations, no parties, guilds, societies, or autonomous institutions of any kind. There is only the individual and the State, and it is hardly coincidental that Wells should choose, as the distinctive hallmark of individuality, a feature—the thumbprint—at the very time that fingerprinting was becoming established as a definitive method of determining the unique identity of the criminal. As in so many earlier utopias, the underlying implication is that humanity remains tainted by Original Sin—and while this is explicitly denied in *A Modern Utopia* (p.299), the fact remains that Wells's vision is of a utopia that will curb and limit individual impulses, rather than allow individuals freedom to fulfill their desires. The overwhelming emphasis is on discipline, rather than freedom.

A still more striking parallel between Wells's utopias and their Renaissance predecessors, however, is that (as in *Looking Backward*) there is almost no discussion of *how* the utopian society was created—an omission perhaps understandable in the Renaissance, but considerably less so in an era where there had been so many examples of radical social and political change. In *A Modern Utopia*, for instance, while its initial premise is that the society described is a utopian mirror-image of the narrator's own— that 'every man, woman, and child alive has a Utopian parallel' (p.24)[26]—this assertion is subsequently modified to the point of outright contradiction by the narrator's admission that such a utopia could only have emerged from a wholly different utopian history. He then goes on to posit a world with a radically different history, in which a utopian tendency had always been apparent: a world in which

> Jesus Christ had been born into a liberal and progressive Roman Empire that spread from the Arctic Ocean to the Bight of Benin, and was to know no Decline and Fall, and Mahomet, instead of embodying the dense prejudices of Arab ignorance, opened his eyes upon an intellectual horizon already nearly as wide as the world. [p.260]

For utopia to exist, in other words, it must *already* have existed: even while Wells attempts to imagine a society capable of change, he severs its link with the world which utopia proposes to alter for the better—his own. In *Men Like Gods*, there is some talk of the utopian society having its roots in an 'Age of Confusion' clearly akin to the world of Wells's own day, but once again (although an entire chapter is ostensibly devoted to it) there is a singular absence of detailed information regarding *how* utopia emerged from such chaotic origins. We learn that 'very slowly Utopia had evolved its present harmony of law and custom and education' (p.190), and that 'as light grew and intelligence spread they [lawyers and politicians] became more and more evidently unnecessary' (p.202)—but the actual *process* involved is never discussed in any concrete detail. Much as in Bellamy's utopia, history is a largely automatic affair, in which the truths of utopia become so self-evident that resistance to them is unthinkable: the old order simply withers away. Even in *In the Days of the Comet*, where the construction of utopia *is* portrayed, it is only made possible by the fantastic premise of a fundamental change in the nature of the human material of which utopia is comprised: after the descent of the comet, and the release of the 'green vapours', everyone suddenly sees reason, and nothing is ever the same again.

Such fantastic narrative devices, like the mirror-image world of *A Modern Utopia*, or the parallel universe posited in *Men Like Gods* (not to mention the century-long sleep of Julian West in *Looking Backward*), are of course a reflection of the changed context in which Wells was writing—one in which the traditional remote utopian locale, somewhere in the southern hemisphere, was no longer available. Yet even so, the fantastic methods whereby Wells effects the visitor's transition to utopia have some curiously traditional features. As has already been remarked, both *A Modern Utopia* and *Men Like Gods* begin with the visitor going on holiday—an activity which in a sense constitutes the modern version of the process of exploration described in the travel narratives on which the Renaissance utopia was modelled. Where in More's time the traveller might well *be* an explorer, by Wells's day exploration has given way to vacation—and in this respect the narrator of *A Modern Utopia* and Mr Barnstaple in *Men Like Gods* (even his name is that of a popular holiday destination in south-west England) may be seen as travellers just as representative of their age as were Hythloday and the Genoese mariner in the days of More or Campanella. (Even in *In the Days of the Comet*, the actual transition to utopia takes place while the narrator is at a seaside resort.)

Nor do the echoes of the Renaissance discovery narrative and its utopian analogue end there. In *Men Like Gods*, Mr Barnstaple sets out on holiday, fleeing, not from the depredations of the Tartars, but rather from the tyranny of his wife and his employer—and finds himself, despite his original intention of driving north to the Lake District, forced by roadworks to turn (in the best utopian tradition) south and west. *A Modern Utopia* likewise begins with a descent: seated at their picnic lunch high on the Piz Lucendro, gazing south at the landscape far below, the narrator and his companion are suddenly transported to their own world's mirror-image, and then make their way down into the utopian counterpart of Switzerland. (Given Wells's passion for order and cleanliness, his choice of Switzerland as starting-point for a tour of utopia is hardly surprising.) There are even hazards associated with the process of transition: Arden and Greenlake, the pastorally named pioneers of contact between parallel universes in *Men Like Gods*, are both killed during their experiments, and there are numerous fatalities during the universal sleep that precedes the world's utopian awakening in *In the Days of the Comet*. In most respects, however, just as holidays are in general safer than voyages of exploration, the utopias of both Bellamy and Wells seem significantly tamer than those of their Renaissance predecessors. Indeed, judging by some of their salient features, it would appear that, if the traveller's tale offered a narrative model for the Renaissance utopia, a more appropriate intertext to the utopias of Bellamy and Wells might be provided by the modern holiday brochure.

Like the modern tourist, the utopian visitor of Bellamy and Wells is offered a guided tour of an unfamiliar world and, also like the modern tourist, generally adopts a passive, spectatorial role. Where the visitor is better off, however, is in that, unlike the average tourist, he has no complaints about the food or hygiene. Everything in utopia is clean, of good quality, and easily accessible by modern methods of transportation. Waiters are polite, the inhabitants are fit and sun-tanned, and everyone speaks perfect English. (In *Men Like Gods* this effect is produced by telepathic activation of the brain's speech centres: when a utopian concept proves too advanced, the visitor suffers the temporary illusion that he has gone deaf.) Wells, in particular, makes much of the physical superiority of the Utopians to their terrestrial counterparts: in *A Modern Utopia* the more perfect society has succeeded in eliminating baldness; while in *Men Like Gods*, Mr Barnstaple discovers on his return home that he has grown nearly three inches during his utopian vacation. The image of perfect physical specimens disporting themselves in idealized surroundings, of course, is now a familiar one. As in life, so in the realm of the imagination: just as in the real world exploration paved the way for colonization, so the territory opened up by utopian imaginings has been seized upon with glee by the modern advertising industry. Part of the tourist brochure's seductive allure lies in its implication that a utopian existence (if only for two weeks) is not only desirable, but *possible*. Utopian images, in other words, can be used not only to arouse the desire for things to be otherwise, but also to contain it: as Bloch suggests, the commercialization of such images still allows for dreams, 'yet it still rations them, even in more distant excursions to the over-blue coast of the travel agent's and beyond: so that they do not explode the given world' (1986, p.34). What Bammer refers to as 'commodified dreams' become 'tools with which to keep deeper and politically more destabilizing dissatisfactions in check' (p.44). The utopian dream, however radical its underlying impulse, is always in danger of being co-opted.[27]

Yet even when not in so debased a form—in the form, that is, of utopian fiction—it is clear that the utopian dream often ends up reinscribing many of the values of the society that it seeks to challenge. As we have seen, even given the most genuine desire for radical social change, for progressive values, for 'kinetic' rather than static social formations, utopian fiction all too often presents an alternative order that remains static, authoritarian, and characterized by many of the most oppressive features of the writer's own society. The precise extent to which this is determined by the narrative form in which the utopian vision is expressed is, of course, difficult to determine; nevertheless, it would seem clear that there are certain features inherent in the traditional narrative paradigm that are particularly conducive to the expression of that vision in authoritarian terms.

To begin with, while the utopian narrative paradigm derives in part from the model of the classical dialogue, that model is, as Bakhtin observes, often profoundly un-dialogic. With the exception of More's *Utopia*, where there *is* genuine debate and interaction between differing viewpoints, the tenor of most utopian dialogue is essentially monologic. The relation of the Knight Hospitaller to the Genoese mariner, of Julian West to Dr Leete, of Mr Barnstaple to a variety of utopian mentors, and even of the narrator in *A Modern Utopia* to his utopian *alter ego* is essentially similar: each involves the passive reception by the one of the authoritative utterance of the other. Even the questions that are asked, even such reservations as are expressed function primarily as rhetorical devices, designed to elicit a further flow of authoritative discourse. And in the eager passivity of the listener ('Tell me more, I beg you,' pleads Campanella's Knight, 'tell me more' (p.29)) we may see figured the ideal reader of the utopian text—one whose function is, above all, to be persuaded.

The unequal relationship between speaker and listener is further reinforced by the inherent dynamics of the traveller's tale. Having seen utopia, Hythloday and the mariners of Campanella and Bacon know it works; having lived there, Dr Leete and Wells's various utopians are even more certain: in the face of their superior knowledge, their practical experience, the assertion of contrary points of view can hardly have much authority. (Even where criticism of utopia *is* allowed to appear—as voiced, for example, by the Botanist and the 'apostle of Nature' in *A Modern Utopia*, its inadequacy is made glaringly self-evident.) As Bellamy puts it, utopia can no more be opposed 'by force than by argument' (p.29). Resistance is futile, as is clear from the fate of Rupert Catskill and his companions in *Men Like Gods*. When asserted with such unshakeable authority, it is perhaps unsurprising that even the most 'progressive' views are liable to seem fixed, static, and authoritarian in tendency.

Equally, it may be argued that the retrogressive elements in the utopian vision are also related to the narrative implications inherent in the discovery narratives on which the traditional utopia is modelled. In its Renaissance formulation, as has been demonstrated, it is by its very nature ambiguous, given that the whole process of exploration and discovery was by no means unequivocally oriented to a search for what was new. Informing the early voyages of discovery was the dream of re-establishing contact with the ancient civilizations of the East, even of attaining the mythical realms of Eden and El Dorado; discovery, it might be argued, was the incidental by-product of a far more ambiguous aspiration. Little wonder, then, that utopian narratives modelled on accounts of voyages of discovery should lend themselves so easily to expression of regressive fantasies of returning to the primal security of the womb, or to the protected world of early childhood.

Moreover, if the motives for the process of exploration charted in the discovery narratives of the Renaissance were ambiguous, so too were its effects. While the voyages of discovery revealed a 'New' world, they were soon followed by a process of colonization geared primarily to the re-establishment and consolidation of the values of the Old. The radically different cultures of the Americas were suppressed or erased; the hierarchies of the Old World were imposed; the resources of the New World were used to shore up the economies of Western Europe; while at the same time the New World functioned as a valuable safety valve, a refuge not only for surplus population, but also for dissidents and malcontents who might otherwise cause trouble at home.[28] What the narrative of discovery enacts, therefore, is paradoxically a process whereby the new is disclosed, yet at the same time re-covered, its space filled and its novelty neutralized as a familiar order is imposed upon it.

This process, as we have seen, is parallelled in the utopias of More and Campanella, both of which articulate fantasies of the conquest and subjection of the indigene. Yet it is also re-echoed in modern rewritings of the conventional utopian paradigm. While the geographically separate locale of the Renaissance utopia may have been replaced by the future, or by a parallel universe, what is still conceived of is essentially *space to be filled*. For such space to be available, however, it must first be *empty*—or, if there are local inhabitants, they must be easily enough moulded (like the subjects of King Utopus, or Peter Martyr's naked savages) to conform to a higher purpose. Thus, when Wells suggests that 'no less than a planet will serve the purpose of a modern Utopia' (*A Modern Utopia*, p.11), it is partly on the grounds that the isolation of the Renaissance utopia is no longer possible under modern conditions, yet at the same time his rationale exhibits a colonialist distrust of the Other—of 'the epidemic, the breeding barbarian' (p.11) lurking beyond the boundaries of anything other than a world state. What is at work here (and implicitly in *Looking Backward*, where nation states still exist, but have all followed the pioneering example of America) is a similar belief in the necessity of colonizing all available space: despite its global extent, there is little room for difference in the modern

topia: while there may be room for a few individual eccentrics, there is
one for other value systems or forms of social organization. To be different,
iven the evident superiority of utopia, is to be inferior, and inferiority is
omething which utopia ultimately seeks to eliminate—generally by means
f selective breeding. (Although Wells asserts, rather alarmingly, in the
nidst of what is generally an argument for racial tolerance, that 'there is
nly one sane and logical thing to be done with a really inferior race, and
nat is to exterminate it' (*A Modern Utopia*, p.337).) Nor is this the only
arallel: another recurrent feature of modern reworkings of the traditional
topian paradigm is the representation of the erasure of what was once
nere. Bellamy's Boston of the future retains the familiar geographical
eatures, but scarcely a vestige of the human structures that once
ccompanied them (the former inhabitants are, with the exception of the
narrator, all dead). In William Morris's utopian rebuttal of Bellamy, *News
om Nowhere*, one of the chief activities of his future society is the
emolition of the ugly evidences of the old order; while in Wells's *In the
ays of the Comet*, as we have seen, the transition to utopia is accompanied
y a 'vast exultant dust of house-breaking' (p.200) as the world's cities are
ummarily levelled prior to the work of utopian reconstruction. The fate
f Edinburgh, Philadelphia, Chicago, as imagined by Wells, is not dissimilar
o that of the great City of Mexico at the hands of the conquistadores.[29]

Given the nature of its narrative models, then, it is not difficult to see
hy the utopian impulse towards radical change so often becomes
edirected, turned back on itself. So long as the paradigm persists, it is
nsurprising that even the most ambitious attempts to resolve the problems
poses by purely *narrative* means should never entirely succeed. In *A
Modern Utopia*, for example, it is striking how often the speculative,
entative tone of voice which Wells strives to preserve slides into the
rescriptive, authoritative utterance with which utopian narrative is so
nuch more at home. The open-ended verbal formations already
nentioned ('Let us suppose', 'in Utopia we should ...') repeatedly give way
o far more authoritative assertions: 'there must be a competition in life of
ome sort to determine who are to be pushed to the edge, and who are to
revail and multiply' (p.137); or 'that, at any rate, is beyond controversy'
.194)—this last occurring, as we have seen, in the context of Wells's
ighly controversial discussion of women and marriage. When this is
ombined with the utopian tendency to determine things down to even
ne most apparently gratuitous detail, it is little wonder that the outlines
f the utopian society which emerge *despite* Wells's attempts at narrative
xperimentation seem so familiar, so reminiscent of the utopian visions of
n earlier era.

Finally, it is clear that the gender dynamics of Bellamy's and Wells's utopian fictions differ surprisingly little from those of their Renaissance predecessors. In part, as Bammer suggests, this reflects the continued utopian privileging of the public sphere over the private—over 'the sphere of everyday life in which politics for women have most often been grounded' (p.13)—and the unspoken assumption that, however sweeping the social changes proposed, the structures of private life will remain comfortingly unaffected. Nevertheless, given not just the frequency, but the extent to which utopian narratives reassert patriarchal norms (even as in the case of Bellamy and Wells, in the context of ostensible proposals for the enhancement of women's rights) it is worth asking whether the traditional utopian paradigm, following the narrative of discovery, does not itself inscribe the power dynamics of gender relations in the society of the time. The very processes of exploration, taking possession of territory repeatedly gendered as female, penetrating into its darkest unknown recesses, renaming it, guarding it against intruders, seem particularly susceptible to description in terms of metaphors of sexual possession. When this is set alongside the psychological implications of that paradigm, with its underlying fantasy of reconstituting maternal security through the institution of a masculine order, it is scarcely surprising to find the subordination of female to male so incessantly re-enacted in utopian fiction—not merely in the structures of the utopian society described, but even in the apparently gratuitous narrative flourishes that so often surround the description. To return, one last time, to Wells's *Men Like Gods*, when Mr Barnstaple finally returns to Earth, inspired by the wonders of utopia, it is with the determination to live his life differently, to live it in such a way as to work towards the realization of utopia upon Earth. He has all kinds of schemes in mind when he finally reaches home, but the only real difference we are *shown* (other than his gain in height and impressive sun-tan) is his new-found ability to assert effortless authority over his hitherto bossy wife.

4. Dystopia: The Dream as Nightmare

Today, examining the utopias of Bellamy and Wells with all the benefits conferred by hindsight, their regimentation appears more than a little alarming. While the subjection of individual conduct to incessant public scrutiny, the subordination of private freedoms to the interests of public welfare, are equally characteristic of the Renaissance utopia, the eagerness of Bellamy and Wells to use the resources of modern technology in the service of an imposed, centralized social order now seems decidedly suspect. To be fair, neither writer had any real experience of what a modern, centralized, totalitarian state could be like—but such innocence of the consequences of seeking to impose order on humanity in its own best interests soon becomes impossible. Where the utopian dream of order appears later in the twentieth century (with the exception of such maverick productions as B.F. Skinner's *Walden Two*), it is most strikingly in the form of parodic inversion—in the nightmare visions of Zamyatin, Huxley, Orwell, and more recently, Atwood.

Challenges to the utopian ideal, of course—whether in the form of direct rebuttal or of parody—are hardly an exclusively modern phenomenon. Examples of the former range from Aristotle's strictures on Plato, through . Lesley's attack on James Harrington, 'A Slap on the Snout of the Republican Swine that rooteth up monarchy,'[1] to the numerous abusive reviews of *Walden Two*; while in the latter category one might include Jonathan Swift's grotesque send-up of the Baconian scientific ideal in Book II of *Gulliver's Travels*, as well as his far more disturbing portrait of the 'perfect' society of the cold, rational, genocidal Houhyhnhnms in Book IV. Bellamy's *Looking Backward* inspired a veritable rash of parodic responses,[2] primarily designed to show what his utopian ideal would lead to in practice—perhaps the most noteworthy being A.D. Vinton's *Looking Further Backward*, which portrays a future United States in which individual initiative has been so far sapped by the abandonment of the capitalist competitive ethic that it easily falls prey to a Chinese invasion.

Yet it is only in the twentieth century that dystopian fiction, combining parodic inversion of the traditional utopia with satire on contemporary society, begins to take on the kind of mythic resonance that underlies the appeal of the traditional utopia from the time of More on. Indeed, many of the very factors that undermine the appeal of the utopian dream of order in the modern era also serve to heighten the relevance of the dystopian parodic inversion. Where utopian fictions gave expression to humanity's growing sense of mastery over both social conditions and the natural world, the works of writers such as Zamyatin, Huxley, and Orwell speak to an audience increasingly disillusioned by the consequences of such controlling aspirations. Where Bellamy's belief in the virtues of an industrial army and Wells's vision of a world where nature is groomed and manipulated to suit human convenience now seem disturbingly naïve, the totalitarian nightmares of Zamyatin and Orwell, or Huxley's portrait of a society dominated by mindless consumerism, seem hardly less apposite now than when they were written.

There are several reasons for this. The first and most obvious—as has already been suggested—is the modern experience of totalitarian governments whose conduct has called into question the traditional utopian premise that strong, centralized authority would act in the best interests of the citizen. Implicit in Vinton's parody of Bellamy, however, is a second concern—that, even were the institution of a benevolent utopian state possible, the consequent resolution of social problems would deprive its citizens of the challenges necessary to sustain progress, and that they would consequently lapse into a state of decadence that would render them easy prey to more vigorous, if less perfect societies. Vinton, in fact, was tapping into an anxiety, current in both America and Britain during the later nineteenth century, that progress had already rendered such decadence a real danger—an anxiety reflected in a whole series of invasion narratives.[3] Perhaps the most memorable of these is Wells's science fictional reworking of the theme in *The War of the Worlds*, yet it is in his earlier *The Time Machine* that he points most clearly to what he fears might be the inherent weakness of a future utopia. Arriving in the distant future, Wells's Time Traveller finds a beautiful, apparently peaceful, pastoral world—yet one whose inhabitants have degenerated into either effete lethargy or mindless cannibalism, and he reflects on the bitter irony that, having achieved its goal of 'comfort and ease, a balanced society with security and permanence as its watchword' (p.97)—a 'perfect world' with 'no unemployed problem, no social question left unresolved' (p.97)—humanity had removed all incentive for further development:

> 'It is the law of nature we overlook, that intellectual versatility is the compensation for change, danger, and trouble ... Nature never appeals to intelligence until habit and instinct are useless. There is no intelligence where there is no change and no need of change. Only those animals partake of intelligence that have to meet a huge variety of needs and dangers.' [p.97]

Implicit in such evolutionary pessimism, however, is not simply the mournful conclusion that resolving our current problems would merely create others, probably much worse, but also what is surely at the root of the dystopian distrust of utopia: the fear that we are simply creatures of our society—that what we take to be our essential identity is in fact socially constructed, and hence susceptible to radical change under different social circumstances. While utopias, as Levitas argues, 'are seen by their opponents as totalitarian because they visibly shape needs and match them with available satisfactions, thus moulding the individual to the system' (*Concept of Utopia*, pp.184–5), they also imply, perhaps more alarmingly, that we are *already* products of our social environment, and that it is only the unpredictable outcome of competing conditioning influences that creates the illusion of individual freedom and essential identity. Not the least of the reasons for the continuing appeal of dystopian fiction is that it addresses this fear, but at the same time mobilizes against it the reassuring notion that there is, after all, some essential and invariant 'human nature' that is in the last analysis immune to such conditioning influences.

In addition, unlike the traditional utopia, dystopian fiction posits a society which—however outlandish—is clearly extrapolated from that which exists. Where utopian fiction stresses the *difference* of the society it depicts, often obscures the connection between the real world and its alternative, and rarely indicates *how* such an alternative might be created, the dystopian writer presents the nightmare future as a possible destination of present society, as if dystopia were no more than a logical conclusion derived from the premises of the existing order, and implies that it might very well come about unless something is done to stop it. Thus Zamyatin, in *We*, while depicting a society of the far future, clearly takes as his starting point Lenin's Socialist Order, and the contemporary artistic fascination with the aesthetic of the machine, to project a world where that order is now absolute, and where the *only* beauty is mechanical. Not the least impressive of Zamyatin's achievements, in fact, is his ability to convey not only the horror and cruelty of his future society, but also something of the terrible appeal of the dream of order which underlies it—the appeal of sensing oneself part of something far greater than the mere sum of its parts. Although *We* charts the process whereby an individual comes to rebel against the authority of the One State, we are given a powerful sense of the difficulty he experiences in breaking away from beliefs and assumptions he has held all his life. Until the seeds of doubt are sown in his mind, D-503 is not merely a good citizen, giving unquestioned allegiance to authority; he is also the designer of the spaceship *Integral*, with which the One State proposes to conquer the universe—a man genuinely committed to the ideas and values of his society. Part of the power of Zamyatin's narrative lies in the vividness with which he dramatizes not just the struggle between the individual and the State, but also the internal struggle which precedes it.

Huxley, by contrast, takes the consumer society of modern capitalism as the starting point for his satiric extrapolation. While the names of some of the characters in *Brave New World*—Lenina Crowne, Benito Hoover, Morgana Rothschild, Helmholz Watson, and so forth—suggest a plague-on-all-your-houses approach, with capitalism, communism, fascism, modern science, all featuring as ancestors of the society of the future, it is Henry Ford who is its presiding deity. Huxley not only takes the production line that Ford pioneered several steps further, applying its principles to the creation of human beings as well as motor vehicles, he also works out the implications of Ford's wage policies, in part designed to assist in creating a market for his own products, and comes up with a vision of a consumer society based on an ethos of endless self-sustaining economic growth which bears a disquieting resemblance to the western society of today. Indeed, there are striking parallels between Huxley's depiction of a world where citizens acquiesce in their own conditioning, where ostensible sexual liberation is instrumental in sustaining oppression, and where solitude is almost impossible, and Marcuse's analysis of postwar American society as one where people are conditioned by a process of 'repressive desublimation' to acquiesce in their own enslavement, and where 'solitude, the very condition which sustained the individual against and beyond his society, has become technically impossible' (*One-Dimensional Man*, p.71).

Orwell's *Nineteen Eighty-Four* returns to communism, this time of the Stalin era, for its inspiration. Although the ambience of Orwell's future society, with its rationing, appalling food, and general seediness is very much that of post-war Britain, there can be little doubt as to who is the model for the mustachioed Big Brother, whose face gazes down from innumerable posters. While certain features of Airstrip One, as Britain has been renamed (such as the use of children to spy on their parents) appear to have been derived from the example of Nazi Germany, the bulk of the parallels—between Goldstein and Trotsky, for example—are clearly with the Soviet Union. Certainly, there is no doubt as to what *Pravda* saw as the main target of Orwell's satire. There, Orwell is described as:

> ... slobbering with poisonous spittle ... he imputes every evil to the people ... It is clear that Orwell's filthy book is in the spirit of such a vital organ of American propaganda as the *Reader's Digest* which published the work. [Quoted in Chilton and Aubrey, p.11]

In the United States, the message appears to have been equally clear. Isaac Deutscher describes being recommended the book by a New York newsvendor with the words: 'Have you read this book? You must read it, sir. Then you will know why we must drop the atom bomb on the Bolshies' (p.265)!

Dystopian fiction, then, for all that it is set in futures of varying degrees of remoteness, reasserts the *connection* between the actual and the imagined which the traditional utopia so often obscures. In its parodic inversion, the essential identity between many features of utopia and those of the world to which it proposes an alternative re-emerges. Where utopian satire on the existing order (such as Bellamy's parable of the coach) stresses the disparity between the real world and its utopian alternative, that difference constituting the measure of the former's deficiencies, dystopian fiction highlights the resemblances between our own world and the projected society of the future. Dystopia, in effect, satirizes both society as it exists, and the utopian aspiration to transform it. From the dystopian perspective, it is by very reason of its roots in existing society that utopia is unable to transcend it: conditioned by what exists, utopia can only offer more of the same, on a larger scale. Utopia's apparently noble dream of creating a better world is seen as arrogant and presumptuous—the reflection of an unquestioning belief in mankind's right to control and manipulate both humanity and nature.

Dystopian Narrative

In terms of narrative impact, this altered relationship between the actual and the imagined carries with it a number of benefits. In parodically inverting the utopian model, the dystopian text succeeds in establishing a dialectic between existing society and the projected alternative which, while to some extent present in More's *Utopia*, is generally lacking in the work of his more literal-minded successors. While the traditional utopia seeks to forestall critical judgement of the alternative society, utopia constituting the standard by which our own world is judged and found wanting, dystopian fiction positively demands that readers judge the projected society by the standards of their own. Confronted by a world where everyone lives in glass boxes, as in *We*, under the constant surveillance of telescreens, as in *Nineteen Eighty-Four*, or under the inescapable influence of both pre- and post-natal conditioning, as in *Brave New World*, it is almost impossible not to conclude that the dystopian projection is less desirable than the world as it stands. Yet at the same time, the evident resemblances between dystopian and existing society encourage a parallel process, whereby readers are encouraged to judge their own society by the extent to which it embodies dystopian features. In its parody of the traditional utopia, the dystopian text at the same time satirizes many features of existing society—and, in the grotesque distorting mirror which it holds up to reality, the reader is enabled to see, in some respects more clearly, the extent to which society manifests the dystopian characteristics of mindless conformity and acceptance of authoritarian control. Rather than being embedded in the static portrait of a more perfect society, the values implicit in the dystopian text emerge from an active interplay between the reader's critical judgements of both actual and imaginary worlds.

This is not to say, however, that dystopian fiction is any less manipulative of the reader than is its utopian counterpart. While the reader of a dystopian text may well experience a greater freedom in passing judgement, that freedom is clearly constrained and determined by the terms in which the comparison between the two worlds is set up. When Huxley, in *Brave New World*, portrays babies being given electric shock treatment to encourage an aversion to books and flowers, followed by an official sermon from the Director of Hatcheries and Conditioning on the benefits of replacing a taste for the simple pleasures of literature and nature by a desire for far more technologically sophisticated—and accordingly expensive—artifacts and pursuits, the reader's response is not hard to predict: initial revulsion, followed by recognition of the obvious parallels between Huxley's dystopia and modern consumer society. Such crude, though undeniably effective, satire is in essence just as clear in its designs on the reader as the standard scene in traditional utopian fiction, where a depiction of utopia's positive aspects is closely followed by a parallel scene in the real world, in which health, cleanliness, and happiness are mirrored by decrepitude, squalor, and misery.[4] The only real difference is that it works better. Where utopian narrative ostensibly juxtaposes two different viewpoints, the utopian and the non-utopian, it is clear that, as Bakhtin puts it:

> This is not a clash of two ultimate semantic authorities, but rather an objectified (plotted) clash of two represented positions, subordinated wholly to the higher, ultimate authority of the author. The monologic context, under these circumstances, is neither broken nor weakened. [*Problems*, p.188]

In dystopian parody, by contrast, the monologic authority of the utopian voice (for example, that of the Director of Hatcheries and Conditioning) is undermined by the parodic context in which it is placed. What is introduced, by implication, is, as Bakhtin suggests, 'a second voice' with 'a semantic intention that is directly opposed to the original one' (p.193)—and in the light of which it is impossible to accept the first voice as authoritative. Where the monologic character and schematic oppositions of utopian narrative are liable to create resistance on the part of the reader ('this is what I am *supposed* to think'), their dystopian parodic counterparts are a far more effective rhetorical device for securing the reader's assent to the author's point of view. In addition, because the dystopian text tends to *dramatize* both the similarities and differences between the real and imagined, rather than spelling them out, the reader is also spared the presence of the usually uncritical narrator or visitor, whose opinions the reader of the traditional utopia is so clearly intended to share. In effect, dystopian fiction demonstrates a greater readiness to trust both the reader's intelligence and the writer's own technical skill.

This is perhaps most clearly evident when the first person narratives of such utopian texts as *Looking Backward* or *A Modern Utopia* are compared with the equivalent use of the device in dystopian fiction. Bellamy's and Wells's narrators, as we have seen, speak with the conviction of the converted: to them, the virtues of utopia are self-evident, and in representing them as desirable they speak with confidence and authority; yet at the same time, they exhibit a curious passivity. Bellamy's Julian West, in the face of the still more authoritative utterance of Dr Leete; Wells's narrator (at any rate during the overtly fictional sections of the text) when confronted by his utopian *alter ego*: each displays an uncritical acceptance of what he is told, and in doing so, as has been suggested, offers an implicit model for the reader. The narrators in Zamyatin's *We*, or indeed Atwood's *The Handmaid's Tale* are more active, by contrast, yet at the same time less confident. D-503 and Offred are hesitant, reluctant to pass judgement, sometimes even confused, and their narratives reveal, not minds already made up, but rather minds in the process of being made up. D-503 reveals himself as engaged in an internal struggle over what to think, over whether to accept or reject the values of the One State, while Offred, although clearly opposed to the fundamentalist values of Gilead, is occupied throughout the book with the question as to what she can or should do about her situation. The narrative, in other words, embodies a process, is— to use Wells's terms—'not static but kinetic,' and as a result offers the reader a very different model with which to identify. In its parodic inversion of the traditional utopia, dystopian fiction portrays a society whose undesirability is far more clearly self-evident than is the desirability of its utopian counterpart, while at the same time it presents a protagonist whose actively critical attitude towards it is far easier to endorse.

Dystopian fiction, then, would seem—at least at first sight—to be free from many of the narrative limitations of the traditional utopia. Gone are the ponderous narrative mechanisms used to account for the visitor's transfer to utopia: the fictions of Zamyatin, Huxley, Orwell, Atwood all begin *in medias res*, often with arresting narrative devices calculated at once to stimulate curiosity and alert the reader to the *difference* of the world being described:

A squat grey building of only thirty-four stories. Over the main

entrance, the words, CENTRAL LONDON HATCHERY AND CONDITIONI
CENTRE, and in a shield, the World State's motto, COMMUNI˙
IDENTITY, STABILITY. [*Brave New World*, p.15]

It was a bright cold day in April, and the clocks were striking thirtee
[*Nineteen Eighty-Four*, p.7]

What then follows is an account of life in the different society filter
through the consciousness, not of the admiring tourist, but of t
inhabitant, living with it day-in, day-out, and lacking any other standar
by which to judge it—unless one counts the rapidly fading memories
Offred and Winston Smith. The only visitor to dystopia, as such, is Huxle˙
Savage, whose background is almost as alien to our own reality as t
society he visits. Hence the details of dystopian society emerge, not in t
course of the traditional guided tour, but in the process of an inheren
far more dramatic narrative of oppositional struggle; while, as we ha
seen, where there *are* expository set pieces, such as the Directory
Hatchery and Conditioning's pompous lecture on the history
conditioning techniques in *Brave New World*, their effect is radica
different, inviting ridicule rather than acceptance.

Nevertheless, for all these differences in narrative strategy, dystopi
fiction continues to reproduce many features of the traditional utopia
and not always just parodically. While extrapolated from the very differe
value systems of Soviet communism, consumer capitalism, a:
fundamentalist Christianity, the dystopias of Zamyatin and Orwell, Huxle
and Atwood all display a family resemblance whose source is not diffic˙
to divine.[5] All constitute parodic reworkings of the traditional utopi
paradigm, but while the primary function of parody is of course to expo
the limitations of the original, the very closeness of its relationship to t
original often means that these limitations are also to some exte
reproduced. Given the degree to which the utopian paradigm
characterized by tension and contradiction, it is perhaps unsurprising tł
these should also inform dystopian parody. As will be seen, some of t
most characteristic features of the traditional paradigm resurface—
sometimes unexpected forms—even in a parodic context.

In terms of what dystopian fiction *exposes*, perhaps the most immediate
striking feature of all the works under discussion is their common empha
on the extraordinarily public character of life in the societies they proje
Like the traditional utopia, dystopia portrays a society which is regiment
and hierarchical—and also one where adherence to the societal ideal
ensured by an almost obsessive concern with surveillance, with t
subjection of the individual to public scrutiny. Not only do its citize
conform to the standards of the monolithic state—they must be *seen*

conform, and it is this visible conformity which is seen as essential to the preservation of stability and order in utopia and dystopia alike. More, in *Utopia*, sees the elimination of privacy as the key to ensuring individual virtue: no one is likely to do wrong 'because they live in full view of all' (p.49). Dystopian fiction simply takes this one step further, exposing it as a fundamental principle of both utopian and dystopian order: ultimately, the only way to be *certain* that society's norms are consistently observed is by watching everyone, all the time. Accordingly in dystopia all the resources of modern technology are employed to ensure that privacy is kept to an absolute minimum. The glass bedrooms of *We*, the telescreens of *Nineteen Eighty-Four* (precursors of the video cameras which grace today's banks, stores, public buildings, and even men's washrooms), the spies and hidden microphones of *The Handmaid's Tale* all serve the same essential purpose as do the social provisions of More's *Utopia*. *Brave New World*, indeed, resembles *Utopia* still more closely, in that the element of overt coercion present in other dystopias, where the consequences of being seen to act antisocially are made abundantly clear, is replaced by a benign confidence in the powers of conditioning. The citizens of *Brave New World* are conditioned to *want* to spend all their time 'in the full view of all'; such privacy as they preserve is devoted to such harmless (and in society's terms, respectable) practices as sleep, recreational sex, and the consumption of stupefying drugs.

Conformity is assured, and so too is uniformity—in the most literal sense. The citizens of all four dystopias wear uniforms, reinforcing the sense that (as in so much utopian narrative) people are types rather than distinct individuals. (Huxley and Atwood make their uniforms colour coded, like electrical wiring, further enhancing the sense that the individual is merely part of the social machine.) In *We*, everyone does everything at the same time, while all four future societies have communal rituals in which individual identity is submerged in that of the group, ranging from public executions, in Zamyatin and Atwood, through Orwell's Two Minutes Hate, to the group sex of Huxley's *Brave New World*.

Even this last may be seen as having its roots in the provisions of the traditional utopia, with its characteristic blurring of the lines between the public and private spheres, which is nowhere more apparent than in its treatment of sexual relations. Campanella, as we have seen, organizes sexual intimacy under the supervision of astrologers, physicians, and matrons, with not only the choice of sexual partner but the exact time of intercourse dictated by the state. Yet this, while extreme, is scarcely an aberration. Implicit in both Bellamy's substitution of sexual for economic rewards, with women providing the ultimate incentive for male productive efficiency, Wells's depiction of marital relations as ultimately the concern of the state, rather than of the individuals involved, is the same impulse to subordinate all aspects of individual experience to the needs of society. Again, dystopian fiction simply takes this one stage further: Zamyatin's sex-vouchers, the universal promiscuity in *Brave New World*, where 'everyone belongs to everyone else,' the reduction of women to mere mechanisms for procreation in *The Handmaid's Tale*, all serve to expose the implications inherent in the sexual provisions of utopia. Ultimately, whether in utopia or dystopia, the message is the same: that individual agency cannot be trusted, even in the most intimate sphere of personal relations; in the end, the overriding interests of the state must prevail.

In taking the utopian emphasis on the virtues of conformity and the need for supervision of every aspect of individual behaviour to its logical conclusion, dystopian fiction makes explicit the extent to which the utopian ideal is premised on the suppression of any distinct individual identity. Such identity is acquired only gradually, in the process of growing up, as individuals begin to make choices and take responsibility for their actions: in effectively removing responsibility and choice from the individual sphere, utopian society minimizes the opportunities for such identity to emerge—which in part explains why attempts to incorporate elements of novelistic characterization into the traditional utopian narrative are so seldom successful. Dystopian fiction, however, portrays a process which renders the implications still clearer: in suppressing the emergence of individual identity in the interests of stability, security, conformity, the dystopian state clearly seeks to discourage the development of any kind of mature, adult awareness—of any form of consciousness sophisticated enough to perceive and articulate the society's limitations. There is in consequence a distinct childishness evident in the behaviourial norms of dystopian society, suggesting that the regressive aspect of the utopian ideal—its desire for a return to womb-like security—has been correctly intuited.

It is Huxley who exposes these implications most clearly. As well as providing an abundance of food, diversion, and guilt-free sexual gratification, his future society reduces work to an undemanding minimum (as the same time conditioning the individual to enjoy it), and leaves the responsibility for running things to a ruling élite of World Controllers. It is a world which is not merely innocent, but quite explicitly infantile: infantile behaviour constitutes the socially approved norm. When Bernard Marx talks to Lenina Crowne of wanting to act like an adult, her response is one of simple incomprehension, and Bernard is later reprimanded for his 'lapse from a proper standard of infantile decorum' (p.85). For well-adjusted citizens, by contrast, the ideal state is one of blissful unconsciousness—the symbolic implications of which are made only too 'lear. When Lenina and Henry Foster conclude their evening out with a rip to the Westminster Abbey Cabaret (featuring the music of Calvin Stopes ınd his Sixteen Sexophonists), their last, drug-enhanced dance together s described in unmistakable terms:

> Lenina and Henry had what they wanted ... They were inside, here and now—safely inside with the fine weather, the perennially blue sky. And when, exhausted, the Sixteen had laid by their sexophones and the Synthetic Music apparatus was producing the very latest in slow Malthusian Blues, they might have been twin embryos gently rocking together on the waves of a bottled ocean of blood-surrogate. [pp.69–70]

In the more hostile environments depicted in other dystopian fictions, ›articularly *Nineteen Eighty-Four*, this aspect is less overt. Nevertheless, the ·limination of individual responsibility, the enforced conformity, the ·ndless organized activities in which the citizens of both Orwell's and ۲amyatin's future societies are obliged to participate all serve to suggest a ›attern almost as regressive. If womb-like security is the ideal of the citizens ›f *Brave New World*, the ambience of *We* and *Nineteen Eighty-Four* is more ۱kin to that of a gigantic boarding-school, governed by routine, ritual, and ۱rbitrary acts of authority. And in all three works, as in *The Handmaid's ۲ale*, any indication of an adult tendency to independent thought or action s the ultimate heresy.

The parallels between the childlike, infantile, or even foetal dependence ۰ostered by dystopian society and the underlying pattern of the traditional ıtopia are clear enough, but the resemblance does not end there. In each ·ase the regressive dependence of the individual is secured by essentially imilar means—by the imposition of a distinctively patriarchal order. In ۷e, it is the larger-than-life figure of The Benefactor who rules the One ۱tate which protects its citizens from the terrors of the unexpected and the langers that might accompany the 'savage state of freedom' (p.19). In fact, ۲he Benefactor is merely a man: 'a bald-headed, a Socratically bald-headed ۱an' (p.205), perhaps modelled on Lenin; but he is normally described in ۰erms that suggest he is gigantic—rather as a father might appear to a small ۰hild. In an interview with D-503, The Benefactor, concerned by his ۱nvolvement with the rebels, significantly invites him to 'talk as grown-ıps do when the children have gone off to bed' (p.204), much as the ›rivileged eldest son might be invited to join with his father in man-to-۱an conversation.[6] Equally significantly, it is a woman who represents the lisruptive force which tempts D-503 to taste the forbidden delights of ۰reedom—and it is a woman whose destruction is essential to the ›reservation of the stability of the patriarchal state. It is the woman's,

E-330's,[7] attempt to take possession of the *Integral*, the phallic spaces
with which the patriarchal One State seeks to penetrate the heavens, t
constitutes the ultimate, unforgivable act of rebellion; when it is thwar
by the intervention of the male Guardians, order is thereby restored.

In *Nineteen Eighty-Four* an almost identical scenario unfolds itself; inde
the parallel is so close that it is clear that Orwell must have been indeb
to Zamyatin for the inspiration. Here it is another woman, Julia, v
arouses the protagonist, Winston Smith, to go beyond mere sul
resentment of the Stalin-like Big Brother and take action against author
Once again, however, the woman proves no match for the patriarchal sta
tortured and brainwashed, Winston disowns Julia, and ends up in ɡ
sodden adulation of Big Brother. Here, however, the power of
patriarchal ruler is mediated by the presence of another male autho
figure, O'Brien, for whom Winston feels much the same instinctive reg
as does the narrator in Wells's *In the Days of the Comet* for the politic
Melmount—although here the homoerotic implications are even clea
Larger and stronger than Winston, O'Brien treats him—even wl
torturing him—with an almost indecent intimacy. All the while Wins
is being subjected to the most unspeakable agonies, O'Brien is there, ha
on his shoulder, to reassure him that it is all for his own good, and,
Gerald Fiderer points out) there is a distinctly masochistic element
Winston's response:

> At sight of the heavy, lined face, so ugly and so intelligent, his he
> seemed to turn over. If he could have moved he would have stretcl
> out a hand and laid it on O'Brien's arm. He had never loved him
> deeply as at this moment ... It made no difference. In some se
> that went deeper than friendship, they were intimates. [p.217]

O'Brien even invades Winston's dreams, which had hitherto be
primarily about his mother, and on this unconscious plane re-enacts
triumphant suppression of the female by the male. By the end, Wins
has betrayed and forgotten not only his lover, but also his mother—b
have been replaced by males.

Amid the rampant heterosexual promiscuity of Huxley's World Sta
the element of patriarchal dominance is less immediately appar
(although the confrontation between the rebels and the World Control
Mustapha Mond, replicates the power dynamics of the equivalent sce
in *We* and *Nineteen Eighty-Four*—indeed, faced by Mond's unassaila
authority, Bernard Marx reverts completely to the status of a child:
bursts into tears, and has to be put to bed). None the less, while men a
women apparently enjoy an equal degree of sexual freedom (or lack o
given that promiscuity is more or less compulsory), it soon becomes cl

that equality ends there. Henry Ford, rather than Lenin or Stalin, is the presiding male deity, in whose name the (apparently all male) World Controllers rule the acquiescent masses. And while humanity is segregated into genetically predetermined castes, which are conditioned to have as little as possible to do with one another, there appears to be an exception which allows for sexual relationships between Alpha males and Beta females. It is a revealing contradiction, indicative of the extent to which Huxley's futuristic extrapolation remains governed by the assumptions of his own time: despite imagining a world whose sexual morality is radically different, Huxley uncritically reproduces the *gender* relations of his own era. Significantly, the only members of the Alpha élite we encounter are male, with the exception of the Headmistress of Eton, who is a 'freemartin'—a female who has been rendered sterile by prenatal doses of male sex hormones. (The status of the central female character, Lenina, is left ambiguous: although Theodor Adorno describes her—rather oddly— as 'a well-groomed and polished American career woman' (p.105), her occupation points to a Beta, rather than an Alpha classification.) In a world whose only sexual taboos are against celibacy and monogamy, and where pregnancy and childbirth have been superseded by mechanical reproductive technology, the word 'Mother' is the ultimate obscenity. ('Father' is only mildly smutty by comparison.) Although there is no counterpart to the subversive females of Zamyatin and Orwell, it is noteworthy that the main opponent of the dystopian society—the Savage—is devoted to his mother. The work ends, once again, with the destruction of the central female character—in this case the hapless Lenina—and the death, rather than the acquiescence of the defeated rebel.

While there may be less overt glorification of male power in *Brave New World* than in *We* or *Nineteen Eighty-Four*, in removing women's reproductive power, and replacing it with a male invention—the production line—Huxley takes the utopian dream of a male-dominated order still further. At the same time, he takes to its logical conclusion the longstanding utopian preoccupation with selective breeding: in *Brave New World*, humanity is quite literally designed to fit the demands of the state. The conformity which in the dystopias of Zamyatin and Orwell is secured by such relatively clumsy means as brain surgery or torture is painlessly ensured in Huxley's World State by the technologies of mass production:

> One hundred and seven heat-conditioned Epsilon Senegalese were working in the foundry. Thirty-three Delta females, long-headed, sandy, with narrow pelvises, and all within 20 millimetres of 1 metre 69 centimetres tall, were cutting screws. In the assembling room, the dynamos were being put together by two sets of Gamma-plus dwarfs.

The two long work-tables faced one another; between them crawl
the conveyor with its load of separate parts; forty-seven blond hea
were confronted by forty-seven brown ones. Forty-seven snubs
forty-seven hooks; forty-seven receding by forty-seven prognathc
chins. The completed mechanisms were inspected by eighte
identical curly auburn girls in Gamma green, packed in crates
thirty-four short-legged, left-handed male Delta-minuses, a
loaded into the waiting trucks and lorries by sixty-three blue-eye
flaxen and freckled Epsilon Semi-Morons. [pp.130–1][8]

To such visions of the future, in which human beings seem hardly l
mechanical than the machines they use, it is hard to respond withou
degree of revulsion—and part of the narrative appeal of dystopian ficti
stems from the writer's ability to exploit the reader's reaction against t
society portrayed. Whereas it is often difficult to share the visitor to utopi
uncritical enthusiasm for the wonders of utopian society, the horrors
dystopia guarantee a sympathetic reaction on the reader's part to anyo
who stands out against the mindless conformity imposed by the monolit
state. On occasions, such sympathy is still further exploited for ironic effe
as when Huxley, having first established Bernard Marx as a sympathe
figure by making him a cogent—indeed, almost the *only*—critic of t
appalling world he lives in, then proceeds to undercut the reader's natu
tendency to identify with such a character by showing him succumbi
all too readily to the lures of success. But this is a comparative rarity: wh
none of D-503, Winston Smith, the Savage, or Offred are by any stret
of the imagination idealized portrayals, they are so much preferable to t
worlds they live in that the actual *nature* of their opposition to dystopi
society may easily escape critical examination—given that in such a socie
any opposition seems better than none at all.

The forms which opposition to dystopia takes, however, are wor
looking at more closely, for it is here that the extent to which dystopi
fiction shares the limitations of the original it parodies begins to becor
apparent. There is in fact a family resemblance, not only between t
patterns of the various dystopian societies, but also between the modes
rebellion against them. Thus, for example, the first form which resistan
takes is invariably the repudiation of the demand that life be lived primar
in public. At E-330's behest, D-503 finds himself conniving in the use
the hours of privacy sanctioned only for sexual purposes for other, mo
subversive purposes. Secret knowledge, secret behaviour are seen as
themselves subversive, almost irrespective of the nature of the secre
involved. Bernard Marx establishes himself as suspicious simply by virt
of his desire to spend time by himself, rather than in the mindle

gregariousness which is seen as normal. And Winston Smith, for all his error of the state's power of physical coercion, deliberately risks his safety in his pursuit of privacy:[9] at first timidly, in the tiny alcove out of sight of the telescreen, where he keeps his journal; and later more boldly, with his illicit liaison with Julia in their secret meeting place above a junk shop.

What is significant, however, is the consistency with which this reassertion of the desire for privacy is associated with the past. The early meetings of D-503 and E-330 take place at the House of Antiquity, a relic of the past preserved for instructional purposes; Winston and Julia pursue their liaison in a room above a shop that sells antiques. Both E-330 and Julia shock and entice their lovers by wearing old-fashioned clothing, while Winston Smith records his subversive thoughts in a lady's keepsake album which is attractive partly because of its age, writing with an old-fashioned pen-nib on 'beautiful creamy paper' (p.11) which is no longer manufactured. And the past, in its turn, becomes the main source of the values in comparison with which dystopian society is judged and found wanting. In *Brave New World*, the energy and verbal richness of the Savage's beloved Shakespeare is used to highlight the clichés and emotional poverty of dystopia; while such ancient texts as the Bible and the writings of William James and Maine de Biran are seen as so subversive that they are kept securely locked away in the safe of the World Controller, Mustapha Mond.

At first sight, the subversive import of such survivals from the past would seem to be largely symbolic. Certainly there *are* relics of the past whose political relevance is immediately evident, as when Winston Smith comes across a newspaper photograph of three party members who officially no longer exist—or indeed ever existed. Here there is objective evidence that the authorities are lying—yet in terms of its impact, the actual use that can be made of the information, there appears to be little effective difference between the photograph and the keepsake album in which Winston keeps his diary. Ultimately, the subversiveness of an interest in the past lies not in the implications of any specific piece of information, but rather in the fact that there was a past at all.

Dystopian society, like that of most traditional utopias, has as its ideal a condition of eternal and static stability. Once perfection (of whatever kind) is achieved, change automatically becomes a threat—and the problem with the past is that, simply by showing that things were once different, it demonstrates that change is at least *possible*. The very existence of the past where things were different implies that society is 'not static but kinetic,' and dystopian societies uniformly go out of their way to obliterate its memory. In *Nineteen Eighty-Four*, history is systematically rewritten to conform to the changing necessities of the present: even so dramatic an event as the replacement of Eurasia by Eastasia as Oceania's

enemy in the endless world war is so effectively glossed over that wit
a matter of days the fiction that Oceania and Eastasia have *always* beer
war is almost universally accepted as fact. To show an interest in what
past was really like is almost certain evidence of thoughtcrime, punisha
by anything from twenty-five years imprisonment to death. In *We*, the ɪ
possesses a certain exotic fascination, but it is generally viewed
hopelessly primitive, infinitely remote from the present: a 'wild epo
(p.34), peopled by 'brutes,' 'apes,' whose behaviour is repeatedly descril
as 'laughable' and 'incredible,' and whose art is referred to as 'w
unorganized, insane ... epileptically distorted' (p.41). Although the Wc
State in *Brave New World* preserves an enclave of tribal society on the N
Mexico Reservation, its squalor, and the 'queer' behaviour of its inhabita
serve primarily as an object lesson to visitors of the horrors from wh
the World State has liberated them; otherwise, the prevailing view of
past is summed up by the celebrated dictum of the Godlike Ford: 'Hist
is Bunk.'

Yet despite its satiric exaggeration, the dystopian attitude towards
past is little more than the logical development of a tendency implicit
the traditional utopia. In *A Modern Utopia*, history proves as malleable
in *Nineteen Eighty-Four*: to render utopia possible, the entire course
human history is blithely rewritten in less than a page. In *Men Like Gc*
the allegedly intellectual curious Utopians show singularly little interes
the more primitive culture of the Earthlings: a single brief conference ser
to tell them all they need to know, and they show scarcely any curios
thereafter. Even in *Looking Backward*, where the arrival of a visitor fr
the past does arouse considerable interest, his account of the past ser
only to confirm existing assumptions. The general attitude of Bellam
utopians to their past is one of self-congratulation for having escaped fr
it so easily: the 'old musty books' (p.166) that talk of the past hold lit
fascination, while in their celebrations of the year 2000 we are told tl
'the almost universal theme ... has been the future rather than the pɛ
not the advance that has been made, but the progress that shall be ma
ever onward and upward' (p.xxii). Skinner's *Walden Two* is har
exceptional in its explicit assertion that the ideal society would deliberat
set out to 'discourage any sense of history' (p.235).

Rebellion in dystopia, then, expresses itself through a series of binɛ
oppositions. It opposes the public with the private, and counters 1
dystopian aspiration to permanence and stability with the destabilizɪ
evidence of history and tradition. In addition, the rebel finds in the ru
pastoral world beyond the confines of dystopian society a space ɛ
freedom otherwise denied. Dystopia shares with the traditional utopiɛ
predominantly urban emphasis, and here again rebellion takes the fo

of simple antithesis. Freedom from the One State in *We* lies beyond the 'Green Wall,' among the more natural, primitive humans who refuse to be conscripted into the conformist world ruled by The Benefactor. It is in the countryside that the Savage seeks refuge from the horrors of Brave New World, and it is in the countryside, too, that Winston and Julia first share the liberation of sexual ecstasy. Where the Wellsian utopia offers a vision of humanity in control of nature, in dystopia the natural world offers virtually the last refuge from the tyranny of the state. Once again, dystopia makes absolute what in utopia is only implicit. Where even Wells allows nature at least some role, however subordinate, dystopia draws the lines more starkly: the natural, organic character of the rural world is inalterably opposed to the controlling human design of dystopian society.

In opposing this controlling impulse, the dystopian rebel inevitably challenges the prevailing ethic of infantile or childlike dependence fostered by the patriarchal state. Not only privacy and tradition, but adult behaviour of any kind are seen by the state as inherently subversive. Thus, when E-330 upholds the value of independent individual initiative, or the Savage argues for the benefits of deferred, rather than immediate gratification, it is primarily their defiance of the regressive norms of their society that constitutes a threat. Yet for all this, the *form* such defiance takes often seems curiously limited in scope: only *We*, for example, portrays any kind of effective *political* challenge to the State. For the most part, resistance manifests itself more in the sexual than the political realm—and then most often in the form of the reassertion of more traditional sexual values.

In *We*, where the *Lex Sexualis* states that 'Every number has the right of availability, as a sexual product, to any other member' (p.37), securing the sexual services of anyone one desires is a simple matter of applying to the authorities for the appropriate pink coupons, which entitle one to have sex during the private sexual hours. And it is this indiscriminate, yet regulated gratification of desire that E-330 resists, both by engaging in sexual activity outside the designated hours, and refraining from it during them. Sexuality is restored to the individual's control, and with it responsibility for the consequences of her actions. Yet it is here that the implications of E-330's challenge to the One State's sexual norms become more equivocal. On D-503's first trip with her to the House of Antiquity, she exchanges her androgynous uniform for more traditional garb:

> She had on a black hat, a short, antiquated, glaringly yellow dress, black stockings. The dress was of light silk: I could clearly see that the stockings were very long, reaching considerably above her knees, while the neckline was low, revealing that shadow between her—
> [p.43]

And here D-503 breaks off, as though barely able to control himself–
he does again on a subsequent occasion, where the nature of the costum
allure is made even more explicit:

> She was in a saffron-yellow dress of an ancient cut. This wa
> thousandfold more wicked than if she had had absolutely noth
> on. Two sharp points, glowing roseately through the thin tissue: t
> embers smouldering among ashes. Two tenderly rounded knee
> [p.65]

Clearly, the utopian project of stripping sexuality of guilt has been less th
successful, given the immediacy of D-503's response to this traditio
stereotype of female sexuality, teasingly provocative in its simultane
offer and refusal of gratification. This, Zamyatin seems to be implying
what human beings (or, more precisely, men) really want, as opposec
the bureaucratically regulated permissiveness of the One State. Yet
opposing one form of objectification to another, in presenting the soci
constructed sexual stereotypes of his own day as more 'natural' than
more overtly regulated sexuality of his future society, Zamyatin effectiv
does little more than reinscribe his own society's norms. While *We* po
a future society with a radically different sexual ethic, the implication:
this are never really thought through: in a world where everyone is sexu
available to everyone else, *We* reproduces the familiar scenario o
traditional bourgeois narrative of adulterous love. D-503 has an offici
approved partner, O-90, who is short and chubby, talks faster than
thinks, and goes on rather tiresomely about wanting to have a baby;
deserts her in favour of E-330, whose sharp white teeth, exotic taste
clothing, and body—'slender, hard, wilfully pliant as a whiplash' (p.24
clearly have a rather different kind of appeal; and the result is disaster
the world of the far future, not a great deal seems to have changed.

In *Nineteen Eighty-Four*, where the prevailing sexual ethic is repress
rather than permissive (there is even a State-sponsored organization ca
the Anti-Sex League), the form rebellion takes is still strikingly simi
Once again, any form of sexual activity other than that sanctioned
authority is seen as inherently subversive. As Winston reflects: 'The sex
act, successfully performed, was rebellion. Desire was thoughtcrir
(p.62). It is the instinctual, spontaneous, uncontrollable quality of sex
desire that makes it a threat to officially imposed conformity, and ind
part of Julia's appeal to Winston lies precisely in her promiscuity, wh
he sees as representing a breach in the 'wall of virtue' which the state
tried to erect:

> His heart leapt. Scores of times she had done it: he wished it had

been hundreds—thousands. Anything that hinted at corruption always filled him with wild hope. Who knew, perhaps the Party was rotten under the surface, its cult of strenuousness and self-denial simply a shame concealing iniquity. If he could have infected the whole lot of them with leprosy or syphilis, how gladly he would have done so! Anything to rot, to weaken, to undermine! [p.111]

Here, at the outset, there is an almost carnivalesque quality to Orwell's depiction of sexuality: even in corruption and disease there is the spark of life, the hope of renewal. 'Simple undifferentiated desire' (p.112) is a force that the official values of society can never wholly contain or repress: 'that was the force that would tear the Party to pieces' (p.112). And Winston is quite clear as to the implications of his desire:

> Their embrace had been a battle, the climax a victory. It was a blow struck against the Party. It was a political act. [p.112]

Yet as the relationship between Winston and Julia develops, this anarchic, carnivalesque celebration of desire soon gives way to something far more conventional. Defiance of the official sexual morality increasingly takes the form, as it does in *We*, of a reinscription of traditional stereotypes. Julia speaks of her desire to wear a 'real woman's frock' rather than trousers, to 'wear silk stockings and high-heeled shoes'—to be 'a woman, not a Party comrade' (p.127). In a scene clearly influenced by Zamyatin's example, Julia enhances her allure, not only with old-fashioned clothing, but even make-up:

> Her lips were deeply reddened, her cheeks rouged, her nose powdered; there was even a touch of something under the eyes to make them brighter. It was not very skillfully done, but Winston's standards in such matters were not high. He had never before seen or imagined a woman of the Party with cosmetics on her face. The improvement in her appearance was startling. With just a few dabs of colour in the right places she had become not only very much prettier, but, above all, far more feminine. Her short hair and boyish overalls merely added to the effect. [p.126]

While it is her 'animal instinct' (p.112) that Winston finds attractive at first, it is paradoxically the old-fashioned artifice of make-up[10] that reveals her 'true' femininity. Moreover, although it is Julia who first takes the lead in their relationship, she soon reveals more stereotypically feminine qualities. Unlike Winston's, her opposition to the Party proves to be instinctual, rather than intellectual: she has little interest in political ideas, falls asleep when he reads her the subversive writings of Goldstein, and regards 'any kind of organized revolt against the Party ... as stupid' (p.117).

It is Winston who initiates their joining what he takes to be the resistanc
at which point the formerly promiscuous Julia declares that, even in t
interests of overthrowing the Party, the one thing she will not countenan
is their separation. Her resourcefulness, so striking at the outset, so
becomes largely confined to finding black market food for them to consur
in the rented room that is 'almost a home' (p.133), where they meet
make love and 'g[i]ve themselves up to daydreams of escape' (p.134).
the end, what is opposed to the massive tyranny of the state is little mc
than a bourgeois domestic idyll, a brief, fragile dream of quasi-marital bli
Like Zamyatin, Orwell opposes to the monstrous sexual conformity of t
dystopian state a purportedly 'natural' sexuality which is in fact no lc
socially constructed.

Brave New World also creates an opposition between the sexual norn
of dystopian society and more traditional values—but here the contrast
less uncritical. Huxley portrays a society more permissive even th
Zamyatin's, where everyone has not merely the right, but the duty to ha
sex with as many partners as possible, both privately and in commur
sex-orgies. Extrapolated as it is from the realities of capitalist society, the
is no bureaucratic regulation of the operations of the sexual free market
which is probably just as well, given that the volume of pink coupo
required would most likely have exceeded the capacity of the World Stat
paper production. In such a world, about the only possible subversive for
of sexual activity is to refrain from it, which is precisely what the vario
rebels attempt to do: Helmholz Watson, though once an 'indefatigal
lover' (p.62) with a track record of six hundred and forty sexual conque:
in less than four years, gives up sex altogether in the hope that the ener
thus saved will enable him to think more clearly, while Bernard and t
Savage justify their aversion to immediate sexual gratification by imagini:
they are in love. Yet while this might seem to suggest a yearning f
authenticity, for something more 'real' than state-sanctioned promiscuif
the fact that in the case of both Bernard and the Savage the object of th
desire is the vacuous Lenina rather undercuts the effect of their roman
idealism. The old-fashioned male ideal of chivalric love, rather than bei
held up as a contrasting positive, is exposed as mere fantasy projecti
(onto a singularly blank screen), quite as ludicrous as the mindless sexu
indulgence to which it is opposed—and for that matter, quite as clea
socially constructed.

Nevertheless, this is not to say that Huxley altogether avoids the tr
of merely reversing the utopian equation, and judging the alternati
society by the standards of today's, rather than vice versa. While the sear
for authenticity in the form of true love may be represented as bogus, it
clear that Huxley does imply *some* absolute standards whereby the valu

f Brave New World can be judged as specious and inauthentic. As Adorno
oints out, although Huxley satirizes conventional morality, showing a
world where promiscuity is just as moral as sexual decorum used to be,
1e ideological bias of his own critique is hardly less conventional:

> In its proclamation of the bourgeois nature of what claims to be
> unbourgeois, [Huxley's] thesis itself becomes ensnared in
> bourgeois habits ... Like that of many emancipated Englishmen,
> his consciousness is preformed by the very Puritanism he abjures.
> He fails to distinguish between the liberation of sexuality and its
> debasement. [p.103]

or Huxley, what is most repellent about Brave New World is not so much
s oppression of its citizens (in any event, he is only really concerned with
1e problems of the Alpha élite), as the vulgarity of its mass culture. Of the
ebels, the only one who is not also the object of satire is Helmholz, the
creative artist who is unable to find an audience in a world of mindless
onformity—a world where even Shakespeare is no longer relevant. What
Iuxley proposes as sources of absolute value by which dystopia is judged
nd found wanting are Art, and still more so, Religion—it is instructive to
iscover what the *really* forbidden books are that Mustapha Mond
eeps locked up in the safe in his office: the Bible, *The Imitation of Christ*,
William James's *The Varieties of Religious Experience*, works by Cardinal
Iewman and Maine de Biran. These, it is implied, represent the objective,
canscendent reality lost sight of in Brave New World's pursuit of subjective
appiness—a reality whose ideological character Huxley never
cknowledges.[11]

Despite such variations in approach, however, the pattern of resistance
1 dystopian fiction remains remarkably consistent: the reassertion of
raditional and individual values is accompanied in each case by the
isplacement of political resistance into the sexual realm. While D-503 and
.-330, Bernard, Helmholz, and the Savage, Winston and Julia all desire
he destruction of the State, at any rate in theory, what is actually
ramatized is more their sexual than political unorthodoxy. Yet perhaps
he most striking similarity of all lies in the fact that, in every case, rebellion
; shown as doomed to defeat. Although in *We* the battle goes on, E-330
; executed, and the lobotomized D-503 renews his allegiance to The
tenefactor; Helmholz and Bernard are exiled, while the Savage commits
uicide; and Winston and Julia betray both themselves and each other. For
ll its parodic inversion of the utopian ideal, one feature which dystopia
eproduces virtually unchanged is the myth that resistance is futile. Indeed,
here is a curious inevitability to the process whereby the individual takes
n the might of the monolithic State, and is ultimately destroyed by it—

an inevitability which perhaps stems from the terms in which confrontation is set up. To begin with, the dualistic opposition betw the values of the individual and those of society ultimately places individual in a situation where defeat can scarcely be avoided. W secrecy and privacy are appealing in the context of the invasive surveilla practiced by the dystopian state, they remain essentially defen strategies; collecting obsolete artifacts, wearing old-fashioned clothing, engaging in anachronistic sexual behaviour offer only symbolic resista to the power of the State, while the individual, alone and isolated, realistically do little to challenge the collective might and technolog resources which society can deploy. As in the traditional utopia, the very little by way of collective organization to mediate between individual and centralized authority. Significantly, Zamyatin's dystop the one where resistance is shown as coming closest to success. It is ha coincidental that it is the only one where resistance is shown as collec and organized, rather than merely an individual gesture of defiance.

Yet the oppositional struggle that dystopian fiction dramatizes is simply that of the individual against society. In its parodic inversion of utopian dream of order, dystopian fiction effectively rewrites its underly fantasy of the patriarchal appropriation of the powers of the mot focusing instead on the dream of the son's unsuccessful rebellion aga the father. It is noteworthy, to begin with, that all the male rebels aga patriarchal authority (with the lone exception of Helmholz) feel themse to be in some way inadequate: D-503 feels his hairiness is somel primitive; Bernard is sensitive about his height; the Savage's insecu goes back to his lonely, fatherless childhood; and Winston is painf aware of his physical frailty. Yet they all take on an authority symboli by a larger-than-life male figure who has all the confidence and po that they lack. D-503 is clearly intimidated by The Benefactor: altho at one point, briefly, he laughs at his baldness, it is rather guilty laugh and for the most part the emphasis is on The Benefactor's aln superhuman power. Bernard is intimidated, and the Savage outarguec the sleekly self-confident World Controller, Mustapha Mond, and symbolic authority of Big Brother is given concrete expression in O'Bri physical domination—most glaringly in the scene where he actually p out one of Winston's teeth with his bare hands.

The outcome of such a confrontation is predictable enough—to extent, indeed, that the actual conclusions of We, Brave New World, Nineteen Eighty-Four are strikingly similar. All three end with the defea the rebellious male, the triumph of paternal authority, and the incide destruction of the female who has been presumptuous enough to us the love which the father-figure sees as rightfully his. In We, the conclus

s particularly disturbing, with the now acquiescent D-503 sitting alongside
The Benefactor as E-330 is tortured:

> Then she was led in under the Gas Bell Glass. Her face became very
> white, and since her eyes were dark and large, this created an
> extremely beautiful effect. When they started pumping the air out
> of the Gas Bell Glass she threw her head back, half closing her eyes
> and compressing her lips: this reminded me of something … This was
> gone through three times— [p.221]

The sexual overtones of D-503's description are unmistakable, and it is
clear that the triple repetition of this quasi-orgasm is not merely an arbitrary
exercise in cruelty, but also a manifestation of superior potency: only The
Benefactor could induce such symptoms three times in rapid succession.

The conclusion of *Nineteen Eighty-Four* is equally indecent, as Winston
is alternately tortured and comforted by the muscular O'Brien. When he
encounters Julia again, after his release, she arouses no feeling in him other
than a vague distaste, and he leaves her to return to the café, where he
can indulge in loving thoughts of Big Brother—and in an almost
voluptuous longing for the bullet which will penetrate the back of his neck:

> He was walking down the white-tiled corridor, with the feeling of
> walking in sunlight, and an armed guard at his back. The long hoped-
> for bullet was entering his brain.
>
> He gazed up at the enormous face. Forty years it had taken him
> to learn what kind of smile was hidden beneath the dark moustache.
> O cruel, needless misunderstanding! O stubborn, self-willed exile
> from the loving breast! Two gin-sodden tears trickled down the sides
> of his nose. But it was all right, everything was all right, the struggle
> was finished. He had won the victory over himself. He loved Big
> Brother. [p.256]

Even in *Brave New World*, where the homoerotic overtones are less overt,
the scenario concludes in a similar fashion. The Savage's mother dies,
Lenina is killed (whether actually or only ritually is never made quite clear),
and the Savage expiates his sexual guilt for having succumbed to
heterosexual desire by hanging himself in, of all things, a lighthouse—
which continues to point to the sky as the Savage dangles dead at its base,
in yet another symbol of triumphant phallic authority.

Thus, while dystopian parody of the utopian ideal exposes many of its
underlying implications, the very closeness of the relationship between
parody and original results in the reproduction of some of the latter's most
problematic features. While designed as an attack on the utopian dream
of a static, all-embracing order, dystopian fiction nevertheless accepts

utopia's underlying premise: that its ideal of a synchronous total system
the only viable alternative to the chaos and flux of history in process.
that differs in dystopia's parodic inversion is that the utopian ideal
presented as undesirable, the corollary being that a return to the world
it is now becomes the goal. As a counter to the threat of a utopian futu
the dystopian writer often ends up merely reasserting the values of t
past.[12] In its own way, in fact, the basic impulse of dystopian fantasy is j
as regressive as that of the traditional utopia, and for all its success
transcending some of the latter's narrative limitations, it may be seen tl
the underlying structure of the traditional utopian paradigm still persi:
Although, as we have seen, dystopian narrative begins *in medias res*, ratl
than with the customary journey to utopia, this is not to say that the journ
motif is altogether dispensed with. Where the utopian narrative starts
the everyday world, moves to utopia, then returns, what dystopian ficti
enacts is the same process, only in reverse. Here the narrative begins a
ends in the dystopian future, but frames a symbolic return to the past.
503's first 'irrational' act is to accompany E-330 to the House of Antiqui
Bernard and Lenina travel to the tribal Reservation; and Winston's fi
illicit assignation with Julia takes the form of a trip out to the unspc
countryside. And while these symbolic journeys may be seen in the liş
of dystopian fiction's overall opposition of the values of the past to thc
of the nightmare dystopian future, their underlying psychologi
implications prove on closer examination to be strikingly similar to thc
of their utopian counterparts.

In *We*, D-503 and E-330 are greeted at the House of Antiquity by an c
crone, whose mouth 'consist[ing] solely of pleats and folds' seems 'grov
over, somehow' (p.40). When she opens this vaginal aperture, much
D-503's astonishment—'it seemed altogether unbelievable that she wou
break into speech' (p.40)—it is to invite them into her house. They asce
a 'wide dark staircase' (p.40) into an apartment whose gorgeous orgai
chaos 'could not be reconciled in any equations whatsoever' (p.41), a
D-503 finds himself unaccountably reminded of the sexual act. Berna
and Lenina, in *Brave New World*, ascend to the reservation by way o:
channel between precipitous banks; after rounding a projection, they th
enter 'a water-worn ravine' (p.92), accompanied all the while by the sou
of drums 'as though the whole air had come alive and were pulsing, pulsi
with the indefatigable movement of blood' (p.92). On finally reaching the
destination they encounter the ultimate object of disgust—a real, li
biological mother, Linda, whose previous employment just happens
have been in the Fertilizing Room. And in *Nineteen Eighty-Four* a simi
pattern is evident: Winston and Julia make their way along a narrow tra
into the woods:

They came to the fallen tree that she had spoken of. The girl hopped over and forced apart the bushes, in which there did not seem to be an opening. When Winston followed her, he found that they were in a natural clearing, a tiny grassy knoll surrounded by tall saplings that shut it in completely. [p.106]

Here they proceed to make love, but before doing so, Winston actually sees the landscape which has been recurring in his dreams—a landscape invariably associated with his mother. As in the traditional utopia, the underlying dream is of finding refuge in the security of the maternal womb.

In addition, albeit from a different perspective, dystopian fiction reenacts the triumph of an essentially masculine dream of order. As we have seen, at the conclusion of dystopia and utopia alike (with the partial exception of *We*, where resistance continues despite the defeat of E-330 and D-503) patriarchal authority is shown as reigning supreme.[13] While this may be undesirable, it nevertheless indicates an implicit acceptance of the premise of the traditional utopia—that the establishment of a permanent, static order is at any rate practicable.[14] Writing in 1939, Orwell declared that:

The terrifying thing about the modern dictatorships is that they are something entirely unprecedented. Their end cannot be foreseen. In the past every tyranny was sooner or later overthrown, or at least resisted, because of 'human nature', which as a matter of course desired liberty. But we cannot be at all certain that 'human nature' is constant. It may be just as possible to produce a breed of men who do not wish for liberty as to produce a breed of hornless cows. The Inquisition failed, but then the Inquisition had not the resources of the modern state. The radio, press censorship, standardized education and the secret police have altered everything. Mass suggestion is a science of the last twenty years, and we do not yet know how successful it will be. [*Essays, Journalism, Letters*, Volume 1, p.419]

Paradoxically, while the concept of some kind of essential, invariant human nature lies at the root of dystopia's critique of the traditional utopia, what dystopia dramatizes is the possibility of that nature being altered—a horrifying possibility which can only be avoided by a return to the past. Thus, while the traditional utopia may be characterized as a narrative 'in which an oppositional impulse is embedded in an essentially conservative form' (Bammer, p.45), dystopian fiction, as Jean Pfaelzer argues, 'is formally and historically, structurally and contextually, a conservative genre' ('Parody and Satire', p.61)—one in which even the 'oppositional impulse' leads back to the status quo.

Nevertheless, there are alternatives to the depiction of order

triumphant: despite the defeatist tendency of much dystopian fiction—
despairing acknowledgment that the worst may very well happen—su
defeatism is not necessarily an inherent feature of the genre. Although t
result of the struggle between the all-too-human individual and virtua
superhuman authority is predictable enough, the outcome of a strug
depends not only on the relative strengths of the opponents, but also
some extent on the terms of the contest. As in real life, to confront a mc
powerful opponent directly is to court defeat, however gallant—to opt
failure, however heroic. D-503 in the presence of The Benefactor, Bern
and the Savage in that of Mustapha Mond, Winston in the hands of O'Bri
have already lost before they even meet their opponents. The transacti
is a foregone conclusion. Yet it remains to be seen whether there are r
other strategies—the fictional equivalent of guerilla tactics, perhaps, wh
the weaker side chooses the conditions of battle, and may ultimat
triumph, even over a stronger opponent.

Rewriting Dystopia: Atwood, *The Handmaid's Tale*

In this context, Atwood's *The Handmaid's Tale* is worth looking at mc
closely. Although, as has been suggested, Atwood's text is in very mu
the same tradition as its dystopian predecessors, it also reveals so
interesting departures from the norm. Gilead, Atwood's vision of
theocratic dictatorship set in the United States of the not-very-dist
future, in many ways closely resembles the worlds portrayed by Zamya
and Orwell: it, too, is an authoritarian, patriarchal state (authority bei
wielded in the name of that ultimate patriarch, God the Father), and
once again a primarily urban society, which relies on extensive surveillar
to enforce both political and sexual orthodoxy. At first sight, indeed,
would appear that the individual is equally powerless in the face
authority. Offred, the protagonist, is as helpless a victim as any of F
fictional predecessors. Even the religious basis of Atwood's dystopia mal
relatively little difference to the essential nature of the society describe
While Gilead's *values* may differ ostensibly from those of Zamyatin's O
State or Orwell's Oceania, the basic principle of insisting on univer
conformity remains constant. Despite abolishing the worship of God,
fact, Zamyatin's, Orwell's, and indeed Huxley's dystopias all effectiv
replace it with quasi-religious cults centred on a patriarchal author
figure. Religion serves, as it does in Atwood's Gilead, as an effecti
instrument of control; if it figures more largely in her dystopia, t
difference is primarily one of emphasis.

Where Atwood's fiction differs most obviously is in the gender of
protagonist, which radically alters the underlying scenario of confl

etween father and son, in which the average male confronts the omnipotent authority or the supermale patriarch, and is doomed to defeat. This is not to say, of course, that Offred *does* any more by way of effectively challenging authority: at best, she is a witness to the challenges of others— her mother's, her friend Moira's, her companion Ofglen's, all of which end in varieties of defeat. Even her attempts at escape are orchestrated by others—by her husband, Luke, or by Nick, her lover. Indeed, in many ways she is the most passive of all the rebels against dystopia. Yet for all her passivity, Offred is by no means *simply* a victim of the all-powerful state. Although she is humiliated, forced against her will into what is tantamount to slavery, separated from her friends, husband, child—even stripped of her name—she never concedes defeat, as do D-503, the Savage, or Winston Smith. In sheerly practical terms she may do even less than they by way of actively challenging authority, but what differs is the way in which her resistance is represented. Far more exclusively than any other dystopian writer, Atwood chooses to focus on the private consciousness of her protagonist—on the one realm that the State cannot successfully invade.

Whether this is in fact the case is, of course, arguable: as we have seen, a central premise of the earlier dystopias is that, in the last analysis, the State *can* control individual consciousness—that the human mind is simply another territory that can be colonized. Lobotomized, D-503 renews his allegiance to The Benefactor and the One State; tortured and brainwashed, Winston Smith lapses into maudlin adoration of Big Brother. Huxley's World State, more confident of its power, sees independent thought as so little of a threat that such radical procedures are not even needed: the small minority of dissidents can easily be contained on the margins of society, in penal colonies in places like the Falkland Islands; only the Savage, lacking the benefit of proper conditioning, tries to lead an existence wholly independent of the State—but ends up killing himself. Yet while this might seem the ultimate admission of defeat, suicide is presented in *The Handmaid's Tale* in a different light, as a radical refusal of the State's authority. Both Ofglen and Offred's predecessor as the Commander's handmaid take that route, and are to an extent honoured for doing so: while self-destructive, suicide is seen as a gesture of defiance, rather than surrender—a willed removal of oneself from the sphere of the State's coercive power. It is not Offred's solution, however: she sets as her goal survival, which in turn involves compromise, though not surrender. What *The Handmaid's Tale* charts is the process whereby Offred, even though a prisoner of the dystopian state, attempts the precarious task of preserving both her life and her integrity.

In focusing on this, Atwood resorts, like Zamyatin, to first person narration. Whereas the narrative perspective of *Brave New World* and

Nineteen Eighty-Four, showing the individual *in* society, serves to heigh
the sense of his helplessness and vulnerability, Atwood's narration sho
the State through the subjective perspective of the individual. The eff
however, is very different from that created by Zamyatin's use of the sa
device. While everything is filtered through D-503's consciousness,
narrative utterance is permeated by the controlling discourse of the St
Even as he is led by E-330 into increasingly active resistance, he enga
in an incessant inner dialogue as he tries to explain and justify his cond
in the light of the official values which he has so thoroughly internaliz
In effect, it is his subjective consciousness that constitutes the m
battleground for the tension between the conflicting ideologies of the St
and the dissidents, whose challenge to assumptions long taken for gran
causes him such acute discomfort. D-503 is already a product of the Sta
the very language he uses reflects the extent to which its values are a p
of him, and when he finally undergoes the Grand Operation to cure h
of 'fantasy'—that is, the power of independent thinking—one sense
certain feeling of relief on his part that the tormenting inner dialogue l
finally been stilled, that things have been made simple once again.

In Offred's case, however, the values of Gilead have never been par
her consciousness: she is a creature of her own past, and while this do
not automatically transform her into an active opponent of the new ord
there is little doubt as to her contempt for it. There is no battle betwe
competing discourses to be fought out within her mind, since she is alrea
clear which side she is on. Although her thoughts are about all she a
have left her, the privacy of her mind remains inviolable. For all
elaboration of the State's surveillance mechanisms, it cannot prevent l
from committing treason in her own mind, from thoughtcrime, to
Orwell's terminology—remembering with affection those whom the St
has sought to destroy, judging the system and its representatives a
finding them wanting. Admittedly, much the same could be said of Winst
Smith, prior to his arrest—but again, the difference of perspective is cruc
By focusing so exclusively on Offred's subjective consciousness, Atwc
privileges her perceptions to a far greater degree. While she is scarcely
a position to take effective action against authority, that authority is se
only through her eyes—a context in which its pretensions become m
than a little ridiculous. 'Context is all' (p.136), Offred remarks at one poi
and her narrative goes a long way towards demonstrating the truth of tl

In the context of Offred's narrative, for example, patriarchal author
no longer looms as large: in place of the superhuman, machine-l
Benefactor, the Godlike Ford, the all-seeing Big Brother, is—a vo
Nominally, Gilead is a society dedicated to the great glory of God the Fath
but from Offred's point of view His is not a presence, but an absence:

His place there are merely rather pathetic surrogates—the Commanders. Unlike the representatives of authority elsewhere (the suave Mustapha Mond, the brutal O'Brien) the Commanders almost invariably appear in contexts which render them ridiculous. Offred's own Commander, with his desire for the forbidden delights of Scrabble, his furtive glee over the schoolboy obscenities scrawled in his Latin textbook, his excitement at a trip to a brothel where sexual allure is provided by old cheerleaders' outfits and secondhand Bunny costumes, is merely ludicrous. Even his real power, his power over life and death, is undermined by being presented in the context of Offred's accompanying awareness of his confusion and incompetence. He appears genuinely puzzled by the course of events, surprised by Offred's dislike of her role, as if dimly aware that the perfect order that has been created is not quite working as it should. And as a representative of God the Father, he is conspicuously lacking in the sexual vitality of the Old Testament patriarchs, being both probably sterile (as even his wife concedes) and sexually inept: 'I've had him,' Moira remarks offhandedly, 'he's the pits' (p.228). Unlike Mond or O'Brien, Offred's Commander appears vulnerable: at the end he is shown as 'worried and helpless' (p.276), visibly shrinking as he sees himself being dragged down by Offred's apparent disgrace—the victim, in effect, of his failure to control someone he had regarded as a mere possession.

Nor do the other male figures fare much better. In her earlier fictions, Atwood's virtuosity in evoking sexual disgust is already apparent: in *Life Before Man*, for instance, a woman describes a sexual encounter with a particularly bland civil servant as like being in bed with 'a large and fairly active slab of Philadelphia cream cheese' (p.213)—and in *The Handmaid's Tale* she allows that virtuosity full rein. At the Prayvaganza, Offred reflects that while the presiding Commander, with his uniform and decorations, may appear impressive enough, she has the power to imagine him otherwise: 'in bed with his Wife and Handmaid, fertilizing away like mad, like a rutting salmon' (p.204). And at the mass wedding ceremony for military heroes newly returned from the front, Offred again imagines the reality of their sexual lives:

> .... momentous grunts and sweating, damp furry encounters; or better, ignominious failures, cocks like three-week-old carrots, anguished fumblings upon flesh cold and unresponsive as uncooked fish. [p.209]   .

Laughter becomes a powerful weapon in *The Handmaid's Tale*. 'It does so do good. It does,' insists Moira (p.208) when Offred (repressing her impulse to giggle) protests at her crude but vivid fantasy of one of the trainees engaging in oral sex with the redoubtable Aunt Lydia. In its

carnivalesque reassertion of the physicality of the body, such laught
implies the hollowness of the régime's official façade of reason ar
spirituality. Laughter asserts the humanity of the person who laughs, whi
at the same time undermining the authority of those who are laughed a
For all its limitations as a practical political tool (although satire and ridicu
have never been particularly welcome to those in power), in the conte
of a fictional narrative it decisively affects the impression made by tl
representatives of the dystopian state. While Zamyatin, too, sees laught
as a liberating force, it works only sporadically: although D-503 may laug
at the bald-headed man who is the reality behind the cast-iron image
The Benefactor, his power is too real to be laughed at for long. Mustapl
Mond and O'Brien are not laughed at at all. In *The Handmaid's Ta.*
however, 'mirth rhymes with birth' (p.138): laughter provides a way o
of the all-embracing security which the State seeks to impose on tl
individuals whom it is striving to mould in its own image. Where tl
dystopian dissidents of Zamyatin, Huxley, and Orwell seek refuge from tl
State's authority in the womb-like security of the past, Atwood presen
liberation as a process of going forward, into the unknown.

In addition, laughter represents the assertion of alternative perspectiv
on reality; it speaks a different language, one which challenges the offici
discourse of the State. Beneath its surface frivolity lies something mo
serious: while the schoolboy dog-Latin—*Nolite te bastardes carborundorum*—
scrawled on the floor of Offred's cupboard may be merely a furtive joke
the Commander, for Offred it is a coded inscription, a gesture of defian
from a woman whose death has put her beyond the reach of the State
authority. While, as Orwell perceived, the standardization ar
impoverishment of language is an essential of the State's control
individual thought, Atwood's rebels exploit the richness and ambiguity
a linguistic realm over which the State has no jurisdiction. (It is significa
that Offred's interactions with the Commander, outside the sphere of the
official relations, involve their playing a competitive word game.) In tl
end, the State's attempt to impose the authority of its own officia
monologic discourse is thwarted by the sheer variety of associations whic
language derives from contexts beyond its control. The very codeword
the resistance—Mayday—is fraught with complex and ambiguo
associations wholly alien to the simplistic fundamentalism of the dystopia
state: Mayday is a call for help in a foreign language, a carnival remind
of pagan fertility rituals, and the chief festival of international socialisn
In the context of the book, it is also a declaration of independence.

In Atwood's hands, then, opposition becomes both more complex ar
more far-reaching than in the earlier dystopias: what she grasps is tl
paradox that the farther the State attempts to extend its power, the mo

arenas it creates where resistance is possible. As Barthes argues in his discussion of Fourier, the utopian impulse to determine everything down to the last detail ultimately deconstructs itself, establishing a system so complex that it inevitably breaks down. Thus, the more that is forbidden, the greater the number of potentially subversive actions becomes. And while Offred makes no effort to conceal her weaknesses, her defeats, her failures in courage, her passivity, her shameful dependence on her lover, her opposition to the monolithic authority of the State is in fact a good deal more effective than she realizes. However passive her resistance, she provides an audience for the resistance of others, a space in which the implications of their actions can resonate. The point that Atwood stresses is that no matter how powerless, how often defeated, the rebel is *not* alone. When Moira escapes from the Re-Education Centre, after overpowering Aunt Lydia in the washroom, hers is not merely a personal bid for freedom; at the same time she exposes the limitations of authority:

> Moira was our fantasy. We hugged her to us, she was with us in secret, a giggle; she was the lava beneath the crust of daily life. In the light of Moira, the Aunts were less fearsome and more absurd. Their power had a flaw to it. They could be shanghaied in toilets. [p.125]

It is, indeed, in Bakhtin's terms, a classic example of the carnivalesque uncrowning of official authority. Aunt Elizabeth, the symbol not only of authority, but of female purity, is overpowered in a lavatory overflowing with excrement; she is led downstairs to the basement, where she is stripped of her clothing, and dressed in the red garments of the Handmaid, while Moira now dons the robes of authority. In one action the official hierarchy of dystopian society is completely reversed.

Thus, despite the extent of the State's attempt to impose the authority of an all-embracing static system, the result is merely to increase the potential scope of opposition. Even something so apparently trivial as gossip becomes subversive: when Offred asks the Commander to tell her 'what's going on', her choice of language implies a process, a continuous dynamic which may at any moment result in change. The necessity of imposing control implies the continued existence of something that has to be controlled. The television news, though rigorously censored by the authorities, implies by its self-evident selectivity the fact of other events, which are *not* reported. The more absolute the authority the State seeks to wield, the more precarious it becomes. This is not to say, of course, that this renders the collapse of authority inevitable. As Stuart Hall observes:

> The multiplication of new points of antagonism ... characteristic of

our emerging 'post-industrial' societies, while making available n⟨
potential sites of intervention, further fragments the political fie⟨
dispersing rather than unifying the different social constituenci⟨
[Quoted in Levitas, *Concept of Utopia*, p.197]

Like Orwell and Huxley, and to a lesser extent Zamyatin, Atwood choo⟨
not to address the question of *how* effective resistance to the all-power
state may be mounted (an evasion which clearly echoes the utopi⟨
reluctance to specify how the more perfect society might be created):
best, she shows more clearly the points at which it is vulnerable.

Nevertheless, it is clear that Atwood effectively transforms both the m⟨
terms in the classic dystopian equation, creating a protagonist whc
passive resistance and satiric eye produce a very different impact than
the direct challenges to authority presented by the male rebels of earl
dystopian fiction, while at the same time stripping patriarchal authority
much of its aura of invulnerability. In addition, she is more sceptical of t
basic premise of utopia and dystopia alike, that the creation of an enduri
total system is actually *possible*. Unlike Zamyatin's One State, Huxle⟨
World State, or Orwell's Oceania, Gilead has clearly indicated limits, bc
spatial and temporal. There are other places to which escape is possib⟨
and it is apparent that, as a social experiment, it has only a finite existence
In the epilogue, Gilead becomes the focus of a twenty-second centu
academic symposium, from which it becomes clear that its existence w⟨
merely a transient historical phenomenon—albeit one which provided
abundance of research opportunities. Unlike the earlier dystopias, whc
terror lies partly in the threat of their being eternal, Gilead is ephemer
deprived of an eternal future in part because of its inability to sever its⟨
from the past. The connection with contemporary reality, which utopi
fiction seeks to obscure, and dystopian society to obliterate, is here clea⟨
manifest. Gilead's fatal weakness lies in its inability to cut itself off frc
history: Atwood demonstrates what is one of the principal limitations
all revolutions, whether for good or ill: the fact that they are made by thc
who have been conditioned by the values of the society which t
revolution seeks to overthrow.

It is the State's belief, of course, that this limitation can be overcom
The 'aunts' repeatedly assure their sceptical charges that, while they m⟨
find it difficult to adjust to the new order, it will be easier for generatio⟨
to come:

> You are a transitional generation, said Aunt Lydia. It is the hard⟨
> for you. We know the sacrifices you are being expected to make.
> is hard when men revile you. For the ones who come after you,
> will be easier. They will accept their duties with willing hearts.

She did not say: Because they will have no memories, of any other way. [p.111]

Until that time, however, memory, with the different perspectives it provides, remains a potent threat to the authority of the State. Offred is just one of innumerable individuals who remember how things were before, who remember the outrages perpetrated in the name of the new order, who can contrast now with then, and consider the implications of the difference. Nor are the rulers themselves immune to the power of memory, to the influence of the past: unable to control their previously socialized lust for women as sex-objects, they recreate the brothels which their puritan revolution was meant to abolish. Between the hypocrisy of the rulers and the mocking laughter of the ruled, it is clear that the new order is constructed on shaky foundations.

In both its narrative approach, then, and in its presentation of the nature of the authoritarian state's limitations, *The Handmaid's Tale* represents a radical extension of the dystopian critique of the traditional utopia. Nor is it only the limitations of utopian idealism or authoritarian trends in contemporary society that Atwood seeks to expose; in places, it is clear that *The Handmaid's Tale* is also addressing the flawed assumptions underlying specific aspects of earlier dystopian fiction. In particular, Atwood challenges Zamyatin's and Orwell's stereotypical depiction of traditional images of female sexuality as more 'natural' than, and hence subversive of the State's sexual norms. As we have seen, both Zamyatin's E-330 and Orwell's Julia resort to old-fashioned methods of sexual allure by way of defying the official sexual ethic of the State, and by doing so render themselves far more attractive than the state-approved partner with whom the protagonist has previously been involved. In *The Handmaid's Tale*, however, the equivalent scene, in which Offred sheds her nun-like uniform and puts on make-up, high heels, and a revealing outfit largely comprised of feathers, is designed to illustrate, not the subversive power of 'natural' female sexuality, but rather the extent to which such stereotypes are merely the obverse of the male fear of female sexuality which informs Gilead's puritanism. While Gilead's stringent moral code is ostensibly designed to protect women from predatory male sexuality, its designers continue to dream of the old stereotypes, and find their sexual outlets at that archetypal locale of male fantasy, the brothel. Perhaps the most ludicrous aspect of Offred's trip to the brothel with her Commander is his pathetic belief that the trip is somehow exciting for *her*. Where Offred defies the State's sexual norms is not in overt displays of male-approved traditional femininity, but in her illicit encounters with the Commander's chauffeur, which take place in the darkness, and which she never really

finds words to describe. The subversiveness of such sexual conduct li
familiarly enough, in its privacy—something which her monthly coupli
in the Commander's marriage bed signally lacks—yet even so, Off
remains dubious as to just how far this too constitutes a form of comprom
with male authority. Where Winston Smith sees his sexual relations w
Julia as 'a battle, the climax a victory ... a blow struck against the Party
a political act' (p.112), for Offred, so simplistic an opposition of 'natu
sexuality to official authority is impossible. Having experienced
unequal sexual power relations not only of Gilead, but of the society t
preceded it, she cannot help but be aware the sexual arena is one whe
while rebellion may be possible, it remains fraught with complicity.

Thus, *The Handmaid's Tale* presents a dystopia where the lines of ba
are far more ambiguously drawn. Offred's challenges to the Stat
authority are not always uncritically presented as positive, and while
memory constitutes an alternative perspective by which the State can
judged, there is far less of the nostalgia that characterizes both *We* a
Nineteen Eighty-Four, where the past is portrayed as somehow m
authentic, more 'real' than the present. By contrast, Offred's recollectic
of contemporary America, with its pornography, its sex industry,
continual threat of rape and violent assault, hardly offer a glitter
alternative to the new morality of Gilead. Indeed, it becomes abundan
clear in the course of the narrative that many of her survival skills,
capacity for secrecy and passive resistance, were learned from
experience as a woman in the society which Gilead replaced. Indeed, wh
Gilead evidently collapses at last, it is clear that the world of the future t
succeeds its fall is far from ideal either. The academic discussion of Gile
with its sexist jokes, its smug refusal to take any kind of moral stance
its discussion of what happened, indicates much the same kind
intellectual elitism and abdication of responsibility that was presuma
one of the preconditions for the establishment of Gilead in the first pla

This sense of the force of historical continuity, of the overlap betwe
past, present, and future, enables Atwood to avoid the often simplis
polarized alternatives of earlier dystopian fiction. The dualistic oppositi
between future and past—the one associated with totalitarian conformi
the other with a vaguely liberal conception of 'freedom'—is replaced
an altogether more complex sense of their interrelationship. The resul
a vision which is critical, not only of utopia, or of the society to wh
utopia proposes an alternative, but also of the dystopian response itself
is this critical—and indeed, self-critical—impulse which may be seen
underlie a series of attempts to likewise transform the nature of the utopi
vision.

DREAMS OF FREEDOM

5. Libertarian Alternatives: Morris, *News from Nowhere*; Bogdanov, *Red Star*; Huxley, *Island*

The basic premise of dystopian fiction, of course, is rooted in the assumption that the utopian ideal is *inherently* repressive—that the establishment of the machinery of State repression nevertheless has its origins in a genuinely utopian impulse. Not the least disturbing aspect of *We*, *Brave New World*, and *The Handmaid's Tale*, in fact, is the apparent sincerity of the belief of those in authority that they are actually doing good. Only in *Nineteen Eighty-Four*, where O'Brien brazenly admits that power is its own reward, is the rationale that authority is wielded in the best interests of society as a whole abandoned—but this is very much the exception rather than the rule. The patriarchal authority figures of the other dystopian narratives—The Benefactor, Mustapha Mond, even the Commanders—share with Wells's Samurai, the officers of Bellamy's industrial army, and the priest-rulers of the City of the Sun, the conviction that authority is a duty rather than a matter of self-interest. Whatever the *effect* of their exercise of that authority, the underlying aspiration remains in keeping with the traditional utopian ideal: the creation of a better, more rational social order, from whose all-embracing security the citizen cannot help but benefit.

Yet a distaste for the generally repressive and authoritarian tenor of the traditional utopia, such as that which activates the dystopian critique of the utopian ideal, can also be combined with very different approaches—approaches which do not necessarily presuppose the utopian aspiration to be flawed in itself. In *News from Nowhere* (1890), for example, William Morris is among the first to call into question the premises of the traditional utopia by proposing an alternative embodying radically different values: libertarian and decentralist, rather than repressive and authoritarian. Morris's vision is of a Communist far future in which the state has withered away, and in this he is followed by Alexander Bogdanov, whose *Red Star* (1908), written in the aftermath of the abortive Russian revolution of 1905, envisages an equally decentralized (although noticeably less pastoral) communist society—removed in space rather than time, however, being set on the planet Mars. Nor is this the only ideological perspective from which the traditional utopia has been reimagined: Aldous Huxley's *Island* (1962) offers another libertarian vision, but one whose emphasis on spiritual values seems explicitly designed to counter the materialist bias of the Wellsian utopia. Whether, however, such conscious challenges to the values and political assumptions of the traditional utopia are any more successful a recipe for resolving the problematic implications of the traditional narrative paradigm than, say, Wells's primarily narrative experimentation, remains to be seen.

While all three works indicate a clear awareness of the tradition of utopian narrative, it is those of Morris and Huxley that most directly address its limitations. Indeed, both *News from Nowhere* and *Island* were conceived of in direct response to what each perceived as the problematic character of specific works in the utopian tradition. *News from Nowhere* was quite deliberately designed as a rebuttal of Bellamy's *Looking Backward*, which Morris had already reviewed in extremely hostile terms in *The Commonweal* the paper of the Socialist League. First published in serial form in the pages of *The Commonweal*, its polemic intent is quite clear: to offer what Morris saw as a genuinely Socialist alternative to the stifling conformity of Bellamy's utopia. Huxley likewise set out, in *Island*, to remedy the deficiencies of an earlier work—in this case his own dystopia, *Brave New World*—which he had criticized in a subsequent Foreword (1946) for its lack of any positive alternative to the 'insanity' of Utopia on the one hand and the 'lunacy' of the Savage on the other (*Brave New World*, p.7). *Island* represents the working out of that positive alternative, whose outlines are first suggested in the Foreword.

News from Nowhere

It is not difficult to see why Morris so disliked *Looking Backward*: almost every aspect of Bellamy's utopia, from its regimentation to the crass vulgarity of its author's conception of the role of culture, represented the virtual antithesis of everything Morris stood for.[1] Nevertheless, it is worth examining in more detail some of the specific objections which Morris raised in his highly critical review, particularly given the light which they shed on the nature of the countervailing ideals which he sought to embody in *News from Nowhere*. To begin with, Morris accurately perceived that while *Looking Backward* purported to offer a vision of a society in which class conflict had been resolved, its values were exclusively those of the middle class:

> The only ideal of life which such a man can see is that of the industrious *professional* middle-class men of today purified from their crime of complicity with the monopolist class, and become independent instead of being, as they now are, parasitical.[2]

As we have already seen, Dr Leete's sympathy for 'the plight of the few educated' in the late nineteenth century, living in a society largely comprised of 'ignorant, boorish, coarse, wholly uncultivated men and women' (*Looking Backward*, p.122), to say nothing of his singular view that the 'rich and cultured' of the period were 'little better off' than the poor (p.122) gives a fair idea of Bellamy's class bias. To Morris, Bellamy's utopian ideal represents, not radical social reform, but rather the maintenance of existing privilege: an ideal utopian only in its abolition of guilt. Where Bellamy offers the vision of a world in which a bourgeois lifestyle is available to all, Morris sees its maintenance as incompatible with the existence of social and economic justice. Culture, for Morris, is an *integral* aspect of society, a superstructural expression of its economic foundations: the transformation of society's economic basis and political institutions must necessarily transform its cultural values and the forms in which they are expressed. What he thought of Bellamy's attempt to preserve unchanged the values of the late nineteenth century bourgeoisie in a radically different socioeconomic context may be divined from his comment, in a letter to Bruce Glasier: 'I wouldn't care to live in such a cockney paradise' (Glasier, p.198).

Nevertheless, it was on the organization of Bellamy's utopia, and the assumptions underlying it, that Morris concentrated most of his fire. The elaborate structure of Bellamy's industrial army, and the complex system of incentives to productive labour, ranging from early retirement to the prospect of a more attractive marital partner, struck him as merely laughable:

> Mr Bellamy worries himself unnecessarily in the seeking (with obvious failure) some incentive to labour to replace the fear of starvation, which is at present our only one, whereas it cannot too often be repeated that the true incentive to useful and happy labour is and must be pleasure of the work itself. [p.506]

The provision of early retirement, in particular—Bellamy's utopian equivalent of the paradisiacal dream of idleness—was something which, in Morris's view, wholly missed the point:

> ....everybody is to begin the serious work of production at the age of twenty-one, work three years as a labourer, and then choose his skilled occupation and work till he is forty-five, when he is to knock off his work and amuse himself (improve his mind, if he has one left him). Heavens! think of a man of forty-five changing his habits suddenly and by compulsion! [p.505]

In *Looking Backward*, work is a necessary evil, its rigours palliated by an elaborate system of honours and rewards, but still sufficiently arduous as to require both strict discipline and a complex supervisory process to ensure

it gets done—the whole being coordinated by the industrial equivalent •
a military high command. Conformity is enforced, while individu
responsibility is minimized—very much, in fact, as it is in the earlier utopi.
of More and Campanella—and to this Morris vigorously objected:

> It is necessary to point out that there are some socialists who do n•
> think that the problem of the organization of life and necessary labou
> can be dealt with by a huge centralization, worked by a kind of mag
> for which no one feels himself responsible; that on the contrary
> will be necessary for the unit of administration to be small enoug
> for every citizen to feel himself responsible for its details, and t
> interested in them; that the individual man cannot shuffle off th
> business of life onto the shoulders of an abstraction called the Stat
> but must deal with it in conscious association with each other; th.
> variety of life is as much the aim of a true Communism as equalit
> of condition, and that nothing but a union of these two will brin
> about real freedom ... [pp.506–7]

Morris also took exception to what he saw as Bellamy's uncritic.
enthusiasm for technology (which, as we have already seen, serves i
Looking Backward largely to conceal the processes of production), and sti
more so to his assumption that the transition to a utopian society could b
a painless, automatic process, devoid of conflict. Nevertheless, it was clearl
the centralization of Bellamy's utopia, the State's authoritarian assumptio•
of responsibility and denial of individual agency, that he saw as mo:
pernicious. One can only imagine, given the vehemence of Bellamy
response to being labelled a 'socialist,' how he must have reacted to Morris
dismissal of his utopia as 'State Communism.'

It is Communism of a very different cast, however, that underlie
Morris's counterblast,[3] *News from Nowhere*—and that Morris, writing i
1890, consciously conceived of his utopia as Communist is wort
emphasizing. While the old-fashioned view of Morris as only incidentall
(if indeed at all) a Marxist has been comprehensively demolished by th•
studies of Paul Meier and E.P. Thompson,[4] a lingering tendency to se•
Morris's utopia as a work of only vaguely radical sympathies persist:
Engels' description of Morris as a 'very rich art enthusiast but untalente•
politician,'[5] and as a 'sentimental socialist,'[6] perhaps encourages such
view—as indeed do such attempts to conscript *News from Nowhere* for th•
anarchist cause as Peter Kropotkin's description of it as 'perhaps the mo:
thoroughly and deeply anarchist conception of the future society that ha
ever been written' (quoted in Meier, Volume 1, p.xxxviii). Morri:
however, was in no doubt as to the character of the society he wa
describing. His own struggles with the anarchists within the Socialis

League had given him a keen sense of the distinction between Anarchism and Communism, and in *News from Nowhere* the form of social organization is explicitly described as being the latter (p.76). While there is no longer formal government as such—decisions being for the most part taken at the local, communal level—this is in keeping with the withering away of the State envisaged in Marxist theory as characterizing Communism's final phase.[7] And while there is of course a millenarian element in such a vision, a static quality very much akin to that of the traditional utopia, where Morris differs is in his refusal to gloss over the process of reaching the desired goal. Unlike Bellamy, whose utopia comes into being with smooth inevitability, by consensus, and 'with absolutely no violence', Morris emphasizes the sheer difficulty involved in the creation of a more perfect society. In marked contrast to the perfunctory accounts of utopia's origins which characterize the traditional narrative paradigm, Morris devotes an entire chapter—the longest in the book—to describing the brutal class conflict from which his utopian society emerged, and the arduous process of reconstruction which was involved.

Throughout the narrative, in fact, Morris consistently calls attention to what other utopian fictions seek to conceal: the problematic nature of the connection between reality and its utopian alternative. Rather than creating elaborate rational explanations to account for the narrator's passage into utopia, Morris deliberately emphasizes the precarious, dreamlike quality of his presence in the society of the future. Both William Guest (as he chooses to call himself, without any pretence that it is his real name) and the utopians show an awareness that his account of himself does not really make sense, and both his embarrassment when their questions become too awkward and their courteous, but at the same time clearly evident avoidance of angles of inquiry that may expose the improbability of his story serve to call attention to the narrative's fictional character—rather as Wells was to do later in *A Modern Utopia*. Often, and especially when the most disturbing aspects of the past are conjured up, the dream seems to fray at the edges—so that even the utopians become half aware of the reality by which the narrator is haunted. Following his long discussion of the past with Old Hammond, Dick (who acts as the narrator's utopian guide) remarks:

> 'I am glad to have you again, and to find you and my kinsman have not quite talked yourselves into another world; I was half suspecting ... that you would be vanishing away from us, and began to picture my kinsman sitting in the hall staring at nothing and finding that he had been talking a while past to nobody.' [p.115]

Clara, Dick's lover, likewise seems aware that something is amiss:

'I don't like this: something or another troubles me, and I feel as if something untoward were going to happen. You have been talking of past miseries to the guest, and have been living in past unhappy times, and it is in the air all round us, and makes us feel as if we were longing for something that we cannot have.' [p.116]

Morris rarely allows the establishment of a comfortable suspension of disbelief: the very precariousness of the dream constantly calls attention to the reality which it only barely veils. As E.P. Thompson suggests:

[Morris] allows an ambiguity to hang over the narrator throughout: he is troubled to understand how he is there himself; the other characters sense him as someone different, and this is a disturbing influence on their relationship; he has premonitions that he must return ... [pp.694–5]

Rather as Wells was to do in *A Modern Utopia*, Morris deliberately draws attention to the fictional character of his utopian vision, and in this Thompson argues that his aim is to make it clear that what is being offered is not so much a blueprint, as a vision of utopian possibility. Rather than setting out in detail the mechanisms of an alternative social order, Morris may be seen as engaged in what Bloch was later to propose as the main goal of utopian speculation—'the education of desire' (Thompson, p.791).[8]

Other critics have gone still further, taking this, along with Morris's conscious references to his own actual political involvements, as prefiguring the self-referential practice of more recent fiction.[9] Yet while it is undoubtedly true that Morris's focus on the problematic nature of the relationship between utopia and reality is relatively unusual, it by no means enables him to avoid entirely the problems inherent in the traditional narrative paradigm. Despite the perceptiveness of his critique of the political shortcomings of Bellamy's utopia, Morris seems less aware of its *narrative* limitations—many of which *News from Nowhere* reproduces. Suvin argues that whereas Bellamy's political stance is reflected in 'a closed and often oppressive narrative structure' (*Metamorphoses*, p.189), Morris succeeds in creating an 'open and airier structure ... homologous to his warmer, nonregimenting politics' (p.189), yet this is surely to understate the extent of the narrative parallels between the two works. For example, while the narrator's interactions with the utopians—with Old Hammond, with Ellen, with Dick and Clara—communicate more of a sense of genuine dialogue than do Julian West's with Dr Leete and his daughter, the essential passivity of the narrator, which the convention of the visit to utopia imposes, remains. While the transmission of information concerning the utopian society is more deftly handled than in *Looking Backward* (even the garrulous Old Hammond is considerably more succinct than Dr Leete), the narrator is still condemned by his ignorance of the nature of utopian society to be the passive recipient of information, to rely on guides to show him what he ought to see. And while Morris's utopians do exhibit slightly more curiosity concerning their visitor's past experience, his first-hand knowledge of the past serves largely (as is the case in *Looking Backward*) to confirm their existing preconceptions as to how awful it was. Morris may be, as Thompson argues, more alive to the political realities involved in the transformation of society than other utopian writers of the period, yet he experiences similar difficulties in translating theory into narrative practice. Although his utopia posits a far more radical departure from the ideological assumptions of his own society than do the utopias of Bellamy and Wells, whose values are in essence those of the contemporary bourgeoisie, translated into a context where they can be perpetuated without the inconvenience of guilt about those less well off, this greater radicalism often seems at odds with the implications of his utopian narrative.

Indeed, for a utopia purportedly grounded in Marxist theory, *News from Nowhere* seems curiously backward looking. Even granted that, as Thompson points out, it 'must not be, and was never intended to be, read as a literal picture of Communist society' (p.696), the degree to which it is permeated by a sense of nostalgia for a world that has been lost is striking.[10] From the moment of the narrator's first plunge into the cleansed and cleansing waters of a River Thames in which the salmon swim once more, the overwhelming emphasis of Morris's description of the utopian future is on restoration rather than innovation. Ugly factories and jerry-built housing have been torn down, and much of the urban wasteland of the late nineteenth century has been reclaimed by fields and woodland, the 'big murky ... centres of manufacture' (p.58) having been replaced by a decentralized network of workshops. Although we are told that 'all work which would be irksome to do by hand is done by immensely improved machinery' (p.82), the work that is actually *described*—be it harvesting, construction, or manufacture—is almost invariably manual labour. While the rags of the Victorian poor and the stiff formal attire of the ruling class have been replaced by elegant costumes of a decidedly mediaeval cast, both these and the artifacts which Morris describes in such loving detail—the glassware, crockery, pipes, furniture—are evidently the work of individual craftsmen. Indeed, so far as what we are actually *shown*, there is little sign of any form of modern technology in Morris's utopia, other than the 'force barges' used to transport goods by water. The railway, we learn, has disappeared, and in the world of the future the only other methods of transport we encounter are rowing boat and horse and carriage. All this, together with the pastoral setting of the latter part of the narrative, lends an almost Arcadian quality to Morris's utopia: in places, his vision of a Communist future reads more like an evocation of some vanished golden age.

What begins to emerge, in fact, is a gap between Morris's imaginative response to the all too evident squalor and suffering which attended the rapid industrialization of a hitherto predominantly rural Britain, and the theoretical stance which informs both his critique of Bellamy and much of Old Hammond's outline of utopian society. While, as a Marxist, Morris acknowledges the *necessity* of Capitalism as a phase in the development of society, an inescapable precondition for the transition to Socialism, his distaste for it is often couched in terms more suggestive of the romanticism of his earlier years. When he talks elsewhere of the need to 'be our own Goths, and at whatever cost break up again the new tyrannous Empire of Capitalism' (quoted in Meier, Volume 1, p.255), his choice of terminology is surely significant, suggestive not merely of the fascination with barbarian culture so often reflected in his other writings, but of an attitude towards existing society whose impulse is primarily destructive. In 1888, in a lecture entitled 'The Society of the Future,' Morris declared that 'my *special* leading motive as a Socialist is hatred of civilization; my ideal of the new society would not be satisfied unless that Society destroyed civilization' (quoted in May Morris, Volume 2, p.457)—and in that emphasis on the destruction, the erasure of the existing order, he seems closer to the spirit of the conservative Romantic critique of modern industrialism than to the Marxist view of Capitalism as a necessary phase in the dialectical process of history.[11] While it is possible to argue that the pastoral character of *News from Nowhere* is in keeping with Engels' insistence on the necessity of the 'abolition of the antithesis between town and country' (p.331),[12] it is at the same time no coincidence that Morris was a great admirer of Richard Jefferies' *After London*, a novel which charts with extraordinary vividness the disappearance of virtually every trace of modern civilization, as resurgent Nature obliterates roads, houses, towns, cities, under a tangle of undergrowth and rampant vegetation. While Morris's vision, in *News from Nowhere*, is one of humanity living in harmony with the natural world rather than struggling to survive, there are clear echoes of Jefferies in his description of a future London where much of Victorian suburbia has been re-covered by woodland which stretches from Kensington 'northward and west right over Paddington and a little way down Notting Hill':

> ... thence it runs north-east to Primrose Hill, and so on; rather narrow strip of it gets through Kingsland to Stoke-Newington and Clapton, where it spreads out along the heights above the Lee marshes; on the other side of which ... is Epping Forest holding out a hand to it. [p.22][13]

To an even greater extent than Wells, who cheerfully demolishes the world's major cities in preparation for the establishment of utopia in *In the Days of the Comet*, Morris celebrates the erasure of his own society as a necessary precondition for the creation of a better future:[14] much of the narrative fascination of the latter part of the book, which charts the narrator's voyage up the Thames, lies in its insistent emphasis on what is no longer there. Where the often obsessive specificity of detail which characterizes the traditional utopian paradigm suggests a colonialist desire to fill the space into which utopia can be imagined, Morris's concern seems rather to make it empty again—or perhaps, more accurately, to render visible once more the outline of an ideal order that is *already there*.

Thus, while the lack of regimentation in Morris's society, its emphasis on freely chosen cooperation rather than imposed conformity, sharply differentiates it from virtually all previous utopian fictions, it remains fraught with contradictions. In part, this can be ascribed to Morris's adherence to a narrative strategy that differs little from that of the traditional utopia. As we have seen, the standard format of the visit to utopia produces the same essential passivity on the part of the narrator, whose interactions with the utopians, while somewhat livelier than is normally the case, are scarcely more inherently dialogic. William Guest has already assented in advance to the desirability of utopia; the utopians have already determined their attitude towards the past which he represents—and it is clear that, as in most such exchanges, the values of the utopians are to be accepted as authoritative. As Morson argues, what is involved is not so much a dialectical interaction between competing value systems, from which a new truth emerges, but rather—as in the traditional utopian paradigm—a final determination of value, different in character from any that preceded it:

> News from nowhere differs from all other news in that it will never be outdated. Thus, when the citizens of Morris' pastoral paradise condemn nineteenth-century urban architecture, they are not simply expressing the opinion of one period and civilization about another. They are, rather, voicing a final determination of aesthetic value, one which, unlike any of our evaluations, will never become but one chapter in the history of taste. Utopia anachronizes anachronism. [p.121]

As a result, all that really emerges from the exchanges in *News from Nowhere* is the traditional linear and episodic narrative in which the distinctive excellences of utopia are revealed. Once again, however, as in the utopias of Bellamy and Wells, a gap emerges between what the narrator is told, and what he is shown.

For example, while *News from Nowhere* contains numerous vivi
descriptions of the look of things—utensils, clothes, furnishings—th
process whereby they are produced (for all Morris's emphasis on the virtue
of unalienated labour) is hardly more evident than is the case in *Lookin*
Backward. Harvesting and construction work are fleetingly glimpsed at a
the narrator and his utopian companions make their leisurely way up th
Thames, but the latter part of the narrative is, significantly enough, a
extended account of *going* to work, but one where the goal is never actuall
reached: the dream breaks off before the actual process of working can b
experienced. Nor, for that matter, is there any more direct evidence of th
processes whereby society is governed. While Old Hammond offers th
narrator a brief account of the participatory democracy obtaining at th
local level, the only interactions we are actually *shown* are purely socia
the pleasant and courteous exchanges that occur over the rituals c
hospitality.

Indeed, for an avowedly Communist utopia, the lack of politica
emphasis is striking. Even Old Hammond's account focuses more on wha
has disappeared than on what exists. Laws have disappeared, as ha
money—the absence of the latter rendering the former redundant—an
shopkeeping has become, quite literally, child's play. Morris's future societ
is one where the Houses of Parliament are preserved only as a
archaeological curiosity, and as a storehouse for horse manure—a
amusing reflection of the anti-parliamentarian stance of Morris and th
Socialist League at the time—and when the narrator inquires as to th
nature of utopian politics, he is told that utopia has none. Any discussio
of politics, Old Hammond tells him, would resemble the chapter in Niel
Horrebow's *Natural History of Iceland*, entitled 'Concerning Snakes,' whic
reads in its entirety: 'No snakes of any kind are to be met with throughou
the whole island' (p.72). As Suvin argues

> ... overcompensating for Bellamy's state apparatus and clear lines c
> power, *News from Nowhere* omits all machinery for determinin
> priorities between communes or any other basic units. Yet a
> production, including very much an automated one, requires—a
> long as it is not simply magical—coordination and a (however trul
> participatory) system of vertical decision making ... *News from*
> *Nowhere* sacrifices human productivity in order to get rid of Statisr
> and technocracy. [*Metamorphoses*, p.182][15]

The markedly apolitical character of Morris's future society in its turi
highlights a further contradiction—the fact that, for all Morris's keei
awareness of the historical process, his is a utopia in many ways hardl
less static than those of his predecessors. The world he portrays, reflectin

s it does that most utopian element in Communist ideology, the belief in he ultimate withering away of the State, is one where the dialectic of class truggle has run its course—and where history has, in effect, come to an nd. In subtitling *News from Nowhere* 'An Epoch of Rest,' Morris even ighlights this aspect—the fact that his utopia, though the *result* of a lynamic process, has reached stasis: 'the present rest and happiness of omplete Communism' (p.160). It is scarcely surprising in consequence to ind that the resultant chronotope differs little from that of the traditional itopia. Extension in space, the journey in the course of which utopia is evealed, fails to conceal the blurring of time so characteristic of the utopian ision. In the eternal summer which Morris's future appears to enjoy, vhere all that changes from day to day is location, time has little more neaning than it does in *Looking Backward*, where a week is all it takes for he otherwise bemused Julian West to secure the hand of Edith Leete in narriage, despite her being some hundred years his junior. Under utopian onditions, the ageing process has been radically affected: although the pectacular longevity of the City of the Sun, where a lifespan of two nundred years in not unknown, may not have been attained, the biblical 10rm of three score years and ten has certainly been surpassed. Old Iammond, for instance, is over a hundred and five, yet the narrator is eminded, on seeing him, of his own face in the mirror. Age, rather than ignalling the passage of time, often suggests that its normal operations 1ave been suspended: the narrator mistakes a woman of forty-two for a wenty year old, while he, though only fifty-five,[16] is taken for a man in iis eighties. Clara, in fact, goes so far as to suggest that prolonged exposure o utopia might even reverse the ageing process:

> 'I think in a few months we shall make him look younger; and I should like to see what he was like with the wrinkles smoothed out of his face. Don't you think he will look younger after a little time with us?' [p.116]

Such dislocations of the normal temporal process are not uncommon n the traditional utopia, where, as Bloch suggests, longevity is often offered is a rationalized substitute for the more fantastic dream of immortality vhich characterizes visions of paradise or the millennium. Yet this is by 10 means the only feature which *News from Nowhere* shares with more raditional utopian dreams of order; indeed, in some respects, it resembles he Renaissance utopia still more closely than do the visions of Bellamy ind Wells. While universal co-operation between nations is the norm, thus obviating the need for the ruthless defensive precautions described in More's *Utopia*, or *The New Atlantis*'s concern with maintaining complete secrecy regarding the location of Bensalem, *News from Nowhere* is none the

less yet another island utopia (the island in this case being Britain), a¹
one characterized by much the same qualities of abundance and freedc
from care so typical of paradisiacal fantasy—indeed, Suvin goes so far
to propose that, generically, the work should be classified as an Eartl
Paradise, rather than as a utopia *per se* (*Metamorphoses*, pp.182–²
Nevertheless, like earlier utopias, Morris's offers a radical simplification
the complexities of living, a rational approach to the problems and anxieti
of everyday existence having caused them virtually to disappear. Thus,
we have seen, while Morris fully acknowledges the necessity of labour,
irksomeness is removed, not by reducing working hours or providing f
early retirement, but rather simply by making it enjoyable—ind:
tinguishable, in the delight it affords, from any other form of recreatio
Commercial problems and financial complexities have disappeared alor
with money itself, with trade largely being conducted by children; ar
while sexual tensions still persist, they are minimized by the removal
legal constraints on human relationships.

Nevertheless, it is curious that this should be the *sole* area which Mor.
chooses to show as remaining problematic—to the extent, indeed, th
despite the otherwise pacific tenor of his utopia, we learn of no fewer tha
four murders occasioned by sexual jealousy. While Old Hammond tells tl
narrator that laws have been rendered superfluous by the abolition of ·
those features of the capitalist economic system which provided incentiv
to crime, this persistence of violence suggests that, as in *Looking Backwar*
the economic imperatives of existing society have been displaced, in utopi
into the sexual sphere. Significantly, when the question of econom
incentives to labour is raised, Morris explicitly equates production ar
reproduction. When the narrator asks what makes people work in tl
absence of any financial reward, Old Hammond responds that work is i
own reward:

> 'Plenty of reward,' said he—'the reward of creation. The wages whic
> God gets, as people might have said time agone. If you are going
> ask to be paid for the pleasure of creation, which is what excellen·
> in work means, the next thing we shall hear of will be a bill sent
> for the begetting of children.' [p.77]

With this exception, however, Morris's utopia is one where innocen·
has largely been restored, and while his emphasis is on individual freedor
rather than order, the underlying zeal for simplification is very similar
that embodied in the traditional utopian paradigm. Even Morris
unusually concrete depiction of the process involved in the creation of
more perfect society has only a localized impact, casting a shadow of 'pa
unhappy times' over the sunlit world of his utopian dream. While h

ecognition of the cost, in terms of lives lost and human suffering, of radical ocial change is in marked contrast to the evasion or glossing over of the onnection with reality which constitutes the utopian norm, the ransitional metaphor in *News from Nowhere*, the account of the process vhereby the narrator reaches utopia, is no less suggestive than is the case 1 fictions where it fulfils a clearly compensatory function. Like Julian Vest, Morris's narrator falls asleep in his own world and wakes in the ttopian future, and while there is none of the preposterous apparatus of ubterranean chambers and hypnosis whereby Bellamy accounts for the 1ystery of his narrator's reawakening, Morris's narrative is not without :s own curiosities. Prior to waking in utopia, Morris's narrator undergoes rather less eccentric subterranean ritual, travelling home by underground ailway (or, as it was already becoming known in Morris's time, by 'tube')— journey during which he 'stews discontentedly' with his fellow travellers 1 'a vapour bath of hurried and discontented humanity' (p.1). On arriving tome, he goes to bed and falls into a troubled sleep from which he finally wakes to find the early winter of reality transformed into the midsummer f the utopian future. His first act, on emerging from this symbolic gestation teriod, is to go for a baptismal swim—he takes on a new name shortly hereafter—and is then taken under the protective wing of Dick the toatman who, along with Clara, displays an almost parental solicitude for tis charge, educating him in the ways of the new world in which he finds timself.

Yet here further ambiguities emerge: while to the narrator it is a new vorld, much of its novelty consists in its restoration of an older one. The ttopian future is several times described as a world enjoying a 'second hildhood'—an ambiguous phrase in which youth and age become merged nto one—which further heightens the sense that Morris's Communist ttopia is as much as anything a paradise regained. While the narrator ncounters much that is unfamiliar, he finds the experience far less insettling than does Julian West on his first exposure to the 'new' Boston— reflection, perhaps of the extent to which Morris's utopia represents a eturn to an old, organic harmony between humanity and nature, rather han the imposition of a new, man-made order. Certainly, the emphasis f *News from Nowhere*, describing as it does a world that has been 'brought o its second birth' (p.112), is on the innocence and freedom which might te associated with childhood, rather than on the security, allied of course vith individual helplessness, of the womb, but the underlying impulse is 1one the less a regressive one. The very direction of the journey that tccupies the latter part of the book is in itself significant: it is a voyage tpstream, against the current, back towards the source. Although, in deological terms, *News from Nowhere* may be seen as representing a radical break with utopian tradition, it remains limited by its adherence to narrative model evolved in a very different historical context, and express a very different political ideal. For all the forcefulness of Morri critique of Bellamy's utopia, his own is equally one which might described as 'Looking Backward.'

Red Star

If Morris's disgust with *Looking Backward* provided the initial inspirati for *News from Nowhere*, Bogdanov's motivation for writing *Red Star* appe to have been more directly propagandistic. As a leading Bolshev (although one on the verge of an irreparable breach with Lenin),[17] he sa the function of his utopia as both educational and inspirational, not or providing its audience with an instructive portrait of a society operati in accordance with Marxist principles, but also offering an enabling visi of revolutionary possibility, designed to counteract the prevailing defeatis and despair following the failure of the 1905 revolution. Perhaps as a resu Bogdanov appears to pay little attention to the *narrative* problems of utoj as such, making few significant modifications to the traditional paradig of the visit to and guided tour of a utopian society. Nevertheless, while tl in turn creates some familiar problems, his acute awareness of the politi implications of some of the resultant contradictions enables him to addr directly issues that earlier utopian writers ignore.

Set in Russia in the immediate aftermath of the 1905 revolution, *F Star* begins with an encounter between Leonid, a seasoned party work with marital problems, and a mysterious envoy from the South, who code name is Menni—and who later turns out to be from Mars. Havi first pointed out the ideological basis of the tensions between Leonid a his wife to such good effect that she promptly leaves him, Menni th invites Leonid to accompany him to Mars, where it turns out a fully-fledg Communist society already exists, one both politically and technologica far more advanced than any on Earth. Seeing in this the opportunity f the acquisition of knowledge and skills that will render him more usef to the revolutionary cause, Leonid agrees, and the trip to utopia begins

For all its science fictional character, however, it turns out to be journ with a number of familiar features: Leonid and Menni leave the latte apartment in a small flying machine, and travel through the night un they reach the 'etheroneph'—a massive spaceship, whose form is describ as 'almost spherical, being flattened at the lower end rather like Columbu egg' (p.35). Although there is no visible means of entry, 'part of the met cover of the structure slowly moved to one side, and our craft sailed in the black opening' (p.33); within, they pass through the by now almo standard utopian terrain of 'elongated' rooms and 'dimly lit' corridors (p.33), until Leonid reaches his cabin, where he falls asleep, his 'brain overpowered by oppressive visions':

> I had a series of dreams which ended in a terrible nightmare. I was standing on the brink of an enormous black abyss. Stars shone at the bottom, and Menni was irresistibly dragging me down into it, telling me that there was no reason to fear the force of gravity and that in a few hundred thousand years we would reach the nearest star. I moaned in my final agonizing struggle and awoke. [p.33]

Awakening from his nightmare, he finds himself in the reassuring presence of the ship's doctor, Netti, who (in a manner reminiscent of the equivalent scene in *Looking Backward*) soothes him back to sleep with a combination of soft lights and hypnotic suggestion. The following morning they depart.

Although the nuclear-powered etheroneph is technologically extremely advanced, the journey to Mars is still a lengthy one, and Leonid takes the opportunity to learn the Martian language, which turns out to be 'of great simplicity' (p.47), so regular that its rules 'have no exceptions whatever' (p.48), and entirely lacking in gender distinctions—indeed, the only thing he finds confusing is that 'the names of all objects and qualities are declined according to their temporal status' (p.48). This evidence of a concern with the passage of time is also reflected in the fact that (in marked contrast to the utopian norm) Leonid is given a good deal of information concerning Martian history[18]—including, as in *News from Nowhere*, an extended account of how the revolution came about. Only once is the otherwise uneventful journey disrupted, when—for reasons that never become apparent—an elderly scientist chooses to conduct in Leonid's presence what turns out to be a highly dangerous experiment, resulting in an explosion that blasts a hole in the ship's hull. Disaster seems inevitable, until the scientist heroically plugs the hole with his own body, saving Leonid's life, but killing himself in the process.

Once he has arrived on Mars, what follows is very much the standard utopian guided tour. As K.M. Jensen points out, its familiar features include:

> ... plenty, uniform standard of living, stable planned economy, free labour, complete satisfaction of needs, personal security and happiness, absence of politics and state, high level of social consciousness, an environment conducive to individual creativity, universal education, scientific efficiency, functional architecture and effective population distribution, urban society, high technology and automation. [p.17]

Like Morris's, Bogdanov's Communist utopia is one where the state ha
withered away, although, in marked contrast to *News from Nowhere, Re*
Star provides a great deal of information concerning the mechanisms c
social organization. Leonid visits (and later works in) a factory wher
automation has reduced the average working day to the equivalent c
between four to six Earth hours, and learns that the elimination of mindles
drudgery, together with the high level of Martian education, has rendere
'each individual … perfectly free to choose his own occupation' (p.67). H
visits a 'Children's Colony', where Martian children are raised an
educated, not only by adults, but also by one another, in an environmen
free of the tensions and traumas of conventional family life, and then tour
a museum where he is introduced to Martian art and architecture, an
reflects on the role and character of art in a socialist society (a discussio
of particular interest, given Bogdanov's later status as one of the leadin
theoreticians of the Proletcult movement).[19] This is followed by a visit t
a hospital, where he learns of the advanced medical technology which
along with the practice of 'mutual blood transfusions',[20] has resulted in
dramatically increased lifespan, and by trips to public meetings and th
theatre.

After several weeks of this strenuous régime, however, Leonid suffer
a complete nervous breakdown—apparently the result of informatio
overload—and is put to bed under Netti's care, which, besides reducin
him to the childlike dependency so characteristic of the traditional visito
to utopia, also serves to introduce a love interest strongly reminiscent o
the relationship between Julian West and Edith Leete in *Looking Backwar*
Netti, to whom he has already found himself strangely attracted, turns ou
not to be a man after all, but a woman—and one moreover, whose passio
for all things terrestrial has already predisposed her to return his eviden
affection:

> Simply and generously, she yielded to my unbridled impulses
> When I recovered from my joyous insanity I again kissed her hand
> with involuntary tears of gratitude in my eyes. My crying, of course
> was due to weakness caused by my illness. Netti said with her swee
> smile:
>
> 'You know, it seemed to me just now that I was holding you
> whole youthful world in my arms. Its despotism, its egotism, it
> desperate hunger for happiness—I felt all that in your caresses. You
> love is like murder. But … I love you, Lenni.' [p.93]

As in *Looking Backward*, the visitor arrives in utopia to be rewarded by th
effortless fulfilment of sexual desire. Yet, as in Wells's utopias, such desir
also turns out to be disturbingly conflated with maternal affection: prio

leaving on yet another interplanetary expedition, this time to Venus, etti leaves him a letter in which she declares:

> I love you not only as a wife, I love you as a mother who guides her child into a new and strange life full of trials and dangers. This love is the strongest bond that can exist between two people. For that reason my promise requires no sacrifice of me.
> Goodbye my darling, my beloved child ... [p.106]

So far, it would appear, so familiar. Despite some often acute political analysis, Bogdanov's utopian narrative repeatedly lapses into a fantasy of infantile dependence. Not the least significant aspect of Netti's letter is that despite the fact that free love is the norm on Mars (and something to which Leonid also claims to be committed), she goes out of her way to reassure him that 'There will never be anyone else' (p.106): what is offered is the utopian promise of absolute security, free from the complications of adult existence. Indeed, even where Bogdanov is at his strongest—as in his commitment to address the *process* whereby the utopian society is created—there are still indications of a regressive simplifying impulse, an underlying desire to evade complexity and difficulty. Revolution on Mars, it transpires, was a far simpler affair than is the case on Earth. Smaller, and with better communications (there being fewer seas to divide people and less gravity to slow them up), Mars had already evolved into a world state with a single language long before the revolution—and as a result there were no national rivalries to interfere with the revolutionary process. While the major industrial crisis that followed the completion of the 'Great Project' (the digging of Mars's 'canals') was accompanied by strikes and uprisings, there was—as in *Looking Backward*—almost no violence:

> The result was a social revolution, but once again the course of events was relatively peaceful ... The owners retreated step by step before the inevitable, and even when the government fell into the hands of the workers' party, the vanquished did not attempt to assert their interests by force. [p.56]

For an active Bolshevik, who had personally witnessed the brutal suppression of the 1905 uprising, it is a remarkable compensatory fantasy.

In addition, *Red Star* displays—if possible, to an even greater extent—the displacement of tension and conflict from the public (political and economic) arena into the private, sexual realm, which has already been observed both in the traditional utopian paradigm and its dystopian parody. At the outset, as we have seen, Leonid is married to a woman with whom he has profound differences—differences which, as Menni points out, have a clearly ideological basis. Nevertheless, despite the importance of the revolutionary struggle in which both are engaged, their *political* charact‹ (Leonid is a Bolshevik, Anna Nikolaevna a Menshevik) is mentioned on‌ in passing, whereas their differences over questions of sexual morality ar discussed at considerable length:

> According to Anna Nikolaevna, in socialist society the class ethics ‹ the proletariat would necessarily become the universal moral cod‹ while I believed that the proletariat was already moving toward th‌ destruction of all morals and that the comradely feeling unitin‌ people in labour, joy, and suffering would not develop fully until had cast off the fetishistic husk of morality … She thought that lov implied certain obligations—concessions, sacrifices, and, above a‌ fidelity for the duration of the union. In actual fact I had no intentio‌ whatever of entering into other liaisons, but I was unable to recogniz fidelity as an obligation. I even believed that polygamy was i‌ principle superior to monogamy, since it provided for both a rich‹ private life and a greater variety of genetic combinations. In m‌ opinion, it was only the contradictions of the bourgeois order whic‌ for the time being made polygamy either simply unfeasible or merel the privilege of the exploiters and parasites, who were all befoule‹ by their own decadent psychology … Anna Nikolaevna deep‌ resented such views, in which she perceived an attempt to mask coarsely sensual outlook with intellectual phrases. [p.25]

Nevertheless, despite this stance, Leonid's reaction on discovering th‌ nature of Netti's sexual history is far from philosophical. Having recovere‹ from one breakdown, he almost suffers another on learning that her pa‌ partners include Letta—the scientist who saved Leonid's life at the cost ‹ his own—and Sterni, another member of the expedition which brougḥ him to Mars, and also an advocate of the colonization of Earth. Ostensibl‌ concerned over the fate of the human race (Sterni argues that colonizin‌ Earth would necessarily involve first exterminating its inhabitants) bᴜ really motivated by sexual jealousy, he seeks out Sterni, and bludgeon‌ him to death. (When Netti describes his love as being 'like murder', sh‌ clearly speaks more accurately than she knows: not content with h‹ assurances of sexual fidelity in the future, he effectively erases her sexuᴀ past.) As in *News from Nowhere*, the only violence in utopia is caused b sexual jealousy, while to an even greater extent than in the case of Bellam and Wells, the visitor's experience of the more rational utopian world i‌ accompanied by symptoms of extreme psychological disturbance: Leonid' last days on Mars prior to his return to Earth are spent in a mental hospitᴀ

At the same time, however, there are some significant differences. Whil the process of the Martian revolution may be radically simplified an smoothed over, the achievement of a utopian society takes on a very different resonance in the light of its connection with Bogdanov's vivid depiction of the revolutionary struggle on Earth. Indeed, whenever the two planets' histories are compared, the far greater scale of the problems of achieving social justice on Earth is repeatedly stressed—yet always with the accompanying assurance that the much greater energy required to overcome such obstacles will ultimately lead to a correspondingly higher pinnacle of achievement. To return to Earth is to return to the realm of difficulty, to the necessity of struggle, and in juxtaposing the situations of the two planets Bogdanov creates a dynamic that to some extent anticipates the narrative strategies of later writers such as Piercy and Le Guin. Despite feeling that he has disgraced himself by his conduct on Mars, Leonid returns determined to continue fighting for a better society on Earth: in the Epilogue, he is critically wounded while leading a commando attack on the government forces.

In addition, while *Red Star* exhibits the familiar displacement of political tensions and contradictions into the sexual realm, there is at the same time evidence of some critical awareness of the resultant implications. While at the outset Leonid is able to reflect on his differences with Anna Nikolaevna in an apparently objective fashion, his encounter with a society where his theories are common practice force him painfully to confront the contradictions arising from his own socialization. On learning not only that Netti had been involved with Letta and Sterni, but that for a time the relationships had overlapped, Leonid reflects:

> ... there are no words to describe how I felt. Why? No reason in particular. Netti was a free person and behaved like a free person. What of it if Letta was her husband? I had always respected him and would have liked him very much even if he had not sacrificed his life for me. Netti was married to two of her comrades at the same time? So what? I have always believed that monogamy among us is due exclusively to our economic conditions, which limit and enslave man at every step. The conditions on Mars were quite different and in no way inhibited personal feelings and relationships. Why then this agitated bewilderment, this incomprehensible pain that made me want to scream and laugh at the same time? Or was it that I did not know how to *feel* as I *thought?* [pp.104–5]

Where both the traditional utopian narrative and its dystopian parody comfortably reinscribe the unequal gender relations of existing society, Bogdanov's emphasis on Leonid's discomfort when faced with women's sexual freedom highlights the extent to which, as a male, he has unconsciously assumed the inequity from which he has hitherto benefited

to be the norm—although the effect of this acknowledgement is somewhat
undermined when Netti returns at the end, monogamous and maternal,
to whisk him back to utopia. As well, Leonid is forced to acknowledge the
contradictions of his class status: while, as a revolutionary intellectual, he
is committed to the workers' cause, he often experiences the genuinely
co-operative culture of Mars as a threat to his own identity. When his
fellow-workers at the factory help him out when he makes mistakes, for
example, he assumes that it reflects badly on his competence, and that
they are constantly keeping an eye on him—whereas in fact such mutual
assistance is the norm. At the end, reflecting on his bouts of mental
instability during his exposure to genuine social equality, he wonders
whether it was not partly the result of his background as an intellectual
'who nine-tenths of the time had worked either alone or in a one-sided
unequal relationship to his comrades and fellow workers' (p.135):

> Perhaps it would be easier for an uneducated worker to become
> integrated into a new and higher order, for although he would have
> to learn much more at first, he would not be forced to relearn as
> much, and that, after all, is the most difficult problem ... Perhaps the
> contradiction would have proved less acute for a man who had
> instead spent nine-tenths of his working life in an environment that
> may have been primitive and uncultivated but was nonetheless
> pervaded by a spirit of comradeship. An environment in which
> equality was real ... [p.135]

Where Bellamy and Wells imagine utopias in which middle-class values
have become universal, and even dystopian parody for the most part
implicitly appeals to those values as normative, Bogdanov stresses the
extent to which a more equal society imposes the imperative to change.
(Although, at the same time, it is significant that despite his dawning
awareness of the contradictions of his own gender position, Leonid never
wonders if a woman might not also find the experience of utopia less
problematic—given that she might be liable to find gender equality rather
less of a threat.)

Finally, while much of the dialogue in *Red Star* functions as little more
than an expository device, there is one episode which features genuine
debate. For there *is* debate on Mars—in part because, for all its utopian
features, it is not a world where all problems have been resolved: although
at the level of social interaction this may be the case, the struggle with the
forces of nature still continues. Despite the 'Great Project', the massive
engineering works that have irrigated the Martian desert, natural resources
are in increasingly short supply, and as one Martian remarks: 'the tighter
our humanity closes ranks to conquer nature, the tighter the elements

close theirs to avenge the victory' (p.79). Since checking population growth 'would be tantamount to capitulating to the elements' (pp.79–80), Martian society is faced with only one solution: the colonization of other planets— and it is this that constitutes the focus of the central debate.

As we have already seen, one recurrent feature of utopian narrative is its rehearsal of the process of colonization so inextricably linked with the narratives of discovery on which it is partly modelled. From More's *Utopia*, where the indigenous inhabitants are remoulded in the image of their conqueror, and then proceed to impose their norms on the nations that surround them, to Morris's and Wells's celebration of the destruction of the architecture and culture that preceded the establishment of utopia, the utopian dream is in part a fantasy of finding space in which a new order can be constructed—and if that space should happen to be occupied, the only logical conclusion is that it will have to be made empty. In terms of utopian narrative, this can be effected in a fairly painless and guilt-free fashion simply by projecting utopia into the future, by which time all those inhabitants of the utopian space *not* committed to utopian values will have died, without the inconvenience of having to either massacre or re-educate them, leaving only their buildings to be demolished (as they almost invariably are). In the case of *Red Star*, however, Bogdanov chooses not to evade the issue of the connection between the process of colonization and the utopian aspiration to create a better world, but instead makes it a central focus of his narrative.

As Bogdanov structures it, the debate focuses on two alternatives—the colonization of Venus, a hostile environment, though rich in natural resources, and the colonization of Earth—and in the view of the astronomer, Sterni, that effectively leaves only one option. Given the dangers of Venus—thunderstorms and winds which can destroy aircraft and demolish buildings, monsters, bacteria, diseases, earthquakes, volcanic eruptions, tidal waves—Earth is the only realistic alternative. However, this presents problems of its own: Sterni maintains that the primitive character of Earth's society renders it impossible to live among them— nationalist propensities meaning that humans are liable to band together against a common enemy. Echoing the discovery narrative's demonization of the indigene as a rationale for what is almost invariably represented as *retaliatory* violence, he argues that humanity's reliance on 'brute strength and violence ... will *force* us to adopt the same attitude toward them' (p.111). An enclave of Martian civilization is unthinkable, given the constant struggle that would be involved, since Socialism is still a long way off, even with Martian assistance—and even if achieved, its character would likely be warped by the violent struggle to attain it. (Sterni at this point offers an eerily prescient vision of the likely consequences of the establishment of 'socialism in one country'.[21]) Given the clear superiority of Martian civilization, extermination is the only answer. Two of Wells's pronouncements in *A Modern Utopia*—that 'no less than a planet will serve the purpose of a modern Utopia' (p.11) and that 'there is only one sane and logical thing to be done with a really inferior race, and that is to exterminate it' (p.337)—here take on a particularly sinister overtone.

It is Netti who counters these arguments in favour of conquest and genocide with what is essentially a plea in favour of *difference*—regarding which, as we have seen, traditional utopian narrative remains highly ambivalent. While Martian civilization is unquestionably more advanced than that of Earth, this does not in Netti's view argue a fundamental superiority:

> If they were identical with us in all respects save their level of development, then one might be able to agree with Sterni: a lower stage is worth sacrificing for the sake of a higher one, the weak must yield to the strong. But the Earthlings are not the same as we. They and their civilization are not simply lower and weaker than ours— they are *different*. If we eliminate them we will not replace them in the process of universal evolution but will merely fill in mechanically the vacuum we have created in the world of life forms. [p.117]

Ultimately, she argues, the greater variety and energy of life on Earth, its diversity of language and culture, while it may render the process of uniting humanity longer and more arduous, will give birth to a socialism in many ways richer and more sophisticated than that of Mars—which is not to say, however, that Mars cannot help it on its way. What Bogdanov dramatizes in this exchange, in effect, is the *relation* between utopia and the world as it exists: not only may one learn from the example of the utopia that lies beyond and above the limitations of the here and now, but by doing so it becomes possible to transcend the regularity and simplification which is utopia's limitation.

What is also significant, however, is the way in which Bogdanov genders the debate. It is Sterni, not merely a male, but an unusually large and powerful one, who expresses the colonialist desire for the suppression and expropriation of the Other, and for the imposition of a single, harmonious order; whereas it is the woman, Netti, who speaks for diversity and the right to self-determination. Where Sterni describes the human race as 'masters of the planet' (p.110), who can simply be replaced by more powerful masters, Netti refers to them as though they are an organic part of it—as a 'stormy but beautiful ocean of life' (p.119)—whose loss would be irreparable. This is not to say that Netti's position is entirely unproblematic: if Sterni embodies the male dream of conquest and

ossession of nature, Netti at points seems to associate herself with the
aternal passivity which Kolodny sees as its polar opposite, while in her
mphasis on the organic character of human development she often comes
lose to suggesting that the achievement of socialism is itself not only a
atural, but an inevitable process. Nevertheless, set in the context of
ubsequent challenges to the largely male-authored traditional utopian
ream of order by feminist writers who seek to incorporate freedom and
nultiplicity into the utopian dream, Bogdanov's treatment of the issue
nay be seen as a decisive step forward. Only one detail serves to darken
he picture. In order to obtain access to the records of the meeting at which
he debate took place, Leonid has to resort to subterfuge, since the librarian
t colonial archives denies such records exist: slipping past him while he
s otherwise engaged, he proceeds to the audio-recording section, where
e is careful to make his request for information sufficiently general not
o cause alarm. Only then does he discover the audio-recording of the
ebate. While Martian society is otherwise represented in a uniformly
avourable light, secrecy and bureaucratic obstructionism are apparently
o strangers to the utopian state.

Island

Jearly forty years later, in the 1946 Foreword to *Brave New World*, Aldous
Iuxley also offered, in outline, a vision of what might constitute the basis
f a libertarian utopia. While *Brave New World* set out to expose what for
Iuxley were the nightmarish implications of the Wellsian utopia, its
veakness, as he saw it, lay in its failure to see beyond the polarized
lternatives it presented—between the irrational brutality of a 'natural' life
n a primitive community, on the one hand, and the mindless conformity
f a rationally planned utopia on the other. As a possible solution, he
uggested 'a third alternative' (p.8)—the 'possibility of sanity' which might
e embodied in a community of exiles and refugees from the utopian World
tate:

> In this community economics would be decentralist and Henry-
> Georgian, politics Kropotkinesque and co-operative. Science and
> technology would be used as though, like the Sabbath, they had been
> made for man, not (as at present and still more so in Brave New
> World) as though man were to be adapted and enslaved to them.
> Religion would be the conscious and intelligent pursuit of man's Final
> End, the unitive knowledge of the immanent Tao or Logos, the
> transcendent Godhead or Brahman. [pp.8–9]

Given that, with only minor modifications, this is very much the ideal which forms the basis for the fully worked-out utopian society depicted in *Island*, it is worth examining Huxley's recipe for a positive alternative to dystopia more closely. Most immediately striking, perhaps, is its spiritual emphasis, which, given the predominantly secular and materialist concern of most earlier writers (including even the devoutly Christian More), would seem to indicate a significant change of focus. It is no coincidence that while lacking the spectacular religious special effects of Bacon's *The New Atlantis*, *Island* is concerned above all to demonstrate the crucial importance of spiritual awareness as a precondition for the establishment of any truly desirable form of social organization. Even the subordination of technology to human needs, which the Foreword advocates, and *Island* illustrates, is only made possible by a sense of purpose which Huxley sees as ultimately religious in character. And while the utopia portrayed in *Island* is predominantly Buddhist, rather than based on the somewhat eclectic mix advocated in the Foreword, its underlying emphasis remains much the same. For Huxley, the ultimate horror of his dystopian future, and indeed of the contemporary society from which it was extrapolated, lay in its mindlessness, its lack of awareness of any goal other than that of immediate gratification. It is this which his utopia, with its focus on the central necessity of spiritual awareness, seeks to counter.

Huxley's evident intuition of the regressive element inherent in the utopian impulse is, of course, reflected in *Brave New World*, whose infantile behavioural norms render explicit an aspect that remains latent in the utopian tradition he parodies. There, as we have seen, Huxley implies that spiritual awareness is the antithesis of such infantilism, and in his utopian society of Pala the religious exercises and rituals that are practised from childhood on are represented as crucial to the development of an independent, adult consciousness, in which the individual is able to perceive her or his own needs in relation to the wider horizons of society, as well as to the 'Final End' referred to in the Foreword. Palanese religion works in tandem with its educational system to encourage a strong sense of distinct personal identity, based on the exploration of one's individual potential, while at the same time emphasizing the individual's responsibility to control any anti-social impulses to which s/he is particularly susceptible. Children learn at an early age to deal with personal problems, to resolve family conflicts within a network of extended families, and to take a mature and responsible attitude towards sexual relationships—in other words, to grow up both faster and more fully. Children are deliberately exposed to *all* aspects of human experience: 'all the important and significant things that human beings do and suffer— working, playing, loving, getting old, being sick, dying....' (p.93), and 'Attention,' a slogan insistently repeated by Pala's talking birds, is perhaps the fundamental motto of Huxley's utopia. Active attention is encouraged to everything: the food one eats, the experience of sexual intercourse, the controversial 'moksha-medicine' (the psychedelic drug which certain of Huxley's less perceptive critics have sought speciously to equate with the narcotics consumed in vast quantities in Brave New World)[22]—the ultimate goal being to promote 'awareness, complete and constant awareness' (p.152) of the infinite variety of the world one inhabits. When this is combined with the active encouragement of a sceptical attitude towards conventional beliefs and received assumptions, it becomes clear that Huxley's utopia is explicitly designed to ensure that its citizens cannot be manipulated by the centralized authority so characteristic of the traditional utopia. The primary purpose of Pala's social, political, and religious institutions is to create a framework that allows for the maximum possible individual freedom: rather than a structure to be imposed on its citizens in their own best interests, utopia here is the sum of the experience of the individuals who compose it.

Interestingly enough, the sharpest contrasts between the virtues of utopia and the deficiencies of the 'real' world are provided by the example of the individual products of the different societies. Opposed to the balance and maturity of Dr Robert and Susila, or even the young lovers Radha and Ranga, is the sulky petulance of the mother-dominated Murugan, or the example of the two distinguished westerners cited by the Palanese Under-Secretary of Education:

> 'I was thinking of two people I met last time I was in England. At Cambridge. One of them was an atomic physicist, the other was a philosopher. Both extremely eminent. But one had a mental age, outside the laboratory, of about eleven and the other was a compulsive eater with a weight problem that he refused to face.' [p.214]

For Huxley, the superiority of utopia resides not so much in the perfection of its social and political structures, as in the extent to which such structures promote growth and maturity: many of the problems of his own society are represented as rooted in the relative immaturity of those who comprise it. When the mentality of the playground is allowed to persist into adulthood, the consequences can be disastrous—the most spectacular example offered being that of Adolf Hitler, who is significantly described as a 'Peter Pan': a classic case of arrested development leading to psychopathic behaviour. In Pala, by contrast, the compulsions that create a Hitler, like the gullibility that caused people to respond to his primitive appeal, are something that can be outgrown.

Even at the level of metaphor the adult quality of utopian society is evident. Palanese medicine, for example, stresses the importance of allowing the body's own self-healing mechanisms to do their work: to prevent the conscious mind interfering in this process, patients are often put into a hypnotic trance. The conscious self is like a 'little boy' who, though only too anxious to help, has to be sent 'to play in the garden so that the grown-ups can do their work in peace' (p.94). When Dr Robert justifies Pala's refusal to import luxuries, such as the expensive foreign cars for which Murugan yearns, it is on the grounds that 'We can't import toys ... only essentials' (p.146). In such a context, it is perhaps hardly coincidental that the only mode of transport available to the Rani, who embodies the bogus spirituality so prevalent outside utopia, should be a 'Baby Austin.'

Nevertheless, however refreshing Huxley's stress on the virtues of maturity, of individual freedom and responsibility may be—particularly in a utopian context, familiar problems arise when it comes to translating theory into narrative practice. *Island* is, yet again, a narrative which adheres to the basic format of a guided tour provided for the visitor to utopia—and one whose didactic intent is no less overt than is the case in the utopias of Bellamy and Wells. Thus, while few would quarrel with the old Raja of Pala's realistic assessment that a certain amount of pain and sorrow is an inescapable part of the human condition (even in utopia), *Island*'s narrative format often makes Huxley's representations of human sorrow seem *merely* propagandistic. Even the movingly described death of Dr Robert's wife, Lakshmi (itself clearly based on the death of Huxley's first wife, Maria[23]) is surrounded by episodes clearly designed to show how well the Palanese deal with it; indeed, as though anxious lest the point be missed, Huxley also provides graphic descriptions of how *badly* death is dealt with elsewhere. In contrast to Lakshmi, the visitor to utopia, Will Farnaby, cites the case of his Aunt Mary, whose death from cancer was marked by nothing but terror and degradation; his own helpless guilt and horror over the death of his wife is set against the strength and dignity with which Susila deals with the death of her husband. Such schematic contrasts, of course, exemplifying as they do the problematic 'double encoding' of utopian narrative as both fiction and some other mode with very different designs on the reader, are only too typical of the traditional utopian paradigm. In the case of *Island*, however, their effect is particularly unfortunate, working as they do against the basic premises of the utopia which it proposes. While the free exercise of individual judgement by the Palanese may be approved, Huxley is evidently reluctant to allow a similar privilege to the reader. As in so many more authoritarian utopias, it is less the inherent implausibility of the society depicted that constitutes the problem (witness the cheerful suspension of disbelief with which readers greet the far more extravagant inventions of much science fiction), than the authorial insistence on spelling everything out, on specifying each detail of the utopian vision. *Island* is yet another utopia whose dialogue is essentially monologic, calculated as it is to assert the authority of a single utterance.

Huxley himself was obviously aware of the problems inherent in the creation of an effective utopian fiction. Writing to his son during the early stages of composition, he described himself as:

> ... wrestling with the problem of getting an enormous amount of diversified material into the book without becoming merely expository or didactic. It may be that the job is one which cannot be accomplished with complete success. In point of fact, it hasn't been accomplished in the past. For most Utopian books have been exceedingly didactic and expository. I am trying to lighten up the exposition by putting it into dialogue form, which I make as lively as possible. But meanwhile I am always haunted by the feeling that, if I only had enough talent, I could somehow poetize and dramatize all the intellectual material and create a work which would be simultaneously funny, tragic, lyrical and profound. Alas, I don't possess the necessary talent ... [*Letters*, pp.875–6]

Coming from the author of *Brave New World*, it is a telling admission, indicative of the much greater compositional problems inherent in utopian narrative as opposed to dystopian parody. Adhering as he does so closely to the traditional utopian narrative model, Huxley is little more successful in transcending its limitations: his attempts at 'lively' dialogue rarely succeed in disguising its fundamentally didactic intent—the fact that once again it is little more than exposition distributed among a range of speakers. Where Huxley does extend the conventions of the traditional narrative paradigm, it is by the inclusion of novelistic elements—in this case, a subplot designed, like that in Wells's *Men Like Gods*, to supplement the somewhat limited narrative appeal of the standard utopian visit.

Will Farnaby, it transpires, is not just a journalist: he is also the agent of the newspaper proprietor and oil magnate, Joe Aldehyde, who is keenly interested in getting his hands on Pala's substantial oil resources—which the Palanese themselves refuse to develop for other than their own needs. Even as, in the course of his guided tour, he becomes increasingly attracted to the Palanese way of life, Will is simultaneously engaged in underhand negotiations with various parties also interested in Pala's oil reserves— including the ambassador of the neighbouring dictatorship. And while this is clearly likely to undermine the independence which is the precondition for Pala's remaining a utopian society, he initially justifies his actions on the grounds that the commission he will earn will enable him to abandon

journalism for the pursuit of Art. As time goes by, however, he grows
increasingly unhappy about the compromises he is being forced to make—
and in this Huxley is doubtless trying to dramatize the connection between
individual practice and the existence of utopian society, and to create a
visitor to utopia who is more than simply a passive presence. The only
problem is that the subplot is so transparently just that: a subplot and no
more. In the end, it doesn't really *matter* what Will does: Pala's fate depends,
not on his negotiations, but on the actions of Murugan, heir apparent to
the Palanese throne, his mother, the Rani, and Colonel Dipa, the
neighbouring dictator. Which brings us to the question of the political
structure of Huxley's utopia.

In the Foreword to *Brave New World*, it will be recalled, Huxley envisaged
a more perfect society whose 'economics would be decentralist and Henry-
Georgian, politics Kropotkinesque and co-operative' (p.8). The economic
principles of the bourgeois prophet of land reform, Henry George, are seen,
in other words, as wholly compatible with political structures based on
entirely different premises—a yoking which shows little sign of awareness
of their essential incompatibility.[24] Huxley's tendency towards a sort of
mix-and-match political eclecticism is of course already apparent in *Brave
New World*, where capitalism, communism, fascism, and modern science
are lumped together as joint progenitors of his dystopian future. Yet while
this presents comparatively few difficulties in the context of Huxley's free-
ranging satiric attack on almost every aspect of modern society (with its
highly conservative underlying premise that almost all change is for the
worse, and should be avoided), such patent lack of discrimination becomes
considerably more problematic when it comes to devising the basis for a
more perfect—and radically different—social order.[25] In *Island*, the
contradictions implicit in the Foreword to *Brave New World* become
glaringly evident—to the point that, in places, it begins to seem that Huxley
himself is not entirely clear as to how his utopian society is run.

At the outset, it would appear that the Palanese utopia was to all intents
and purposes established by *fiat*, in the context of a political structure best
described as benevolent despotism. It is the creation of two men: the Raja
of Pala and Dr Andrew MacPhail, the Scottish surgeon who, after first
saving the Raja's life, becomes his chief adviser—Prime Minister in all but
name. While their recipe for a more perfect society—in essence a fusion
of Western scientific and technological know-how with the wisdom and
spiritual awareness of the East—may differ radically in character from those
of More and Bacon, their mode of putting it into effect differs little from
that of King Utopus or King Solamona. While the Raja and Dr MacPhail
go to great pains to win the Palanese over to their new ideas, there is no
doubt that in the first instance it is the existence of an inherently

authoritarian political structure that enables them to impose their will.

By the time Will Farnaby reaches utopia, however, Pala appears to have moved—at least to some extent—with the times. Pala has become a constitutional monarchy' (p.40): there is a Cabinet, a Privy Council, a House of Representatives. Elsewhere Dr Robert boasts:

> '... we have no omnipotent politicians or bureaucrats. Pala's a federation of self-governing units, professional units, economic units—so there's plenty of scope for small-scale initiative and democratic leaders, but no place for any kind of dictator at the head of a centralized government ... the eloquent rabble-rouser, like Hitler, or our neighbour across the Strait, Colonel Dipa, just doesn't have a chance here in Pala.' [p.149]

Yet here, once again, as in so many utopias, what we are told is at odds with what we are shown. The virtues of Palanese society are unfortunately lost on the heir apparent, Murugan, who appears to be the lone Palanese *not* to have benefited from its educational system. Instead, he has been brought up by his mother, the Rani, on quite different principles: the result is a sulky, gay playboy, whose favourite reading is the Sears-Roebuck catalogue. With a mother eager to use Pala's oil resources to finance a religious crusade reminiscent of Moral Re-Armament, and a lover who just happens to be the same Colonel Dipa from across the strait, Murugan has rather different priorities from those of his subjects. On his coming-of-age, the constitutional aspect of his monarchy is conveniently forgotten: Colonel Dipa's troops arrive to assist in establishing the new order, and Pala reverts to being part of the all too imperfect real world.

Huxley's decision to make his utopia, of all things, a monarchy— particularly given that it is precisely this feature that ensures its destruction—is surely a curious one, more in keeping with the political norms of the Renaissance than those of the mid-twentieth century. It does, however, serve to highlight the contradiction inherent in Huxley's account of his utopia's origins: the fact that it is a libertarian society created by essentially authoritarian means. It is this contradiction which resurfaces at the end of *Island*, when it becomes clear that the whole libertarian panoply of independent initiative and self-determination can be erased as easily as it was created. Once again, it would appear that the persistence of the traditional narrative paradigm serves to undermine the author's attempts to transcend its limitations. Even as Huxley strives to demystify the question of utopia's origins, he exposes the essential similarities between his vision of a utopia based on freedom and the authoritarian models that precede it. Nor do the resemblances end there: as its title suggests, *Island* also represents a return to the traditional location of earlier utopian narrative—an island in some unspecified southern sea. Rather than embracing the whole world, as do the utopias of Bellamy and Wells, Huxley's isolates itself from it—an isolation rather unconvincingly explained as being due to its lack of a natural harbour. This, in its turn, has some interesting consequences, for, unlike its neighbour, Rendang, Pala is thus spared the ill-effects of successive waves of colonization:

> 'Rendang has a magnificent harbour. That brought them an Arab invasion in the Middle Ages. We have no harbour, so the Arabs left us alone and we're still Buddhists or Shivaites—that is, when we're not Tantrik agnostics … After the Arabs, it got the Portuguese. We didn't. No harbour, no Portuguese. Therefore no Catholic minority, no blasphemous nonsense about it being God's will that people should breed themselves into subhuman misery, no organized resistance to birth control. And that isn't the only blessing. After a hundred and twenty years of the Portuguese, Ceylon and Rendang got the Dutch. And after the Dutch came the English. We escaped both those infestations. No Dutch, no English, and therefore no planters, no coolie labour, no cash crops for export, no systematic exhaustion of our soil. Also no whisky, no Calvinism, no syphilis, no foreign administrators. We were left to go our own way and take responsibility for our own affairs.' [pp.80–1]

What Pala has escaped, in other words, is almost the entire course of modern history. Like Wells in *A Modern Utopia*, Huxley effectively severs utopia from existing reality: utopia can only emerge from a context that is *already* different from that obtaining in the present. In addition, like Bacon's *The New Atlantis*, *Island* offers a scenario in which communication between utopia and the rest of the world is essentially one-way. Utopians from both societies go out into the world to learn from it, but contamination by visitors is discouraged.

Given this self-imposed isolation, of course, it becomes necessary to offer some form of narrative explanation for the visitor's presence—and once again this takes the by now sufficiently familiar form of a highly suggestive rite of passage. Shipwrecked on the coast of Pala after sailing alone beyond the safe confines of Rendang harbour, Will Farnaby miraculously ends up on 'the only sandy beach in all those miles of Pala's rockbound coast' (p.6). At the head of the little cove in which he finds himself there is 'a kind of headlong ravine where a little stream came down in a succession of filmy waterfalls, and there were trees and bushes growing between the walls of grey limestone' (p.6), and he proceeds to climb. The ascent, however, becomes increasingly nightmarish: the narrow path into Eden, it turns out, is infested with snakes, and after nearly stepping on one, he falls, badly injuring his leg. The light begins to fail, and even when he finally reaches the top, the nightmare continues. As he lies in a woodland glade in a state of semi-delirium, a series of painful memories return to haunt him. He recalls his wife, Molly, dying in the hospital after a car crash; he remembers his guilt-wracked sexual encounters with the woman for whom he left her, nights of mingled ecstasy and degradation in a room which the light of the neon gin advertisement outside periodically transforms into 'a womb of mud' (p.3); and finally, with something like revulsion, he recalls his mother. Only after being taken through the trauma of his climb (and fall) by a ten-year-old girl does he escape from his nightmare and find release in a fit of hysterical crying. As in Bellamy's *Looking Backward*, the entry to utopia is accompanied by tears.

What follows is among the most paradisiacal of all utopias, rife with the symbols of Eden. On his recovery from his perilous ascent he finds himself lying at the foot of a tree; the girl he first encounters gives him fruit which he eats (although, to be fair, it is not an apple, but a banana); and the psychotherapy which she then proceeds to practice on him involves, significantly enough, curing him of his fear of snakes. Pala seems very much a paradise regained, with its birds that talk, its luxuriant but well-groomed tropical landscape, and its security—which is in the first instance provided by a number of comforting adult presences. Unable to walk, Will is first treated for his injuries by the wise and fatherly Dr Robert (shades of Dr Leete), then carried off to bed, where he is soothed to sleep by an attractive yet motherly woman, Susila. For all the emphasis of Huxley's utopia on the virtues of adult responsibility and independence, its opening sequence, with its tears, its helplessness, its reassuring parental presences, reads very much like an account of a return to infancy. After Will sinks into his trance-like slumber, Susila notes that his face 'seemed suddenly very young, childlike in its perfect serenity' (p.29): once again the reversal of the direction of time, that most fantastic of all utopian aspirations, is made to seem almost possible.

Pala is, in addition, yet another world where innocence has been in large measure restored: such powerful potential inducers of guilt as religion, sexuality, and the family have been rationalized in order to minimize the problems to which they normally give rise. This in turn is symptomatic of a more general impulse towards simplification and demystification, which also manifests itself in such dubious panaceas as a return to the gold standard, which is touted as a solution to the complex problems of modern finance—although it may equally be seen as exemplifying the utopian desire to eliminate the gap between appearance and reality so strikingly evident in *The City of the Sun*. As so often, utopia is a world where what you see is what you get. Death, as we have seen, is dealt with with far more openness, courage, and understanding than is the case elsewhere, and if its terror cannot be eliminated altogether, nor the pain of bereavement abolished, Huxley's utopia is yet another where the *minimizing* of the causes of pain and confusion acts as a figure for their erasure. In keeping with Bacon's belief that humanity, by its own efforts, could at least 'in some part' repair the consequences of the Fall, Huxley creates another rationalized Eden—a world in which 'the Fall was an exploded doctrine' (p.219).

Where *Island* departs most strikingly from the traditional narrative paradigm, in fact, is in its conclusion, where the utopian dream is decisively shattered, not merely by the visitor's awakening, as in *News from Nowhere*, but by the actual destruction of utopia by the invading armies of Rendang. What emerges, however, is a pattern almost identical to that of the dystopias of Zamyatin, Orwell, and Huxley himself. At the end, a woman (Lakshmi) lies dead, the male representative of positive values (Dr Robert) is destroyed, and a more powerful male authority (Colonel Dipa) is triumphant. As in both *We* and *Nineteen Eighty-Four*, a heterosexual interaction involving the relationship of a fallible male to a stronger and more resourceful woman—here the dawning attraction between Will and Susila—is swept aside by a very different kind of partnership, which in this case in quite explicit in its homo-eroticism. Yet while the unholy alliance of Murugan and Colonel Dipa signals the end of utopia, it also highlights the fact that the original utopian dream was also the product of a male union. For all its emphasis on free, equal relations between the sexes, and its portrayal of strong, independent women, *Island* nevertheless depicts a society which is the brainchild of two men. Pala's utopian society is quite explicitly presented as the fruits of a marriage between the best aspects of Eastern and Western civilizations, the one represented by the Raja of Pala, the other by Dr MacPhail. And while the villains—Murugan, Dipa, Mr Bahu, Joe Aldehyde—are also men, it is significant that the strongest expressions of contempt are reserved for the Rani, the embodiment both of False Spirituality and of Motherhood. Underlying Huxley's utopian vision is much the same tacit assumption of male dominance as informs the traditional utopian dream of order. Despite a theoretical commitment to a greater degree of freedom and independence for women, Huxley only *shows* them playing relatively conventional roles—nursing, teaching, nurturing—while it is males who continue to take the lead. While there is one brief passage towards the end which seems to acknowledge the extent to which conventional images of women are merely male projections, when Will, under the influence of *moksha*, sees Susila in quick succession as Mater Dolorosa, 'a dark Circean goddess' (p.289), 'a laughing girl with a weakness for kisses' (p.290), and a cross between Juliana of orwich and Catherine of Genoa, at the very end the traditional order is estored. Although throughout the narrative Susila has been depicted as stronger and wiser than Will, the narrative ends with her sobbing in Will's comforting arms, as the troops of Colonel Dipa move in to take control.

Gender and Utopian Narrative

Huxley, however, is hardly alone in his reinscription of the power structures of existing gender relations. Morris, in fact, reproduces still more daringly his own society's assumptions as to the 'natural' role of women. As Levitas points out, in her otherwise positive assessment of *News from Nowhere*, one thing it shares with Bellamy's *Looking Backward* is its 'failure . to give any serious attention to the questions of the position of women or the care of children' (*Concept of Utopia*, p.109). For all his emphasis on freedom, as opposed to the regimentation of Bellamy's utopia, Morris's vision of freedom remains very much that of a Victorian male, eating excellent food and drinking fine wine, while waited on by beautiful women. Indeed, when William Guest expresses surprise at finding that women still do all the housework, he is greeted by Old Hammond with the nearest he comes to scorn:

'... perhaps you think housekeeping an unimportant occupation, not deserving of respect. I believe that was the opinion of the "advanced" women of the nineteenth century, and their male backers. If it is yours, I recommend to your notice an old Norwegian folk-lore tale called How the Man minded the House ... the result of which minding was that, after various tribulations, the man and the family cow balanced each other at the end of a rope, the man hanging half-way up the chimney, the cow dangling from the roof.' [pp.50–1]

Having thus naturalized the apparent male incapacity for domestic labour by appealing to the authority of a tale rooted in the cultural assumptions of an entirely different social formation, Old Hammond goes on to ask:

'... don't you know that it is a great pleasure to a clever woman to manage a house skilfully, and to do it so that all the house-mates about her look pleased, and are grateful to her? And then, you know, everybody likes to be ordered about by a pretty woman: why, it is one of the pleasantest forms of flirtation.' [p.51]

As the 'everybody' makes clear, *News from Nowhere* is once again a utopian vision in which the marginal status of women is reinscribed. In the final chapters, indeed, the extent to which it embodies specifically *male* desire becomes still clearer, as the narrator's unconsummated love for the beautiful Ellen is made to act as a figure for the ungraspability of utopia. The bitter-sweet melancholy that suffuses the conclusion stems as much from thwarted sexual yearning as from the loss of utopia as a whole.

Even Bogdanov, as we have seen, although he goes further than either Morris or Huxley in foregrounding the contradictions between his narrator's theoretical commitment to sexual equality and the effects of his social conditioning, falls into some of the same traps. As in *Island*, for all the insistence on the unimportance of gender distinctions (women and men are physically more difficult to tell apart, while the Martian language, as has been noted, has no gender distinctions) women are only *shown* in traditional nurturing roles. Of the three the main female characters, Netti is a doctor, Nella, her mother, works at the Children's Colony (in fact, the only people we actually *see* involved in child care are all women), while Enno, although an astronomer, is only shown in the roles of teacher, lover, and an unhappy wife who nearly commits suicide when she is unable to have a child by the man she loves.

Thus, while the utopian premise that humans will behave differently under different social circumstances implies acceptance of the socially constructed character of human identity, in all three cases the notion of an essential, 'natural' femininity persists. Taken in conjunction with the obstinate survival of an archaic narrative paradigm, this repeated reinscription of conventional patterns of gender relations even in the context of radical modifications of the social structure as a whole poses the question whether what is most problematic about utopian narrative is not so much the basic premise of imagining a more perfect society *per se*, as the extent to which it embodies a specifically male fantasy of establishing a familiar security. If its narrative problems seem largely associated with an inability to break away from an increasingly anachronistic narrative model, the aspects of existing social relations that it seems most consistently unable to reimagine are those to do with gender. However, not all narratives with roots in the past are necessarily regressive in their implications: while Morris's Old Hammond may appeal to the example of the Norwegian folktale of How the Man Minded the House to naturalize existing modes of gender inequity, the example of another folktale, 'Hansel and Gretel' might be helpful in establishing a context for examining ways in which utopian narrative may be rewritten from a different gender perspective.

In the early stages of the tale, the initiative is taken by the male, while the woman's role remains marginal—yet at the same time, Hansel's initiative consists solely in devising means of finding the way home, or returning to a situation that is familiar; it is only when the prospect of return is denied the children, and they find themselves confronted with the dangers of the altogether new, that Gretel takes the lead. When, having outwitted the Witch, she leads her brother back home, it is not by the old path but by an entirely new one—one which involves crossing water, symbolically marking their break with the past—and when they do return, it is no longer to the old pattern of a hierarchy in which they are subordinate. Instead, they arrive back older, wiser, and independent. As Bloch argues, the utopian desire for a world where one is truly at home is by no means the same as a desire to return to the way things once were— although it is always possible for the former to be contaminated by the latter. Without drawing too crude an analogy between 'Hansel and Gretel' and the history of utopian narrative as a whole (to see women writers as necessarily displaying Gretel-like resourcefulness in dealing with the problems involved is to lapse into another kind of essentialism), what does become clear from at least some feminist rewritings of utopia is that the introduction of a different gender perspective can result in fundamental changes to the narrative paradigm we have so far seen at work. It is with these that the final two chapters will deal.

6. A World of One's Own: Separatist Utopias

If the patriarchal character of the traditional utopian narrative paradigm is reflected not only in the social and political provisions of the Renaissance utopia, but also in the distinctively masculine character of the fantasy which underlies them, it is scarcely surprising that where the influence of this paradigm persists, its doubly patriarchal bias should be so hard to escape. As we have seen, the conscious attempts of writers such as Bellamy, Wells, and Huxley to provide for a greater degree of sexual equality are undermined by the contradictions that emerge within the narrative—which perhaps indicates the extent to which the paradigm itself serves to potentiate the latent assumptions of male dominance rooted in the culture which utopia seeks to transcend. Even dystopian attacks on the premises of the traditional utopia rarely avoid a reinscription of the utopian suppression of the female: except in Atwood's *The Handmaid's Tale*, dystopian narrative enacts an erasure of the feminine no less striking than that embodied in Bacon's *The New Atlantis*.

It would seem to follow, therefore, that a successful challenge to the inherently patriarchal assumptions of the traditional utopia might be likely to have more far-reaching narrative repercussions than those produced by Wells's primarily narrative experimentation, by libertarian reworkings of the traditional utopia's authoritarian premises, or even dystopian parody. Such a challenge is clearly the goal of a number of writers who have envisaged societies not merely no longer dominated by men, but wholly exclusive of them. And while some of these (those of Monique Wittig, Joanna Russ, or Suzy McKee Charnas, for example) are only tangentially utopian,[1] others—notably Charlotte Perkins Gilman's *Herland* (1915) and Sally Miller Gearhart's *The Wanderground* (1979)—offer fully developed accounts of a more perfect society whose most fundamental premise is the absence of men.

Herland

Of the two, *Herland* seems, at least at first sight, far closer to the traditional paradigm. Whereas Bellamy, Morris, and Wells had already acknowledged the implications of the end of the age of discovery by either projecting their utopias into the future, or else positing such science fictional scenarios as the existence of a parallel universe, Gilman adheres to the time-honoured convention of the geographical utopia, lying in some unspecified

outhland, inaccessible and undiscovered. Like More's Utopia and Bacon's
Bensalem, it once had links to the outside world, but these were decisively
evered—although not, in this instance, by the conscious decision of a male
authority figure. Where King Utopus decreed the cutting of the isthmus
connecting Utopia to the mainland, and King Solamona took the political
decision to isolate his kingdom from the rest of the world, Herland's
solation came about as the result of a natural catastrophe. At one time,
we learn, the plateau on which Herland is located was inhabited by what
s referred to as 'a bi-sexual race' (p.54), which formerly possessed all the
accoutrements of a patriarchal society: 'ships, commerce, an army, a king'
p.54)—not to mention slaves. However, like Campanella's Solarians, they
are forced by the depredations of more warlike races to retreat to the
ecurity of an impregnable stronghold—in this case, a mountain fastness
connected to the outside world only by a single pass. It is while their army
s off defending the pass that a volcanic eruption takes place, completely
blocking it—and leaving the army on the wrong side of the impenetrable
obstruction. Very few men are left behind, and those who are are promptly
wiped out by a slave uprising, followed in turn by a desperate struggle in
he course of which the surviving women kill all the male slaves. In the
end, we learn, 'There was literally no one left on this beautiful high garden
and but a bunch of hysterical girls and some older slave women' (p.55).

   With the closure of the pass it would appear that the women are doomed
not merely to isolation, but to inevitable extinction, deprived both
symbolically and literally of access by the impregnating male presence. It
s at this point, however, that they are rescued from racial oblivion by one
of their number (described as a 'wonder-woman') developing the capacity
for parthenogenesis. This proves to be an inherited trait: each of the five
daughters she bears produces five daughters in her turn, and they, with
characteristically utopian symmetry, give birth to a further five daughters
each, and so on. From the first 'Queen-Priestess-Mother' a new race of
ultra-women' (p.57) is born. In what is almost a precise mirror-inversion
of the male utopian fantasy of masculine appropriation of the womb,
Gilman imagines a womb-like environment from which the male is forever
excluded. In contrast to the Baconian dream (and Huxleian nightmare) of
rendering women superfluous to the reproductive process, Gilman posits
a scenario where it is men who are redundant.

   In most other respects, however, Gilman's all-female society conforms
closely to the traditional utopian pattern. There is the familiar emphasis
on peace and security: Herland's inhabitants are notable for their
confidence and self-assurance, which is born of their having nothing to
fear. Nature has been domesticated with an almost Wellsian single-
mindedness: wild animals have been eliminated, and while there is a

profusion of cats (which have been trained not to eat birds), there are no dogs to foul the pathways of what is repeatedly described as like a gigantic park or garden—even the trees are 'under as careful cultivation as so many cabbages' (p.14). Indeed, at times it almost seems that it is *only* in the gender of its inhabitants that Gilman's utopia differs significantly from the traditional norm. It, too, provides the womb-like security and untroubled, innocent happiness of the typical rational Eden—although it is significant that Gilman does depart from the island location so beloved of male authors of utopian fiction, isolating her utopia instead by perching it on top of a 'piece of geography [which] stands up like a basalt column' (p.38).

Gilman's major innovation, in fact, has less to do with the structure of her utopia as such, than with her handling of that most traditional feature of utopian narrative, the visit (with its attendant guided tour). Here the issue of gender becomes crucial, for Gilman chooses to problematize the relationship between visitor and utopia by making the visitors (three in number) to her all-female utopia male. This, in its turn, has a number of consequences. As we have seen, in its traditional formulation, the visit to utopia tends to impose passivity on the visitor: inevitably ignorant of how things work, of the basic facts concerning utopian society—its customs, its history, and so forth—he has therefore to be told or shown everything of importance by the more knowledgeable inhabitants. What results is a scenario which, while ostensibly dialogic in format, is actually monologic in effect: the visitor fills the role of passive and acquiescent audience, whose primary function is to elicit and be persuaded by the authoritative utterance of his utopian mentor. In *Herland*, however, the situation is radically different: the interactions between Gilman's explorers and the utopians who act as their captors, instructors, and even partners have little in common with the cosy camaraderie which exists between Julian West and Dr Leete, or William Guest and Old Hammond; nor, for that matter, is there much sign of the schoolmasterly indulgence with which Dr Robert treats Will Farnaby, let alone the self-abasing reverence of Bacon's narrator in the presence of the representative of the House of Salomon. There is, to begin with, a marked difference in emphasis. Gilman devotes far less space than usual to direct disquisitions on the wonders of utopia, and far more to the reactions of the visitors to what they experience, while at the same time exploiting the difference in gender to sharpen the contrast between their perspective and that of the inhabitants. Although the *dynamic* of the relations between visitors and utopians remains in keeping with utopian tradition, the effect could hardly be more dissimilar: in *Herland*, it is women who have the knowledge and power, the men who have to adjust to the values and expectations of the society in which they find themselves—and by enacting this reversal of conventional gender roles, Gilman calls

tention to the *situation* of the visitor in a way that most utopian fictions
) not. In place of the uncritical transmission of information which the
sitor normally provides, as if his sole purpose were to provide the reader
ith the most faithful and unmediated account possible of the merits of
topia, Gilman's visitors respond to their new situation in a manner which
often confused, reluctant, or even frankly hostile. Rather than trying to
ose the gap in perception between the utopians and their visitor/s as fast
; possible, Gilman stresses its existence, at the same time encouraging the
ader to judge the judgements of the visitors. *Herland*, in other words,
ncourages what most utopian fictions seek to suppress: an active critical
articipation on the part of the reader.

Nor is this the only change in emphasis. Inaccessible though Herland
—to the extent that it has gone undiscovered for two thousand years—
ne of the most striking features of the opening sequence is the relative
ase with which the visitors get there. While the physical barriers—
nscalable cliffs, waterfalls, mountain ranges, and so forth—which isolate
erland from the rest of the world may seem formidable enough at first
ght, surmounting the challenge which they represent involves none of
e pain, hardship, or trauma so apparent in works such as *Looking Backward*
r *Island*. Faced by such apparently insuperable geographical obstacles,
ilman's narrator and his companions avoid the normal arduous rite of
ansition by resorting to the aid of modern technology: they simply fly
ere. The enormous wealth of Terry (the most traditionally male of the
ree) provides a steam yacht to cover the first part of the journey, a
otorboat to enable them to penetrate the upper reaches of the river above
hich Herland rises, and an aeroplane to ferry them to the plateau itself.
f all journeys to utopia, it is by far the most comfortable and best-
quipped; in marked contrast to the normal utopian pattern, the visitors'
roblems begin only after they get there.

Almost from the moment of their arrival, Gilman's visitors encounter
ifficulties—which in itself distinguishes them from the majority of their
llow explorers, for whom acceptance into utopia is normally a relatively
ncomplicated process. At most, there may be a few minor bureaucratic
roblems, as in *A Modern Utopia*, or a seeking of preliminary assurances, as
Bacon's *The New Atlantis*, but in general utopian societies are notable for
e trust and hospitality with which they welcome strangers. While Julian
Vest may initially be somewhat overwhelmed by the shock of finding
imself in a new world, his utopian hosts are quick to put him at his ease,
ffering him wine, food, tobacco, and the hand of their daughter in
arriage; and the periodic unease of Morris's William Guest or Wells's Mr
arnstaple is largely attributable to their sense that utopia is almost too
ood to be true. Even in *Men Like Gods*, where almost the first action of the

visitors is to kill someone with their motor car, the first reaction of the god-like utopians is one of benevolent curiosity: the visitors actually have to shoot two of them before they finally take action.

In *Herland*, however, the situation is markedly different. Not only are the inhabitants considerably more wary of strangers, but the visitors also show themselves to be more than usually aggressive: almost their first action on arriving is to attempt to take one of the inhabitants captive. As a direct consequence, they find themselves forcibly confined—and while they are well treated, things are by no means made easy for them. It is they who have to learn the local language, there being no comfortable fiction that utopia is naturally English-speaking, and it is their masculine assumptions that have to be radically revised in the face of an exclusively female society that evidently works considerably better than their own. (It takes them some time, in fact, finally to abandon their conviction that there must be *some* men in charge, somewhere, given that everything runs so smoothly.) In response to such unaccustomed hardships, the three make an early attempt to escape, to reassert their freedom of action—only to find themselves recaptured with humiliating ease. Nor is this by any means the only humiliation they experience: in many fields of endeavour which they have been conditioned to view as exclusively male preserves, the utopian women prove themselves to be decisively superior; in a world where the 'natural' superiority of the male is not assumed, their attempts somehow to demonstrate it are repeatedly frustrated. The result is a growing sense of unease: even as early as their first confrontation with the women of utopia, the narrator confesses to

> ... the funniest feeling—a very early feeling—a feeling that I traced back and back in memory until I caught up with it at last. It was that sense of being hopelessly in the wrong that I had so often felt in early youth when my short legs' utmost effort failed to overcome the fact that I was late to school ... We felt like small boys, very small boys, caught doing mischief in same gracious lady's house. [p.19]

It is an image which recurs—and one which highlights one of the most traditionally utopian aspects of the narrative, namely, the state of childlike dependence to which the visitors are reduced. While the narrative starts out with all the trappings of a tale of conventional male derring-do, in the tradition of Rider Haggard's *She* or Conan Doyle's *The Lost World*, it soon takes a very different direction. On their arrival they are physically overpowered:

> Each of us was seized by five women, each holding arm or leg or head; we were lifted like children, straddling helpless children, and borne onward, wriggling indeed, but most ineffectually. [p.23]

'Struggling manfully, but held secure most womanfully' (p.23), they are carried inside, anaesthetized, undressed, washed, and put to bed, as even the macho Terry ruefully acknowledges, 'like so many yearling babies' (p.25)—and whereas in most utopian fictions such imposed passivity seems to constitute an important part of utopia's appeal, in Gilman's case it is exploited for comic and satiric effect. While for Julian West or Will Farnaby being tucked up in bed and put to sleep may be an unmixed blessing—a welcome return to the blissful security of childhood—for Gilman's intrepid explorers it is an unending source of embarrassment. Their evident resentment at their subordinate status in a world run by women becomes a consistent source of humour. A rarity among utopias, *Herland* is (among other things) genuinely funny.

Part of the humour, of course, lies in the conspicuous gap between the visitors' expectations and the reality they encounter. Terry, we are told, has 'visions of a sort of sublimated summer resort—just Girls and Girls and Girls' (p.7) and talks—only half-jokingly—of becoming a latter-day King Solomon. The situation in which he in fact finds himself—a prisoner, guarded and watched over by the all-too-capable women of Herland—is a source of acute discomfiture. In addition to finding it hard to come to terms with the nature of the society in which they find themselves, however, the visitors find equally unnerving the utopians' sharp eye for the gaps and contradictions that emerge from their own somewhat selective account of the world they have come from. Despite what Van, the narrator, describes as 'a tacit endeavour to conceal much of the social status at home' (p.80) the visitors frequently find themselves revealing the most discreditable features of their own society as they struggle to answer the awkward questions they are so often posed: 'such ... questions as might have intimidated a university professor' (p.65). Much to the visitors' alarm, Herland's women prove singularly adept at drawing deductions not only from what they are told, but also from 'the things we palpably avoided saying' (p.80) and reveal a disconcerting ability to put two and two together in such a way as to expose the falsity of many of their claims. Terry's comforting fiction that women enjoy a privileged position in a male-dominated society, for example, soon falls apart in the face of questioning:

> 'Tell us—what is the work of the world, that men do—which we have not here?'
>
> 'Oh, everything,' Terry said grandly. 'The men do everything, with us.' He squared his broad shoulders and lifted his chest. 'We do not allow women to work. Women are loved—idolized—honored—kept in the home to care for the children.'
>
> ... Zava begged: 'Tell me first, do *no* women work, really?'

'Why, yes,' Terry admitted. 'Some have to, of the poorer sort.'
'About how many—in your country?'
'About seven or eight million,' said Jeff … [pp.60–1]

Even from quite minor details—casual remarks about the treatment of cat
and dogs in the visitors' world—the utopians are able to draw much large
inferences as to the questionable nature of the assumptions informing thei
society as a whole. Innocent though they may be in many respects, th
utopians are far from naïve. As the narrator comments:

> … just as a clear-eyed, intelligent, perfectly honest, and well-meanin
> child will frequently jar one's self-esteem by innocent questions, s
> did these women, without the slightest appearance of malice or satire
> continually bring up points of discussion which we spent our bes
> efforts in evading. [p.62]

As a satiric device, of course, this is hardly new: Swift achieves mucl
the same kind of effect in *Gulliver's Travels*, when the King of Brobdingna
interrogates the boastful Gulliver, and accurately intuits from his replie
the unsavoury reality underlying his guest's account of European society.
Gilman's focus is rather narrower, her main concern being to expose th
inherent contradictions of her own society's sexual politics, rather than t
offer Swift's blanket condemnation of hypocrisy, injustice, cruelty
corruption—of all that renders civilization, in his view, an organized lie—
yet the device itself is similar. Where the real difference lies is in th
presence of such satire in a utopian context—for Gilman's purpose is no
merely satiric. Damaging though her critique of male values undoubtedl
is, there is nevertheless a sense of genuine dialogue at places in the text
not only do the visitors undergo a painful process of learning t
acknowledge the virtues of utopia (as opposed to accepting then
uncritically from the outset, as is so often the case), the utopians themselve
reveal an unusual degree of openness to change. Although only too awar
of the shortcomings of the visitors' world, they remain eager not only t
learn about it, but to learn, if possible, from it. While Gilman's intent is n
less didactic than that of earlier utopian writers, there are far fewer of th
ponderous, one-sided set pieces that characterize traditional utopia
narrative: dialogue, instead, becomes an interaction in which actua
communication takes place, rather than merely serving to mask th
unidirectional and monologic transmission of information.

One side-effect of this is that the actual *character* of the visitor takes o
a significance seldom encountered in the traditional utopia. While Gilman'
visitors often make fools of themselves, what they say actually *matters*, i
a way that is rarely the case in narratives where the visitor's main functio

is merely to be persuaded by what he is told, and to act as a medium for the communication of the utopian message. Normally, as we have seen, such individualizing traits as the visitor may possess—the impatience of Campanella's sea-captain, the weariness of Morris's narrator, or the mawkish sentimentality of Julian West—are rarely more than vestigial. Even the Botanist in *A Modern Utopia*, whose main function appears to be to provide some variety in terms of characterization, rapidly becomes a rather tiresome distraction from what is clearly Wells's main concern—the theorizing of a more perfect form of social organization. In Gilman's hands, however, the characterization of the visitors, although certainly schematized, has a genuine function. Whereas the character traits of most visitors to utopia are more or less interchangeable—it would make little difference to the actual narrative if it were Will Farnaby who arrived in Bellamy's future Boston, or Julian West who landed in Pala—in *Herland* they make a difference, representing as they do radically different possible interactions between the values of utopia and those of the outside world. Thus, while the narrator himself may be seen as conforming fairly closely to the traditional norm, inasmuch as he is quickly persuaded of the superiority of the utopian way, he is flanked by two companions whose long-held assumptions prove less susceptible to alteration by exposure to the utopian ideal.

The more immediately striking example of this, of course, is Terry, the ultra-masculine leader of the expedition, whose only real interest in women is as objects of sexual desire. When the reality proves to be conspicuously different than his anticipations, it is he who prompts their unsuccessful escape bid, who shows the clearest frustration at the constraints imposed upon them, and who is most consistently critical of utopian society. Yet here again Gilman's focus is less on the perfections of utopia, than on the glaring inadequacies of the visitor's response. Brave, resourceful, charismatic, 'a man's man' (p.9), Terry seems at first sight the archetypal explorer of (male-authored) romance. Yet in the context of Herland's value system his 'manliness' often seems indistinguishable from childish petulance. His evident resentment of women who do not conform to his expectations regarding appropriate female behaviour expresses itself at first in rather schoolboyish attempts at humour: he makes digs at the 'Colonels' or 'Grandmas', as he characterizes their captors, and contrives extremely forced puns on the names of the tutors assigned to them. But his hostility does not end there: instead, his frustration at the 'old-maid impudence' (p.33) that prevents him mixing with the 'real girls,' together with his conviction that 'There never was a woman yet that did not enjoy being *mastered*' (p.131), culminates in an attempted rape. Despite the example of an entire society of women controlling their own destiny and being happy doing so, he continues to cling to his fixed belief that what a woman 'really' wants is to be forced to submit to the 'superior' power of the man. Not even the dismal failure of his attempt at a practical demonstration seems to move him: while the response of his intended victim (a powerful kick in the testicles) would seem to constitute a convincing refutation of his thesis, he remains unpersuaded: '"I'd give a year of my life to have her alone again," he said slowly, his hands clenched till the knuckles were white' (p.143).

By itself, this might seem perilously close to caricature—which is not to say that a great deal of conventional male behaviour might not also be described in the same terms—but Terry's crude attempts at asserting male superiority are only one aspect of Gilman's representation of male responses to the threatening reversal of gender expectations which Herland represents. In addition to Terry and the narrator, the party has a third member—Jeff, the doctor—whose views differ markedly from those of either of his companions. Jeff, we are told, 'idealized women in the best Southern style. He was full of chivalry and sentiment, and all that. And he was a good boy; he lived up to his ideals' (p.9). As a result, it is Jeff who is by far the most enthusiastic about the matriarchal society they encounter—to the extent, indeed, that his companions begin to regard him as 'something of a traitor—he so often flopped over and took their side of things' (p.51). Yet Jeff also has his limitations: while he displays none of the closed-minded opposition which Terry exhibits, neither does he seem in any way *changed* by his experiences, as the narrator is. Where the narrator is shown as *becoming* increasingly sympathetic to the society in which he finds himself, Jeff seems almost a parody of the passive, uncritical observer of the traditional utopia (a device which has the side-effect of making the actual narrator seem more objective, and hence reliable). He has always idealized women, and seen them as other than they are—the narrator complains of his tendency to put 'rose-colored halos' (p.9) on them—with the result that when he encounters women who differ markedly from those he is used to, his attitude remains virtually unchanged: the irony that in Herland women's superiority is practical rather than theoretical one that appears to elude him. Significantly, Jeff is the only one of the three who appears unperturbed when the 'marriages' they contract in Herland turn out not to include sexual relations other than for strict procreational purposes. Unlike Terry, who attempts to rape his 'wife,' the narrator, whose resultant emotional difficulties are rendered in some detail, Jeff apparently finds the absence of sex quite as natural as do the utopians—for whom sexuality had ceased to be an issue some two thousand years before.

In seeking to illustrate the gap between the expectations of the male visitors, which are rooted in the sexual politics of their own society, and those of their utopian wives, Gilman provides a curious analogy:

> ... imagine a devoted and impassioned man trying to set up housekeeping with a lady angel, a real wings-and-harp-and-halo angel, accustomed to fulfilling divine missions all over interstellar space. This angel might love the man with an affection quite beyond his power of return or even of appreciation, but her ideas of service and duty would be on a very different scale from his. Of course, if she was a stray angel in a country of men, he might have had his way with her; but if he was a stray man among angels—! [p.123]

While hardly the most fortunate of comparisons, it does serve to suggest the extent of what Gilman terms 'the gulfs of difference' (p.94) between the utopians and their visitors. Of course, given the absence not only of sexual relations, but of any equivalent to either home or family in Herland, the fact that the utopians should consider contracting marriages with their visitors at all remains something of an unresolved contradiction. Nevertheless, the marriages do highlight what in many utopias is passed over—the fact that the inhabitants of a society radically different from our own are themselves liable to be radically different. Unlike Bellamy's Leete family, who differ hardly at all from the middle-class norms of the late nineteenth century, Gilman's utopians *are* different—despite which Jeff accepts their unorthodox views on marriage without as much as a flicker of surprise:

> He accepted the angel theory, swallowed it whole, tried to force it on us—with varying effect. He so worshipped... not only Celis, but what she represented; he had become so deeply convinced of the almost supernatural advantages of this country and people, that he took his medicine like a—I cannot say 'like a man,' but more as if he wasn't one. [p.123]

As with so many visitors to utopia, Jeff, while uncritically approving of utopia's superiority, seems oddly immune to any sense of its otherness. Utopia is better—but it is not *strange*. Like Julian West, William Guest, Mr Barnstaple, Jeff is already a convert: no process of persuasion is necessary for him.

Yet while Gilman's often satiric presentation of the interactions between the utopians and their visitors effects an unsettling reversal and defamiliarization of conventional sexual assumptions, the actual picture of utopian society that emerges mirrors many of the most familiar features of the conventional utopia. The cult of supreme male authority, implicit in the traditional utopia, seized upon and made explicit in its dystopian

inversion, is here replaced by an idealization of the feminine no 1
pronounced. With its Altar of Motherhood, its great ruling Over Motl
its repeated references to 'super-', 'ultra-', and 'wonder-women', *Herl*
offers merely a reversal, rather than any radical transcendence of
conventional narrative paradigm.[3] Although at first sight its matriarc
society could hardly seem further removed from the patriarchal norm:
utopian tradition, this reversal of one of utopian narrative's major premi
in fact leaves many of its dynamics unaffected. As Susan Gubar points c
'Gilman's strategy of reversal [often] threatens to invalidate her femini
by defining it in precisely the terms set up by the misogynists it wo
repudiate' (p.198). While the feminine values which *Herland* endorses
represented as a positive alternative to the abuses of the patriarchal soci
of the three explorers, they nevertheless reflect a conception of feminir
which is very much the creation of precisely that male-dominated soci
whose values Gilman rejects. In what amounts to its fetishization of
virtues of Motherhood, its emphasis on the sacred duties of child care, a
its repeated stress on the purity and virtue of the utopian women, *Herl*
reveals what Bammer terms an 'unsettling convergence between a visi
of what women, under utopian conditions, *could* be, and the normat
definition of what a woman, according to the prevailing ideology *sho*
be' (p.31).[4] As has often been pointed out, *Herland* is a utopia in wh
woman's sphere remains the home; the only difference is that here 1
home has expanded to embrace the entire community. When Terry sne
that '[t]here isn't a home in the whole pitiful place' (p.98), Jeff retorts tl
'[t]here isn't anything else, and you know it' (p.98). Herland is a coun
which has been entirely domesticated: there are no wild areas—even 1
forests have been groomed and 'petted' (p.13) to be useful as well
beautiful; the entire country has been purged of pests and mess-creati
animals; and overall, we learn, 'their country was as neat as a Dui
kitchen' (p.53). Despite two thousand years of separate developme
Herland's women manifest precisely those idealized qualities ascribed
them by the patriarchal ideology of early twentieth-century No
America.

   In thus effectively naturalizing her own society's socially construct
gender roles, Gilman endorses a view of 'woman' which, as Bamn
argues, is 'revalued, but not redefined' (p.93), and which ultimately ser
to reaffirm 'the very ideology of separate gender spheres on which t
suppression of women had been based' (p.35).[5] Nevertheless, wh
Gilman's vision of a utopia which is essentially the private sphere writ la
enshrines the concept of domestic virtues prevailing at the time,
emphasis on order is also wholly in keeping with the visions of utoj
offered by male writers. From More's *Utopia*, where even the cities are bc

dentical and equidistant, to Wells's *Men Like Gods*, which shares Gilman's passion for cleanliness to the point of eliminating not only all pavement-ouling animals, but even 'the untidier sorts of small birds' (p.122), utopian narratives repeatedly represent worlds where everything is in its place, known and accounted for. As in the best run homes, utopia provides an environment where nothing ever goes wrong—indeed, where nothing ever *happens*. Process and change—anything that is liable to disturb order—are normally conspicuous in utopia only by their absence.

Herland is no exception in this regard. As in so many utopias, the actual course of utopian history is vague and in places even contradictory: from a developmental level described as being equivalent to 'that of Ancient Egypt or Greece' (p.67) they have apparently advanced to the point where electric cars travel along their modern roadways, but very little appears to have *happened* in the interim. The utopians, we are told, are 'agreed on most of the basic principles of their life; and not only agreed in principle, but accustomed for these sixty-odd generations to act on those principles' (p.122), yet despite this continuity, they exhibit little interest in the past. When the narrator asks his wife-to-be 'Have you no respect for the past? For what was thought and believed by your foremothers?' she replies simply: 'Why, no... Why should we? They are all gone. They knew less than we do.' The women of Herland, he reflects, 'had ignored their past and built daringly for the future' (p.111). And this characteristically utopian vagueness concerning history has its counterpart, at the level of narrative, in a consistent vagueness with regard to the passage of time: 'the weeks ran into months' (p.33) is a typical formulation, and while we learn at the end that the visitors' stay has lasted 'more than a year' (p.137) there is virtually no specific indication of *when* anything takes place during that period. Given the opening words of the book—'This is written from memory, unfortunately' (p.1)—it would appear that this is a deliberate narrative strategy.

Yet what is perhaps most problematic in *Herland* is not so much the lack of action as (as a number of critics have pointed out) the absence of *desire*, which has apparently disappeared along with the men: the sexual tensions which trouble even so idyllic a world as that of *News from Nowhere* have simply vanished. Herland's citizens are women whose 'great life-view had no shady places; they had a high sense of personal decorum, but no shame—no knowledge of anything to be ashamed of' (p.101). As Van, the narrator, later remarks: 'No wonder this whole nation of women was peaceful and sweet in expression—they had no horrible ideas' (p.111). Free from even such 'pleasant vices' (p.98) as drinking and smoking, it is a world which, in the more acid words of Terry, is 'like a perpetual Sunday school' (p.99). Yet while this clearly reflects contemporary stereotypes of

'feminine' virtue, it is—once again—also very much in keeping w
utopian tradition. Like its Renaissance predecessors, *Herland* exhibits
characteristic utopian impulse towards simplification: problems are no
much resolved, as avoided by the elimination of their source. As in Mo
Utopia, it is difficult to get into trouble, primarily because there is so li
trouble to get into—but in some ways Gilman goes even farther. Wh
earlier utopias sought the restoration of innocence through the *contro*
desire (as for example in *The City of the Sun*, where intercourse is supervi
by a team of gym instructors, matrons, doctors, and astrologers), Gilm
eliminates it altogether.

One of the resultant problems, however, is that in doing so Gilman e
up reinstating the infantilization of the visitor which she began by satirizi
Whereas the reduction of the explorers on their arrival to the state
helpless children, undressed and put to bed, offers an effective parody
the customary passivity of the traditional visitor to utopia, it is harder
discern any such complicating irony in Gilman's later representation of 1
'marriages' contracted between the explorers and three of the inhabitar
Part of Gilman's purpose, of course, in putting forward the notion
marriages which include neither cohabitation nor sexual relations, is
focus attention on the assumptions of the male explorers, whose hor
at the absence of what they had hitherto taken for granted is rendered
some detail. (Or rather, to be more precise, the horror of two of them:
we have seen, the idealistic Jeff does not appear to notice that there
anything unusual about the arrangements.) Yet while this serves to expe
the realities underlying so much male rhetoric regarding the sanctity
marriage, Gilman's actual descriptions of Herland's unconventional mar
arrangements contain some curiously revealing analogies. When his w
refuses to accept sexual relations as a 'natural' part of marriage, Van fi
tries to rationalize this by quite literally, and apparently uncritica
comparing her to an 'angel' (p.123), and then praises her success—'gr
superwoman that she was' (p.130)—in distracting him from his sex
preoccupations:

> ... no child, stormily demanding a cookie 'between meals,' was e
> more subtly diverted into an interest in house-building than wa
> when I found an apparently imperative demand had disappear
> without my noticing it. [p.128]

Here the process of infantilization, elsewhere reinforced by his wife's u
of such epithets as 'you blessed child' (p.110), is represented in a larg
positive light—as is also the case when Van finally renounces his sex
desires in favour of his wife's purer ideal of gender relations. Indeed, t
abject submissiveness with which he acknowledges her super

judgement, in addition to reproducing the blurring of the distinction between wife and mother so strikingly apparent in the utopias of Wells and Bellamy, almost seems to prefigure the dystopian abasement of D-503 and Winston Smith in the face of the larger-than-life representative of the dominant ideology:

> After I got over the jar to my pride … I found that loving 'up' was a very good sensation after all. It gave me a queer feeling, way down deep, as of the stirring of some ancient prehistoric consciousness, a feeling that they were right somehow—that this was the way to feel. It was like—coming home to mother. [pp.141–2]

While the power relations envisaged in *Herland* may differ radically from those of the traditional male utopian fantasy, inasmuch as what is imagined is not the male recovery of prenatal security, but rather the restoration of some lost world of prehistoric matriarchy, the regressive character of the utopian dream remains very much in evidence.

One of *Herland's* most puzzling features, however, involves what would seem at first sight to be a clear departure from the utopian norm. Given that the traditional utopia so often represents a state of perfection or near-perfection, it follows that any change is likely to be for the worse, and the majority of male-authored utopias, as we have seen, include provisions to prevent such an eventuality—whether by the maintenance of formidable armies (although only, of course, for purposes of self-defence), keeping its location concealed, or extending its compass to include the entire world, thereby eliminating external enemies. In *Herland*, however, despite its inhabitants' evident satisfaction with things as they are, and in the face of all they have been able to deduce regarding the evils of the world outside, the women seem astonishingly open to the possibility of renewed relations with men—and in an attempt to render this plausible, Gilman stresses the possibility that the interaction of the male visitors with the strong, independent women of Herland may lead not only to the re-education of the former, but also to a fuller range of experience for the latter. Van's future wife, for example, declares:

> 'We are only half a people. We have our woman-ways and they have their man-ways and their both-ways. We have worked out a system of living which is, of course, limited. They must have a broader, richer, better one.' [pp.97–8]

Yet despite repeated assertions that a 'bi-sexual' society must necessarily be 'much more stirring' with 'new possibilities of growth' (p.135), their effect is undercut by the force of Gilman's own satire. Such optimism hardly seems compatible with the bleak picture which the utopians have deduced from their visitors' account of the outside world—and while this does, of course, open the way for a sequel (duly provided in *With Her in Ourland*, in which Van and his wife undertake a tour of his world), one of the least convincing features of *Herland*'s decidedly abrupt conclusion is the utopians apparent readiness to accept their visitors' word of honour as gentlemen 'not in any way to betray the location of this country' (p.145). Although Terry, angry and humiliated following his unsuccessful rape attempt immediately protests (in language strongly reminiscent of colonialist fantasies of the land as a female body awaiting penetration) that '[t]he first thing I'll do is to get an expedition fixed up to force an entrance into Ma land' (p.146), the women are apparently quite content to rely on the entirely alien concept of a gentleman's word[6]—to the extent that a mere six line later his promise has been accepted, and their departure ensues.[7]

This tacit acceptance of the values of the society to which *Herland* offer an alternative, however, is hard to reconcile with Gilman's repeated emphasis on the incompatibility between Herland and its visitors (relationship which differs radically from that obtaining in the traditional utopia). Simply by reason of their being male, they represent both a threat and a challenge to the utopian order in a way that the traditional visitor does not. Although Morris's narrator may be unable to sustain his utopian dream, and while Wells's Mr Barnstaple may consent to return to his own world, there is normally no *inherent* incompatibility between the visitor and utopia. Once converted to the utopian way, there is no reason why the visitor should not be co-opted and absorbed by the more perfect society (as is Julian West, for example). In *Herland*, by contrast, the visitors impose on utopia the imperative to change: unless the visitors are deported imprisoned, or done away with,[8] their mere presence implies that utopia will ultimately have to adapt to new and potentially disruptive forms human relationship. While the focus is primarily on the ways in which the visitors are forced to adjust, it is clear that utopia, too, will be changed by their continued residence. This, in its turn, is a reflection of the fact that Gilman's utopian society is one whose basis is biologically, as well as socially determined—and while this is in part responsible for the more dynamic character of the relations between utopia and its visitors, it is clear that also creates certain problems.

Whereas the traditional utopia posits a society structured in such a way as to promote more desirable conduct on its members' part, Gilman's make inherited characteristics—namely sexual difference—equally, if not more fundamental: the basis of her more perfect society is genetic as well environmental. As a result, the male visitor becomes an alien, differing from the utopians not merely in terms of values, but in terms of his very being. The superiority of the utopians is, implicitly, innate, rather than being something to which the visitor, given sufficient exposure to a utopian environment, might aspire. While in theory, Gilman's separatist utopia may be seen as offering a model from which the rest of the world might well learn, the problems inherent in the notion of a society whose superiority has, even in part, a genetic basis remain unresolved. If sexual difference can provide such a basis, one might well ask, then why not race? Gilman's own racist tendencies have been commented on,[9] and it is scarcely reassuring to learn that Herland's inhabitants are most likely 'of Aryan stock, and were once in contact with the best civilization of the old world' (p.54). We are also informed that 'They were 'white,' but somewhat darker than our northern races because of their constant exposure to sun and air' (p.54). And while such overt statements are very much the exception in Herland,[10] the unsettling implications remain: Gilman's is yet another in which some of the least appealing features of the dominant ideology of the time are still more starkly reproduced.

The Wanderground

Where such implications can lead may be seen more clearly in Sally Miller Gearhart's The Wanderground, in which women's superiority, rather than emerging from the confrontation of a female utopian society with the crass assumptions of males from the outside world, becomes a given—a fact to be celebrated. Written from the perspective of a feminism far more radical than Gilman's, it portrays a world in which sexual difference is likewise far more polarized. While the women of the Wanderground possess (as we shall see) quite literally supernatural powers, which are used not only for their own protection, but for that of the planet, the men of the City are described as 'Driven in their own madness to destroy themselves and us and any living thing' (p.3). Men and women are adversaries, between whom the dialogue which is so striking a feature of Herland is no longer even an option:[11] 'We once had hope for them, but even that hope they snuffed out' (p.2), laments one of the Hill Women. Even with the gentles'—the small minority of men 'who, knowing that maleness touched women only with the accumulated hatred of centuries, touched no women at all' (p.2)—communication is a precarious affair, fraught with hostility and suspicion.

Yet it is not merely the patriarchal ideology of the traditional utopia that Gearhart challenges: The Wanderground also represents—at least at first sight—an equally radical break with the traditional narrative paradigm. It is a utopia without visitors (the only contacts with outsiders take place beyond its borders), without compensatory metaphors of transition, and without even any real linear, connected narrative. In its place are a series

of loosely overlapping episodes concerning the lives of the Hill Women
which only a handful of characters recur, yet from which there neverthe
emerges a comprehensive picture of how Gearhart's utopians deal w
the realities of love, death, danger, religious experience, and interact
with the natural world. They are portrayed in conference on question
policy, engaging in defence duty, and—most unusually—mak
concerted efforts to preserve the memory of the past from which th
utopia emerged: as in *News from Nowhere*, the section dealing with the p
is by far the longest in the book. In addition, *The Wanderground* is a w
in which the element of fantasy is far more crucial than in any of the utop
so far discussed.

As we have seen, despite such episodes as the miraculous apparition
an advance copy of the Bible in *The New Atlantis*, it is noteworthy that
majority of traditionally conceived utopias content themselves w
relatively modest extrapolations from the realities of their time. The contr
between Wells's exuberant exploration of the possibilities of weig
lessness, invisibility, time travel, and interplanetary travel in his scie
fiction, for example, and the modesty of invention evident in his utop
could scarcely be more marked. Gearhart, by contrast, shows little reg
for the constraints of relative plausibility, which lay something of a de
hand on the inventiveness of so many earlier utopian works. Whereas
traditional utopia tends to rely as little as possible on exceeding the lin
of existing human or technological possibilities (leaving aside whate
bizarre elaborations may surround the process of getting there),
Wanderground makes no pretence at realism. Like *News from Nowhere*, o
to a far greater degree, Gearhart's utopia offers, not so much a poten
blueprint for a more perfect society, as a prefigurative vision of fut
possibilities—presumably designed, like those of Morris and Bogdanov
energize and inspire a readership already engaged in various forms
political and personal struggle towards goals to which utopian fiction is a
to give a more concrete image than any provided by contemporary soci

Set at an unspecified point in the future, *The Wanderground* posits a wo
in which the total destruction of the environment by a male-domina
society has only been forestalled by what is termed the 'Revolt of
Mother' (p.158)—the Earth's refusal to consent any longer to its violati
No explanation is offered as to the cause of this, but its effects are drama
Machines and weapons suddenly cease to function; animals refuse to
ridden by males; and men lose their sexual potency outside the urb
enclaves within which most of them live. Nevertheless, the threat that m
may one day recover both their sexual and technological power remai
and it is the prevention of such a disaster that constitutes one of the m
priorities of the Hill Women, who represent Gearhart's vision of an

female utopian society. Like the inhabitants of Herland, the Hill Women have developed the capacity for parthenogenesis, but whereas that was virtually the sole element of the marvellous in Gilman's utopia, in Gearhart's it is merely one wonder among many. Over the years, the Hill Women have developed their psychic powers to the point where their abilities are, quite literally, supernatural—a premise which also allows Gearhart to bypass some of the more problematic aspects of women's situation in existing society. Thus, in response to the growing feminist awareness during the 1970s that women were the prisoners (or even the creation) of linguistic as well as social structures, Gearhart fantasizes a world beyond language altogether: although the 'discipline' of speaking aloud is sometimes practiced 'for the refining of present images and the generation of new ones' (p.60), communication between the Hill Women is otherwise almost exclusively telepathic.[12] In addition, having learned to channel their mental energies, they have developed the capacity to fly ('windriding'), lift enormous weights ('toting'), swim for long distances underwater, engage in psychic healing, and participate in energy exchanges with trees. As well as being able to communicate with cats, dogs, birds, snakes, horses, and fish, they enjoy empathic communion not only with the Earth and the Moon, but even with such unlikely objects as holes in the ground and cakes of dried tuna. Indeed, in one scene, a pair of lovers even use their combined psychic powers for the rather prosaic purpose of making tea:

> The early morning ritual of beginning together proceeded that day along familiar lines: in mutual mind effort from across the room they enfolded the tea water, requesting it to boil, aiding it, with its consent, in doing so. [p.20]

More commonly, however, their powers are employed for less mundane ends: as well as maintaining a constant telepathic watch along the border that separates the Wanderground from the Dangerland—beyond which lies the male-dominated City—the Hill Women also maintain a presence in the City itself. Disguised as men, and assisted by the 'gentles,' a network of strong, psychically powerful women use their powers to prevent the male energy of the City extending beyond its confines. The necessity for this is confirmed by the consequences reported when the rotation of the Hill Women in the City is temporarily disrupted:

> 'Several years ago when three hill women were caught and killed in the City whole parties of celebrating men and their women poured into the countryside. They revved up deserted farm machinery and hauled truckloads of copulating couples around a field all night long.

Things stopped rather suddenly, a cessation that corresponded precisely to the arrival in the City of the hill women's replacements ... Last year when some crisis called four ... women home without warning, some would-be hunters holding rifles that had not fired for generations found that live ammunition worked. There were several rapes at that time, too—country men of their wives or of women living alone who thought they were safe. When the hill women returned or were replaced the effect took hold again. No shots. No rapes.' [p.175]

Except for the gentles, who are accorded a distinctly wary and qualified respect, men are presented exclusively as would-be rapists, wholly responsible for the ills that have befallen the planet. In contrast to the flat rage that often surfaces, expressing itself in 'visions of manslaying, of man mangling' (p.128), Gilman's satire seems positively genial.[13]

Like Gilman's, however, Gearhart's is a utopia of which the fundamental premise is basically a *reversal* of the traditional utopian pattern: patriarchal authority is once again replaced by an exclusively female system of social organization. Yet while Gearhart makes this the starting point for a far more radical imagining of the resultant possibilities, a curiously familiar picture begins to appear when one examines the work in detail. Again, as in *Herland*, what emerges is less a departure from the utopian norm, than its mirror inversion—in which many of the same contradictions are apparent. For all its narrative innovation, in fact, *The Wanderground* shares a surprising number of the characteristic features of the traditional utopia. While the existence of the Hill Women is anything but the comfortable, problem-free idyll depicted in *Looking Backward* or *News from Nowhere*, their almost obsessive (though understandable) defensive precautions have much in common with those of More's Utopians or Campanella's Solarians. As in *Utopia* and *The City of the Sun*, the more perfect society is only made possible by the exclusion of the outside world. Likewise, although Gearhart's emphasis on the virtue of privacy (violation of another's privacy is referred to as 'man's crime') may seem something of an anomaly in a utopian context, the pervasiveness of telepathic communication among the Hill Women creates an atmosphere as oppressively public as anything to be found in the work of More or Wells. As in *A Modern Utopia* and *Men Like Gods*, everyone's location is known, and while the intent of the following passage is presumably to suggest the power of women's solidarity, its portrayal of the submersion of individual identity in that of the group conjures up echoes of the dystopian visions of Zamyatin and Huxley:

Hot bodies surrounded her: Juda's head to her left at waist level, Tolatilita's to her right; Yva and Rhoda prone on each of her legs.

Lyssa and Phtha hovering over her own head. They wiped her face, her body, with sharp-smelling leaves. The incantations swirled around and over her, words circling her head, her body, words sliding over her skin, drooping around her ribs and over her brow, under her fingernails and through the curling forest of the mountain slopes and planes; words leapt and pounded in the sockets of her spine; words bent and broke in the crevice of her brain. A thousand hands now moved on her flesh, a thousand eyes now peered at the window of her soul, a thousand lips caressed at the door of her deepest self. [p.51]

Elsewhere, following the 'Gatherstretch'—a telepathic conference involving most of the Hill Women—one of the children awakens and comes downstairs to find the exhausted adults lying in a tangle which she describes as 'like a kitten pile' (p.132), and this is merely one of many scenes in which security is provided by physical contact. Womb imagery abounds, here overt and explicit, rather than oblique and indirect, as is so often the case in male-authored utopias: indeed, the image of organic, nurturing enclosure is central to the work itself, reflected in the Hill Women's nest-like dwellings; in the subterranean passages of the Remember Rooms, where they recall the past; in the tunnels of the 'Deep Cella', where the rite of impregnation is enacted; and even in their characteristic mode of telepathic communication, often referred to as 'enfoldment.'

Nor is the geography of *The Wanderground*, for all its inversion of the traditional utopian pattern, any less suggestive. Whereas the majority of utopias are located in the mythical southland of male fantasy, the territory of the Hill Women is in the north, *above* the regions inhabited by men. (Herland, likewise, is portrayed as rising above the surrounding region.) The Hill Women themselves live mainly in the twin 'ensconcements,' the breast-like curves of whose borders overlook the 'Dangerland'—a disputed area over which neither women nor men have established hegemony— beyond which lies the City, the enclave where male sexuality still functions. In the map which prefaces the text, the implications are still harder to ignore: within a geographical configuration that strikingly resembles a woman's body, the male-dominated City occupies the space where the genitalia would be. What Gearhart's utopia unquestioningly accepts, in other words, is the traditional utopian identification of the land as female— the difference being that it is no longer territory available to be colonized by the male, but rather a domain to be reclaimed by the formerly colonized female.[14] In effect, *The Wanderground* embodies a fantasy of returning to a state of being that formerly existed, before the damage was done. As Bammer argues:

... the unpredictable and contradictory dynamics of change are finally collapsed into an almost mystical vision of harmony defined as the restoration of natural order. Gearhart's utopian vision ... is in the end based not on an estranged view of history, but on the attempt to transcend it. [p.89]

While the *kind* of past that Gearhart seeks to recover may differ radically from that imagined in the traditional, male-authored utopia, the regressive character of the underlying fantasy is no less apparent.

The principle of reversal extends still further, however: where the traditional utopia seeks to re-establish the security of the womb by the imposition of a distinctively masculine order, *The Wanderground* depicts a world in which many aspects of that order are recreated—only by means which Gearhart represents as essentially female. While the Hill Women are, for example, adamantly opposed to any form of technology (which they see as merely a tool of male domination), it is clear that their refusal of technology goes hand-in-hand with a conscious decision to pursue many of its goals by other means. And here again contradictions begin to emerge. On the one hand, we are told that 'women could have built what's been called "western civilization"; we knew how to do all of it but rejected most such ideas as unnecessary or destructive' (p.145). Yet at the same time it becomes apparent that, by pursuing the development of their own psychic powers, the Hill Women have in fact become capable of achieving everything that technology once made possible: 'We can do anything that the old machines could do. And with a good deal less effort' (p.145). With their rituals, incantations, telepathy, intuition, and psychic strength, the Hill Women have effectively realized virtually the entire technological programme first adumbrated in Bacon's *The New Atlantis*: flight, underwater exploration, long-range communications—not to mention the ability to create life without resorting to conventional methods of reproduction—all are there. Bacon's longstanding dream of regaining the 'dominion over creation' lost by the Fall has all but come true: although the Hill Women would no doubt reject the terms in which it is expressed as overly suggestive of the male desire for mastery over nature, the Wanderground is nevertheless a world where nature does their bidding. Indeed, as Bammer points out, the science-fictional neologisms that Gearhart coins to describe the Hill Women's powers evoke 'an image of power more congruent with the high-tech potential of an age of radars, lasers, and micro-computers than with the forces of nature [they are] meant to signify' (pp.91–2); although she attempts to go outside existing language to find terminology to describe the Hill Women's utopian reality, the result ultimately subverts the binary opposition she seeks to establish between woman/nature on the one hand and man/power on the other.[15] While the Hill Women are of course, justifiably proud of their refusal to reproduce many of the negative features of technology, such as bombs, nerve gas, and so forth—his satisfaction begins to seem more than a little complacent when it becomes apparent that what they *have* developed is a potentially genocidal superweapon of their own. In the Gatherstretch, it would appear, the combined psychic energies of hundreds of Hill Women generate a channeled power which could prove literally lethal—and it is a power which a sizeable faction seem eager to use for destructive ends: 'Let us wipe the City out now. One directed gatherstretch ...' (p.129)

The implications are, to put it mildly, alarming—not least in that the enemy is genetically determined. Men, it is claimed, 'are no longer of the same species' (p.115), while the Hill Women, for their part, disclaim all responsibility for the evils that have befallen the Earth. In their incantations in the concluding section, all blame is laid squarely at the door of Man:

> The Crown of Creation.
> He is the slayer.
> His is the litany.
> We are the slain ... [p.193]

His crimes are enumerated, women's freedom from complicity in them is celebrated, and after the briefest possible expression of remorse for such part as women might have played in aiding Man's enormities, the ceremony moves on to imagine the final death of Man through his own destructive impulses, leading to the affirmation: '*With water and blood we can wash away the slayer. / With water and blood we can wash away the race.*' It is in many respects a characteristic utopian fantasy—one of being able to remain as one is (in this case, true to an ahistorically conceived essential femininity), but without guilt.[16] There are some qualifications, certainly: that women have occasionally collaborated with the male oppressor is reluctantly conceded, while elsewhere it is even acknowledged that 'It is too simple ... to condemn them all or to praise all of us' (p.2). Yet this concession is promptly undermined by the qualification that immediately follows it: 'But for the sake of earth and all she holds, that simplicity must be our creed' (p.2). There may be men—the gentles, for instance—who are not all bad, but for the sake of a higher cause the simplifying fiction must be upheld, even in the face of evidence to the contrary. It is a logic with which Goebbels would certainly have been familiar.

An unfair comparison? Perhaps—although it is hardly one that *The Wanderground* does a great deal to discourage. As Bammer points out, the uncomplicated ascription of woman to the realm of nature was also a central feature of Nazi ideology—as was the appeal to a glorified mythic past (although not, as in Gearhart's case, a matriarchal one) whose recovery

becomes a central goal. If More's and Campanella's visions of a ratio
social order have been seen (whether justifiably or not) as prefiguring
communist dream of an end to human exploitation, Gearhart's emph
on the mystic properties of the blood, the unlimited powers of the hun
will, the appeal of group ritual, and above all the simplistic attributior
all ills to a genetically determined Other, suggests a rather different para
Part of the appeal of fascism, as Bloch has argued, lies in its awarenes:
the utopian allure of the simple solution. To blame economic crisis on
Jews, or mass unemployment on foreign immigrants is *simpler* than seek
the source of such problems in the complexities of modern capitalism
the same time, by identifying the Other as responsible for whatever
gone wrong, fascist ideology absolves of guilt all those to whom it appe
And, so long as problems persist, it takes only a small step to identify
simple, not to mention the final solution—the elimination of those w
are to blame: Jews, immigrants, or, in Gearhart's case, men—taking c
first, of course, to deny their essential humanity. Once the other has b
identified as an 'inferior race,' or 'no longer of the same species' (p.1
there is likely to be only one outcome: to return once more to We
declaration in *A Modern Utopia*—'[t]here is only one sane and logical th
to be done with a really inferior race, and that is to exterminate it' (p.3
What lies beyond the final solution is, of course, utopia: a world where
'natural' order has been restored, and where guilt and evil have b
banished along with those who were their source. Even as it seeks
challenge and subvert the norms of the traditional male utopia,
Wanderground shows all too clearly how the utopian impulse to pur
premises to their logical conclusion often serves to unmask their m
alarming implications.

At the same time, it is clear that much of the dynamism of Gearha
narrative—the sense it communicates (highly unusual in utopian fictic
of people having experiences that actually matter—is dependent on
very fact of the existence of the hated Other. The violent and disturb
struggle between the two lovers, Seja and Alaka, stems from Se
uncontrollable rage over another woman's rape; the anxiety, tensi
anger that surfaces during the Gatherstretch are occasioned by the prop
that the Hill Women meet with men officially (only 'gentle,' but men nc
the less); even the Hill Women's highly un-utopian preoccupation w
the past is rooted in their need to maintain awareness of the dangers t
have escaped. However much they may deny their connection with
men of the City, it is against the men that they define themselves; fr
the Other that they derive part of their own identity.[17] In this it is h
not to see both a reflection of the political realities of Gearhart's own socic
and at the same time yet another example of the curious utopian tende

:o displace those realities into the realm of sexual politics. In *Looking Backward*, as we have seen, Bellamy replaces the economic incentives of :he late nineteenth century free market by sexual ones, while not even Morris, who envisages a far more radical transcendence of the realities of contemporary society, can imagine the total disappearance of the desire for possession, which translates itself into the violent sexual jealousy which constitutes the lone disruptive element in his idyllic future. Likewise, in :he polarized oppositions of *The Wanderground*, what we encounter is surely a reinscription of the simplistic dualism of the Cold War: In God We Trust versus The Evil Empire; us versus them; women versus men. Gearhart's is yet another utopia which reproduces, albeit on a different plane, the limitations of the reality which it seeks to transcend.

Gender and Utopian Narrative (part two)

While both *The Wanderground* and *Herland* offer a direct challenge to the patriarchal assumptions of the traditional utopia, what becomes clear is the extent to which even this leaves some familiar problems unresolved. Although Gearhart and Gilman avoid some of the narrative pitfalls inherent in the traditional paradigm, their strategy of simply reversing the terms of the conventional utopia results—as is so often the case in dystopian narrative—in the reproduction, rather than resolution of many of its most problematic features. What is perhaps most striking, however, is the degree to which both writers share the traditional utopian tendency to accept as natural a conception of essential femininity that itself derives from the gender relations of their own society. Clearly, neither Gilman nor Gearhart share Campanella's assumption of women's weakness, which undermines the apparently enlightened vision of gender equality which his utopia proposes, or Bellamy's conviction that women's true role is to provide the incentive for male industrial productivity. Nevertheless, their ahistorical ascription to women of precisely those qualities traditionally associated with them by patriarchal society creates problems which are by no means resolved simply by presenting such qualities in a more positive light. Gilman's utopians may well be stronger and more athletic than their counterparts in the real world, but they continue to manifest the virtues of purity, goodness, and maternal kindness to children which constitute the ideal of femininity in the patriarchal society of her own era; and while the Hill Women are still more spectacularly accomplished, they are again represented as loving, nurturing, spiritually aware, and closely associated with Nature.

What this fails to conceal, however, is the extent to which these 'essential' qualities are in fact relational. Although Gilman's fantasy of a

'natural' femininity grown strong enough to withstand male oppressi
differs in emphasis from Gearhart's vision of out-and-out separatism, ea
depends on the existence of an Other to which such essentialized feminin
can be opposed. Both, in effect, are fantasies of redemption: the on
liberal feminist vision of bringing peace and harmony to existing soci
through the influence of values which are themselves a product of tl
society; the other a radical feminist dream of rescuing the Earth from t
demonized Other, and being rewarded by the restoration of an untroubl
symbiotic union with Nature. Nevertheless, as Thürmer-Rohr argues:

> We cannot simply say: Patriarchy has turned out to be a form
> society whose predominant members, men, saw as valual
> something that turned out not to be valuable. Therefore we wom
> are finally taking our different morality out of the closet, setting t
> priorities ourselves, replacing and occupying the empty spaces. I s
> this fine challenge as an ahistorical illusion. We are not boundi
> into unoccupied territory; such territory doesn't exist. Besides, v
> have nothing in our possession, or not enough, with which to occu
> this no place in our own way—a completely different, brand-n
> way. [p.104]

Although the gender basis of Gilman's and Gearhart's utopias serves
heighten the sense of their difference from existing society, they are
many ways as hampered by the baggage of the past as their male-author
counterparts. Once again, the connection between utopia and real wo
may be obscured, but it cannot be altogether concealed.

  In another sense, however, the separation between reality and uto
becomes more pronounced. While it may be argued that the narrati
premises of *Herland* and *The Wanderground* are not in themselves any m
fantastic than the positing of hundred-year sleeps, parallel universes,
life on Mars by earlier authors, there is a crucial difference in terms of wh
Levitas terms the 'perceived possibility' (*Concept of Utopia*, p.194) of t
utopian society envisaged. While none of the utopias so far discussed a
concerned with the actual *prediction* of the nature of a future society, the
can be little doubt that works such as *Looking Backward, A Modern Utop*
or *Red Star* are based on the assumption that a society something like th
imagined by the writer would be both possible and desirable. With *Herla*
and *The Wanderground*, however, this is clearly not the case. For all h
emphasis on women's strength, and on the inequities of existing socie
there is never a sense that Gilman is actually *advocating* separatism as
solution—as is clear from the rather unsatisfactory conclusion; and wh
Gearhart might well see her imaginary society as *desirable*, it is clearly n
her intent to represent features such as human flight, parthenogenesis,

telepathic tea-making as possible in the same sense as, say, Bogdanov's representation of Martian child care arrangements.

There are, of course, certain benefits in such an approach, particularly in narrative terms. As Levitas remarks, '[w]here utopia is not expected to be realised, one is constrained only by what it is possible to imagine, not by what it is possible to imagine as possible' (*Concept of Utopia*, p.193): one side-effect of the greater imaginative freedom made possible by the abandonment of the criterion of 'perceived possibility' is that both *Herland* and *The Wanderground* exhibit a narrative dynamism far removed from that of the traditional ponderous utopian guided tour. At the same time, however, there is a cost involved. While, as we have seen, the traditional utopia is often evasive about the process whereby a more desirable society might be created, the retreat from the notion of utopia as at least possible results in a still further diminished sense of agency. In the case of *The Wanderground* in particular, the reliance on quasi-divine intervention—the 'Revolt of the Mother'—as the premise for the establishment of a utopian society has a decidedly millennialist flavour, somewhat reminiscent of the native American Ghost Dancers' belief in the great wave of earth that would cross the continent, obliterating the white man as it passed. Yet, as Levitas goes on to argue, millennial fantasies of divine intervention are most frequent among 'groups which perceive themselves, often correctly, as unable to exert control over the course of history' (p.194). While they may provide the incentive to acts of opposition (usually doomed), they may equally reflect a fatalism which she suggests is 'the key issue' (p.195) when it comes to the writing of utopias:

> Where it is no longer assumed that social organisation is inherently controllable by human agents, or where it is no longer believed that the agents who are in control can themselves be made accountable to the rest of us, much of the motive for the construction of utopias as goals is lost. They cease to be images of a hoped-for future and become again expressions of desire. The role of fantasy increases and utopia is less and less intended as a literal goal, and less bound by constraints of literal plausibility. [pp.195–6]

In the case of *The Wanderground* in particular, for all its undeniable narrative benefits, this removal of hope to 'the realm of fantasy and myth,' as Bammer puts it, leads inevitably to a utopia which presents 'a separation from reality rather than a process of intervention' (p.89). Whether this represents a step forward is a question that will be addressed in the final chapter.

7: Dreams of Freedom: Piercy, Le Guin, and the Future of Utopia

What begins to emerge in both the libertarian visions of Morris, Bogdan(and Huxley, and the separatist utopias of Gilman and Gearhart, is increasing sense that the relationship between utopia and reality is one which conflict is inherent. In *News from Nowhere*, as we have seen, t transition to utopia is marked by violence and bloodshed, while t memory of the squalor and brutality of the narrator's own time repeate(threatens the precarious fabric of the utopian dream, ultimat(overwhelming it altogether. *Red Star* not only begins and ends in the mi(of revolutionary struggle, but also includes serious consideration by t utopians of a possible war of extermination against the human race followed by the murder of its chief proponent by the visitor from Ear while in *Island*, utopia is quite literally overwhelmed by a hostile outsi world. In *Herland*, likewise, it is clear that the utopians' wariness of th(visitors from outside is amply justified: in the light of their initial atten to capture one of the local inhabitants, not to mention Terry's subseque attempted rape, or his threat to organize an expedition 'to force an entrar into Ma-land' (p.146), the decision to imprison them until 'tamed a trained to a degree they considered safe' (p.72) seems eminen reasonable. The visitors from 'our' reality have, so to speak, to be utopia ized before being allowed their freedom. And in *The Wanderground*, course, relations between the utopian Hill Women and what remains modern civilization are marked by outright hostility.

It may be objected, however, that such antagonism is already impli in the Renaissance utopia. The ruthless defence policy of More's Utopia the massive fortifications of the City of the Sun, and the precautions whi Bacon's Bensalemites observe to prevent the discovery of their land har(suggest that congenial relations with the rest of the world are seen as like Nevertheless, there is a difference: in each case, utopia's strength sufficient to render it secure: such is the military might of the Utopia and Solarians, not to mention the technological superiority of t Bensalemites, that there is never the slightest suggestion that the outsi world represents a threat to their stability. Conversely, their remoten(renders them models which may safely be admired—at a comforta(distance. Even where More explicitly contrasts the virtues of Utopia to t shortcomings of his own society, there is little sense that the more perf(

rder imposes anything so threatening as an imperative to change. As the
narrator himself remarks in conclusion: 'I confess there are many things
1 the Commonwealth of Utopia which I wish our own country would
mitate—though I don't really expect it will' (p.91).

In the utopias of Bellamy and Wells, of course, even the implication
aat utopia and reality are inimical all but vanishes. In *Looking Backward*,
s we have seen, utopia supersedes the old order without so much as a
int of opposition; while *In the Days of the Comet* depicts humanity emerging
om its slumber unanimously committed to the construction of a better
/orld. More speculative in tone, *A Modern Utopia* allows that some of the
etails of the more perfect society may be open to debate, but the *desirability*
f a utopia along the general lines suggested remains a given. Only in *Men
ike Gods* is there active opposition to the utopian ideal, in the shape of
upert Catskill and his companions, but even this intrusion from the past
epresents little real challenge: once they become too troublesome, they
re swept aside like so many irritating insects. The utopian truths are self-
vident to all but a benighted few, who will soon be left behind by the
nevitable course of history. Utopia, worldwide and unchallenged, is in
ach case represented as a form of manifest destiny.

Morris is thus perhaps the first writer seriously to challenge the
omforting fiction that the transition to utopia would be painless, injurious
o no one's vested interests—and it is no coincidence that his is among the
rst utopias to stress the *precariousness* of the utopian vision, not to mention
he fact that even the capacity to dream requires some degree of liberation
om the bare necessities of life. Yet even while Morris acknowledges the
ecessity of struggle, and the sheer difficulty of creating a better world, his
ctual *representation* of conflict remains marginal to the utopia he depicts.
lthough the chapter entitled 'How the Change Came' is the longest in
he book, the account it offers remains self-contained, isolated from the
nain body of the text. For most of the utopians, such conflict is a thing of
he past: the struggles whereby 'the world ... was brought to its second
irth' (p.112) are hardly more than a dream. It is not until much later that
ve encounter utopian fictions in which the conflict between utopia and
eality which Morris recognizes becomes more central—integral to the
epiction of an alternative social order in which utopia is neither a static
lternative, remote from reality, nor the inevitable destination of a linear
istorical process, but rather a disputed territory, to be fought for in the
ere and now.

It is this focus on change and conflict that Moylan identifies as central
o what he terms the 'critical utopia'—which he sees as distinguished by
n 'awareness of the limitations of the utopian tradition ... [rejecting]
topia as blueprint while preserving it as dream' (*Demand the Impossible*,

p.10), by its concern with 'the conflict between the originary world and the utopian society opposed to it so that the process of social change is more directly articulated' (p.10), and by a focus 'on the continuing presence of difference and imperfection within utopian society itself' (pp.10–11). In addition, the 'apparently unified, illusionary, and representational text of the more traditional utopia' (p.46) is replaced by a more fragmented and self-reflexive narrative, in which the single, authoritative vision of the traditional paradigm is never allowed to establish itself. As examples, Moylan cites works by Russ, Le Guin, Piercy, and Delany—and given that he sees these as in large measure resolving the problems, both narrative and ideological, inherent in earlier utopian writing, it is to a consideration of these that we will now turn.

In two of Moylan's examples, in fact, Russ's *The Female Man* and Delany's *Triton*, utopia is stripped altogether of its privileged position as the central focus of the text, coexisting instead with other, non-utopian (or even frankly dystopian) portrayals of society—the effect being to create a multiplicity of perspectives, in which the utopian is seen as only one of a variety of possibilities. In *The Female Man*, for example, the action shifts back and forth between four different settings, only one of which is utopian, and in the process we are offered fragmentary glimpses, rather than a comprehensive vision of the utopian world of Whileaway—an all-female society in which extremely advanced technology and minimal government combine to maximize individual freedom. In *Triton*, the hapless protagonist moves through a range of worlds, some desirable, some quite the reverse, at home in none of them—the crowning irony being his inability to take advantage of utopian possibilities even when they present themselves. Yet while both fictions go some way to resolving many of the problems which have been identified as characteristic of traditional utopian narrative, they do so at a certain cost. In each, the notion of utopia as 'perceived possibility', whose coexistence with the opposing notion of utopia as an unattainable ideal creates such a fertile and life-giving tension in so many earlier fictions, again gives way—as in *Herland* and *The Wanderground*—to what is more in the nature of a thought-experiment, where utopia becomes primarily a device for defamiliarizing and calling into question the assumptions which we bring to reality. It is significant that in both *The Female Man* and *Triton* the utopian society itself remains a given, made possible largely by means of the sort of technological fix so beloved of earlier writers. In Russ's Whileaway the problem of labour has been all but eliminated by means of the 'induction helmet', which allows for direct mental control of machinery; while on Triton, one of the moons of Neptune, Delany depicts a society where a whole battery of standard science fictional devices— gravity shields, cybernetic technology, advanced surgical and psychotherapeutic techniques—make possible not only universal abundance, but also overnight changes in both gender and sexual orientation. What each offers, in effect, is another form of simplification by exclusion: the solution of certain problems is taken as read, thereby making it possible to focus more exclusively on others. For both Russ and Delany, the elimination of basic economic problems by technology allows them to focus primarily on questions of sexual politics (a displacement which, as we have seen, is by no means atypical of traditional utopian narrative) in which they are clearly far more interested.

Yet while both Russ and Delany succeed in avoiding some of the most characteristic weaknesses of the traditional utopia—its ponderous didacticism, its imposition on the reader of a specific (and often authoritarian) vision, its unquestioning reproduction of existing patterns of gender relations—they abandon in the process much of what renders utopian fiction utopian. Russ offers only a fragmentary vision of the more perfect society, while Delany's *Triton*, as we have seen, refuses the title of 'utopia' altogether. And while this may be no bad thing (indeed, commentators such as Bammer argue that it is only in such fragmentary glimpses or 'partial visions' that genuinely utopian alternatives can be advanced), the question remains whether or not it is possible to create a fiction in which the outline of an at least plausible social ideal continues to be central, yet which at the same time resolves some of the perennial narrative and ideological problems inherent in the genre.

In this regard perhaps the most interesting experiments are provided by two of Moylan's other examples, Piercy's *Woman on the Edge of Time* and Le Guin's *The Dispossessed*, and also by Le Guin's later *Always Coming Home*, all of which offer detailed visions of utopian society, only no longer in isolation, linked to reality only by the presence of the visitor. In both *Woman on the Edge of Time* and *The Dispossessed*, utopia's troubled, precarious, yet at the same time life-giving relationship with reality emerges from a pattern of alternating episodes, in which events in utopia are counterpointed to those in the 'real' world. And while *Always Coming Home* represents a utopia far removed in time from the world of our own day, the sense of the relationship between the two remains strong: if utopia is haunted by the nightmare of our reality, equally our reality is permeated by a saving awareness of the utopian dream.

Like Russ and Delany, both Piercy and Le Guin use the conventions of science fiction to provide the vehicle for their utopian extrapolations: the more perfect societies of *Woman on the Edge of Time* and *Always Coming Home* are displaced into the far future, while that depicted in *The Dispossessed* is remote in space, located on one of a pair of planets in the system of Tau Ceti. Yet for all that, futuristic technology is far less central to the actual workings of the societies presented than is the case in either *Triton* or *The Female Man*. Indeed, in both *Woman on the Edge of Time* and *Always Coming Home* (the latter representing an almost exclusively agrarian society) the utopias depicted seem hardly less Arcadian in some of their aspects than the future imagined in *News from Nowhere*.

In *Woman on the Edge of Time*, for example, although there is no lack of advanced technology, its uses are relatively unobtrusive—to the extent that when Connie Ramos, the twentieth-century visitor to the future, arrives in the year 2137, she is at first struck by how primitive everything seems, and even wonders whether she has not travelled *back* in time instead. The inhabitants of Piercy's utopia wear small portable computers which are used both for purposes of communication and as actual extensions of human memory; sophisticated weaponry is deployed in the ongoing struggle with the last vestiges of the old military-industrial complex; and, most notoriously, there is the 'brooder'—where human embryos are now grown, thus liberating women from the disabling effects of pregnancy and reproduction. Yet none of this alters the fact that Piercy's is a largely agrarian utopia, consisting of a network of largely self-supporting village communities. There is an elaborate system of trade and communication between them, as well as provision for a decision-making process to deal with broader issues concerning more than one community, but as one of the utopians tells Connie, they are 'all peasants' (p.70). Everyone, no matter how technically skilled, is obliged to engage in manual labour, since machines are for the most part used only when there is a clearly demonstrated need—as in the case of dangerous, or boring and repetitive work. We learn that mining is performed entirely by machines, and we are given a brief glimpse of a fully automated pillow factory, but in general, as in *News from Nowhere*, the narrative emphasis is less on innovation than on restoration, on the need to repair the damage done to the environment by urban industrialism. Connie's puzzled comment, 'Forward, into the past?' (p.70) captures perfectly the ambiguous temporal direction which Piercy's utopia shares with that of Morris.

Indeed, if one were to take Piercy's representation of utopian society by itself, it might well seem, for all the distinctiveness of many of its details, conventional enough in general outline. While the peace and harmony of Piercy's utopia do not depend on the regimented order envisaged by More or Campanella, its inhabitants share with the Utopians and Solarians an uncompromising commitment to their society's defence: virtually everyone takes turns at military service, and indeed in the course of the narrative one of the main characters, Jackrabbit, is killed in combat. There are the familiar utopian benefits of abundance (although a cautionary note is sounded regarding the need to ration such comparatively wasteful uxuries as coffee and tea), health, and (marginally) longer life. As in so many earlier utopias, possessiveness has vanished along with private property, and once again sexuality has been rendered guilt-free. Most of the sources of injustice, oppression, pain and suffering have been eliminated—with predictable consequences in terms of human behaviour. Less cynical and repressed, more openly and freely expressive of their feelings than their twentieth-century counterparts, Piercy's utopians seem both more innocent and more childlike as a result. Indeed, it is precisely this quality that strikes Connie most powerfully on her first visit:

> Like a child! She could not imagine any woman of the age they must share saying in El Barrio or any place else she had lived, 'Me myself, I drum magnificently!' Indeed, they were like children, all in unisex rompers, sitting at their long kindergarten tables eating big plates full of food and making jokes. [p.75]

Piercy is clearly aware of the problems this can cause: to Connie, the utopians seem in consequence simply that much less real. Contrasting her dead lover, Claud, with the utopian, Bee (who strongly resembles him), she reflects: 'Pain had honed Claud keen. This man was a child by comparison' (p.104). It is Claud's suffering—in large measure due to his being a black man in a racist class society—that gives him much of his identity: to imagine him in a world from which racism and class oppression have been eliminated is more than she can manage. As her sarcastic response suggests—' You saying there's no racism left? Paradise on earth, all God's children are equal?' (p.104)—utopia seems to her quite literally too good to be true.

This is, of course, a familiar problem in utopian narratives—but Piercy's attempted solution goes beyond the mere acknowledgement that it exists. To begin with, like Morris, Piercy seeks to avoid mere idealized abstraction in her evocation of the utopian future. Even more so than in *News from Nowhere*, there are unusually concrete descriptions of the look and feel of things: of what people eat and what they wear, of their utensils and furnishings, their music and their visual art. And while, like Morris, she emphasizes the pleasure that work can involve (rather than merely reducing the hours), she not only shows it in process, but makes it clear that even under the most utopian conditions it is far from an unmixed blessing; in particular, Piercy does not shirk representing the often exhausting rounds of meetings and negotiations involved in communal and inter-communal decision making.

Moreover, in the search for utopian solutions, Piercy tries so far as possible to avoid the utopian tendency toward oversimplification. In the area of sexuality, for example, there are neither the restrictive exclusions

of Campanella, who outlaws sodomy, nor Gearhart, who represent
heterosexuality as solely a form of male oppression, nor the somewhat
naïve faith of Morris (and to a lesser extent Huxley) that the simple removal
of legal and social constraints will take care of things. Nor, for that matter
does Piercy fall into the familiar trap of merely reproducing (as 'natural'
her own society's patterns of gender relations: in *Woman on the Edge of Time*
homosexuality, heterosexuality, bisexuality, celibacy, promiscuity, and
even juvenile sexual experimentation are all represented as perfectly
acceptable—yet at the same time there is no pretence that the absence of
a single restrictive norm does more than alleviate the problems inherent
in human relationships. While her utopians are no longer troubled by
sexual guilt, the problems of jealousy, pain, loss remain—on occasion
becoming so disruptive that action at the communal level is required in
order to deal with them. While possessiveness and dependence are
countered by strong communal ties, by the separation of sexuality and
parenthood (there is no longer a biological relation between parents and
children), and by the provision of specific social mechanisms to deal with
jealousy, or the grief caused by loss and separation, there is no suggestion
that all problems are thereby resolved. As the rivalry between two of
Jackrabbit's lovers, Luciente and Bolivar, shows, the confrontation of
jealousy and personal antagonism remains a painful process; while the
reactions to Jackrabbit's subsequent death on military service reveal that
even the provision of rituals allowing for the expression of grief and coming
to terms with loss can only mitigate, not remove the pain involved.

What Piercy emphasizes, in effect, is the process of problem-solving.
Hers is not a utopia in which all the major problems have already been
dealt with. Instead, to an even greater extent than Bogdanov, she
represents a world where decisions are still in the process of being taken.
A war is still being fought, both in time and space; there are constant
negotiations to resolve disputes between communities; and there is also
what is referred to as the 'shaping controversy'—a worldwide debate over
the ethical issues involved in using genetic manipulation to increase human
ability. More than most utopias, Piercy's is one where change still appears
to be taking place, and as a result, for all the childlike characteristics which
the utopians exhibit, the element of regressive fantasy is far less apparent.
There is freedom, but not freedom from responsibility; security, but only
as a result of unceasing struggle.

Where *Woman on the Edge of Time* departs most strikingly from the
traditional utopian narrative paradigm, however, is not so much in the
way the society is portrayed (Connie is, after all, given the standard guided
tour) as in the surrounding narrative context. Were it merely a narrative
of Connie's visit to utopia, Piercy's blend of socialist feminism, ecological

consciousness, and do-it-yourself psychotherapy might seem little more than a 1970s update of the traditional model, in much the same way that *Island*, with its free love, eastern mysticism, and sacramental use of psychedelic drugs, might be seen as reflecting the spirit of the preceding decade, or Wells's utopias that of the early years of the century. What makes Piercy's utopia radically different in its effect is its juxtaposition of the traditional visit to utopia with a narrative which serves to highlight the troubled relationship between utopia and reality. The narrative begins, in fact, not with the arrival of the visitor in utopia, but rather with the intrusion of utopia into the all-too-squalid reality of modern-day New York. At the outset, Connie is troubled by disturbing glimpses of a stranger, who claims to come from the future—glimpses which cause her, not unreasonably, to doubt her own sanity. In fact, shortly after her first extended conversation with the stranger she finds herself incarcerated in a mental hospital—although not because she is thought to be suffering from utopian delusions. Instead, her committal is the result of her breaking the nose of her niece's pimp with a wine jug, after he has beaten up the niece for refusing to have an abortion. In the non-utopian world of twentieth-century America, the pimp's false testimony, together with a past history of mental problems, proves more than enough to get her locked up. In the hospital she is again visited by the stranger, who proves able to transport her telepathically to a utopian future, and there then ensues a sequence of alternating episodes, juxtaposing scenes in utopia with the contemporary reality of the mental hospital.

The effect of this narrative strategy is to foreground both the connection between utopia and reality, and the essential conflict between them. To begin with, Piercy's vivid representation of the glaring abuses present in her own society makes the need for alternatives seem that much more pressing, and in consequence her utopian imaginings appear less arbitrary than is often the case. Set against the description of Connie's suffering as a child, a lover, a parent in a world which makes a decent life for the poor and disadvantaged a virtual impossibility, even the more extreme of Piercy's utopian inventions—the severing of the biological links between parent and child, the provision of three, rather than two parents for each child—seem a good deal more persuasive than they might if taken in isolation. And while Piercy's attempt to imagine language appropriate to a genuinely utopian future (with 'per' as a non-sexist replacement for the possessives 'his' and 'her', and a studied avoidance of expletives rooted in sexual taboos) often seems awkward, too obviously invented and unnatural,[1] that very awkwardness—the fact that it is hard not to notice—makes all the more effective the contrast with such 'natural' verbal formulations as the pimp Geraldo's greeting to Connie: 'Caca de puta. Old

Bitch. Get your fat and worthless ass out of my way' (p.13)—or indeed h
still more charmless 'Hey, cunt, stop blubbering' to a woman he has ju
beaten up. Juxtaposed, the representations of the real and the utopi
encourage a reexamination of the assumptions which the reader brings t
each: utopian artifice becomes a device for exposing the limitations of th
real.

This is not to say that Piercy's narrative approach is altogether new
More's *Utopia*, after all, owes much of its force to its juxtaposition c
Hythloday's indictment of the injustices and abuses current i
contemporary England with his subsequent account of Utopian societ'
and the somewhat schematized counterpointing of utopian perfection t
the squalor of reality is, as we have seen, a recurrent feature in many c
its successors. Yet in no case is there the *degree* of interaction, the dialect
between the real and the utopian which Piercy succeeds in establishin;
Utopia is presented not merely as a more desirable alternative to realit'
but as a possibility which implies the necessity for reality to change. Lik
other utopias, *Woman on the Edge of Time* is of course a product of the societ
to which it proposes an alternative, but it is also shown to be th
embodiment of an ideal which changes as the nature of that societ
changes. While the utopian future is the product of past decisions, pa
struggles, it is not therefore fixed and static. Instead, it is actively engage
not only in a continuing military struggle with what remains of the ol
order, but also in taking decisions that affect both the future *and the pas*
The telepathic experiment which brings Connie to the utopian future
part of a battle to ensure that contemporary reality *does* give birth to a bett
future; the utopian is not the only possible future, for as Piercy also show
there are other, much less desirable futures also struggling to be born. Fc
the utopia she depicts to come into being, reality has to change in way
which powerful interest groups in society will fight to the death to preven
for such groups to gain their ends in the here and now will be finally t
eliminate utopia as a real possibility. In *Woman on the Edge of Time* the spac
opened up by utopian imagining is not an empty one—it is dispute
territory, over which the battle is already being fought.

Thus, while a number of features of Piercy's utopia might be seen a
conventional in themselves, the context in which they appear radicall
changes their impact. What is stressed is not peace and security—th
simplified bliss of a utopia to which one might dream of escaping—bu
rather the lessons to be learned from a utopia which is more than merel
a dream or an abstraction. Connie, the visitor to utopia, is described by th
utopians as a 'catcher': someone unusually open to telepathic suggestio
from the utopian future—but what is also clear is that she is more tha
usually alive to the utopian potential even of her own deprived existenc

In the ultimate deprivation of the mental hospital, she sees her everyday life as in a sense utopian, as representing something more:

> No more Thorazine and sleeping pills, the brief high and the endless sluggish depths. Nights of sleep with real dreams. She would go hungry for a week for the pleasure of eating a real orange, an avocado. All day long nobody would tell her what to do. Miraculously she would walk through the streets without an attendant. She would breathe the beautiful living filthy air ... Her life that had felt so threadbare now spread out like a full velvet rose—the rose that Claud had once brought her, loving it for its silkiness, its fragrance, and not knowing it was dark red. Her ordinary penny-pinching life appeared to her full beyond the possibility of savouring every moment. [p.28]

Mattapoisett in the year 2137, however, goes as far beyond the possibilities of her everyday life as that life goes beyond the possibilities of her existence in the mental hospital—to the extent that, once she has overcome her initial scepticism, it almost seems as though it *were* the fulfilment of a dream. In utopia she finds herself free again, sexually attractive, valued for herself, yet the true power of the dream ultimately derives from what it reveals concerning the possibilities of individual human beings—possibilities which her own society denies. In utopia, Connie encounters the utopian embodiment of what her lover, her first husband—both dead—and her child, taken from her for adoption, might have become; while in Luciente, the stranger from the future, a woman so formidable and self-assured that she initially mistakes her for a man, Connie sees an image of what she herself could be—a fighter for the good of others, rather than a helpless victim of society. Far more than most visitors to utopia, Connie is actually changed by her experiences. Indeed, it is Connie's education, her development, that constitute the main focus of the narrative. In a sense, *Woman on the Edge of Time* might be seen as a utopian *bildungsroman*, an account of an individual's growth toward becoming fully a person, the climax coming when Connie realizes that utopia is *not* in fact the ideal, self-evident, automatically-arrived-at solution to society's ills typical of so many earlier utopian narratives, but rather a state whose very existence depends on decisions taken by individuals in the here and now. As her own plight worsens (she becomes one of the subjects in an experimental programme involving electronic brain implants), she has glimpses of other futures—nightmarish projections of other possible directions society might take, if those with power over her continue to have their way. Instead of passively accepting the security provided by a more perfect society, she learns to fight for utopia in this one. In what amounts to a declaration of war on the society that has stripped her of even the little she has, she

effectively puts an end to the brain implant programme by fatally poisoning
four of the team responsible with pesticide stolen from her brother's
greenhouse. Far from being static, Piercy's is a utopia that is kinetic with
a vengeance, concerned less with demonstrating the superiority of a
utopian social structure than with highlighting the urgency of utopian
desire—of the *need* for things to be changed.

Always Coming Home

The utopian society that Piercy actually envisages, consisting as it does of
a cooperative network of self-supporting, predominantly agrarian
communities, is in some respects not dissimilar to that imagined in Le
Guin's *Always Coming Home*. But whereas *Woman on the Edge of Time* stresses
the mutually transformative relationship between utopia and reality, it
would appear—at least at first sight—that Le Guin's intention is to
demonstrate their remoteness from one another. Where Piercy's utopia is
projected a mere century and a half into the future, Le Guin's is set in a
future just as conditional, but far more distant—as is apparent from the
opening words: 'The people in this book might be going to have lived a
long, long time from now in Northern California' (p.ix). Even the apparent
familiarity of the spatial location soon proves illusory: it transpires that
earthquakes and volcanic action have completely altered the region's
geography, submerging most of the old coastline, and raising other areas
above sea-level. The Kesh, the people whose culture is described in great
detail in the text, live in a valley near the 'Inland Sea', beneath which San
Francisco apparently lies buried.

In addition, Le Guin provides very few clues as to the nature of the
events separating the utopian future from contemporary reality. There are
indications that large areas of the planet have been rendered desolate by
radioactivity or toxic chemicals, but no specific details are given as to the
cause of this. The present era is remembered, if at all, mainly in the form
of myths, of which Le Guin provides a number of examples, all suggestive
of a time when humanity was radically out of touch with the rest of the
natural world, and also with most of the values that are central to the
culture of the future utopia. So far as the Kesh conceptualize our time
they do so in terms of a spatial, rather than a temporal metaphor:

> Civilisation, as we know it, appeared in Valley thought as a remote
> region, set apart from the community and continuity of
> human/animal/earthly existence—a sort of peninsula sticking out
> from the mainland, very thickly built upon, very heavily populated,
> very obscure, and very far away. [p.160]

n the tales of the Kesh, the people of our era are generally referred to
ilmost as an alien species—as having their heads on backward, or as living
outside the world' (p.160), rather than inside it, as do the Kesh and other
peoples of the utopian future. Otherwise, few vestiges of 'the historical
period, the era of human existence that followed the Neolithic era for some
thousands of years in various parts of the earth' (p.160), survive—unless
one includes the various degenerative diseases caused by genetic
impairment due to chemicals and radioactivity, from which the Kesh
continue to suffer.

Yet while such separation of utopia from history might seem familiar
enough, it is presented from a perspective that is in many respects a reversal
of the traditional pattern: where More's Utopia was once a peninsula, not
an island, joined to the outside world by an isthmus which King Utopus
severs as a prelude to the creation of Utopia, here it is our world that is the
peninsula. Utopia becomes the norm, our reality the exception. And while
Le Guin, unlike Piercy, seems concerned to stress the tenuousness of the
connection between utopia and reality, the nature of the relationship
between them emerges in a rather different fashion. In the person of
Pandora', who constitutes a quasi-authorial presence in the text, Le Guin
makes often comical attempts to find out what happened, to discover how
utopia came into being—only to be thwarted by the Kesh's apparent inability
to understand her questions, or indeed the reasoning processes that underlie
them. The Kesh, whose economy is based on a combination of hunting-and-
gathering and small-scale agriculture, live in intimate relationship with the
natural world, and their cultural values have much in common with those
of the aboriginal peoples of North America. Hence, to their way of thinking,
Pandora's questions often appear quite literally meaningless: her
preoccupation with *when* things happened, her desire for precise answers
formulated in terms of an abstract, linear concept of time, seem to them
barely comprehensible. When Pandora asks the inhabitants of the Valley
about the origins of their society, their answers are often oblique, as though
couched in the terms of an altogether different frame of reference:

> 'How long have your people lived in the Valley?'
> 'All along.'
> But she looks puzzled, a little uncertain of the answers, because
> the question is strange. You wouldn't ask, 'How long have fish lived
> in the river? How long has the grass grown on the hills?' and expect
> an exact answer, a date, a number of years ... [p.171]

Instead of the precise information she craves, Pandora is given a number
of colourful creation myths, which the Kesh no doubt regard as conveying
a truth at least as valid as any schedule of dates and times. In the end, asked

to define what she means by 'history', Pandora suggests that it is 'the stu‹
of Man in Time' (p.181):

> There is a silence.
> 'You aren't Man and you don't live in Time,' I say bitterly. 'Y‹
> live in the Dream Time.'
> 'Always,' says the Archivist of Wakwaha. 'Right through Civil‹
> ation, we have lived in the Dream Time.' And her voice is not bitt‹
> but full of grief, bitter grief. [pp.181–2]

What emerges, in effect, is a conception of utopia as dream—but a drea‹
that is more than simply prefigurative (as is the case, say, in *News fr‹
Nowhere*). Instead, it holds much the same significance that dream possess‹
in many aboriginal cultures: not so much wish fulfilment, or an exploratic
of possibility, as an alternate way of perceiving reality. The society of t‹
Kesh is portrayed not only as a future possibility, but as, in a sense,
separate reality whose chronotope is coexistent with that of contempora‹
reality: what utopia proposes is another way of seeing:

> It is very difficult to be sure of ... meanings when dealing with
> language and way of thought in which no distinction is ma‹
> between human and natural history or between objective a‹
> subjective fact and perception, in which neither chronological n
> causal sequence is considered an adequate reflection of reality, a‹
> in which time and space are so muddled together that one is nev‹
> sure whether they are talking about an era or an area. [p.160]

Such blurring of the categories of space and time is of course n
uncommon in utopian fiction, where, as we have seen, the erasure of tin‹
often involves a compensatory extension of the spatial. What is clear
Always Coming Home, however, is that the ambiguity is deliberate. Whi‹
the society depicted appears to be relatively static, its stasis is used as
device to interrogate our own conceptions of time—and in particular t‹
ways in which modern society tends automatically to conceptualize chan‹
over time as representing progress. What Le Guin seeks to embody, in t‹
often fragmentary and overlapping narratives which comprise the wor‹
is a sense that the two different temporal frameworks—that of utopia, a‹
that of contemporary reality—are not in fact exclusive of one another. O‹
own reality is depicted as permeated by utopian time, by the perenni‹
dream of things being otherwise; while the utopian future is still haunt‹
by the vestiges of our own time—not only in the form of the persiste‹
effect of the environmental damage wrought in our era, but also in t‹
resurfacing of patterns of thought and action clearly rooted in our ways
perceiving the world.

For all its apparent temporal remoteness, Le Guin's utopia reveals its connection with reality in a number of ways. While, like Morris's, it is in many respects a paradise restored, rather than a new and improved version of the society at present existing, the overall effect is very different. In contrast to the somewhat idealized medievalism of Morris's utopia, Le Guin's has its roots in a past ostensibly more 'primitive'—that represented by the cultures of the native American societies that predate European settlement of the New World. Which, in a sense, represents another kind of return to utopian roots, since it was precisely the example of such societies that inspired More to conceive his own image of a society without money or private property. Le Guin's future harks back to the era when the New World still represented a dream of infinite possibility, before its space was explored, colonized, recreated in the image of the Old World to which it had once offered the dream of an alternative. At the same time, however, the memory of our society is by no means erased. What Le Guin presents instead is a world which, rather than offering mere security, protection from the forces that render our own society less than utopian, is characterized by an underlying balance and harmony that is able to *contain* disruptive forces. *Always Coming Home* provides examples of violence and conflict at almost every level from the personal up—while the longest narrative in the book, the story of Stone Telling, deals with the attempt of a warrior people, the Condor, to impose their authority over the surrounding region. In every case, however, violence proves primarily self-destructive, largely because the society as a whole lives by a logic which does not allow conflict to gather momentum.

The case of the Condor, in fact, is particularly instructive. Their culture—monotheistic, hierarchical, militaristic—has clear parallels in our own world, yet their dreams of military conquest are ultimately thwarted (as those of Colonel Dipa in *Island* are not) by the prevailing social and economic context. To begin with, it is clear that the role of technology in the utopian future is far from conducive to large-scale military enterprise. While humans have access to the 'City of Mind'—a self-sustaining network of computers and cybernetic devices—and there is exchange of information between the City and the human communities across the planet, it is clear that technology is no longer central to the functioning of society as a whole:

> Thoughtful and educated people in the Valley recognised the incalculable treasure put at their disposal by the City of Mind; but they were not disposed to regard human existence either as information or as communication, nor intelligent mortality as a means to the ends of immortal intelligence. In their view, the two species had diverged to the extent that competition between them

was nonexistent, cooperation limited, and the question of superiority
and inferiority bootless. [p.159]

The Kesh utilize certain forms of what might be described as 'modern
technology': electricity, steam locomotives, guns, long-range
communications—but very little else. The *information* exists as to how to
construct devices far more sophisticated than anything the Kesh employ—
up to and including nuclear weapons—but in the absence of the industrial
base necessary for their production, they remain purely theoretical
concepts. While the Condor actually succeed in constructing a tank, and
later several aeroplanes, the cost and effort involved virtually cripples their
economy. In addition, their centralized, urban society proves less and less
viable in a non-industrial world: forced to range further and further afield
in search of food and supplies, they become increasingly vulnerable to
retaliation by the communities that surround them. After doing a
considerable amount of damage, their society finally disintegrates, torn
apart by its own contradictions.

Nevertheless, Le Guin does not present their destruction as a simple
matter—let alone an inevitable one. Warrior societies grow up in many of
the surrounding communities, ostensibly to fight back against the Condor,
but also in imitation of many of their ways—and these cause almost as
much disruption as the Condor themselves. Describing the eventual
dissolution of one such society, one of the Kesh reflects:

> I have come to think that the sickness of Man is like the mutating
> viruses and the toxins: there will always be some form of it about,
> or brought in from elsewhere by people moving and travelling, and
> there will always be the risk of infection. What those sick with it said
> is true: It is a sickness of our being human, a fearful one. It would
> be unwise in us to forget the Warriors ... lest it need all be done and
> said again. [p.411]

Le Guin's utopia is not one where the past is ignored, or forgotten; nor is
it a paradise from which Original Sin has been banished: the human
capacity to do evil remains—utopia is the provision of a context which is
as conducive as possible to doing otherwise. Our own era is not merely a
bad dream: it must be remembered, lest it recur; conversely, in our own
era, utopia is not merely a dream, either—it must be worked toward, lest
our own era continue.

Underlying Le Guin's representation of utopia as almost unimaginably
remote from our own world, then, is a vigorous polemic directed against
the values by which modern society lives. There *is* a connection between
the two, but its nature is suggested by what Le Guin makes the central
metaphor of her text: the *heyiya*, or hinge—most commonly depicted as a

air of interlocking spirals. This constitutes a common decorative motif, the basis for their town design (houses in one spiral, communal buildings in the other), and a metaphor for any kind of link between opposing states: life and death, dream and waking, earth and sky. It implies both a connection and a separation, a link which also involves some form of dislocation. As a metaphor for the complex relationship between utopia and reality, its implications are very different from those of the painful transitions depicted elsewhere, suggestive of both return to and re-emergence from the womb. The hinge, joining surfaces which move in different directions, is the mechanism whereby doors are opened, disclosing gaps in the wall, and revealing new spaces into which movement is possible.

The complex implications of this central metaphor, simultaneously suggesting both difference and relationship, are further reinforced by Le Guin's narrative strategy, which represents a departure from the utopian norm even more radical than Gearhart's *The Wanderground*. *Always Coming Home* contains a number of sequential narratives varying in length from less than a page to the three-part story of Stone Telling, which is practically a novella in its own right; there are examples of Kesh biography, history, fiction, poetry and myth, interspersed with accounts of their customs, rituals, architecture, medical practice, and religious beliefs. And while it is a reflection of the non-utopian character of our own society that the accompanying tape cassette of utopian music is available only to those who can afford the hardback edition, the utopian recipes contained in the section helpfully labelled 'The Back of the Book' can be made by anyone.[2] How all this is read—how much, and in what order—is left up to the reader, and it becomes clear that part of Le Guin's purpose is to avoid the creation of a utopia which is complete, self-contained, and separate from the reality of writer and reader alike. In the words of the quasi-authorial Pandora:

> Pandora doesn't want to look into the big end of the telescope and see, jewel-bright, distinct, tiny, and entire, the Valley. She shuts her eyes, doesn't want to see, she knows what she will see: Everything Under Control. The doll's house. The doll's country. [p.56]

What is offered instead, disparate yet connected, is 'Bits, chunks, fragments, shards, Pieces of the Valley, lifesize'—along with the advice: 'Let the heart complete the pattern' (p.56).

As a challenge to the often authoritarian narrative practice of the traditional utopia, Le Guin's experiment could scarcely be more thoroughgoing. From the 'bits, chunks, fragments, shards' there emerges a picture of life lived under possible utopian conditions which has a concreteness far removed from the abstraction which characterizes many

earlier utopias; yet at the same time, there is little of the relentless specifici
of detail typical of the traditional paradigm. *Always Coming Home* does n
seek to fill the space opened up by utopian imagining, but rather to sugge
its extent: even within the relatively limited geographical confines of I
Guin's future Northern California a good deal of variety is evident, ar
while we are told that 'the rest of the world was not a matter of very urge
concern to most people of the Valley' (p.483), they are clearly aware th
their own is only one of an infinite variety of ways of being—distinct, y
not unrelated. Beyond the mountains to the East that constitute tl
boundary of their immediate geographical world, 'the lands go on and o
to the sea again, you know ... and so on round till you come back to tl
Valley' (p.483). In addition, while no less serious than its predecessor
Always Coming Home is singularly free of the earnestness that so often atten
utopian speculation: like More, whose example in this regard has on
infrequently been followed, Le Guin is alive to the element of game,
play, even of self-indulgence inherent in the utopian project—and sl
engages, particularly in the Pandora sequences, in a considerable amou
of self-mockery. While her utopia offers serious criticism of our ow
society, a more than usually concrete delineation of possible alternative
and a range of sophisticated narrative experiment, it is also, in the wor
of the Archivist of Wakwaha:

> ... a mere dream dreamed in a bad time, an Up Yours to the peopl
> who ride snowmobiles, make nuclear weapons, and run prison cam
> by a middle-aged housewife, a critique of civilisation possible on
> to the civilised, an affirmation pretending to be a rejection, a glass
> milk for the soul ulcered by acid rain, a peace of pacifist jeanjacqueri
> and a cannibal dance among the savages in the ungodly garden
> the farthest West. [p.336]

For Le Guin, at least, the ambiguity, the potential multiple significatior
of utopian fiction are clearly something to be celebrated.

As an attempt to resolve the problems inherent in the extende
depiction of a coherently developed utopian ideal, *Always Coming Hon*
clearly differs radically from *Woman on the Edge of Time*, even whi
addressing many of the same issues. Both works, however, suggest ne
directions in terms of the relation between ideology and narrative practic
In Piercy's utopia, there is clear evidence of a commitment both to feminis
and to a revolutionary socialism whose somewhat eclectic character
suggested by the names of some of the people and places in her utopia
society—there are characters called Red Star, Bolivar, Sacco-Vanzetti, an
Luxembourg, not to mention a greenhouse named after Amilcar Cabra
Le Guin's leanings are equally clearly anarchist (as is likewise apparent i

The Dispossessed); elsewhere, she defines her anarchism as 'not the social-Darwinist economic "libertarianism" of the far-right; but anarchism, as prefigured in early Taoist thought, and expounded by Shelley and Kropotkin, Goldman and Goodman' (*Wind's Twelve Quarters*, p.285). In contrast to Morris's Marxism, however, or the vaguer and more confused radicalism of Huxley, the political beliefs of Piercy and Le Guin do appear to find a reflection in their respective narrative practice. It is hardly coincidental, for example, that Piercy chooses not only to make the central focus of her narrative a woman's oppression, but also to structure the narrative around the dialectic which she establishes between contemporary reality and the utopian future: a dialectic in which utopian ideals can be seen as both a product of and a commentary on the political actualities of the present. Equally, Le Guin's abandonment of an ordered, linear narrative may be seen as motivated by a desire to return to the individual reader a measure of control over the way in which the text itself is constituted, and to resist so far as possible the imposition on the reader of a single, predetermined vision.

Even so, it is necessary to guard against too rigid or facile an equation of ideology and narrative strategy: as has already been seen, an authoritarian, centralist utopian vision need not exclude radical narrative experiment, nor a libertarian one the retention of the traditional narrative paradigm. While Piercy and Le Guin do succeed in avoiding many of the narrative pitfalls evident in earlier utopias, it is clear that resolving the problems inherent in utopian narrative is more than a simple matter of adopting a libertarian stance and then adopting a narrative schema to reflect it. Indeed, it is significant in this context that Le Guin's earlier utopia, *The Dispossessed*, whose narrative strategy closely resembles that of *Woman on the Edge of Time*, with a structure of alternating episodes which once again seeks to establish a dialectic between the real and the utopian, has nevertheless been subjected to a veritable barrage of criticism directed at its alleged political shortcomings.

The Dispossessed

The Dispossessed, which Moylan sees as the most problematic of the critical utopias he discusses, has been found fault with on a number of grounds. Nadia Khouri, for instance, criticizes it precisely for what she sees as its failure to embody a dynamic interaction between utopia and reality—for its 'reduction of the dialectic to binary oppositions, with points of gravity congealed into static equilibrium' (p.51).[3] Despite the recurrent contrasts between the utopian world of Anarres and its twin planet, Urras—clearly analogous to our own—Khouri argues that 'nothing in fact changes in *The*

Dispossessed except that an individual's awareness has acquired a sounder perception of truth' (p.53). The individual in question has also come in for his share of criticism. Shevek, the utopian physicist and mathematician, whose return to Urras constitutes the narrative link between utopia and the analogue of our own reality, is viewed by a number of critics as little more than a classic stereotype: the 'Great Scientist' (male, of course), who leads humanity forward by both his discoveries and his example.[4] Worse, he is also a heterosexual male who, in a society where there is no marriage, nor any social taboos against multiple relationships, deliberately chooses to live in a monogamous partnership. While other modes of sexuality are positively portrayed—Bedap, for example, easily the most politically astute character in the book, is gay—this is dismissed as sheer tokenism.[5] In addition, the relative lack of positive portrayals of women is seen as problematic, indicative of a privileging of traditional sex roles and familial structures.[6] Overall, while her utopia may radically question many of the norms of existing society, Le Guin is viewed as ultimately reinscribing one of its most fundamental bases—namely, patriarchal authority: like so many utopias before it, *The Dispossessed* reinscribes the very norms of gender relations that it purports to challenge.

Such criticisms, however, imply certain normative assumptions of their own as to what utopian fiction should be like. Taken collectively, they suggest a preference for a utopia in which change is inherent ('not static, but kinetic'), connected to reality, yet as far removed from it as possible in terms of its sexual politics—ideally, Moylan suggests, one where

> ... the more collective heroes of social transformation are presented off-center and usually as characters who are not dominant, white heterosexual, chauvinist males but female, gay, non-white, and generally operating collectively. [*Demand the Impossible*, p.45]

What is preferred, in other words, is a utopia not unlike Piercy's. Yet even granting the validity of at least some of the criticisms cited above, it is troubling, to say the least, to find the prescriptive character it has taken writers of utopian narrative so long to escape resurfacing in the form of a new orthodoxy among commentators on such narrative. While perspectives such as those which Moylan lists obviously provide a valuable, even essential corrective to the comfortable white, middle-class, male assumptions of a Bellamy or a Wells, it is simplistic to conclude that works that do not embody them automatically reinscribe the norms of existing society. As Terry Eagleton remarks:

> Simply to counterpose difference to identity, plurality to unity, the marginal to the central, is to lapse back into binary opposition, as the

more subtle deconstructors are perfectly aware. It is pure formalism to imagine that otherness, heterogeneity and marginality are unqualified political benefits regardless of their concrete social content. [*Ideology*, p.128]

What Le Guin's narrative choices reflect is not so much an unthinking reproduction of her own society's normative gender ideology, nor indeed the stasis of the traditional utopia, but rather the fact that she is engaged in a rather different interrogation of the utopian project than that provided by Russ, Delany, and to a lesser extent by Piercy. Perhaps in this context it might be helpful to cite the words of one of Piercy's own characters, Sojourner, during a debate over the issue of art and political correctness:

> 'Every piece of art can't contain everything everybody would like to say! I've seen this mistake for sixty years. Our culture as a whole must speak the whole truth. But every object can't! That's the slogan mentality at work, as if there were certain holy words that must always be named.' [pp.210–11)

While it is true that the utopia Le Guin depicts perpetuates certain of the norms of her own society, the question of the relationship between what changes in utopia and what remains the same, already addressed in the context of the discussion of earlier works, here becomes more than usually ambiguous. For example, while Shevek's relationship with his partner, Takver, conforms to the conventions of twentieth-century Western society, it is clear that the pattern which it represents is hardly fundamental to Le Guin's utopia in the way that, say, More's or Bacon's representation of the patriarchal family is central to the societies depicted in *Utopia* or *The New Atlantis*. Heterosexual monogamy on Anarres is a choice—one among many—rather than the model to which economic and social pressures encourage the individual to conform. As in Piercy's society of the future, there is no reason to be anything—celibate, promiscuous, monogamous; homo-, bi-, or heterosexual—unless it is the individual's wish. Obviously, Le Guin's privileging of monogamous heterosexual partnership as the central relationship in the book, notwithstanding the absence of the economic and social structures that sustain it as the norm in our own society, may be seen as tacitly suggesting that such relationships are 'natural', as opposed to socially constructed; yet at the same time it is apparent that Shevek's 'normality' in this regard serves a narrative function that goes beyond the mere reinscription of conventional values in a utopian context. Certainly, it is true that Le Guin does not address, or addresses only in passing, many of the questions of sexual politics, sexual identity, sexual practice that are central concerns in the work of writers such as Delany and Russ; however, it might be argued that, just as Russ's and

Delany's reliance on the convenient fiction that economic problems are resolvable by technological advances frees them to focus on questions of sexual politics, so Le Guin uses Shevek's apparent conformity to conventional sexual values as a means of exposing other forms of difference. For Shevek is far more than the mere conventional hero to which Le Guin's critics reduce him: in his role as a visitor, not to, but from utopia, his inability to be persuaded by the values of the society he encounters (the reverse of the traditional visitor to utopia's almost immediate conversion) serves to unmask many of its limitations.

It is clear, for example, that it is precisely Shevek's surface 'normality' that enables him to be accepted on Urras in a way that someone more threatening to *its* patriarchal norms—an independent woman, a gay man, or (heaven forbid) a lesbian—would not. (The Urrasti scientists are shocked, and indeed rather put out to discover that Shevek's teacher, Gvarab, was a woman.) Instead of the overt rejection, not to say persecution, which such alternative visitors might have experienced, Shevek encounters welcome, acceptance, attempted co-option, and as a result gains a more immediate insight into the insidiousness of Urrasti culture than would be possible for a more obvious outsider. Indeed, rather as in *Herland* the unguarded comments of the visitors enable the 'innocent' utopians to deduce the realities that underlie them, so Shevek's equally innocent questioning often serves to expose the real state of affairs. While he is told by an Urrasti scientist (in terms reminiscent of Terry in *Herland*) that 'a beautiful, virtuous woman ... is an inspiration to us—the most precious thing on earth' (p.60), this proves hard to reconcile with the response to his innocent question after attending a gathering of dignitaries who are nearly all male: 'Where are other women?'—which his Urrasti hosts automatically interpret as a request for some form of hired sex. Unwilling—or perhaps unable—to accept that someone from a radically different society might be *fundamentally* different from themselves, the Urrasti accept him as someone from whom it is unnecessary to conceal their assumptions.

Yet while Shevek's personal life may appear conventional enough, he is in other respects exceptional. His acceptance on Urras may be a reflection of his apparent normality, but the main reason for his welcome is the fact that he is the foremost physicist on either planet, the pioneer of a theory of time which may render possible instantaneous communication across the galaxy. To criticize Le Guin for making Shevek a stereotypical 'Great Scientist', however, is surely to miss the point—for in the context she creates, what Moylan reads as the 'privileging of male, intellectual, solitary heroics' (*Demand the Impossible*, p.110) in fact raises as many questions about the nature of utopia as his acceptance on Urras raises about our own reality. The problem is that, on Anarres, Shevek is out of the ordinary: Le Guin's utopia is not one characterized by Fourieresque profusion, with 'thirty-seven million mathematicians the equal of Newton'—Shevek is very much one of a kind, and as such he represents a threat to certain tendencies within utopia, namely those toward stasis and conformity. Just as in a capitalist society such as Le Guin's own North America (or its Urrasti analogue, A-Io), which trumpets the virtues of individualism, it is solidarity and collective action that pose the greatest threat, so in the collective society of Anarres it is visible individuality that causes the most problems. In her portrayal of Anarres, Le Guin offers not merely a representation, but also a critique of utopia, and in showing the difficulties occasioned by Shevek's individuality, she dramatizes one of the chief dangers inherent in a utopian society: the possibility that collective solidarity may degenerate into mere conformity (a very real one, judging by the number of utopias that provide specific, and often draconian penalties for dissidence). Even a society run on the most libertarian principles cannot *guarantee* freedom, and what Le Guin sets out to explore is the extent to which, in a society based on collective co-operation, freedom is measured by the ability to accept difference (always provided such difference is not actively antisocial). While fully accepting that his duty to society involves performing arduous physical labour, as well as simply thinking great thoughts, Shevek at the same time insists on his freedom, his right as an individual to do his own work as well—and in doing so becomes part of a larger struggle to keep utopia utopian, not by striving to preserve it as it is, but by forcing it to continue changing. The outcome of an earlier revolution on Urras, the utopia on Anarres is in danger of stagnation, having cut itself off from its roots: Shevek's return represents the reestablishment of a connection between the real and the utopian of which both are in desperate need. The corrupt and increasingly repressive world of Urras needs the hope that utopia represents in order to bring about revolutionary change; Anarres needs the threat which Urras represents to oblige it to keep changing. Arguing for his right to make the trip back to the world Anarres's anarchist revolutionaries had left generations before, Shevek stresses the need to avoid the dangers of pursuing security at all costs:

> '… what we're after is to remind ourselves that we didn't come to Anarres for safety, but for freedom. If we must all agree, all work together, we're no better than a machine. If an individual can't work in solidarity with his fellows, it's his duty to work alone. His duty and his right. We have been denying people that right. We've been saying, more and more often, you must work with the others, you must accept the rule of the majority. But any rule is tyranny. The duty

of the individual is to accept *no* rule, to be the initiator of his own
acts, to be responsible. Only if he does so will the society live, and
change, and adapt, and survive. We are not subjects of a State founded
upon law, but members of a society founded upon Revolution
Revolution is our obligation: our hope of evolution. "The Revolution
is in the individual spirit, or it is nowhere. It is for all, or it is nothing
If it is seen as having any end, it will never truly begin."' [pp.288–9]

The clear message of *The Dispossessed* is that the only real revolution i
permanent revolution—a continuing process, not something to be
achieved once and for all.[7]

On Urras, however, it is Shevek's failure to be *merely* exceptional that
proves disconcerting to his hosts. The Great Scientist they can cope with,
the fact that, for all his difficulties on Anarres, he remains a utopian is more
difficult to comprehend. While they would like to treat him simply as a
dissident genius, gratefully embracing the offer of 'freedom', the Urrast
gradually learn that they cannot seduce, bribe, or intimidate him into
accepting their values. Nor are they able to obtain 'his' secret, the new and
revolutionary temporal theory, since he does not perceive it as a possession
Their efforts to co-opt him ultimately fail, as do their attempts to cast him
in the role of as genius unappreciated by his society, in which his unique
gifts are merely part of his identity, rather than something that makes him
better than others. If he fights for his own freedom, it is at the same time
for a freedom to which everyone should be entitled. It is this, more than
anything, that the Urrasti ruling class are unable to understand. On
Anarres, Shevek's struggles serve to expose some of the problems inherent
in a utopian society; on Urras, by contrast, it is the virtues of utopia that
become apparent. For it is not Shevek's brilliance as a *scientist* that enables
him to see so clearly what is wrong with a society based on greed and
injustice—it is the perspective he has gained from his socialization while
growing up in utopia. For Le Guin's utopia is not simply a society that
provides an equitable distribution of resources, where 'nobody goes hungry
while another eats' (p.229)—although that is of course the essential
precondition for all its other qualities—it is also a world, unlike our own,
that provides for its members the possibility of growing to something like
their full potential. What Le Guin attempts to imagine is what it might be
like to *be* a utopian. Shevek is not a Dr Leete, who is simply a prosperous
nineteenth-century professional living in more congenial surroundings;
nor even a Dr Robert, the well-balanced antithesis to Huxley's eminent
atomic physicist with 'a mental age, outside the laboratory, of about eleven'
(*Island*, p.214): rather, he represents Le Guin's vision of what it might be
like to be an exceptionally gifted individual growing up in a society which

does not seek to co-opt those gifts and make them serve the interests of existing power structures.

Nevertheless, the extent to which Shevek is a product of utopia, rather than merely a stereotypical 'Great Scientist', only becomes fully apparent when he is placed in the context of Le Guin's analogue of the real world—and here, as elsewhere, it is clear that much of the impact of *The Dispossessed* is due to its narrative strategy. Out of the different contexts provided by the twin worlds of Urras and Anarres, separate, yet related, there emerges a larger perspective that embraces both. Taken in isolation, Le Guin's depiction of utopian society shows it in an almost dystopian light; it is through the contrast with Urras that the splendour of the utopian dream is restored. As in *Woman on the Edge of Time*, it is the focus on the relationship between the real and the utopian that gives to the latter the sense of urgency, that utopia is worth fighting for, so singularly lacking in most earlier utopian fictions. Like Piercy's utopia, *The Dispossessed* begins with a reversal of the traditional arrival of the visitor in utopia: it is Shevek, the utopian, who sets out for the counterpart of our own reality. Nor does the parallel end there: just as Luciente comes from a utopian future whose roots lie in our own present, Shevek is likewise returning to his past, to the world from which his ancestors emigrated, seeking refuge from the injustice which on Urras still persists. The gap in space which Shevek crosses is also, in a sense, a gap in time.

Where there is a difference of perspective, however, is in the controlling point of view from which both utopia and reality are portrayed. Here Piercy's is closer to the traditional approach, focusing on the consciousness of Connie, the visitor to utopia, who assesses utopia in the context of her own oppression in the here and now. Le Guin, by contrast, makes the utopian the norm by which reality is judged—which in turn lends a more overtly satirical edge to the narrative. Rather as earlier satirists used the insights of the innocent outsider—the Noble Savage, the Persian traveller—to expose the follies and corruption of European civilization, Le Guin employs Shevek's innocent utopian eye to unmask the absurdity of a number of aspects of Urrasti (and of course our own) society. Unfamiliar with Urrasti norms, Shevek requires explanations for much that his hosts take for granted: the capitalist economic system, the hierarchical military structures used to defend it, the role and status of women, and even the oddities of the university grading system.[8] Like Gilman's utopians, Shevek has a well-developed propensity for asking awkward questions.

Nevertheless, as in *Herland*, the satire is of secondary importance in comparison to the focus on the individual's changing experience of a new society. Le Guin's main emphasis is on Shevek's own struggles as he confronts the contradictions and complexities of a world other than his own, with its own distinctive assumptions as to the nature of reality. A first he is excited by its richness and diversity, by what initially seem to be its wider horizons, by the apparently greater personal freedom he enjoys even the evident injustice and visible oppression seem at first like discord in a larger, richer harmony. But gradually his enthusiasm, stimulated by the newness of his experience, gives way to disillusion. The surface splendour and richness of Urras seem less inspiring when it becomes clea that they are available only to a privileged minority. Frustrated on Anarre because of the difficulties he experiences in doing his own work, he begin to realize that on Urras he is denied the freedom to do anything else. I Anarres places restrictions on his individual freedom, Urras refuses him the right to participate with others in struggling for larger, collectiv freedoms: on both worlds there is the need for rebellion, resistance, change And yet there remains a difference: whereas on Anarres nonconformity arouses the threat of violence—when Shevek leaves for Urras there is fracas in which rocks are thrown, and one person is killed—there is no equivalent for the organized violence of the Urrasti state. It is only afte witnessing helicopter gunships firing on an unarmed demonstration tha Shevek finally understands that there *is* a reason for military hierarch after all—that it is not merely 'a coercive mechanism of extraordinar inefficiency' (p.245):

> ... he now understood why the army was organized as it was. It wa indeed quite necessary. No rational form of organization would serv the purpose. He simply had not understood that the purpose was t enable men with machine guns to kill unarmed men and wome easily and in large quantities when told to do so. [p.245]

As in *Woman on the Edge of Time*, it is only in the course of the narrativ that Shevek comes to realize, like Connie, why utopia is so urgentl necessary.

At the same time, Shevek's relation to the utopian world of Anarre undergoes an equally significant process of growth and change. Interwove with the sequence of chapters dealing with his experiences on Urras is parallel account of Shevek's life on Anarres, beginning with infancy, an ending at the point where he departs for Urras. The Shevek of the Anarre chapters is younger, just as Anarres itself is the younger society, but th impression created by the young Shevek is constantly modified by it juxtaposition to the sequences which portray the adult he has become Similarly, the actions of the older man, his responses to the world of Urra can be seen to be in many respects determined by his past experience or Anarres. The different stages in Shevek's development, in other words, ar presented in such a way that the child, the youth, the young man, th mature adult can be seen as part of a whole being, existing in both space and time: human character is no more static than human society; the changes which the one undergoes are reflected in the other.

Indeed, Le Guin's presentation of the individual, Shevek, in many ways parallels her depiction of utopian society as a whole. For Anarres, too, changes as the narrative unfolds: it likewise faces many of the problems that confront the individual—the dangers of stagnation, conformity, sterile compromise, ceasing to grow; Shevek's avoidance of them also enacts that of his society. For while all these dangers suggest a society on the brink of lapsing into the stasis of the traditional utopia, or even a dystopian enforced conformity, it is clear that such a fate is not inevitable. Anarres is not perfect, not static: it is a utopia, but one shown to be the product of unceasing human effort, not created once and for all, but rather perpetually recreated. Its very precariousness, in fact, is what gives it life, and lends urgency to the efforts of the individuals who comprise it. Even its limitations shed light on the nature of its twin world, the reality to which it is both linked and opposed. Significantly, it is Urras, the analogue of our own reality, which is portrayed as richer and more fertile, more colourful, various, and alive; Anarres, by contrast, is arid, barren, devoid of any life forms other than scrubby vegetation and the humans who have colonized it. There are no animals on Anarres: like any utopia, it is purely a human creation— and in its inhabitants' ceaseless struggle to make fertile their barren world, Le Guin provides a richly suggestive metaphor for the process of trying to breathe life into and give substance to a political abstraction. Like any ideal, utopia can only be made real through human action. By contrast, Urras— reality—for all its fertility, is a world full of fear, suffering, oppression, death: it needs the ideal which Anarres represents to give it hope and direction, just as Anarres needs the life giving energy which Urras embodies. The two, real and ideal, are inseparably linked, for all the attempts that have been made to maintain a separation between them. The Urrasti effort to preserve the status quo by licensing the departure of the revolutionary element to Anarres has proved a failure; so too has the Anarresti attempt to preserve the purity of the utopian ideal by cutting themselves off from Urras: in isolation, the one society is in danger of stagnating, the other of falling apart. On Urras, the inequalities and injustice that once prompted revolution are getting worse in the absence of the revolutionary forces who chose exile over continuing struggle;[9] while on Anarres, cut off from the world which prompted their revolution, the Anarresti find themselves slipping into the sterile conformity so typical of the traditional utopia. In opting for isolation, they have opted out of the dialectic of the real and the ideal, choosing instead a solution that is utopian in the worst sense. Like *Woman on the Edge of Time*, *The Dispossessed* is

concerned with the relationship between the real and the utopian: for L
Guin, the utopian ideal can neither replace reality nor exist in isolatio
from it. Instead, the two are inextricably linked—although not in the stati
binary opposition that Khouri suggests; rather, what is portrayed is
symbiotic relationship in which each gives the other what it lacks—th
reason to go on changing.

In conversation with an alien diplomat from Earth (which is represente
as having undergone an environmental catastrophe of such magnitud
that it makes Urras seem a paradise by comparison) Shevek reflects on th
connection between the real and the ideal, the past and the future:

> 'You don't understand what time is ... You say that the past i
> gone, the future is not real, there is no change, no hope. You thin
> Anarres is a future that cannot be reached, as your past cannot b
> changed. So there is nothing but the present, this Urras, the ricl
> real, stable present, the moment now. And you think that i
> something which can be possessed! You envy it a little. You thin
> it is something you would like to have. But it is not real, you know
> It is not stable, not solid—nothing is. Things change, change. Yo
> cannot have anything ... And least of all can you have the presen
> unless you accept with it the past and the future. Not only the pas
> but also the future, not only the future but also the past! Becaus
> they are real: only their reality makes the present real. You wi
> not achieve or even understand Urras unless you accept the realit
> the enduring reality, of Anarres ... we are the key.' [pp.280–1]

Utopia is a future, but one constantly changing in response to both pas
and present, whose nature it also shapes. Like Piercy, Le Guin succeeds i
creating what Wells only talks of—a utopia that is not static, but kinetic

It is here that the real significance of Shevek's vocation become
apparent. As a physicist and mathematician, he is engaged throughout th
course of the narrative in an attempt to find a theory that will reconcil
the concept of time as linear and sequential with what are termed 'th
Principles of Simultaneity'—a conceptual model in which all moments ar
seen as, in a sense, present. This exploration of the nature of time become
in its turn, another of the work's central metaphors, reflecting as it does
narrative structure which, while linear, also juxtaposes and shows the link
between different moments in time. Shevek's experiences in the presen
reality of Urras are not merely counterpointed to, but moulded by his pas
experiences in a utopia which at the same time constitutes an embodimen
of a possible future. *The Dispossessed* is a utopia which might also be terme
a chronotopia.

Given this dynamic conception of the nature of utopia, it is hardl coincidental that *The Dispossessed*, like *Woman on the Edge of Time*, shows little sign of the traditional utopia's tendency toward a regressive simplification of the complexities of adult experience. While money has been abolished on Anarres, as in so many other utopias, this does not affect the economic realities of trying to grow enough to feed the inhabitants of a singularly unforgiving physical environment. Sexuality is not complicated by irrational taboos and legal constraints, but it remains problematic, a human relationship which resists both systematization and easy solutions. And while labour is rendered more rewarding by its having a demonstrably useful purpose—the furthering of the common good, rather than the enrichment of an employer—Le Guin provides none of the traditional rational substitutes (*very* early retirement, *very* short working days) which so often mask the essentially fantastic dream of paradisaical idleness. Still less is there the pretence that work can be transformed into a form of creative play, as tends to be the case in *News from Nowhere*: not all work *is* good for the health, or offers the aesthetic satisfactions of mediaeval craftsmanship. John Fekete, in fact, criticizes Le Guin for her 'choice of a scarcity and necessity-dominated environment' (p.135) rather than dealing with 'the more interesting range of speculative questions, having to do with permanent revolution and the forms of freedom in a libertarian post-scarcity society' (p.135).[10] For Le Guin, however, it is clear that there is a utopian aspect to the overcoming of difficulty, the sharing of hardship. The utopian ideal present in *The Dispossessed* is not the recovery of childhood, but the achievement of brotherhood, sisterhood—a solidarity which begins, in Shevek's words, 'in shared pain' (50). While, like all utopias, Le Guin's is a human construct, a simplification which can never fully match the richness and complexity of reality, it remains one in which the human element is not a limitation, but a strength. While attending a party at the luxurious home of a wealthy Urrasti, Shevek makes this very point, contrasting the richness of Urras to the poverty of Anarres:

> 'Anarres is all dust and dry hills. All meager, all dry ... The towns are very small and dull, they are dreary. No palaces. Life is dull, and hard work. You can't always have what you want, or even what you need, because there isn't enough. You Urrasti have enough. Enough air, enough rain, grass, oceans, food, music, buildings, factories, machines, books, clothes, history. You are rich, you own. We are poor, we lack. You have, we do not have. Everything is beautiful, here. Only not the faces. On Anarres nothing is beautiful, nothing but the faces. The other faces, the men and women. Here you see the jewels, there you see the eyes. And in the eyes you see the splendor, the splendor of the human spirit. Because our men and

women are free—possessing nothing, they are free. And you th
possessors are possessed. You are all in jail. Each alone, solitary, wit
a heap of what he owns. You live in prison, die in prison. It is all
can see in your eyes ...' [p.184]

Following which, having indulged for the first time in the Urrasti custo
of drinking alcohol (another of Anarres' many lacks), he proceeds to vom
copiously over an elaborate tray of canapes. Yet even here we see
metaphor of the relationship between utopia and reality. The gross physic
act whereby Shevek renders the delicate, expensive pastries repulsive an
inedible is itself, to use Bakhtinian terminology, a form of carniv
uncrowning, unmasking the reality that underlies the official version: fro
a utopian perspective such displays of conspicuous consumption in th
midst of poverty and starvation are inherently disgusting—Shevek's gro
physical action merely makes this apparent. Although concerned wit
ideals, Le Guin does not therefore idealize those who uphold them: h
'Great Scientist' is also a fallible human being with stinking breath and
bad hangover the following morning—an apt enough representative of th
utopia which produced him. Le Guin's utopia is one which acknowledge
reality, rather than seeking to escape it, not least because it presents i
ideological concerns within a narrative framework which serves t
foreground the relationship between utopia and the reality from which
stems, yet to which it proposes an alternative. Like Piercy's, it is a utopi
which shows the future as conditional, rather than perfect.

The Future of Utopia

In the introductory chapter it was suggested that critical responses t
utopian narrative are themselves a form of narrative—most often of
journey away from the monolithic ideal of the traditional utopia, an
toward a variety of destinations. For some commentators it is a narrativ
with an at least potentially happy ending, as in the case of readings wher
the fragmentation of the monolith into a variety of 'partial visions', (
multiform and self-reflexive narratives, is seen as a positive developmen
enabling a renewed engagement with the problematics of oppositiona
struggle under the conditions of late capitalism; or where the stasis an
authoritarianism of the traditional utopia are seen as being made open t
dialogue by the active reading strategies of reader-response theory. Fc
others, the narrative is more problematic: while such new developmen
(not to mention the critical interest in them) may be taken as a welcom
indication that utopian hope is still alive, they also serve to highlight th
difficulties of finding ways of *acting* on that hope under the condition
obtaining in contemporary society—difficulties which have led some critic

ɔ the more pessimistic conclusion that the relevance of utopia has been xhausted, and that the journey is one that merely leads to a dead-end.

In the case of the present discussion, it might seem that the narrative of the more optimistic variety, tracing as it does a movement toward the esolution of many of the narrative problems on which earlier chapters ɔcused. Yet at the same time it is clear that this has not been achieved vithout cost. While the utopias of Piercy and Le Guin delineate societies ar removed from the regimented visions of the past, and do so in ways hat resolve many of the formal and aesthetic difficulties apparent in raditional utopian narrative, it remains unclear whether this renders them ny more effective in promoting social transformation than their redecessors. As Levitas reminds us, while both the form and content of ttopia are of central importance, there is also the question of *function*— nd it would seem that in this regard the movement away from the norms ıf the traditional utopia has also involved a retreat from the notion of ttopia as representing a coherent possible alternative to existing society. Vhat has become clear, in effect, is that the *role* of utopia has changed: the urpose of utopian narrative has become less the advocacy of specific lternative sociopolitical formations, and more the stimulus and education ıf desire.

Clearly, the issue of the education of desire is a crucially important one— articularly given the existence of a vast capitalist dream machine dedicated ɔ colonizing the imagination in the interests of the maintenance of the tatus quo. As Bammer argues, ours is a society which also seeks to educate lesire, but in the service of far from utopian goals:

> ... to the extent that consumer economies are based on the principle of perpetual increase, a systemic effort is made to commodify desire as a need that can be satisfied through the acquisition of objects. Desire is thus (re)constructed in material terms and directed to become profitable within the sphere of production and exchange. As visions of the good life (romance, adventure, wealth, and power) are marketed as lucrative diversions from the stress and tedium of everyday routines, commodified dreams become tools with which to keep deeper and politically more destabilizing dissatisfactions in check. Seduced by our own desires as we see them reflected in the promises for fulfilment on display, we buy into fantasies that prevent us from acknowledging (much less pursuing) what might be more authentic needs. [p.44]

Not the least insidious aspect of this process is its transformation of desire from a potential engine of change to a tool of social control. Indeed, part ɔf the ideological legitimacy of late capitalism rests on its success in making us believe that our desires *are* being met, or that if not they *can* be met— or, failing that, that if not, the fault lies with the individual rather than the system: that this is the way things *are*, and that change is neither possible nor desirable. Obviously, for change to *be* possible, it is necessary for people to be able to imagine change as both possible and desirable, and given the extent of what Kenneth Roemer refers to as 'speculative illiteracy' in modern society, the need for powerful images of alternative possibilities is all the more pressing. In a society where utopia has become a brand name for soft drinks and canned tomatoes, and where even highly educated young students, to use Roemer's example, asked to imagine a utopian transformation of their own environment, with unlimited resources available to accomplish the task, are unable to conceive of anything more than better parking facilities and a winning season for the local baseball team (*Utopian Literature* p.394), the need for the educative potential of utopia scarcely needs to be argued.[11]

Nevertheless, while utopian literature offers a potential mechanism for the education of desire in new directions, an awareness of the importance of the task can lead to an overestimation of the success with which it is being carried out. Thus, while Moylan, for example, argues that '[f]rom Gerard [*sic*] Winstanley's designs of a democratic and just society in the seventeenth century to the elaborate systems of the utopian socialists in the nineteenth, great alternate systems in print did little to generate fundamental social change' (p.5), this sober assessment of the limitations of the traditional utopia gives way to an almost messianic zeal when he turns to the 'critical utopia' of his own time:

> The critical utopias ... have restored the utopian impulse to the general oppositional movement. Therein radically hopeful figurations can become part of the collective, participatory, and non-hierarchical project of tearing down the present dominant system and meeting the historical, material, and situationally specific needs of all people rather than of the few who benefit from the current structure ... The critical utopias ... help achieve a breach in the ideological and cultural structures that surround us and thus help create that oppositional public sphere in which the play of alternatives can be elaborated. In their self-reflexive and deconstructive questioning of utopian discourse they free the utopian impulse for the ongoing task of social change. [pp.212–13]

This, however, begs a number of questions. Leaving aside the question of how far the utopianism of Winstanley and others *was* in fact effective in informing the radical oppositional consciousness of earlier eras, Moylan's claims for the much *greater* effectiveness of what are after all a relatively

mall number of utopian fictions, written in a single country during a
elatively brief period of time, do seem to indicate an exaggerated sense of
he importance of cultural production to the larger sphere of oppositional
truggle—which in Levitas's view can be attributed in part to what she
escribes as 'an alarming if increasingly common misconception of
;ramsci, claiming that Gramsci identified "the terrain of ideology and
ulture as *the* [rather than a] major site for contesting the dominant power"'
Concept of Utopia, p.174). Yet while it is not uncommon for those engaged
1 intellectual and cultural production to overestimate the importance of
heir own sphere of endeavour, such underlying assumptions can lead on
ccasion to flagrant absurdity, as for example when Moylan cites Stanley
ronowitz's assertion that:

> ... the struggle over culture, rather than the struggle for economic
> advantage, is connected to the problematic of historical change, since
> under late capitalist conditions economic struggles no longer retain
> their subversive content. [Quoted in Moylan, p.208]

)uite what would happen if one were to inform striking workers, fighting
or their jobs against the corporate agenda of transnational capitalism, that
hey would be better deployed writing postmodern utopian fiction is
erhaps better left to the imagination—and, indeed, it might equally be
[uestioned whether the freedom fighters of East Timor, fighting against a
égime that continues to enjoy close ties with the North American academic
stablishment that also supports the expanding study of utopianism, would
dentify their struggle as primarily a cultural one. While the task of
enerating images of alternative possibilities is an important one, there is
ittle to be gained from exaggerating its significance.

Yet while Moylan is clearly aware of the continued necessity of utopian
lternatives, the same can hardly be said of Peter Ruppert, who, while also
vriting in the aftermath of the wave of utopian writing hailed by Moylan
s a breakthrough, takes an almost antithetical view of its continuing
elevance. According to Ruppert:

> The essence of utopian thinking has always been a desire for a
> thorough restructuring of social relations and a radical
> transformation of social life. Such a restructuring implies the
> possibility of a perspective outside of and in opposition to the status
> quo. In a homogeneous society such as our own, so completely
> standardized, systematized, and programmed by mass culture, such
> a perspective is more and more difficult to achieve. There are simply
> fewer areas of discontent and fewer remaining dissatisfactions in a
> society that delivers the goods and provides so many distractions.

The net result is that many forms of utopian expression surviving today seem vacuous and lacking in genuine utopian content [pp.164–5]

With statements like this, it is hard to know where to begin: delivers the goods to whom? To the US prison population, one of the largest *per capita* in the world? To the inhabitants of its urban ghettoes? To the Third World? Were the Los Angeles riots in the aftermath of the Rodney King beating merely one of the 'fewer areas of discontent' in a 'homogeneous society'? Nevertheless, depressing though this, the revelation that it is possible to write an entire book on utopian literature and still ask whether we have not 'reached precisely the kind of well-being and happiness that those old utopian dreamers dreamt about' (p.164) does suggest that the effectiveness of utopia in challenging the dominant ideology may be rather less than Moylan claims.

In thus universalizing the experience peculiar only to his own class and culture, Ruppert betrays a parochialism which is, however, not unfamiliar in a utopian context: the world in which Ruppert *imagines* he lives is in fact not far removed from that of Bellamy's Dr Leete—a comfortable middle-class reality whose norms are supposed to be universally shared. And while Moylan is not guilty of such crassness, his inflated assessment of the oppositional utility of the critical utopia is in some respects hardly less ahistorical than Ruppert's suggestion that utopia may finally have arrived. Whereas Ruppert appears to believe that we have finally arrived at a state hardly distinguishable from Fukuyama's 'End of History', where utopian alternatives are redundant, Moylan's exuberant claim that the critical utopia has *at last* overcome the irrelevance of its predecessors, and unlocked a range of entirely new oppositional strategies strikes an almost equally millennial note.

What does seem to be the case is that even as utopian writing has resolved many of its narrative problems, it has lost some of its immediate relevance. In the face of the more extreme claims made for the importance of contemporary utopian writing, it is worth bearing in mind Kumar's reminder that no recent utopia has succeeded in stimulating anything like as much public debate as did works such as *Looking Backward* or *A Modern Utopia* (*Utopia*, p.420). Kumar sees this as being due in part to formal considerations, arguing that the more limited appeal of works such as *The Dispossessed* is a direct result of its use of a science fiction format, rendering it 'difficult to break out of its specialized literary ghetto' (p.420)—and while this may be somewhat overstated, it offers a useful corrective to the tendency, fostered by the expanding study of science fiction in the academy, to overestimate the universality of its appeal. In addition, as

Levitas points out, the self-conscious, self-reflexive ambiguity of much recent utopian writing, for all its artistic and intellectual appeal

> is not merely exploratory and open, it is also disillusioned and unconfident ... The presentation of alternative futures, multiple possibilities and fragmented images of time reflects a lack of confidence about whether and how a better world can be reached. [*Concept of Utopia*, p.196]

Perhaps as a result, the wave of new utopian writing, however exciting its implications, has proved to be a relatively short-lived phenomenon—indeed, it might be argued that the expansion of the academic study of utopias during the last decade has been in inverse proportion to their continued production.

At the same time, a more sober assessment of the role and significance of utopian writing need not necessarily entail a pessimistic view of its future, still less an acceptance of the complacent assumption that utopia is no longer necessary in the 'homogeneous' and supposedly eternal world of late capitalism. What utopian writing is still capable of doing is highlighting the socially constructed, and hence potentially transformable character of existing reality, and also of providing images of the utopian moment—glimpses of the almost infinite possibilities that are opened up at the moment of revolutionary social transformation. Such glimpses occur in real life, as well as imaginative literature: witness the testimony of observers of the early days of the Russian and Chinese Revolutions, such as John Reed's *Ten Days That Shook the World*, or William Hinton's *Fanshen*—or more recently the Portuguese Revolution where, in the immediate aftermath of the fall of Caetano, it was at least briefly possible to erect a sign in Lisbon's central railway station reading 'We are trying to create a better society—please help us by paying your fare' and actually be taken seriously. Perhaps one of the continuing functions of utopian writing is to remind us that such moments need not be merely a thing of the past.

What *happens* after such moments, of course, is often disillusioning: the past all too often resurfaces in an only slightly different guise. In the Soviet Union there soon emerged a leader as brutal and authoritarian as any Tsar; in China one as self-aggrandizing as any Emperor; while in Portugal there now exists a capitalist state little different from any other in Europe. Perhaps one of the functions of the *study* of utopia is to encourage reflection on the causes of this recurrent tendency of even the most hopeful social developments to collapse back into the semblance of the very thing to which they were opposed. For utopia, as we have seen, constantly reproduces features—often the most troubling and problematic ones—both of its predecessors, and of the society to which it proposes an alternative; it, too, repeatedly falls short of what it might be; in looking to the future, it all too often re-enacts the past. And yet at the same time, it is still capable of pointing the way, however hesitantly, toward something new. In looking at its failures, we may perhaps learn more about our own tendency to repeat the past, whether that tendency is rooted in personal psychology, our broader socialization, or simply the narratives in which we find ourselves taking part. To recognize a narrative is the first step toward deciding whether or not we wish to participate in it, and then looking for ways to be part of another story—and in this context utopia provides innumerable examples from which we may learn. While utopia may tell the same story over and over again, one of its lessons is that it does not always *have* to be repeated.

Notes

Preface
1. For a more detailed discussion of these questions, see Levitas (1997).
2. Reader-response criticism goes still further, suggesting that *all* utopian fiction can—or even should—be read in such a way. Ruppert provides perhaps the most sustained example of this approach.
3. For a helpful discussion of the state of contemporary utopian studies, which includes a critique of Moylan's concept of the 'critical utopia', see Levitas (1990), pp.156–200. For Moylan's response, see Moylan (1992), pp.89–94.

Chapter 1. Introduction
1. See Morson pp.164–75. Morson argues, in fact, that editorial decisions regarding the inclusion of this material as part of the text often reflect the editor's assumptions as to the work's nature: 'It appears that those who either view *Utopia* as an unambiguous endorsement of a particular ideology or regard the distinction between literary and tractarian works as unimportant tend to offer shorter versions than those who read it as an ironic, playful, and ambiguous literary work' (p.166).
2. Suvin, *Metamorphoses*, pp.37–62; also Morson, pp.70–2 and 173–5, on the dangers of regarding utopian narrative as merely 'the literary mould' into which utopian political theory is poured.
3. See for example Ruppert, who examines utopian fiction in the light of reader-response theory. More broadly, there is a growing body of criticism which seeks to re-read earlier utopian fiction in the light of more recent fictional practice, as exemplified by works such as Russ, *The Female Man* (1975), Delany, *Triton* (1976), or, more recently, Le Guin, *Always Coming Home* (1986). For a discussion of what he terms the 'critical utopia', see Moylan, *Demand the Impossible*.
4. Although see Morson, who suggests that utopian visions 'are designed, in short, not to be convincing, but to convince', i.e. that aesthetic success, rather than being an end in itself, nevertheless remains secondary to the persuasive intent.
5. The remark is attributed to Marx in Sorel, p.150.
6. Kumar likewise suggests that '[a]s so often, the teacher came to be the enemy of the artist. Like Wells, Huxley grew impatient with purely literary form, and came to see the message as infinitely more important than the medium' (*Utopia*, p.226).
7. See Levitas (1990), pp.35–58 for a more extensive discussion of the views of Marx and Engels on utopianism; see also Geoghegan, pp.22–34. Both Levitas (1990), pp.83–105, and Geoghegan, pp.87–97, also provide valuable discussions of the work of Ernst Bloch. See also Levitas (1997).
8. See Geoghegan, pp.98–139 for an examination of how this insight has been developed by a range of more recent Marxist or neo-Marxist thinkers. See also Bammer, pp.48–53.

9. See note 2, above.

10. For a discussion of the distinctions between various types of utopian fantasy, see Davis, pp.12–41. For a discussion of the essential differences between millennial and utopian fantasy, see Olson.

11. Suvin argues that while science fiction is 'collaterally descended from utopia... if not a daughter, yet a niece of utopia' (*Metamorphoses*, p.61), its subsequent expansion has led to an 'englobing of utopia' (p.61). It is thus in retrospect that utopia can be seen as 'the *sociopolitical subgenre of science fiction*' (p.61). For a spectacular misreading of this argument see Ruppert, who asserts that in 'extending the boundaries of utopia to *include* [italics mine] science fiction, Suvin is attempting to gain greater recognition and acceptance of the latter by associating it more closely with the utopian tradition. This is somewhat ironic since utopian literature is itself not highly regarded as literature, although it apparently has achieved greater recognition and regard than the science fiction texts Suvin is seeking to justify' (p.39). This in a study published in 1986—when the study of science fiction can hardly be said to have been in its infancy.

12. See also Levitas (1990), pp.9–34, for a more recent overview, in which she argues that working definitions of utopia, rather than resulting from the 'consistent application of ... identifiable criteria' are in fact 'the outcome of habitual assumptions' (p.11).

13. In his more recent (1997) discussion of the problematics of defining utopia, Suvin concedes that his earlier formula was 'perhaps too narrowly focused' (p.135), and suggests that, for all his reservations concerning what he terms Ernst Bloch's 'pan-utopianism' (p.132), Bloch's broader conception of the utopian as a category offers a way out of the definitional impasse. This discussion also provides an illuminating examination of the relation between the utopian text and its reader.

14. This would also appear to be Richard Gerber's position in *Utopian Fantasy*, where he appears to argue that the most successful utopian narratives are those which most closely approximate to the norms of the realist novel, and suggests that the evolution of utopian narrative is in fact towards the novel: 'The development towards the novel is part of the logical evolution of the myth-creating utopian imagination, which impatiently proceeds from the general idea to ever greater actualization' (p.120). See Morson, pp.72–4 for a critique of this position.

15. Kumar takes a similar view of Le Guin's *The Dispossessed*, which he suggests 'so qualified its optimism as to appear to many readers to be offering merely the material for contemplation, rather than endorsing a new order' (*Utopia*, p.420). However, he also argues that its failure to fulfill the persuasive function of the traditional utopia is also a reflection of generic considerations: 'Presented in science fiction guise, it tended in any case to find it difficult to break out of its specialized literary ghetto' (p.420).

16. For Ruppert, this process is evident even in a hostile reading, such as William Morris's response to Bellamy's *Looking Backward*. Ruppert argues that '[w]hat remains incomplete in Bellamy's vision has been spelled out in great detail in William Morris's dialectical reading of Bellamy's text ... Morris's critical response to Bellamy, in other words, attempted to complete Bellamy's fragmented and inconclusive vision ...' (pp.76–7).

17. Jameson, however, argues that the plot devices of traditional utopian

narrative are in fact so perfunctory that the relative absence of plot and character creates a kind of estrangement effect, undermining the reader's expectations, conditioned by more conventional fictional narrative, and 'jar[ring] the mind into some heightened but unconceptualizable consciousness of its own powers, functions, aims and structural limits' ('Islands and Trenches', p.11). See Bammer, pp.15–21, for a critique of this position.

18. Such proposals for a radically reduced working day are a continuing feature of utopian speculation—and not merely by authors of utopian *fiction*: witness, for example, August Bebel's suggestion, in *Woman Under Socialism* (1879), that the working day might be reduced to two-and-a-half hours.

19. 'Les utopies apparaissent comme bien plus réalisables qu'on ne le croyait autrefois. Et nous nous trouvons actuellement devant une question bien autrement angoissante: Comment éviter leur réalisation définitive? ... Les utopies sont réalisables. La vie marche vers les utopies. Et peut-être un siècle nouveau commence-t-il, un siècle ou les intellectuels et la classe cultivée reveront aux moyens d'éviter les utopies et de retourner à une société non utopique, moins 'parfaite' et plus libre.' Not the least interesting aspect of Berdiaeff's statement is its clear implication that utopian dreaming is essentially only the business of the cultivated élite—rather than the lower orders who might actually benefit from the transformation of the existing order.

20. Other examples include L.P. Hartley's *Facial Justice*, Kurt Vonnegut's *Player Piano*, Anthony Burgess's *A Clockwork Orange*, and Ira Levin's (admittedly rather derivative) *This Perfect Day*—while dystopian futures are a staple feature of modern science fiction. Kumar, however, argues that more recent dystopian writing suffers from the same malaise that he detects in utopian writing: 'Anti-utopia shares in the fate of utopia. As utopia loses it [sic] vitality, so too does anti-utopia' (*Utopia*, p.422). He also suggests that 'No anti-utopia since *Nineteen Eighty-Four* has truly captured the popular imagination or become the centre of public debate' (p.422).

21. See for example Lefanu, pp.130–46. Also Khouri, pp.49–60.

22. See Jameson, *The Political Unconscious*, in which he argues that a study of the ideology of form serves not merely to 'reveal the active presence within the text of a number of discontinuous and heterogeneous formal processes' but makes it possible 'to grasp such formal processes as sedimented content in their own right, as carrying ideological messages of their own, distinct from the ostensible or manifest content of the works' (p.99).

23. To counteract the impression of total conformity, some writers (William Morris, H.G. Wells in *A Modern Utopia*) do include a token dissenter, but it is fair to say that this transparently schematic device seldom creates the impression of there being any genuine debate in utopia.

24. See for example Morson, pp.146–55; also Ruppert, pp.123–30.

25. A comparable utopian prevision of humanity transformed by radical changes in social organization may be found in Trotsky's *Literature and Revolution*, where he suggests that 'Social construction and psycho-physical self-education will become two aspects of one and the same process ...Man will become immeasurably stronger, wiser and subtler; his body will become more harmonized, his movements more rhythmic, his voice more musical. The forms of life will become dynamically dramatic. The average human type will rise to the heights of an Aristotle, a Goethe, or a Marx. And above this ridge new peaks will rise' (p.256).

26. Bloch argues that the bourgeois imagination, while much given to dreams, 'still rations them, even in more distant excursions to the over-blue coast of the travel agent's and beyond: so that they do not explode the given world. People with wishes of this kind live beyond their own means, but never beyond the generally existing means' (*Principle of Hope*, p.34).This, of course, becomes less of a problem for writers whose utopian fictions are conceived of within the generic conventions of Science Fiction—Russ and Delany being cases in point.

Chapter 2. The Utopian Dream of Order

1. Frye argues, in fact, that 'utopian romance does not present society as governed by reason; it presents it as governed by ritual habit, or prescribed social behavior, which is explained rationally' ('Varieties', p.27).

2. Yates, *Giordano Bruno and the Hermetic Tradition*, p.1–19.

3. See Yates (*Bruno*, pp.205–9); also McNulty, pp.300–5.

4. See Webster, pp.6–31.

5. The publication in 1989 of the long-missing 'Letter to the Sovereigns' announcing the Discovery has made this clearly apparent: '...through the divine grace of Him who is the origin of all good and virtuous things, who favours and gives victory to all those who walk in His path, in seven years from today I will be able to pay Your Highnesses for five thousand cavalry and fifty thousand foot soldiers for the war and conquest of Jerusalem, for which purpose this enterprise was undertaken' (Zamora, p.7). See Zamora for a translation of the letter, and a discussion of its implications.

6. Columbus's theories as to the location of the earthly paradise are contained in his account of his third voyage. See Jane, Volume 2, pp.28–38.

7. See A.E. Morgan, *Nowhere Was Somewhere*.

8. Vespucci's were by no means the only discovery narratives whose authenticity was questioned: Walter Ralegh's *The Discoverie of the large, rich, and beautifull Empire of Guiana* (1596) was published in part to refute accusations that, far from exploring Guiana, he had 'hidden in Cornewall' (p.273), and that the gold samples he brought back had in fact been purchased in Barbary (p.278).

9. So vague is More's description, indeed, that one otherwise perceptive critic locates Utopia 'somewhere in the South Atlantic' (Kumar, *Utopia*, p.71)!

10. For a more detailed discussion of the search for the earthly paradise and its implications, see Bloch (*Principle of Hope*, pp.772–81); also Sanford, pp.36–45. Vespucci also declared that 'if the terrestrial paradise be in any part of this earth, I esteem that it is not far distant from these parts' (*Letters*, p.48), although this is in a letter widely held to be spurious.

11. The text of this letter, and the following one cited, are translated by Robert Adams, and are included in his edition of *Utopia*—although their textual status is rendered somewhat equivocal by their being separated from what is labelled 'The Text of *Utopia*', and included instead in an appendix which also contains selections from earlier writers and subsequent critical discussions.

12. In actual fact, this view is attributed to Simon Magus by a hostile critic, St Hippolytus, in *The Refutation of all Heresies*. See Manuel and Manuel, p.43.

13. See Bakhtin, *Rabelais*, p.11.

14. See *The Principle of Hope*, pp.51–77. Bloch argues that conscious dreams,

whatever their unconscious basis, 'are all dreams of a better life. No doubt there are among them base, dubious, dismal, merely enervating escapist dreams full of substitution, as is well-known. This kind of escape from reality has often been combined with approval and support of the status quo; as is revealed most strongly in the empty promises of a better hereafter. But how many other wishful daydreams have sustained men with courage and hope, not by looking away from the real, but, on the contrary, by looking into its progress, into its horizon. How many have reaffirmed their refusal to renounce, in the course of anticipation, of venturing beyond and its images. The amount of venturing beyond that takes place in daydreams thus indicates nothing repressed, even psychologically, nothing that has simply sunk down out of consciousness that already existed, nor any atavistic state which was simply left over from or breaks out of primeval man. The venturer beyond does not occupy a shaft in the ground beneath existing consciousness, with a single exit either into the familiar daylight world of today, as in Freud, or into a romanticized diluvium, as in C.G. Jung and Klages. What hovers ahead of the self-extension drive forwards is rather ...a Not-Yet Conscious, one that has never been conscious and has never existed in the past, therefore itself a forward dawning, into the New' (pp.76–7).

15. Kolodny provides an extensive examination of this aspect of the discovery narrative. For more recent discussions, see Parker, pp.126–54, and Montrose.

16. For a detailed discussion of the gender implications of the narratives of Ralegh and Keymis, see Montrose.

17. For an extended critique of the assumptions underlying such essentialist views of what constitutes the feminine, see Thürmer-Rohr.

18. Bammer argues that utopian fantasies in fact reinscribe a whole range of the inequities to which utopia purports to offer an alternative: 'as we look more closely at the visions of supposedly ideal worlds from Plato's *Republic* to contemporary science fictions, we find that hierarchies of class and caste and inequalities of race and gender are everywhere reinstated. Indeed ... many of the most virulent prejudices of the time and place in which a given utopia was written are likely to reappear, alive and flourishing, in the new world that purports to present an alternative' (p.19). Yet while this is undoubtedly true of *some* utopias (existing class prejudices, for example, are strongly evident in the utopias of Bellamy and Wells), it is by no means true of all of them. What this study argues is that existing gender hierarchies and assumptions regarding gender relations are far more consistently reproduced (at any rate, in male-authored utopias) than any of the other inequalities to which Bammer refers.

19. There are clear parallels here with Ralegh's later *Discoverie*, in which he represents the indigenous inhabitants of the lands bordering on Guiana as desperately eager for English rule, given that only the English appear able to defeat the hated Spaniards—although in order to sustain this eagerness, whether real or imagined, Ralegh is at pains to conceal that Spaniards and English alike 'came both for one errant, and that both sought but to sacke & spoile them' (p.335).

20. In Montrose's view, the renaming process exemplifies 'an emergent colonialist discourse that works to justify and, symbolically, to effect the expropriation of what it discovers. Typically, this discourse denies the natural right of possession to indigenous peoples by confirming them to be heathens,

savages, and/or foragers who neither cultivate the land nor conceptualize it as real property; or it may symbolically efface the very existence of those indigenous peoples from the places its speakers intend to exploit' (p.184).

21. J.C. Davis, however, cites a number of authorities who argue that *The New Atlantis* was in fact left by Bacon in the form in which he had intended its publication. See Davis, pp.121–4.

22. See Gilison, p.24.

23. See Yates, *Bruno*, p.375.

24. See Morley, p.vi. As Richard Stites points out in his edition of Bogdanov's *Red Star*, this is by no means the only such expurgation: 'a recent Soviet edition of Bogdanov's novel saw fit to omit Leonid's ruminations on marriage and sex' (p.9).

25. This is only one of a number of details that suggests the influence of Diodorus Siculus's account of the Isles of the Blessed, written in the second century BC, which Cohn describes as typical of 'the kind of egalitarian phantasy which the ancient world was to bequeath to the Middle Ages' (p.189), and which was repeatedly translated during the Renaissance. It too depicts a society of sun-worshippers—the Heliopolitans, among whom private property, marriage, and the family are all unknown, and whose lifespan is a hundred and fifty years.

26. This claim is echoed, some three hundred years later, by H.G. Wells in a lecture entitled 'The Discovery of the Future', in which he declares: 'In the past century there was more change in the conditions of human life than there had been in the previous thousand years' (quoted in Kumar, *Utopia*, p.173). See also Kumar, p.437 for a discussion of the possible sources of this remark.

27. See Kumar, *Utopia*, pp.29–36. While Kumar suggests that *The New Atlantis* provided 'the model of the dynamic utopia which was at the same time felt—at least by his followers—to be a realizable project' (p.34), he also points to the problematic character of the link between science and utopia: 'the dynamism of science was bound to press against the finished, perfect order of utopia' (p.30).

28. Despite its explicitly Christian character, Kumar, rather oddly, describes *The New Atlantis* as 'of all the seventeenth-century utopias the one least obviously indebted to Christian conceptions' (*Utopia*, p.19), although he does go on to point out that the House of Saloman 'is modelled fairly clearly on the monastery' (p.19).

Chapter 3. Bellamy and Wells

1. Frye, for instance, argues that 'because technology is progressive, getting to the utopia has tended increasingly to be a journey in time rather than space, a vision of the future and not of a society located in some isolated spot on the globe (or outside it ...' ('Varieties', p.28). Moylan, similarly, suggests that 'in late nineteenth-century utopias, subversive visions were relocated in a future time when the process of revolutionary, historical change brought about the utopian society. At this point in the development of the genre, history more directly entered the texts, and utopian novels more regularly provided accounts of the required transition from the present to utopia' (*Demand the Impossible*, p.6). Yet in fact, with the honourable exception of Morris's *News from Nowhere*,

it is striking how *seldom* such transitions are described in anything other than the most perfunctory detail: the evasion of the connection with existing society remains a recurrent feature of utopian narrative until well into the twentieth century.

2. In fact, this narrative device first appears as early as 1771, in Louis-Sebastien Mercier's *L'An 2440*, which Clarke describes as 'the first influential story of the future in world literature' (p.23).

3. Leacock farcically restages the scene where Julian West is taken to a rooftop by Dr Leete and shown a vista of the utopian Boston of the future: 'Great Heavens! Was this the city I had known! Whither had gone the tall skyscrapers reaching to the clouds? Where was the long reach of the wide Hudson, the vast suspension bridge hung like an aerial web from shore to shore? Where was it all gone, or how had it changed to this? I turned to Dr. Oom, who stood beside me, quietly smiling at my evident and utter astonishment. "Can this," I said, pointing to the vision around me, "can this be New York?" "New York?" said Oom, "no, of course not. This is London." The exhilaration which had kindled in his face died out of it. In fact he looked rather crestfallen ... "What made you think it New York?" "Why, I fell asleep in New York," I said. "I believe that's right," said Dr. Oom, reflecting, "you did, very likely. There was a sort of patriotic exchange of hundred-year sleepers between England and America and you must have come over in that lot. In fact, now I think of it, you did."' (p.13).

4. For a more extensive discussion of Bellamy's influence, see Bowman.

5. While this is one of the most universally criticized features of Bellamy's utopia, Bellamy was hardly alone in proposing such solutions. See for example Trotsky's argument, in *Terrorism and Communism*, that the 'militarization of labour' was essential to solve the economic problems facing the new Soviet Union—at least on a temporary basis—although he was at the same time careful to distinguish between the structures of Soviet-style military organization and those of conventional armies (pp.133–57).

6. Bleich suggests, rather unkindly, that the otherwise pacific Bellamy's preoccupation with such militaristic analogies might be rooted in his youthful failure to gain admission to West Point (p.52).

7. Kumar suggests a different parallel, arguing that the structure of Bellamy's utopian society 'comes very close to the actual Saint-Simonian proposal of a triumvirate of industrialists, scientists, and artists as the directing agency of the socialist society. As with Saint-Simon, the specific organization of the "free professions" introduces a much-needed liberal and "pluralist" element in an otherwise highly co-ordinated and integrated structure based on industry' (*Utopia*, p.158).

8. See for example Jean Pfaelzer, 'Immanence', p.53.

9. As Kumar remarks, 'Such a régime of sexual *apartheid* might please some of the radical feminists of today. But it can scarcely satisfy socialists, and seems to owe more to Bellamy's Victorian patriarchalism than to any anticipation of feminine separatism' (*Utopia*, p.164).

10. Morson points out that such apocalyptic imagery is a recurrent feature in *Looking Backward* (p.121). In a subsequent discussion with Dr Leete, Julian West suggests that 'this is indeed the "new heavens and the new earth wherein dwelleth righteousness," which the prophet foretold' (p.112)—a view which he is informed is shared by a number of the citizens of the future, including,

it would appear, the preacher towards the end of the book, who declares that in the world of AD 2000 '"For the first time since the creation every man stood up straight before God"' (p.159).

11. The comment actually occurs in a letter to William D. Howells, written 17 June 1888.

12. See Milton Cantor, 'The Backward Look of Bellamy's Socialism' in Pata (*Looking Backward*, pp.21–36) for a discussion of this aspect of Bellamy's utopia See also Kumar, pp.158–63.

13. A further gap between what is described and what is dramatized becomes apparent when one considers that, as Kumar observes: 'Julian never meets anyone outside the nuclear family circle of Dr Leete, nor is anyone else even mentioned as a neighbour, colleague or friend' (*Utopia*, p.164). This despite the fact that a whole range of communal social structures have been created which render the role of the family in many respects redundant.

14. Not the least remarkable feature of this curious love-scene is the extent to which it reaffirms the narrator's passivity. Far from having to win Edith' love, he arrives in utopia to find that she is *already* in love with him—although she is at the same time anxious to forestall any thoughts he might have that she was '"over quick to fall in love … After you know who I am, you will be found to confess that it was nothing less than my duty to fall in love with you at first sight, and that no girl of proper feeling in my place could do otherwise"' (p.167).

15. A radically different reading of Bellamy's text is offered by Rosemont who sees the romance between Julian West and Edith Leete as centrally important, rather than merely novelistic window-dressing: '*Looking Backward* is, among other things, a love story, telling of a love that conquers, symbolically at least, not only time but death itself. This marvellous erotic triumph exemplifies another essential feature of Bellamy's revolutionary project: the supersession of time' (p.150). This must rank as one of the rare occasions when the imaginative powers of the critic outstrip those of the author under discussion. See also Pfaelzer, who argues that 'the representation of Julian West has the richness, intimation, and ambiguity of the symbolic, and it is through the hero's developing consciousness that we adhere to the latent potential for a redeemed society within industrial capitalism' ('Immanence' p.56).

16. Some of Bellamy's fiction none the less remains of interest in a utopian context. Given the ambiguous relation of utopia to its own past, it is worth noting that in his novel *Dr Heidenhoff's Process* (1880) Bellamy imagines a procedure whereby memory can be erased; while in his short story 'The Blindman's World' (1898) he portrays a society in which precognition is the rule, memory the exception.

17. See for example Kumar, pp.190–205, who argues that '[t]he attractiveness and originality of the form is undoubtedly one reason for the book's popularity and success. Unlike most utopias [it] evokes a vision as much as, and perhaps rather more than, it proclaims a programme' (p.190). For a discussion of *A Modern Utopia* as 'meta-utopia', see Morson, pp.146–55. See also Ruppert, pp.123–30, who discusses the work in the light of reader-response theory.

18. See note 19, below.

19. In his *Experiment in Autobiography* Wells declares that while his thinking

was 'run very close to communist lines ... my conception of a scientifically organized classless society is essentially of an expanded middle-class which has incorporated both the aristocrat and plutocrat above and the peasant, proletarian and pauper below' (Volume 1, p.94).

20. The naturalizing of class distinctions by giving them a biological, rather than social basis is a recurrent feature in Wells's fiction—most glaringly in The Time Machine (1895), where the aristocracy have degenerated into the effete Eloi, and the working class into the subhuman Morlocks. In this scenario, the vigorous and resourceful Time Traveller is able to fulfill a range of middle-class fantasies by sleeping with a representative of the former, and massacring the latter in large numbers.

21. Frye regards Wells's fourfold division of humanity as 'particularly uncharitable considering that the only essential doctrine in Wells's utopian religion is the rejection of original sin. Wells's writing in general illustrates the common principle that the belief that man is by nature good does not lead to a very good-natured view of man' (p.35). Hence, perhaps, Wells's insistence on the need to transform humanity's biological nature; despite his rejection of the doctrine of original sin, he continues to assume the existence of innate laws which need to be bred out, as opposed to being modified by social conditioning.

22. As if to underscore the Edenic quality of the world into which the narrator awakens, when he does discover his discarded revolver, it is described, rather curiously, as 'a blue-black thing, like a dead snake at my feet' (p.155).

23. Cf. 1 Corinthians 15:20. 'But now is Christ risen from the dead, and become the first fruits of them that slept.' Here Wells echoes a passage descriptive of the Resurrection, and the final and irrevocable establishment of the authority of the Father.

24. Certainly both Campanella and Bacon imagine the possibility of scientific inventions extending human mastery over nature, but in neither case does the possibility really influence the character of the utopian society they imagine—whereas in Wells's utopias the possibility is vividly dramatized. Wells, however, does refer approvingly to the 'dynamic' character of The New Atlantis, and on one occasion asserted that 'the Utopia of Bacon's [sic] has produced more in the way of real consequences than any other Utopia that was ever written' (quoted in Kumar, Utopia, p.198).

25. See Kumar, Utopia, pp.230–42, however, for a discussion of the wildly ambitious speculations of contemporary scientists such as J.B.S Haldane and J.D. Bernal, who envisaged a future in which the human physique would be radically transformed (a possibility already considered by Wells in works such as 'The Man of the Year Million' (1893) and The War of the Worlds (1898)), and where energy would be provided by the transformation of the stars 'into efficient heat engines' (quoted in Kumar, p.234). Wells's vision of the extent of the possible transformation of nature by human agency is also rivalled by Bogdanov, in his descriptions of the colossal engineering projects of the Martians in Red Star and Engineer Menni, and even surpassed by Trotsky, whose Literature and Revolution (published the year after Men Like Gods) looks forward to a future in which 'the present distribution of mountains and rivers, of fields, of meadows, of steppes, of forests, and of seashores, cannot be considered final' (p.251), and where 'Man ... will learn how to move rivers and mountains, how to build people's palaces on the peaks of Mont Blanc and at the bottom

of the Atlantic' (p.254).

26. The narrator continues: 'From now onward, of course, the fates of thes two planets will diverge, men will die whom wisdom will save there, an perhaps conversely here we shall save men; children will be born to them an not to us, to us and not to them, but this, this moment of reading, is the startin moment, and for the first and last occasion the populations of our planets a abreast' (pp.24–5). There is, however, no explanation of how this is to b reconciled with the radically different human history that Wells goes on t imagine.

27. Utopia, of course, is hardly the only form of radical expression to b thus co-opted: witness the use of Bob Dylan's 1960s protest song 'The Tim They Are A-Changing' in a recent Bank of Montreal TV commercial, or th Vodafone ads featuring models wearing clothes, and striking poses, clearl borrowed from Soviet revolutionary posters—all in the cause of celebratin the 'freedom' provided by a cellular phone.

28. Ralegh, for example, in his *Discoverie*, uses as an important argumer for his proposed colonization of Guiana the fact that 'Her Majestie may in th enterprize employ all those souldiers and gentlemen that are younger brethrer and all captaines and chieftaines that want employment, and the charge wi be onely the first setting out in victualling and arming them' (p.349).

29. Even where less than a global utopia is imagined, colonialist aspiratior still resurface: witness Skinner's *Walden Two*, which at first sight appears t propose the relatively modest possibility of the establishment of a single utopia community. Later on, however, we discover that in addition to Walden Two there are also Waldens Three, Four, Five, and Six—and that Walden Two founder imagines the possibility of their growing and subdividing 'once ever two years. Then in ten years Waldens Two and Six will give birth to some sixt odd communities ... In *thirty* years ... we could absorb the whole country man times over' (p.228).

Chapter 4. Dystopia

1. See Blitzer, pp.3–4.

2. These include Conrad Wilbrandt, *Mr East's Experiences in Mr Bellamy World* (1891), and J.W. Roberts, *Looking Within* (1893). Like Vinton's *Lookin Further Backward*, they offer farcical visions of what Bellamy's future woul 'really' be like: Wilbrandt imagines a world where chronic inefficiency combined with overspending induced by the use of credit cards, oblige everyone to work until the age of 65; Roberts envisages a society wher uniformity has gone so far that everyone actually *looks* the same, wearin specially moulded masks.

3. Examples of such narratives include Sir George Chesney, *The Battle* Dorking (1871), Sir William Butler, *The Invasion of England* (1882), William L Queux, *The Great War in England in 1897* (1894), M.P. Shiel, *The Yellow Dange* (1898).

4. Such scenes appear in the concluding sections of *Looking Backward, Nev from Nowhere, A Modern Utopia,* and *Walden Two*—to name but a few.

5. It has often been suggested that this 'family resemblance' is in fact reflection of the dystopian genre's debt to Zamyatin. Ruppert, for instanc declares that '*We* has achieved the status of an exemplary work whose influenc

can be seen in numerous imitations: Huxley's *Brave New World*, Orwell's *Nineteen Eighty-Four*, Golding's *Lord of the Flies* ... and many others' (p.105). However, there are a number of problems with this. While *Nineteen Eighty-Four* is clearly indebted to the example of *We* (in places almost to the point of plagiarism), Huxley explicitly denied ever having read it (Collins, p.351), and, as Kumar argues, such resemblances as exist between *Brave New World* and *We* can readily be explained by their common acquaintance with Wells's utopias (*Utopia*, pp.225, 462), and their both using the 'Legend of the Grand Inquisitor' from *The Brothers Karamazov* as inspiration for the set piece debate between the rebels and authority (pp.122–3). In addition, the extent of Zamyatin's own originality is open to question: as Stites points out, N. Fedorov published a science fiction novel in 1906, entitled *An Evening in the Year 2217*, which features 'numbered citizens, monstrous conformity, abolition of marriage and family, sex by appointment, and a lifeless socialist urban milieu of glass and stone'— a virtual prototype for Zamyatin's *We* (p.5).

6. As Morson points out, 'the scene in which the ruler acknowledges the falsehood to a rebel who has detected it' (p.126) is a recurrent feature in dystopian fiction, and one which parodies 'those numerous utopian exchanges in which the delineator reveals the truth. The climax of these dystopias, in other words, is the Revelation of the Lie' (p.126). As Kumar points out, however, such scenes are less parodies of utopia, than reworkings of Dostoevsky (p.122).

7. This is the transliteration used in Guerney's translation; in other translations the character often appears as I-330.

8. While Ford's production line is the most obvious inspiration for Huxley's fantasy of a world whose citizens are both mentally and physically moulded to fit the needs of the State, Kumar points out that another possible model is Wells's *The First Men in the Moon*, with 'its portrait of the ant-like civilization of the Selenites ... anticipating in detail the purported anti-Wellsian critique of *Brave New World*' (*Utopia*, p.178).

9. Fiderer comments on a number of aspects of this scene: its emphasis on the erotic quality of the creamy paper, the immaturity of the scrawl with which he covers it, the almost deliberate courting of disaster by leaving the book open—all of which he sees as lending credence to his thesis that the novel is in part a masochistic fantasy of erotic submission to the power of a superior male, all leading up to the climactic admission that 'He loved Big Brother'.

10. While it may be hard to see the use of make-up as particularly subversive, it is worth bearing in mind that in the utopian context of Campanella's *The City of the Sun* using cosmetics is a capital offence.

11. For Adorno, it is this opposition that constitutes *Brave New World*'s major weakness: 'The crude alternative of objective meaning and subjective happiness, conceived as mutually exclusive, is the philosophical basis for the reactionary character of the novel' (p.112).

12. The extent to which dystopian fiction is *inherently* reactionary remains the subject of debate. Jameson argues, for example, that 'Utopia is a transparent synonym for socialism itself, and the enemies of Utopia sooner or later turn out to be the enemies of socialism' ('Islands and Trenches', p.3). Ruppert, on the other hand, suggests that 'The enemy of both utopia and anti-utopia is the status quo, which both seek to transform' (p.104), and that 'anti-utopias compel the reader to the same dialogue, to the attempt to answer the same

questions inspired by utopias' (p.103). This is, however, difficult to reconcile with his later claim that 'anti-utopias are also inherently reductive, leaving us with a single menacing vision of society, a vision, moreover, which may have the unproductive effect of affirming the status quo' (p.122).

13. Atwood argues that in the case of *Nineteen Eighty-Four* the State's apparent triumph is undermined by the concluding Appendix ('The Principles of Newspeak'): 'he ended it with the note on Newspeak, which is written in the past tense in standard English ... which means that he didn't think Nineteen-Eighty-Four was going to last forever. And you rarely see that point made, except by me ...' (quoted in Alaton, C1).

14. Zamyatin is more sceptical than Huxley or Orwell in this regard: witness his assertion '... all truths are mistaken; the dialectical process is precisely that today's truths become tomorrow's errors; there is no last number' (quoted in Morson, p.120)—although he elsewhere suggests that stasis might be reached by a process equivalent to entropy.'Revolution is everywhere, in everything. It is infinite. There is no final revolution, no final number ...It is a cosmic, universal law, like the laws of conservation of energy and of the dissipation of energy (entropy) ... When the flaming, seething sphere (in science, religion, social life, art) cools, the fiery magma becomes coated with dogma—a rigid, ossified, motionless crust. Dogmatization in science, religion, social life, or art is the entropy of thought. What has become dogma no longer burns; it only gives off warmth—it is tepid, it is cool' (*A Soviet Heretic*, pp.107–8). In any event, *We* is unlike *Brave New World* and *Nineteen Eighty-Four* in representing the rebellion as continuing.

15. See Alaton, where Atwood acknowledges that this is partly influenced by her reading of *Nineteen Eight-Four*, as indicated in note 13, above.

Chapter 5. Libertarian Alternatives

1. For a fuller account of Morris's reaction to *Looking Backward*, see Meier, Volume 1, pp.73–93.

2. Morris's review of *Looking Backward* appeared in *The Commonweal*, 22 June 1889. It is reprinted in May Morris, Volume 2, pp.501–7.

3. While it seems clear that Morris, having undertaken the demolition of *Looking Backward* in his review, intended *News from Nowhere* as an alternative vision of utopian possibility, Ruppert argues that Morris, in his response to Bellamy, 'attempted to complete Bellamy's fragmented and inconclusive vision; Morris tried to reveal the exclusions that a dialectical reading of Bellamy's text uncovers and intensifies' (pp.76–7). This view of the text as *completed* by the reader is a recurrent feature of Ruppert's application of reader-response theory to utopian narrative (rather as though reader and text come together to form the seamless monad which traditional utopian narrative can only aspire to create). However, to see Morris as trying to 'complete Bellamy's ... vision'—as opposed to blasting it off the face of the earth—seems somewhat extraordinary.

4. There are, however, important differences between their readings of Morris; indeed, in the second, revised edition of his work on Morris, Thompson is sharply critical of Meier's representation of Morris as an orthodox Marxist. For Thompson, Morris's utopianism has its roots as much in the Romantic critique of capitalism as in Marxist theory, and has as its goal 'the education

of desire' (p.791), rather than a literal depiction of what a future Communist state would look like. Levitas provides a useful overview of this debate, situating it in the broader context of Marxist discussions of the relationship between Marxism and utopianism (*Concept of Utopia*, pp.106–30).

5. Letter to Karl Kautsky, 22 June 1884. quoted in Meier, Volume 1, p.230.

6. Letter to Frederick Sorge, 29 April 1886. quoted in Meier, Volume 1, p.234.

7. For a critique of this view of *News from Nowhere*, see Buick, p.20.

8. Bloch's own attitude to what he termed Morris's 'Gothic socialism' *Principle of Hope*, p.551) was by no means unsympathetic. While he describes *News from Nowhere* as a 'backward-looking utopia ... reminiscent of the longings at the time of the Restoration, of the Romantic infatuation with the Middle Ages and the wish to see it approaching again from the future' (p.614), he also concedes that 'the conservative political brief which the Romantics had over a hundred years before is missing ...Morris' backward utopia was not intended in a politically reactionary way. It wanted progress from the standpoint of an abandoned position, agrarian-artisan reaction for the sake of a revolutionary new beginning' (pp.614–15).

9. See for example Wilding, p.90.

10. Beilharz, for instance, describes *News from Nowhere* as 'an idyll anticipating *Wind in the Willows* [*sic*]' (p.5).

11. Kumar argues that '*News from Nowhere* might be read more as a powerful indictment of a large-scale mechanical civilization than as a utopian portrait of a future society. It would be more akin, that is, to something like Rousseau's *Discourse on the Origin of Inequality*, with its similar ambivalence between a primitivist utopian and an anti-utopian critique of the writer's own society' *Utopia*, pp.126–7). He also draws attention to the influence on Morris of *After London*, a work whose depiction of 'savagery and brutality ... mark[s] it out clearly as an anti-utopia' (p.127).

12. See for example Levitas, *Concept of Utopia*, pp.40–5, 106–30.

13. For a differing view of the relation of *News from Nowhere* to *After London* see Suvin, *Metamorphoses* pp.187–93. While acknowledging Morris's debt to Jefferies, Suvin argues that *News from Nowhere* in fact charts a "third way" between the visions of *Looking Backward* and *After London*, 'transcending the opposition between Bellamy's ethicoreligious pacification and Jefferies's politicogeological devolution' (*Metamorphoses*, p.188).

14. Despite the wholesale demolition, a few exceptions are made: for example, the British Museum is preserved, on the grounds that 'it is not a bad thing to have some record of what our forefathers thought a handsome building'—although at the same time 'many people have wanted to pull it down and rebuild it' (p.43). In fact, bearing in mind Morris's own tastes, its survival is most probably due to its being a repository of 'all kinds of antiquities, besides an enormous library with many exceedingly beautiful books in it' (p.43).

15. It is largely on the basis of this 'absence of sociopolitical organization' *Metamorphoses*, p.182) that Suvin denies *News from Nowhere* the formal status of a utopia.

16. When asked his age, the narrator describes himself as 'hard on fifty-six' (p.14)—which was Morris's own age when *News from Nowhere* began appearing in serial form in *The Commonweal* in January 1890.

250   NARRATING UTOPIA

17. The differences of opinion between Lenin and Bogdanov were bot philosophical and tactical. It was shortly after the publication of *Red Star*, i fact, that Lenin produced the extended polemic, *Materialism and Empiric Criticism* (1908), in which he denounced what he saw as the perniciou revisionism of Bogdanov and others, whom he accused of lapsing (among othe things) into Berkeleian idealism. In addition, Lenin disagreed with Bogdano over the latter's insistence that a successful armed insurrection remained realistic possibility in the aftermath of 1905. Both Jensen and Stites provid useful background on the political context for the composition of *Red Star*; fc a discussion of the philosophical differences between Bogdanov and Lenin, se Ballestrem (although the latter's bias may be deduced from his description c *Materialism and Empirio-Criticism* as 'a philosophical catastrophe' (p.283)).

18. A good deal more information is provided in Bogdanov's next nove *Engineer Menni* (1913), which deals with the period of the 'Great Project', th building of the Martian canals some time prior to the Martian revolutior centering on the father/son conflict between Menni, the great capitalis engineer who conceives the project, and Netti (who this time really *is* a man) the committed unionist who succeeds him.

19. While for the most part Bogdanov sees art as reflecting the changin economic and political circumstances of the society that produces it, there i one point where Bogdanov tries to hold up traditional artistic conventions a 'natural', rather than socially constructed. When Leonid expresses surpris that Martian poetry still uses strict meter and rhyme, asserting that 'it i commonly thought among us that such form was generated by the tastes o the ruling classes of our society, and that it reflects their fastidiousness an predilection for conventions which restrict the freedom of artistic expression (p.78), he is firmly corrected: 'Nothing could be further from the truth .. Regular rhythmicality seems beautiful to us not at all because of any liking fo conventions, but because it is in profound harmony with the rhythmica regularity of our processes of life and thought. As for rhyme, which resolve a series of dissimilarities in uniform final chords, it is intimately related to tha vital bond between people which crowns their inherent diversity with th unity of the delights of love, the unity that comes from a rational goal in work and the unity of feeling in a work of art. Without rhythm there is no artisti form at all' (p.78).

20. Bogdanov was not only an economist, philosopher, novelist, an revolutionary: he was also a physician, and a pioneer of the—at that time— imperfectly understood process of blood transfusion. He in fact died as th result of an experiment in which he exchanged blood with a patient desperatel ill with malaria and tuberculosis (Graham, p.252).

21. Sterni argues that the uneven development of different nation state means that in some it is possible that 'the cause of socialism will be frustrate for decades' (p.113). In such an event 'the individual advanced countries i which socialism triumphs will be like islands in a hostile capitalist and even t some extent precapitalist sea. Anxious about their own power, the upper classe of the nonsocialist countries will continue to concentrate all their efforts o destroying these islands. They will constantly be organizing militar expeditions against them, and from among the ranks of the former large an small property-holders in the socialist nations themselves they will be able t find plenty of allies willing to commit treason. It is difficult to foresee th

outcome of these conflicts, but even in those instances where socialism prevails and triumphs, its character will be perverted deeply and for a long time to come by years of encirclement, unavoidable terror and militarism, and the barbarian patriotism that is their inevitable consequence. This socialism will be a far cry from our own' (pp.113–14).

22.   Kermode, for example, remarks that 'The *soma* which was once anathematized as a cheap escape from the ardours of reality is now essential to social health' (p.472); see also Birnbaum: 'A freedom induced by a drug extracted from mushrooms seems hardly different from the euphoria induced by *soma* in *Brave New World*' (p.174). In fact, even the most cursory comparison of *Brave New World* and *Island* reveals that the two drugs have dramatically different effects. For a discussion of Huxley's views on, and use of psychedelic drugs, see Ferns (pp.193–212).

23.   Huxley describes Maria's death in a letter to Humphry Osmond, 21 February, 1955 (*Letters*, pp.734–7). Not only is the process of hypnotic suggestion described in *Island* almost identical to that used during Maria's final days, but some of Dr Robert's words to Lakshmi are taken *verbatim* from Huxley's own.

24.   William Morris, it should be said, was in no doubt as to the gap between George's position and that of the anarchists. It was George's disowning of the Chicago anarchists, four of whom were executed on trumped-up charges, that prompted him to write in *The Commonweal*: 'Henry George approves of this murder; do not let anybody waste many words to qualify this wretch's conduct. One word will include all the rest—TRAITOR!!' (quoted in Thompson, 1955, p.593)

25.   For a more detailed discussion of Huxley's shortcomings as a political thinker, see Ferns, pp.23–54; a more sympathetic account of Huxley's political views is provided by Firchow, pp.77–116.

Chapter 6. A World of One's Own

1.   Wittig, *Les Guerillères* (1969); Russ, *The Female Man* (1975); Charnas, *Motherlines* (1978).

2.   For a more detailed discussion of the parallels between *Herland* and *Gulliver's Travels*, see Keyser, who argues that *Herland* can more profitably be read as a satire than as a utopia *per se*.

3.   While it is argued here that the utopian narrative paradigm itself is at the root of the more problematic features of Gilman's narrative, other critics have seen these as having more specifically ideological causes. Mary Hill, for example, argues that some of *Herland*'s shortcomings stem in part from the influence on Gilman of Bellamy's Nationalist Movement: 'like most Nationalists ... [Gilman] was more effective in describing conditions which deprive human life of dignity and meaning than she was in projecting viable solutions' (p.173).

4.   In an illuminating discussion of the historical context from which *Herland* emerges Bammer argues that this is characteristic, not only of *Herland*, but of a number of women's utopias written in America during the preceding century (pp.28–47); she also suggests that the 'dangerously romanticizing adulation of woman as the embodiment of virtue and goodness' (p.35) is one of the chief weaknesses of the mainstream feminism of the period.

5. See also Thürmer-Rohr, pp.132–52, for a critique of idealized conceptions of an 'essential' femininity. As she points out: '[t]hose qualities ascribed to femaleness, the fantasy images of women, display astonishing consistency over a hundred and fifty years. This is not without its comic side, if you can still find any of this comical. The "extraordinary" nature of the feminine, which is situated beyond the masculine order of progress, exploitation, and expansion in a disorderly realm devoid of developmental logic, is still celebrated for its "creatively liberating qualities" : emotionality, sensuality, surrender, imagination, sensibility, receptivity, empathy, harmony, patience, gentleness, understanding, and above all the capacity to love, to sacrifice, and to be selfless' (pp.134–5).

6. Gilman is by no means alone in attaching such exaggerated importance to a gentleman's word of honour. Bellamy, in fact, (whose work Gilman much admired) goes still further: in *Looking Backward*, Dr Leete informs his visitor from the nineteenth century that 'the world has outgrown lying' (p.153); when the latter expresses surprise, he then goes on to make the astonishing claim that 'Falsehood, even in your day, was not common between gentlemen and ladies, social equals ... Because we are now social equals ... the contempt of falsehood is so universal that it is rarely that even a criminal in other respects will be found willing to lie' (p.153).

7. Still more curious, perhaps, is the fact that it is Terry—of all people— who gives the country its name: 'Herland' is represented as his invention, not that of the inhabitants (whose name for their country we never learn). In more ways than one, Gilman's utopia is reliant on the word of a gentleman.

8. A more logical (not to mention more disturbing) exploration of these options is provided in James Tiptree's 'Houston, Houston, Do You Read?'

9. See for example Ann J. Lane's discussion of the issue in her introduction to *Herland* (pp.xvii–xviii). For a different perspective, see Mary Jo Deegan's introduction to *With Her in Ourland* (pp.1–57).

10. They prove more prevalent, regrettably, in Gilman's sequel, *With Her in Ourland* (1916), which contains an analysis of anti-semitism almost as anti-semitic as the views it analyses, as well as fears of America's racial contamination 'by crowding injections of alien blood, by vast hordes of low-grade laborers' (p.106). Deegan, however, argues that these represent 'a few (and it really is only a few) ethnocentric lapses' (p.6), which are balanced by Gilman's denunciation of Western colonialism and theories of racial superiority elsewhere in the book.

11. The possibility of dialogue is still further diminished by the fact that (with the partial exception of the 'gentles') men are incapable of the telepathy which constitutes the Hill Women's main mode of communication.

12. Whether a reality external to language is even *possible*, let alone desirable, is another question. For a valuable critique of the concept of a 'pre-discursive reality', and in particular its association with notions of the maternal as a category prior to the institution of a patriarchal culture, see Butler.

13. This seems to present problems for some male readers of the work. To respond objectively (that is, if one assumes an objective response to utopian fiction to be possible, or even desirable) is clearly more difficult for readers who find themselves identified as belonging to a different species—and, possibly as a result, male critical accounts of Gearhart's utopia often leave a good deal to be desired. Kingsley Widmer, for example, although styling himself

a 'feminist fellow traveller,' dismisses the work as mere 'coterie writing,' an assertion backed up by out-of-context quotation and a derisive summary which at points descends into mere abuse (pp.62–4).

14. While *The Wanderground* is by no means alone in drawing the analogy between women and the colonized, Bammer argues that Gearhart's literal-minded equation of colonialism with patriarchy, and her unproblematic identification of women with the land constitute 'a disturbingly dehistoricized appropriation of the colonial critique' (p.85)—based, among other things, on the construction of woman as victim, free of complicity in the historical process which has led to the nightmare from which the Hill Women seek to escape.

15. For a more detailed discussion of the problems inherent in Gearhart's attempt to imagine a reality outside the patriarchal structures of existing language, see Bammer, pp.79–92: while 'Gearhart realizes that in order to write she must position herself within language; simply put, she must use words ... *The Wanderground* discursively counters its own premise that woman can be written outside of culture by reinscribing her within it' (pp.91–2).

16. For a forceful critique of the belief in women's freedom from complicity with the structures of patriarchy, see Thürmer-Rohr, pp.39–63.

17. Such 'disjunctive binarism', Butler argues, 'paradoxically, institutes precisely the relation of radical dependency it seeks to overcome: Lesbianism would then *require* heterosexuality. Lesbianism that defines itself in radical exclusion from heterosexuality deprives itself of the capacity to resignify the very heterosexual constructs by which it is partially and inevitably constituted. As a result, that lesbian strategy would consolidate compulsory heterosexuality in its oppressive forms' (p.128). Rather than 'troubling' (to use Butler's term) straight society's structures of gender relations, Gearhart's fantasy of their disappearance ultimately leaves them intact.

Chapter 7. Dreams of Freedom

1. Lefanu takes a different view of this, describing Piercy's utopian discourse as 'vivid, racy, and economical'; in particular, she suggests that it is 'remarkable how quickly, as a reader, one becomes accustomed to its lack of gendered pronouns and begins to enjoy this' (p.63).

2. They are disappointing: perhaps the quality of the ingredients is better in utopia.

3. Khouri argues that Le Guin's Taoist-based philosophy embodies a stasis incompatible with the rendering of a genuinely dialectical process. Although by the end of the novel the contradictions inherent in the societies of both Urras and Anarres (and indeed the relations between them) seem on the brink of producing far-reaching transformations in each, this is discounted, as is also the case in Lefanu's discussion of the work: 'At the end of *The Dispossessed* differences are resolved without conflict or change' (p.142). Khouri also criticizes Le Guin for being 'forced to resort to a contrived and non-functional ending—a *deus ex machina*—the incarnation of the author's narrative superego in the form of the unexpected appearance of the Hainish at the end of the novel' (p.53). (The Hainish are the galaxy's oldest known human civilization; a Hainish cosmonaut elects to accompany Shevek on his return to Anarres.) It is difficult to reconcile this assertion with anything the text actually contains. For a more perceptive discussion of the relation between Le Guin's Taoism and

the dialectical process, see Suvin, 'Parables', pp.265–74; see also Bloch's more general discussion of the relationship between Taoist philosophy and dialectic in *Principle of Hope*, pp.1225–30.

4. See Moylan, *Demand the Impossible*, pp.91–120; also Delany, *Jewel-Hinged Jaw*, pp.239–308. Delany's critique is in many respects a persuasive one, although he sometimes appears to get carried away by his polemic intent, as for example when he compares the narrative structure of *The Dispossessed* to that of Edgar Rice Burroughs' *Tarzan* novels!

5. See Moylan, pp.109–10; Lefanu, p.141; Delany *passim*. While Delany, as suggested above, makes a plausible case in this regard, the same can hardly be said of Lefanu, whose assertion that 'homosexuality is tolerated as adolescent experimentation but nothing more' (p.141) is certainly not borne out by the text. In fact, when Shevek and Bedap *renew* the homosexual relations they had briefly engaged in during adolescence they discuss the matter first, recognizing that adult sexuality is a more complicated affair (*Dispossessed*, p.139).

6. Lefanu goes furthest in this regard, denouncing Le Guin for her failure to provide any positive portrayals of women other than 'Poor old Takver, the token strong woman, [who] keeps the home fires burning while Shevek is off changing the future of mankind ...' (Presumably the fact that Anarres was the product of a revolution led by a woman does not count.) Takver, a marine biologist who engages in the apparently unforgivable sin of child care, seems to cause Lefanu particular irritation. Elsewhere she refers to her simply as '... Takver. Oh dear, Takver' (p.133).

7. For an opposing view, see Fekete, pp.129–43.

8. Although *The Dispossessed* was published in 1974, Le Guin's critique is strongly reminiscent of that of the student activists of the late 1960s. Shevek, we learn, 'was appalled by the examination system, when it was explained to him; he could not imagine a greater deterrent to the natural wish to learn than this pattern of cramming information and disgorging it at demand. At first he refused to give any tests or grades, but this upset the University administrators so badly that, not wishing to be discourteous to his hosts, he gave in. He asked his students to write a paper on any problem in physics that interested them, and told them that he would give them all the highest mark, so that the bureaucrats would have something to write on their forms and lists. To his surprise a good many students came to him to complain. They wanted him to set the problems, to ask the right questions; they did not want to think about questions, but to write down the answers they had learned. And some of them objected strongly to his giving everyone the same mark. How could the diligent students be distinguished from the dull ones? What was the good in working hard? If no competitive distinctions were to be made, one might as well do nothing. "Well, of course," Shevek said, troubled. "If you do not want to do the work, you should not do it"' (p.103).

9. Le Guin's representation of the consequences of the mass emigration of the revolutionary elements in Urrasti society echo Marx's concerns, as expressed in 'Citizen Cabet's Plea for Emigration', published in *La Revue Communiste* 1 (1858): 'If those honest people who struggle for a better future leave, they will leave the arena completely open to the obscurantists and the rogues. Europe would certainly fall. Europe is that part of the world where communal wealth can be put forward first and most easily, simply for statistical

and economic reasons. Instead, fire and brimstone will descend upon suffering humanity for centuries to come' (quoted in Marin, pp.271–9).

10. Leaving aside the fact that permanent revolution is precisely what *The Dispossessed is* about, Fekete's clear preference for Delany's comforting fiction that such a society can be achieved through continuing technological progress may itself be seen as reflecting certain prevailing ideological assumptions which were already being questioned in the late 1970s. Two decades later, his dismissal of the 'problems flowing out of scarcity and having to do with distributive justice' as 'less interesting' than those posed by the notion of a 'post-scarcity society' (leaving aside its irrelevance to anyone outside the more well-to-do élite of advanced capitalist societies) is beginning to seem more than a little dated.

11. Roemer's experience is hardly an uncommon one. In my own classes I have sometimes conducted a similar exercise, based on the folk-tale, 'The Three Wishes', which Bloch cites as a paradigm of the problematics of utopian desire. As an imaginative exercise, the students were asked to suppose their instructor temporarily gifted with magical powers capable of granting *any* three wishes they might have—only provided that they were able to write them down within the space of three minutes. Although a number of students came up with honourable abstractions such as 'World Peace', or such clearly desirable goals as 'A Cure for Cancer', what was striking was the poverty of their *personal* visions, which would often take the shape of the desire to 'marry my boyfriend', 'get an A on the course', or even 'get a job at Mount Saint Vincent University'. Perhaps the closest to the banality which Roemer records was the student who wished for a sports-car—it was only a Mazda—although even this outstrips the student whose capacity for utopian desire was limited to the acquisition of 'a forest-green Jetta'.

Bibliography

Adams, Percy G. *Travel Literature and the Evolution of the Novel*. Lexington: University of Kentucky Press, 1983.

Adorno, Theodor W. *Prisms*. Trans. Samuel and Shierry Weber. London: Neville Spearman, 1967.

Alaton, Salem. 'A Tale in the Making'. *The Globe and Mail*. 13 May 1989. C1.

Albinski, Nan Bowman. *Women's Utopias in British and American Fiction*. London: Routledge, 1988.

Armitt, Lucie, ed. *Where No Man Has Gone Before: Women and Science Fiction*. London: Routledge, 1991.

Atwood, Margaret. *The Handmaid's Tale*. Toronto: Seal Books, 1986.

———. *Life Before Man*. Toronto: Seal, 1979.

Bacon, Francis. *The Philosophical Works of Francis Bacon*, Ed. J.M. Robertson. London: Routledge, 1905.

Bakhtin, M.M. *The Dialogic Imagination*. Ed. Michael Holquist. Trans. Caryl Emerson and Michael Holquist. Austin: University of Texas Press, 1981.

———. *Problems of Dostoevsky's Poetics*. Ed. and Trans. Caryl Emerson. Minneapolis: University of Minnesota Press, 1984.

———. *Rabelais and His World*. Trans. Hélène Iswolsky. Bloomington: Indiana University Press, 1984.

——— and P.N. Medvedev. *The Formal Method in Literary Scholarship*. Trans. Albert J. Wehrle. Baltimore: Johns Hopkins University Press, 1991.

Ballestrem, Karl G. 'Lenin and Bogdanov.' *Studies in Soviet Thought* 9.4 (1969), pp.283–310.

Bammer, Angelika. *Partial Visions: Feminism and Utopianism in the 1970s*. London: Routledge, 1991.

Barr, Marlene S. Ed. *Future Females: A Critical Anthology*. Bowling Green: Bowling Green State University Press, 1981.

———. *Alien to Femininity: Speculative Fiction and Feminist Theory*. Westport: Greenwood, 1987.

Barthes, Roland. *Sade, Fourier, Loyola*. New York: Hill and Wang, 1976.

Bartkowski, Frances. *Feminist Utopias*. Lincoln: University of Nebraska Press, 1989.

Baruch, Elaine Hoffman. 'A Natural and Necessary Monster: Women in Utopia.' *Alternative Futures* 2.1 (1979), pp.29–49.

Baxandall, Lee and Stephan Morowski, Eds. *Marx and Engels on Literature and Art*. New York: International General, 1974.

Beilharz, Peter. *Labour's Utopias: Bolshevism, Fabianism, Social Democracy*. London: Routledge, 1992.

Bellamy, Edward. *Looking Backward 2000–1887*. New York: Bantam, 1983.

Benjamin, Walter. *Illuminations*. New York: Harcourt, 1968.

Bennett, Tony. *Formalism and Marxism*. London: Methuen, 1979.

Bergonzi, Bernard. *The Early H.G. Wells*. Manchester: Manchester University Press, 1961.

Berneri, Marie Louise. *Journey Through Utopia*. New York: Schocken, 1971.

Bierman, Judah. 'Ambiguity in Utopia: *The Dispossessed.' Science Fiction Studies* 7 (1975), pp.249–56.

———. 'Science and Society in the *New Atlantis* and other Renaissance Utopias.' *PMLA* 78.4.1 (1963), pp.492–500.

Birnbaum, Milton. *Aldous Huxley's Quest for Values.* Knoxville: University of Tennessee Press, 1971.

Bleich, David. *Utopia: the Psychology of a Cultural Fantasy.* Ann Arbor: UMI Research Press, 1984.

Blitzer, Charles. *An Immortal Commonwealth: The Political Thought of James Harrington.* New Haven: Yale University Press, 1960.

Bloch, Ernst. *The Principle of Hope.* 3 vols. Trans. Neville Plaice, Stephen Plaice, and Paul Knight. Cambridge, Mass.: MIT Press, 1986.

———. *The Utopian Function of Art and Literature.* Trans. Jack Zipes and Frank Mecklenburg. Cambridge, Mass.: MIT Press, 1988.

Bogdanov, Alexander. *Red Star: The First Bolshevik Utopia.* Ed. Loren Graham and Richard Stites. Trans. Charles Rougle. Bloomington: Indiana University Press, 1984.

Bonansea, Bernardino. *Tomasso Campanella: Renaissance Pioneer of Modern Thought.* Washington: Catholic University of America Press, 1969.

Booker, M. Keith. *The Dystopian Impulse in Modern Literature: Fiction as Social Criticism.* Westport: Greenwood, 1994.

———. *Dystopian Literature: A Theory and Research Guide.* Westport: Greenwood, 1994.

Booth, Wayne C. 'Yes, But Are They Really Novels?' *Yale Review* 51 (1962), pp.630–1.

Borges, Jorge Luis. 'Death and the Compass.' *Labyrinths.* Ed. Donald A. Yates and James E. Irby. New York: New Directions, 1964, pp.76–87.

Bowman, Sylvia E. *Edward Bellamy Abroad: An American Prophet's Influence.* New York: Twayne, 1962.

Buick, Adam. 'William Morris and incomplete Communism: a critique of Paul Meier's thesis.' *Journal of the William Morris Society* 3.2 (1976), pp.16–32.

Butler, Judith. *Gender Trouble: Feminism and the Subversion of Identity.* New York: Routledge, 1990.

Callenbach, Ernest. *Ecotopia.* Berkeley: Banyan Tree, 1975.

Callinicos, Alex. *Against Postmodernism: A Marxist Critique.* Cambridge: Polity, 1989.

———. *Theories and Narratives: Reflections on the Philosophy of History.* Cambridge. Polity, 1995.

Campanella, Tomasso. *The City of the Sun: A Poetical Dialogue.* Trans. Daniel J. Donno. Berkeley: University of California Press, 1981.

Charnas, Suzy McKee. *Motherlines.* New York: Berkley, 1979.

Chilton, Paul and Crispin Aubrey, Eds. *Nineteen Eighty-Four in 1984: Autonomy, Control and Communication.* London: Comedia, 1983.

Clarke, I.F. *The Pattern of Expectation 1664–2001.* New York: Basic, 1979.

Cohn, Norman. *The Pursuit of the Millennium: Revolutionary Millenarians and Mystical Anarchists of the Middle Ages.* London: Paladin, 1970.

Columbus, Christopher. *The Journal of Christopher Columbus.* Trans. Cecil Jane. London: Anthony Blond, 1960.

Cranny-Francis, Anne. *Feminist Fiction: Feminist Uses of Generic Fiction.* New York: St Martin's, 1990.

Daniel, Jamie Owen and Tom Moylan, Eds. *Not Yet: Reconsidering Ernst Bloch* London: Verso, 1997.

Davis, J.C. *Utopia and the Ideal Society*. Cambridge: Cambridge University Press 1981.

De Bolt, Joseph. Ed. *Ursula Le Guin: Voyager to Inner Lands and to Outer Space* Port Washington: Kennikat, 1978.

de Certeau, Michel. *The Writing of History*. Trans. Tom Conley. New York Columbia University Press, 1988.

Delany, Samuel R. *The Jewel-Hinged Jaw: Notes on the Language of Science Fiction* Elizabethtown: Dragon, 1977.

———. *Triton*. New York: Bantam, 1976.

Delbanco, Andrew. Introduction. *Looking Backward*. By Edward Bellamy. New York: Bantam, 1983, pp.ix–xix.

Deutscher, Isaac. *Russia in Transition*. New York: Grove, 1960.

Donawerth, Jane L. And Carol A. Kolmerten. Eds. *Utopian and Science Fiction by Women*. Syracuse: Syracuse University Press, 1994.

Eagleton, Terry. *Criticism and Ideology*. London: New Left Books, 1976.

———. *Ideology: An Introduction*. London: Verso, 1991.

———. *The Illusions of Postmodernism*. Oxford: Blackwell, 1996.

Elliott, R.C. *The Shape of Utopia: Studies in a Literary Genre*. Chicago: University of Chicago Press, 1970.

Eliade, Mircea. 'Paradise and Utopia: Mythical Geography and Eschatology. *Utopias and Utopian Thought*. Ed. Frank E. Manuel. Boston: Beacon, 1967 pp.260–80.

Eliav-Feldon, Miriam. *Realistic Utopias*. Oxford: Clarendon, 1982.

Engels, Friedrich. *Herr Eugen Duhring's Revolution in Science*. Chicago: Charles H. Kerr, 1935.

Fekete, John. '*The Dispossessed* and *Triton*: Act and System in Utopian Science Fiction.' *Science-Fiction Studies* 18 (1979), pp.129–43.

Ferns, C.S. *Aldous Huxley: Novelist*. London: Athlone, 1980.

Fiderer, Gerald. 'Masochism as Literary Strategy: Orwell's Psychological Novels.' *Literature and Psychology* 20 (1970), pp.3–21.

Firchow, Peter. *The End of Utopia: A Study of Aldous Huxley's* 'Brave New World' Lewisburg: Bucknell University Press, 1984.

Firestone, Shulamith. *The Dialectic of Sex: The Case for Feminist Revolution*. New York: Bantam, 1970.

Fitting, Peter. 'Impulse or Genre or Neither?' *Science-Fiction Studies* 66 (1995) pp.272–81.

Fisher, Judith L. 'Trouble in Paradise: The Twentieth-Century Utopian Ideal. *Extrapolation* 24. 4 (1983), pp.329–39.

Foucault, Michel. *The Archaeology of Knowledge*. London: Tavistock, 1972.

———. *The History of Sexuality*. New York: Pantheon, 1978.

Frye, Northrop. *Anatomy of Criticism*. Princeton: Princeton University Press 1957.

———. 'Varieties of Literary Utopias.' *Utopias and Utopian Thought*. Ed. Frank E. Manuel. Boston: Beacon, 1967, pp.260–80.

Fukuyama, Francis. *The End of History and the Last Man*. New York: Free Press 1992.

Garvey, Brian. 'The Utopian Imagination.' *Science-Fiction Studies* 45 (1988) pp.244–5.

Gearhart, Sally Miller. *The Wanderground*. Boston: Alyson, 1984.

Geoghegan, Vincent. *Utopianism and Marxism*. London: Methuen, 1987.

Gerber, Richard. *Utopian Fantasy: A Study of English Utopian Fiction Since the End of the Nineteenth Century*. London: Routledge, 1955.

Gilison, Jerome M. *The Soviet Image of Utopia*. Baltimore: Johns Hopkins University Press, 1975.

Gilman, Charlotte Perkins. *The Charlotte Perkins Gilman Reader*. Ed. Ann J. Lane. London: The Women's Press, 1981.

———. *Herland*. London: The Women's Press, 1979.

———. *With Her in Ourland: Sequel to Herland*. Ed. Mary Jo Deegan and Michael R. Hill. Westport: Praeger, 1997.

Glasier, J. Bruce. *William Morris and the Early Days of the Socialist Movement*. London: Longmans, 1921.

Goodwin, Barbara and Keith Taylor. *The Politics of Utopia: a Study in Theory and Practice*. New York: St Martin's, 1982.

Gove, Philip B. *The Imaginary Voyage in Prose Fiction*. London: Holland, 1961.

Graham, Loren R. 'Bogdanov's Inner Message.' *Red Star: The First Bolshevik Utopia*. By Alexander Bogdanov. Ed. Loren Graham and Richard Stites. Trans. Charles Rougle. Bloomington: Indiana University Press, 1984, pp.241–53.

Gramsci, Antonio. *Selections from the Prison Notebooks*. New York: International, 1971.

Greenblatt, Stephen. *Marvelous Possessions: The Wonder of the New World*. Chicago: University of Chicago Press, 1991.

Gubar, Susan. '*She* in *Herland*: Feminism as Fantasy.' *Charlotte Perkins Gilman: The Woman and Her Work*. Ed. Sheryl L. Meyering. Ann Arbor: UMI Research Press, 1989, pp.191–202.

Helgerson, Richard. *Forms of Nationhood: The Elizabethan Writing of England*. Chicago: University of Chicago Press, 1992.

Hertzler, Joyce Oramel. *The History of Utopian Thought*. New York: Macmillan, 1923.

Hexter, J.H. *The Vision of Politics on the Eve of the Reformation*. New York: Basic, 1973.

Hill, Eugene D. 'The Place of the Future: Louis Marin and his *Utopiques*.' *Science-Fiction Studies* 27 (1982), pp.167–79.

Hill, Mary A. *Charlotte Perkins Gilman: The Making of a Radical Feminist*. Philadelphia: Temple University Press, 1980.

Hillegas, Mark. *The Future as Nightmare: H.G. Wells and the Anti-Utopians*. Carbondale: University of Illinois Press, 1974.

Hutcheon, Linda. *The Politics of Postmodernism*. London: Routledge, 1989.

Huxley, Aldous. *Brave New World*. London: Granada, 1977.

———. *Island*. New York: Harper, 1972.

———. *Letters of Aldous Huxley*. Ed. Grover M. Smith. London: Chatto, 1969.

Irigaray, Luce. *This Sex Which is Not One*. Ithaca: Cornell University Press, 1985.

Jackson, Rosemary. *Fantasy: The Literature of Subversion*. London: Methuen, 1981.

Jameson, Fredric. *Marxism and Form: Twentieth Century Dialectical Theories of Literature*. Princeton: Princeton University Press, 1971.

———. 'Of Islands and Trenches: Neutralization and the Production of Utopian Discourse.' *Diacritics* 7.2 (1977), pp.2–22.

——. *The Political Unconscious: Narrative as a Socially Symbolic Act*. Ithaca: Cornell University Press, 1981.

——. *Postmodernism, or, The Cultural Logic of Late Capitalism*. London: Verso 1991.

——. 'Progress Versus Utopia; Or, Can We Imagine the Future?' *Science Fiction Studies* 27 (1982), pp.147–59.

——. 'World Reduction in Le Guin: The Emergence of Utopian Narrative. *Science-Fiction Studies* 7 (1975), pp.221–31.

Jane, Cecil. Ed. *Select Documents Illustrating the Four Voyages of Columbus*. 2 vols London: Hakluyt Society, 1930, 1932.

Jensen, K.M. '*Red Star*: Bogdanov Builds a Utopia.' *Studies in Soviet Thought* 23.1 (1982), pp.1–34.

Jones, Libby Falk and Sarah Webster Goodwin, Eds. *Feminism, Utopia, and Narrative*. Knoxville: University of Tennessee Press, 1990.

Kalin, Martin G. *Utopian Flight From Unhappiness: Freud Against Marx on Social Progress*. Totoway: Littlefield, 1975.

Kateb, George. *Utopia and its Enemies*. New York: Free Press, 1963.

Kautsky, Karl. *Thomas More and his Utopia*. London: Lawrence and Wishart 1979.

Kermode, Frank. 'Fiction Chronicle.' *Partisan Review* 29 (1962), pp.472–3.

Kessler, Carol Farley. *Charlotte Perkins Gilman: Her Progress Toward Utopia, with Selected Writings*. Syracuse: Syracuse University Press, 1995.

——. *Daring to Dream: Utopian Fiction by United States Women Before 1950* Syracuse: Syracuse University Press, 1995.

——. '*Woman on the Edge of Time*: A Novel "To Be of Use".' *Extrapolation* 28. (1987), pp.310–18.

Keulen, Margarete. *Radical Imagination: Feminist Conceptions of the Future in Ursula Le Guin, Marge Piercy, and Sally Miller Gearhart*. Frankfurt am Main Peter Lang, 1991.

Keymis, Laurence. *The second voyage of Guiana performed and written in the yeer 1596, by Laurence Keymis gentleman. The Principall Navigations of the English Nation*. By Richard Hakluyt. Vol 7. London: Dent, 1907, pp.358–93.

Keyser, Elizabeth. 'Looking Backward: From *Herland* to *Gulliver's Travels. Critical Essays on Charlotte Perkins Gilman*. Ed. Joanne B. Karpinski. New York Hall, 1992, pp.159–72.

Khouri, Nadia. 'The Dialectics of Power: Utopia in the Science Fiction of Le Guin, Jeury, and Piercy.' *Science-Fiction Studies* 20 (1980), pp.49–61.

Kolodny, Annette. *The Lay of the Land: Metaphor as Experience and History in American Life and Letters*. Chapel Hill: University of North Carolina Press 1975.

Kumar, Krishan. *Utopia and Anti-Utopia in Modern Times*. Oxford: Blackwell, 1987

——. *Utopianism*. Milton Keynes: Open University Press, 1991.

Lane, Ann J. Ed. *The Charlotte Perkins Gilman Reader*. London: Women's Press 1981.

——. Introduction. *Herland*. By Charlotte Perkins Gilman. London: The Women's Press, 1979, pp.v–xxiv.

——. *To Herland and Beyond: The Life and Work of Charlotte Perkins Gilman*. New York: Pantheon, 1990.

Lasky, Melvin J. *Utopia and Revolution*. Chicago: University of Chicago Press 1976.

Leacock, Stephen. *Afternoons in Utopia: Tales of the New Time*. London: Bodley Head, 1932.

Lefanu, Sarah. *In the Chinks of the World Machine: Feminism and Science Fiction*. London: Women's Press, 1988.

Le Guin, Ursula K. *Always Coming Home*. New York: Bantam, 1986.

———. *The Dispossessed*. New York: Avon, 1975.

———. *The Language of the Night*. London: Women's Press, 1989.

Lem, Stanislaw. *The Chain of Chance*. Trans. Louis Iribarne. Harmondsworth: Penguin, 1981.

Lenin, V.I. *Materialism and Empirio-Criticism: Critical Comments on a Reactionary Philosophy*. Moscow: Foreign Languages Publishing House, 1952.

———. *What Is To Be Done?* Peking: Foreign Languages Press, 1975.

Levitas, Ruth. *The Concept of Utopia*. Syracuse: Syracuse University Press, 1990.

———. 'Educated Hope: Ernst Bloch on Abstract and Concrete Utopia.' *Not Yet: Reconsidering Ernst Bloch*. Ed. Jamie Owen Daniel and Tom Moylan. London: Verso, 1997, pp.65–79.

Lukács, Georg. *History and Class Consciousness*. Trans. Rodney Livingstone. London: Merlin, 1971.

———. *The Theory of the Novel*. London: Merlin, 1971.

Macherey, Pierre. *A Theory of Literary Production*. Trans. Geoffrey Wall. London: Routledge, 1978.

Mannheim, Karl. *Ideology and Utopia: An Introduction to the Sociology of Knowledge*. New York: Harcourt, 1936.

Manuel, Frank E. Ed. *Utopias and Utopian Thought*. Boston: Beacon, 1966.

———., and Fritzie P. Manuel. *Utopian Thought in the Western World*. Cambridge, Mass.: Belknap, 1979.

Marcuse, Herbert. *Eros and Civilization*. Boston: Beacon, 1955.

———. 'Marxism and Feminism.' *Women's Studies* 2, 3 (1974), pp.279–89.

———. *One-Dimensional Man*. Boston: Beacon, 1964.

Marin, Louis. *Utopics: Spatial Play*. Trans. Robert A. Vollrath. New Jersey: Humanities, 1986.

McNulty, Robert. 'Bruno at Oxford.' *Renaissance News* 13 (1960), pp.300–5.

Meier, Paul. *William Morris: The Marxist Dreamer*. Brighton: Harvester, 1978.

Mellor. Anne K. 'On Feminist Utopias.' *Women's Studies* 9 (1982), pp.241–62.

Meyering, Sheryl L. Ed. *Charlotte Perkins Gilman: The Woman and Her Work*. Ann Arbor: UMI Research Press, 1989.

Montrose, Louis. 'The Work of Gender in the Discourse of Discovery.' *New World Encounters*. Ed. Stephen Greenblatt. Berkeley: University of California Press, 1993, pp.177–217.

More, Sir Thomas. *Utopia*. Ed. and Trans. Robert M. Adams. New York: Norton, 1975.

Morgan, A.E. *Nowhere Was Somewhere*. Chapel Hill: University of North Carolina Press, 1946.

Morris, May. *William Morris: Artist, Writer, Socialist*. 2 vols. New York: Russell & Russell, 1966.

Morris, William. *News from Nowhere*. Ed. James Redmond. London: Routledge, 1970.

Morley, Henry. Ed. *Ideal Commonwealths*. London: Routledge, 1885.

Morson, Gary Saul. *The Boundaries of Genre: Dostoevsky's* Diary of a Writer *and the Traditions of Literary Utopia*. Austin: University of Texas Press, 1981.

Morton, A.L. *The English Utopia*. London: Lawrence and Wishart, 1952.
Moylan, Tom. *Demand the Impossible: Science Fiction and the Utopian Imagination*. London; Methuen: 1986.
————. 'Utopian Studies: Sharpening the Debate.' *Science-Fiction Studies* 1 (1992), pp.89–94.
Negley, Glenn. *Utopian Literature: A Bibliography*. Lawrence: Regents Press of Kansas, 1977.
Norris, Christopher. *The Truth About Postmodernism*. Oxford: Blackwell, 1993.
Olander, Joseph D. And Martin Greenberg. *Ursula K. Le Guin*. New York Taplinger, 1979.
Olson, Theodore. *Millennialism, utopianism, and progress*. Toronto: University of Toronto Press, 1982.
Orwell, George. *Nineteen Eighty-Four*. Harmondsworth: Penguin, 1983.
————. *The Collected Essays, Journalism and Letters of George Orwell* (4 vols). Ed Sonia Orwell and Ian Angus. Harmondsworth: Penguin, 1970.
Parker, Patricia. *Literary Fat Ladies: Rhetoric, Gender, Property*. London: Methuen 1987.
Parrinder, Patrick. 'Imagining the Future: Zamyatin and Wells.' *Science-Fiction Studies* 1 (1973), pp.37–41.
Patai, Daphne. Ed. *Looking Backward, 1988-1888: Essays on Edward Bellamy*. Amherst: University of Massachusetts Press, 1988.
————. *The Orwell Mystique: A Study in Male Ideology*. Amherst: University of Massachusetts Press, 1984.
Pfaelzer, Jean. 'Immanence, Indeterminance, and the Utopian Pun in *Looking Backward*.' *Looking Backward, 1988–1888: Essays on Edward Bellamy*. Ed. Daphne Patai. Amherst: University of Massachusetts Press, 1988 pp.51–67.
————. 'Parody and Satire in American Dystopian Fiction of the Nineteenth Century.' *Science-Fiction Studies* 7 (1980), pp.61–71.
————. 'A State of One's Own: Feminism as Ideology in American Utopias 1880-1915.' *Extrapolation* 24 (1983), pp.311–28.
————. *The Utopian Novel in America 1886–1896: The Politics of Form*. Pittsburgh University of Pittsburgh Press, 1984.
Piercy, Marge. *Woman on the Edge of Time*. London: Women's Press, 1979.
Rabkin, Eric. *The Fantastic in Literature*. Princeton: Princeton University Press 1976.
————., Martin H. Greenberg and Joseph D. Olander. *No Place Else: Exploration in Utopian and Dystopian Fiction*. Carbondale: Southern Illinois University Press, 1983.
Ralegh, Sir Walter. *The Discoverie of the large, rich, and beautifull Empire of Guiana with a relation of the great and golden citie of Manoa (which the Spaniards call E Dorado) ... Performed in the yeere 1595 by Sir Walter Ralegh. The Principal Navigations of the English Nation*. By Richard Hakluyt. Volume 7. London Dent, 1907, pp.272–350.
Roemer, Kenneth M. *The Obsolete Necessity: America in Utopian Writings 1888–1900*. Kent: Kent State University Press, 1976.
————. 'Prescription for Readers (and Writers) of Utopias.' *Science-Fiction Studies* 44 (1988), pp.88–93.
————. 'Utopian Literature, Empowering Students, and Gender Awareness.' *Science-Fiction Studies* 23 (1996), pp.393–405.

Rosemont, Franklin. 'Bellamy's Radicalism Reclaimed.' *Looking Backward, 1988–1888: Essays on Edward Bellamy*. Ed. Daphne Patai. Amherst: University of Massachusetts Press, 1988, pp.147–209.

Rosinsky, Natalie. *Feminist Futures: Contemporary Women's Speculative Fiction.* Ann Arbor: UMI Research Press, 1984.

Rowbotham, Sheila, Lynne Segal and Hilary Wainwright. *Beyond the Fragments.* London: Merlin, 1979.

Ruppert, Peter. *Reader in a Strange Land: The Activity of Reading Literary Utopias.* Athens: University of Georgia Press, 1986.

Russ, Joanna. *The Female Man.* New York: Bantam, 1975.

———. *To Write Like a Woman: Essays in Feminism and Science-Fiction.* Bloomington: Indiana University Press, 1995.

Sanford, Charles L. *The Quest for Paradise: Europe and the American Moral Imagination.* Urbana: University of Illinois Press, 1961.

Sargent, Lyman Tower. *British and American Utopian Literature, 1516–1985: An Annotated Chronological Bibliography.* New York: Garland, 1988.

Scholes, Robert. *Structural Fabulation: An Essay on the Fiction of the Future.* South Bend: Notre Dame University Press, 1975.

———., and Eric Rabkin. *Science Fiction: History, Science, Vision.* New York: Oxford University Press, 1977.

Skinner, B.F. *Walden Two.* New York: Macmillan, 1962.

Somay, Bulent. 'Towards an Open-Ended Utopia.' *Science-Fiction Studies* 32 (1984), pp.25–38.

Sorel, Georges. *Reflections on Violence.* Trans. T.E. Hulme. New York: Peter Smith, 1941.

Stites, Richard. 'Fantasy and Revolution: Alexander Bogdanov and the Origins of Bolshevik Science Fiction.' *Red Star: The First Bolshevik Utopia.* By Alexander Bogdanov. Ed. Loren Graham and Richard Stites. Trans. Charles Rougle. Bloomington: Indiana University Press, 1984, pp.1–16.

Suvin, Darko. 'Locus, Horizon, and Orientation: The Concept of Possible Worlds as a Key to Utopian Studies.' *Not Yet: Reconsidering Ernst Bloch.* Ed. Jamie Owen Daniel and Tom Moylan. London: Verso, 1997, pp.122–37.

———. *Metamorphoses of Science Fiction.* New Haven: Yale University Press, 1979.

———. 'Parables of De-Alienation: Le Guin's Widdershins Dance.' *Science-Fiction Studies* 7 (1975), pp.265–74.

———. *Positions and Presuppositions in Science Fiction.* London: Macmillan, 1988.

Thompson, E.P. *The Poverty of Theory and Other Essays.* New York: Monthly Review, 1978.

———. *William Morris: Romantic to Revolutionary.* London: Merlin, 1977.

Thürmer-Rohr, Christina. *Vagabonding: Feminist Thinking Cut Loose.* Trans. Lise Weil. Boston: Beacon, 1991.

Tiptree Jr., James. 'Houston, Houston, Do You Read?' *Star Songs of an Old Primate.* New York: Ballantine, 1978, pp.164–226.

Trotsky, Leon. *Literature and Revolution.* New York: Russell & Russell, 1957.

———. *Terrorism and Communism.* Ann Arbor: University of Michigan Press, 1961.

Unamuno, Miguel de. *The Tragic Sense of Life.* New York: Dover, 1954.

Vespucci, Amerigo. *The First Four Voyages of Amerigo Vespucci.* London: Bernard Quaritch, 1893.

————. *The Letters of Amerigo Vespucci*. Ed. Clements R. Markham. London Hakluyt Society, 1894.

Vološinov, V.N. *Freudianism: A Marxist Critique*. Trans. I.R. Titunik. New York Academic, 1976.

————. *Marxism and the Philosophy of Language*. Trans. Ladislav Matejka and I.F Titunik. Cambridge, Mass.: Harvard University Press, 1986.

Walker, D.P. *Spiritual and Demonic Magic From Ficino to Campanella*. London Warburg Institute, 1958.

Walsh, Chad. *From Utopia to Nightmare*. Evanston: Northwestern Universit Press, 1964.

Webb, Sidney. *Socialism in England*. London: Swan Sonnenschein, 1890.

Webster, Charles. *The Great Instauration*. London: Duckworth, 1975.

Wells, H.G. *Experiment in Autobiography*. 2 vols. London: Cape, 1969.

————. *In the Days of the Comet*. London: Hogarth, 1985.

————. *Men Like Gods*. Harmondsworth: Penguin, 1987.

————. *A Modern Utopia*. Lincoln: University of Nebraska Press, 1967.

————. *The Time Machine*. New York: Bantam, 1976.

Widmer, Kingsley. *Counterings: Utopian Dialectics in Contemporary Contexts*. An Arbor: UMI Research Press, 1988.

Wilding, Michael. *Political Fictions*. London: Routledge, 1980.

Williams, Raymond. *Culture and Society*. Harmondsworth: Penguin, 1958.

————. *The Long Revolution*. Harmondsworth: Penguin, 1975.

————. *Marxism and Literature*. London: Oxford University Press, 1977.

————. *Problems in Materialism and Culture*. London: Verso, 1980.

————. 'Utopia and Science Fiction.' *Science-Fiction Studies* 16 (1978) pp.203–14.

Winstanley, Gerrard. *The Law of Freedom and Other Writings*. Ed. Christophe Hill. Harmondsworth: Pelican, 1973.

Wytenbroek, J.R. '*Always Coming Home*: Pacifism and Anarchy in Le Guin Latest Utopia.' *Extrapolation* 28.4 (1987), pp.330–9.

Yates, Frances. *Giordano Bruno and the Hermetic Tradition*. London: Routledge 1964.

————. *The Rosicrucian Enlightenment*. London: Routledge, 1972.

Zamora, Margarita. 'Christopher Columbus's "Letter to the Sovereigns" Announcing the Discovery.' *New World Encounters*. Ed. Stephen Greenblatt Berkeley: University of California Press, 1993. 1–11.

Zamyatin, Yevgeny. *A Soviet Heretic: Essays by Yevgeny Zamyatin*. Ed. and Trans Mirra Ginsburg. Chicago: University of Chicago Press, 1970.

————. *We*. Trans. Bernard Guilbert Guerney. Harmondsworth: Penguin 1983.

Index